Running with Bonnie and Clyde

Running with Bonnie and Clyde

The Ten Fast Years of Ralph Fults

by
John Neal Phillips

University of Oklahoma Press
Norman

Library of Congress Cataloging-in-Publication Data

Phillips, John Neal, 1949–
Running with Bonnie and Clyde: the ten fast years of Ralph Fults /
by John Neal Phillips.
p. cm.
Includes bibliographical references and index.
ISBN 0-8061-2810-0 (cloth)
ISBN 0-8061-3429-1 (paper)
1. Fults, Ralph. 2. Criminals—Texas—Biography. 3. Barrow, Clyde, 1909–1934. 4. Parker, Bonnie, 1910–1934. 5. Prison violence—Texas—Huntsville. 6. Simmons, Lee, b. 1873. I. Title.
HV6248.F87P55 1996
364.1′552′092—dc20
[B] 95-42771
CIP

Text design by Cathy Carney Imboden. Typeface is Janson Text.

The paper in this book meets the guidelines for permanence and durability of the Committee on Production Guidelines for Book Longevity of the Council on Library Resources, Inc. ∞

2 3 4 5 6 7 8 9 10

For Andre and Angela

Contents

Illustrations

Figures

Maps

Preface

Ralph Fults was only nineteen when he first met Clyde Barrow, but he was already a five-year veteran of crime and detention. He had been shot while fleeing from an Oklahoma officer, had escaped from numerous jails and juvenile institutions, and had been brutalized by guards at the State Juvenile Training School, a reformatory in Gatesville. On April 8, 1930, Fults and three other convicts escaped from solitary confinement at Texas's maximum security Eastham Prison Farm, nicknamed "the bloody 'ham"[1] because of the atrocious conditions in existence there. Lawmen would need five months to recapture Fults.

During his return journey to the penitentiary, September 18, 1930,[2] Fults engaged in a fateful conversation with a twenty-one-year-old convicted burglar facing a lengthy prison term. That burglar was Clyde Barrow. Within a month of their meeting, spurred on by the violence perpetrated against them and their fellow inmates by Eastham's guards, Fults and Barrow formed a pact. They vowed to one day win their freedom, recruit a gang on the outside, return to the prison farm, raid it, and release as many prisoners as possible. The resulting union would later become known as the Barrow gang, or, more popularly, Bonnie and Clyde.

Fults and Barrow finalized the plans for the raid while still in prison. Eventually they won pardons and began recruiting a gang in North Texas.

They robbed their first bank to support the gang and finance the raid. In April 1932 they sent word to their contacts at Eastham that the raid was imminent. Then a series of mishaps resulted in the capture of all but one of the gang members. Only Clyde Barrow remained at large. Ralph Fults, shot and captured along with Bonnie Parker, faced a multitude of charges.[3]

Fults, who plea-bargained for Bonnie Parker's release, was sent back to prison. Bonnie returned to Clyde, but the raid was postponed. Then on January 16, 1934, Bonnie and Clyde finally staged the raid on Eastham, not for the benefit of Raymond Hamilton as is widely believed, but for the sake of any convict wanting to escape from what Barrow termed "that hell-hole," per the original plan. Ironically, that raid, Barrow's only real goal in his brief, violent career, would ultimately seal his doom and that of his girlfriend. The ambush of Bonnie and Clyde five months later was arranged by Col. Lee Simmons, general manager of the Texas prison system, in direct response to that raid.[4]

The year after the killing of Bonnie and Clyde, Ralph Fults won yet another pardon. Almost immediately he joined forces with Death-Row fugitive and former Barrow accomplice Raymond Hamilton. Fults and Hamilton robbed banks to finance a friend's appeal for a stay of execution,[5] passed information to a Houston investigative reporter about brutality in the Texas Prison System, and eluded countless posses, including troops of the National Guard, before both men were recaptured for the last time in April 1935.

Hamilton was executed, but Fults successfully resisted two states' attempts to have him put to death. He also survived a deadly confrontation with a high-ranking Texas prison official, who tried in vain to use Fults to discredit a Houston reporter attempting to expose the rampant brutality in Texas's prisons.[6] The resulting state investigation, coupled with the publication of a report on U.S. prisons that listed Texas as among the worst in the nation, greatly embarrassed Colonel Simmons.[7] On September 2, 1935, the very day Ralph Fults was sentenced to two fifty-year terms, Simmons resigned as general manager of the Texas prison system.

The raid on Eastham and the prison brutality that gave rise to its planning are at the heart of this story. Everything hinges on these factors.

Fults said more than once that while in prison he watched Clyde Barrow "change from a schoolboy to a rattlesnake," so strong was his reaction to the injustices perpetrated against him and his fellow inmates.

Without the brutality, there would have been no raid, no retaliation from Texas prison officials,[8] no state investigation into charges of officially sanctioned brutality[9] in the Texas prison system, and no resignation of Colonel Simmons.[10]

Five years of intensive research has gone into the production of *Running with Bonnie and Clyde*. Appearing throughout the text of this book is dialogue that I created from direct recollections of actual participants in the story, including Ralph Fults. More than twenty hours of interviews with Fults provided the foundation for the dialogue and indeed the whole story. Subsequent interviews with fifty-eight other eyewitnesses, coupled with testimony from police depositions, court transcripts, and contemporary news sources expanded the dialogue to its final form.

I decided to reproduce such an extensive amount of dialogue because of the authentic flavor and unity it lends to the overall story. The dialogue and facts presented here are documented. Wherever possible they have been corroborated by one or more independent sources. Nothing was fabricated, and nothing was accepted as fact merely on the word of an eyewitness. All testimony, even that of Ralph Fults, was subjected to further research.

Much of what Fults said about Bonnie and Clyde differed entirely from the popular picture painted of them. Not that Fults tried to romanticize them or his participation in their crimes. Initially, though, some of his recollections seemed beyond the bounds of truth—for instance, the capture of a fifteen-man posse by Fults and Raymond Hamilton in Mississippi. Time and again, however, Fults's stories checked out, including the capture of the posse. Further research augmented the story and solidified Fults's credibility.

Naturally, not everything could be corroborated, given the nature of the subject—the secretive nether world of an era many would rather forget. Indeed, some of those interviewed, those involved directly with Bonnie and Clyde, only agreed to make a statement because of Ralph Fults and only then if no tape recorders were used. These complications underscored the need for careful research and corroboration whenever possible. My decision whether or not to include uncorroborated material in the text was based on the consistent reliability of the source, especially eyewitnesses. Most were found to be very reliable. A few, however, could not always be wholly believed, and their uncorroborated statements were therefore eliminated from the final draft.

The statements of Ralph Fults are a major focal point of the story, although they comprise only one of a great many sources used in the preparation of the text. Nevertheless, I did not find it necessary to cite every instance of Fults's testimony. I only did so in cases where it was necessary to distinguish Fults's testimony from other sources. Any passages in the book not specifically cited should therefore be attributed directly to Fults.

In the interest of clarity and continuity, I also eliminated a number of minor characters and events from the story. Certain other characters, either still living, or in deference to the wishes of their surviving relatives, have been identified by first name only, or, where applicable, by some nickname known only to the individual concerned.

Apart from a few isolated articles, this book marks the first time an active participant in the crimes of Clyde Barrow and Bonnie Parker has given an author the inside story of one of the most notorious gangs in U.S. criminal history and of the era and circumstances that gave rise to its existence.

From the time of his prison release in 1944 until his death in 1993, Ralph Fults sought to understand the events of his early life, to put into perspective the forces that drove a handful of Depression-era Texas youths beyond the brink of self-destruction.

In later years Ralph Fults was haunted by the fact that he had survived when so many of his associates, twenty-one in all, had either been shot, stabbed, beaten to death, or executed by the state. For him, there was but one reason why he was spared: to tell the story, the whole story, revealing the darkest aspects of his past in hopes of awakening young and old alike to the wholly unromantic, unglamorous, and very real world of juvenile delinquency and adult criminal behavior.

Acknowledgments

I would like to thank all the people who gave so freely of their time and expertise and to thank those who allowed me to probe the past with them, knowing that the memories would not always be pleasant: Sgt. Bobby Adams, Texas Department of Criminal Justice, Institutional Division (TDCJ-ID), Eastham Unit; Blanche Barrow; Marie Barrow; Charles Brown, Texas Department of Criminal Justice, Institutional Division (TDCJ-ID), Public Relations Office; Mary Carey; Kermit "Curley" Crawford; Barbara Dechant; Assistant Warden Joe R. Driskell, Texas Department of Criminal Justice, Institutional Division (TDCJ-ID), Eastham Unit; Jimm Foster, Dallas Public Library, Texas/Dallas History Archives Division; Kenneth R. Fults; Ralph Fults; Ruth Fults; Johnny Hayes; Mr. and Mrs. John W. "Preacher" Hays; L. J. "Boots" Hinton; Sammie Hinton; Ken M. Holmes, Jr.; Jack (pseud.); Lt. Lonny Johnson, Texas Department of Criminal Justice, Institutional Division (TDCJ-ID), Walls Unit; Warden Morris Jones, Texas Department of Criminal Justice, Institutional Division (TDCJ-ID), Walls Unit; Peter Kurilecz, Dallas Public Library, Texas/Dallas History Archives Division; Charles T. "Tim" Leone; Warden Charles R. Martin, Texas Department of Criminal Justice, Institutional Division (TDCJ-ID), Eastham Unit; Cecil Mayes; Louise Polly Palmer, Bienville Parish Library; Dr. Robert

Pierce, Texas Prison Archives, Texas Department of Criminal Justice, Institutional Division (TDCJ-ID), and the Texas Prison Museum; John Pronk, WFAA–TV, Dallas, Texas; Bruce Quisenberry, Joplin Historical Society; James Ritchie, *Celina Record*; Carol Roark, Dallas Public Library, Texas/Dallas History Archives Division; Robert H. Russell; William B. Searles; Lt. Gene Stewart, Texas Department of Criminal Justice, Institutional Division (TDCJ-ID), Walls Unit; Carol Waller, *The Landmark*; Dr. Robert Weesner, Dexter Historical Society; Patty Wood.

I would also like to thank the following sources for supplying the many fine photographs and other materials needed to research this subject: Barker Texas History Center, Austin, Texas; Barrow Collection; Bienville Parish Courthouse, Arcadia, Louisiana; Bienville Parish Public Library, Arcadia, Louisiana; *Celina (Tex.) Record* Archive; Crawford Collection; Dallas Historical Society, Dallas, Texas; Dallas Public Library, Texas/Dallas History Archives Division; Denton County Public Library, Denton, Texas; *Des Moines Register* Photo Archives, Des Moines, Iowa; Dexter Historical Society, Dexter, Iowa; Ford Collection; Fults Collection; Hayes Collection; Hinton Collection; Holmes Collection; Houston County Historical Commission, Crockett, Texas; Houston Public Library, Houston, Texas; Joplin Historical Society, Joplin, Missouri; Kaufman County Public Library, Kaufman, Texas; Leone Collection; Lorenzo de Zavalla Library, Austin, Texas; Mayes Collection; McKinney Public Library, McKinney, Texas; Mississippi Department of Archives and History, Jackson, Mississippi; Missouri Highway Patrol Archives; Moody Ranger Museum, Waco, Texas; North Texas State University Library, Denton, Texas; Robert H. Russell Collection; Sam Houston State University Library, Huntsville, Texas; Searles Collection; Shelby County Public Library, Memphis, Tennessee; Stonewall County Historical Society, Aspermont, Texas; Tarrant County Community College District Library, Northeast Campus, Fort Worth, Texas; Texas Prison Archives, Department of Criminal Justice, Institutional Division (TDCJ-ID), Huntsville, Texas; Texas Department of Criminal Justice, Institutional Division (TDCJ-ID), Eastham Unit, Weldon, Texas; Texas Department of Criminal Justice, Institutional Division (TDCJ-ID), Walls Unit, Huntsville, Texas; Texas Prison Museum, Huntsville, Texas;

United States Government Archives, Fort Worth Branch, Fort Worth, Texas; Wichita County Public Library, Wichita Falls, Texas.

Running with Bonnie and Clyde

May 23, 1934

"Hey, Fults," a voice called out, cutting through the random sounds of farm tools clicking against sun-parched earth. "They finally got them little punk friends of yours this morning." Fults, hoeing weeds in a furrow of green cotton plants, straightened his lean, six-foot frame and glanced first to the shotgun barrel pointed at his chest, then to the smiling face of the guard who gripped the weapon. In all directions uniformed men stood, guns ready.

"Bonnie and Clyde," the guard went on to say. "Shot their goddamned butts to pieces over in Louisiana, not more than two hours ago."

The guard seemed to savor the news. He stared at Fults through dark glasses, fingering the safety catch on his shotgun. Fifty yards away a horseman sat erect on his mount, a high-powered rifle resting on his leg. It looked like a setup.[1]

Fults had seen it before—guards goading convicts into making stupid moves. It was nothing new, especially for Eastham, "the bloody 'ham," reputedly the toughest prison farm in Texas. But such things had little effect on Fults. He had lived with it for nearly ten years, from reform school to the penitentiary, through beatings, shootings, and knifings. He was numb to it, not the least bit surprised by anything he saw or heard in prison, including the information conveyed by the guard standing before him.

Fults had always known that death was the only way out for his friends Bonnie and Clyde. Everyone knew it, even Bonnie and Clyde—especially Bonnie and Clyde. Still, Fults could not help being moved. He had been through a lot with Clyde Barrow and had always held nothing but the greatest affection for Bonnie. Nevertheless, he was not about to give his shotgun-wielding friend the satisfaction of knowing his true feelings. There would be enough celebrating among the ranks of the Eastham guards without that. To every employee of the prison system, the deaths of Bonnie and Clyde settled a score.

A fellow guard, a man named Crowson, had been killed five months earlier during Clyde's infamous raid on Eastham. It did not seem to matter that Clyde was not the actual triggerman. Nor did it matter that the real killer, a sickly convict stricken with ulcers, asthma, and perhaps tuberculosis, was said to have been the frequent recipient of Crowson's brutal beatings—the result of not being able to keep up with the other prisoners in the fields. Indeed, Crowson had been earmarked for death long before Clyde Barrow arrived that winter morning.[2]

Regardless, Clyde Barrow was the man with the name, a celebrity of sorts. His raid had embarrassed many Texas prison officials, particularly Col. Lee Simmons, the general manager who once swore to curb the high incidence of prison escapes. It was Simmons who implemented the fatal ambush in Louisiana.[3]

"I want you to put Bonnie and Clyde on the spot and shoot everyone in sight," Simmons told Capt. Frank Hamer, a retired Texas Ranger hired to put an end to the Barrow gang.[4] There would be no arrest, only action arranged for by Simmons and sanctioned by the governor of Texas, Miriam Ferguson.[5]

Not that Clyde Barrow was about to submit to an arrest. He vowed never to be taken alive. Certainly, others had made similar statements only to recant their words at the last minute. However, after the deaths of nine lawmen and one civilian, it was apparent that Barrow would stand by his word.[6]

Now Clyde was dead—and Bonnie too. Despite the headlines, Bonnie never smoked cigars and was not the promiscuous gun moll she was supposed to be. Her part in the raid consisted of waiting in the car and sounding the horn so that Clyde, James Mullens, and the escaping prisoners could find their way through the thick fog enveloping the area.[7] In time others would die for their part in the terrible raid of January 16, 1934. Few people tangled with prison management and survived.[8]

Had the guard standing before him only known of Fults's involvement in the raid, he would have killed him right there in that cotton field, no questions asked. But only a small group of people knew the truth about the raid, and most of them were either dead or facing execution. Those who remained were not inclined to talk. Fults looked away from the guard and went back to work.

That night Fults couldn't sleep. He just lay there in his bunk, eyes wide open, thinking of the card he had received from Barrow and Parker just two weeks before. Fults was still inside prison walls in Huntsville when it arrived. Signed "Joe and Mary," but unquestionably penned by Bonnie, the note hinted at the possibility of a future attempt to free Fults: "Thinking of You. Hope to see you soon. Hope we all live to see the flowers bloom." Fults destroyed the card and waited for the break that never came. On hearing of the ambush, he thought of that last line. Its significance would haunt him for the rest of his life.

The sounds of snoring men interrupted Fults's thoughts. A voice called out, "I'm getting up now, Captain." The guard motioned, and soon bare feet could be heard slapping across the pine floor boards, heading for the line of exposed toilets at the far end of the Camp 2 dormitory.

In an act of sheer desperation Clyde had killed his first man in front of the Camp 1 toilets, a mile to the north. Most of Clyde's violent acts stemmed from desperation. Prison had taught him the word's starkest meaning. His experiences at Eastham had changed him from a schoolboy to a rattlesnake right before Fults's eyes.[9] But there was once a time when Clyde didn't have his back against the wall. Fults could still remember those times. Even after nearly four years he vividly recalled the day he first met Clyde Barrow. He could still see his face. He could almost hear his voice.

September 18, 1930

It was a hot, dusty Texas day. Even for September the heat was stifling.[1] Perspiration beaded on Fults's brow and trickled down the sides of his face. His black and white striped denim uniform stuck to his skin like a moist towel. The prison van kicked up choking gusts of hot wind as it knifed its way through the humid air of east-central Texas, en route to "the walls," the main penitentiary unit at Huntsville.

Fults had not seen the inside of the Texas penitentiary since his escape from Eastham Prison Farm nearly six months earlier. During those months he had been lucky, drifting as far north as Illinois and as far west as California, without as much as a second glance from a policeman. But in Missouri his luck ran out. A St. Louis detective caught him burglarizing a large commercial business. Fults was arrested and found to be an escaped convict from Texas.

Escapees were not tolerated in Texas. To demonstrate this, prison officials there sent legendary transfer agent Bud Russell all the way to St. Louis to retrieve Fults.[2] The nineteen-year-old convict could easily envision the type of reception that awaited him at Eastham, but he tried not to dwell on it. Instead, he sat in silence, smoking a cigarette and daydreaming. Around his neck a heavy chain and padlock pulled and pinched his skin each time the prison transport hit a bump in the road.

The opposite end of the chain was attached to another chain suspended at eye level between the two rows of prisoners seated in the rear of the big truck.

Throughout much of the return journey to Texas Fults had ridden alone, his only companion the reflection of Bud Russell's eyes that glared at him from one or more of the strategically placed mirrors used to monitor the prisoners. Following all-night layovers in Dallas and Waco, however, on the sixteenth and seventeenth, respectively, additional prisoners joined Fults. On the morning of September 18 Russell drove away from the Waco jail, his truck filled to capacity.

Fults stared at the passing fields of dry Johnson grass, blurs of brown and gold. Sometimes abandoned farm houses stood in the fields, foreclosure notices posted on them. Other times groups of people could be seen camping along the roadside, their vehicles either broken down or out of gas, their dreams of California broken as well. Fults had seen many such things in the months since his escape.

In Kansas City he witnessed a vast community of homeless people, most of them farmers, living in wooden crates and cardboard boxes adjacent to the main railroad switching yard. The residents called their little city "Hoover Town," after the president. Many were malnourished. Some were desperate enough to trap rats and boil them. "Hoover hogs," they called them.[3] Fults felt sorry for those people. He could not forget their faces. He took a puff from his cigarette and closed his eyes.

Suddenly a strange voice called through the din of road noises, "Say, ain't you been on that prison farm, the one they call Eastham?"

Unaware that the question had been directed to him, Fults failed to respond.

"Say, fella, haven't you been on Eastham before?"

Fults glanced from the roadside to a young man seated directly across from him—a late arrival from the Waco jail. His face was lean and smooth. Coal black hair and deep brown eyes contrasted sharply with otherwise delicate features. Dressed in a jacket and tie, he looked more like a schoolboy than a convict.[4]

"Yeh," said Fults. "I've been on Eastham before."

"What's it like?" asked the young man.

"Well, it ain't no damned picnic," said Fults. "There's two things they'll just flat out kill you for—not working, and running. You run once, they'll just rough you up a little. You run again, they take you over some hill and put a slug in the back of your head. 'Attempted escape,' they call it. We call it 'spot killing' "[5]

"Shoot, they can't do stuff like that," said the youth, grinning.

"Man, they've got the guns and they've got the law. They can do any damned thing they want to. There's a pretty good-sized graveyard over at Camp 1 just full of guys who thought otherwise," said Fults, studying the young man closely. He was probably not more than five feet, six inches tall and could not have weighed more than 125 pounds. Fults wondered how long he would last in prison.

"You got a name?" asked Fults.

"Yeh," said the young man. "I'm Clyde Barrow."

"My name's Ralph."

"What are you in for, Ralph?" asked Barrow.

"Burglary," Fults answered.

"Yeh, me too," said Barrow.[6] "I've been in Huntsville, behind them walls. They've had a bench warrant on me. They kept running me here and there, charging me with every burglary and car heist in the state.[7] This last one in Waco got thrown out of court. Hell, they all did. Now I'm hearing I'm supposed to get shipped out to Eastham. That's why I was asking you about it.

"I had an older brother in the joint. He got sent up for burglary too. I was thinking I'd get to see him, but he escaped—just walked out the front gate and drove off in some guard's car.[8] Hell, I don't think those dumb-asses even know he's gone.[9] You got family, Ralph?"

Fults hesitated. Throughout his adolescence, nearly a third of his life, he had probably spent less than two weeks at home.

"Yeh," Fults answered, "I guess so."

"Slim Jim"

Ralph Fults was born in the tiny north Texas town of Anna on January 23, 1911. His parents, Audie and Sophie Fults, moved to Texas shortly after the turn of the century when Audie was offered a better paying job with the United States Postal Service. The family moved again, to nearby McKinney, when Audie was transferred by the Postal Service shortly after Ralph's birth.

McKinney, forty miles north of Dallas, was a quiet agricultural community of approximately 6,600 inhabitants.[1] Early in this century, dusty little gravel streets meandered through rolling hills of oak and mesquite. Around the square, red-brick streets were lined with small shops. It was a typically quiet, rural Texas scene, to which the Fultses and their ever-expanding family adapted well, except for Ralph.

Of the eight children born to Audie and Sophie Fults, only Ralph developed a pattern of troublesome behavior. While his brother and six sisters worked hard to attain good grades in school, Ralph became less and less attentive in class. He thought the curriculum banal. He seemed forever bored and restless, brimming with energy.

Fults grew combative, both verbally and physically. Perhaps he sought a vent for his energy, or possibly he resented being a part of such a large family and wanted to stand out in the crowd. For whatever reason, he soon developed a reputation as a vicious street fighter. At first he fought his schoolmates; soon he was battling grown men.[2]

It is difficult to pinpoint the cause of such behavior. The Fultses apparently maintained a comfortable, middle-class lifestyle. The family was never in want of anything. Without exception, Ralph's parents are described as having been gentle, soft-spoken people, easygoing and exceedingly humorous. Audie Fults was known throughout the county as a storyteller and wit.[3] What, then, caused Ralph Fults to seek and apparently enjoy violence?

Some psychological studies indicate that perpetrators of violent acts had often themselves witnessed violence as children.[4] Despite the ideal setting of his home life, Fults saw four violent deaths before he reached the age of sixteen. His first experience involved the last public execution carried out in McKinney.

The prisoner, a convicted murderer who had stuffed his victim into a water well, was led onto the scaffold. The thick rope, drawn tight against the condemned man's throat, looped upward behind his left ear. With a sharp jerk of the lever, the double doors opened with a horrible crash. The fall, grossly miscalculated, nearly tore the man's head from his body.[5] Fults reeled away in horror, the image burned into his mind.

Within a week Fults would see a man gunned down in cold blood on the town square. Then, after he left home, the boy witnessed a shooting in Oklahoma, and later he saw the slitting of a man's throat in California. By the age of eighteen Fults was in prison, where death was an everyday experience. How could this happen to a child from a small town in America?

Fults came of age during the 1920s. Despite the popular image of flappers, jazz, and prosperity, the decade was one of contrasts, marred by riots, depression, and dire poverty.[6] Scandals in baseball[7] and in the administration of President Warren G. Harding,[8] racial intolerance and the expansion of the Ku Klux Klan,[9] coupled with the revelation that Treasury Secretary Andrew Mellon had doled out $3.5 billion in corporate tax breaks during his tenure through three administrations, helped shape a generation of cynical, uneasy youths.[10]

Parental control relaxed during this period as families became more democratic. The availability of automobiles made it easier for teenagers to escape the constraints of the family. Popular images created by radio, movies, and magazines furthered this trend.[11] Political cartoonists and humorists made sport of bankers, big business, and politicians.[12] Certain Sunday comics like "Slim Jim" made a hero out of an outlaw and reflected growing cynicism.

Ralph loved "Slim Jim." Appearing in most rural newspapers throughout the twenties, it depicted a clever young bandit who always managed to escape from the law, no matter how hopeless the situation seemed.

To an impressionable boy like Ralph, "Slim Jim" was a hero to believe in, something for a child from a sleepy North Texas town to seek as a model for excitement. It all seemed like a fun game—to live the life of an outlaw, a modern day Robin Hood, laughing at a corrupt world. Ralph wanted to be "Slim Jim."[13]

This is not to say that Fults was indolent. Though amply provided for, the youngster nevertheless worked a number of odd jobs to earn extra money. He sold fireworks, worked in the local Coca-Cola bottling plant, and maintained a paper route. He spent most of his earnings on silent movies, particularly westerns in which the outlaw triumphed. When Fults was fourteen, he went to work for a local bicycle repairman, a man named Larson.

While in Larson's employ, Fults developed a keen interest in two of the repairman's other areas of expertise—guns and locks. The boy had never been around firearms, but under Larson's instruction he soon learned to handle and repair almost any weapon. Fults also acquired a basic working knowledge of locks, from the most common variety to complex systems like Mosler safes.

The boy began putting his newfound understanding of locks to practical use, as a game at first, hoping to emulate the character of "Slim Jim." A sudden rash of midnight burglaries swept McKinney. The sheriff suspected children because the items taken were candy and cigarettes. One Sunday he grabbed Fults by the arm.

"I know you've been breaking into these stores around here," he said. "Another kid's folks caught him with a bunch of cigarettes, and he said he got them from you. You bring your folks down to my office tomorrow morning so we can straighten this thing out."

"Yes sir," Fults said obediently. As soon as the sheriff was out of sight, the boy ran down to the railroad switching yard and hopped the first train headed north. Two years would pass before his family would find out what had happened to him.

After he left McKinney, Fults staged a number of burglaries in Oklahoma before drifting out to West Texas. In the town of Aspermont he was caught with a suitcase full of stolen goods and placed in the county jail, a heavy, two-story limestone building located just east of the town square. Fults called himself Raymond Johnson, an orphan from Oklahoma.[14] The sheriff wrote the information down while Fults memorized the layout of the building. Downstairs was divided between the sheriff's office and his living quarters. The top floor of the jail contained a single block of six cells, with eight unglazed windows affording the only light. Each window contained vertical bars to keep the prisoners in and shutters to keep the weather out.[15] The cells were secured by means of a large, primitive padlock hooked through a heavy iron hasp. A padlocked door sealed off access to the stairway. At night, or when he was away, the sheriff always bolted the heavy iron exterior doors.[16]

Within a week Fults had fashioned a key from a Prince Albert tobacco can he had smuggled into his cell. While the sheriff and his family attended a county fair two blocks away, Fults tripped the lock of his cell with the homemade key and escaped, freeing all the other prisoners in the process. Seeing the escapees running through a field of corn, someone telephoned for help. Momentarily a hastily gathered posse raced after the fleeing prisoners. Several shots rang out. Fults kept running. A bullet whistled past his head—then another. He stopped, but the others kept on going. Only Fults, the instigator of the escape, was recaptured. The rest, including a convicted bank robber, vanished.[17] The sheriff was livid. At Fults's trial he pressed to have the boy remanded to the state reformatory. The judge agreed. Thus, at age fourteen Ralph Fults was sentenced to the notorious State Juvenile Training School at Gatesville.[18]

Gatesville

The State Juvenile Training School, later called the Gatesville State School for Boys, chartered in 1887, had a reputation for graduating hardened criminals. Veterans of the institution stood a 90 percent chance of one day being sentenced to the penitentiary.[1] The reformatory compound extended over several hundred acres of land and encompassed wooded areas as well as open fields. The yards were well manicured, with many gardens and fine lawns. Benches dotted the numerous shaded areas, but few people used them. Crops such as cotton and corn were cultivated to help offset the cost of operating such a large facility. The offices, classrooms, and living quarters were uniformly positioned around a pristine parade field. The campus resembled a military compound. Indeed, life at the school was conducted in strict military fashion.

Each morning before dawn the youths were mustered onto the parade grounds for inspection. A series of calisthenics then ensued, followed by drill practice. After breakfast most of the boys attended classes for half a day. However, those who had already graduated from the high school went straight to work. Some boys deliberately failed to keep from working a full day, but Fults finished school as fast as he could, preferring the outdoors to books.

Within two years Fults's urge to roam caught up with him. He scraped together all of his gambling money, gambling being the major source of income at the school, and purchased seven hacksaw blades from a fellow he knew in the metal shop. Each evening he worked on the bars of his dormitory window. On April 16, 1927, Fults and thirteen others lowered themselves to the ground and scattered.[2]

Two weeks later in Duncan, Arizona, Fults pulled up to a diner in a stolen coupe. A local deputy noticed the Texas license plates.

"That car belong to you, kid?" inquired the officer. Fults nodded. The deputy showed the boy a telegram from the Department of Justice, listing the vehicle as stolen. Fults was arrested. No one bothered to search him for weapons, however. When the people of Duncan settled down for their afternoon siesta, Fults came to life. He produced a knife and jabbed it into the old lock that secured the door of his cell. The jail was a one room adobe hut several feet from the sheriff's office. Fults thought it was an outhouse when he first saw it. It was easy to break out. Within hours of his incarceration he was forging deep into the Arizona desert. But he had never before dealt with the extremes of a desert climate. The sweltering summer sun burned high overhead. Soon everything started looking the same. Throughout the day Fults wandered aimlessly in the desert. By nightfall he was desperate. He did not even care if the sheriff picked him up. Then, at 1:00 A.M. he spotted several wagons. A road crew was camped alongside an unfinished spur of the main highway.

Fults crept into the campsite. He found an empty bottle and quietly filled it with water. Grabbing a few biscuits, he started following the freshly graded road back toward the main highway. At daybreak he hitched a ride west.

In Tucson, however, Fults was arrested on a vagrancy charge and once again went to jail. Late the following evening officials from the Texas reformatory arrived by train. They identified Fults as Raymond Johnson, and after making arrangements to extradite the boy, retired to a local motor court. Fults knew he was running out of time. He spotted an air duct in his cell and began backing off the screws that secured the grate.

Someone in the next cell said, "No one can fit in that shaft, so you may as well not try, boy." Fults crawled into the duct without saying a word.

The young fugitive took a bus to Seminole, Oklahoma, where a friend named Hardluck operated a shooting gallery. Through Hardluck, Fults met several members of Oklahoma's underworld community. Blackie Thompson and Whitey Walker were a pair of inexperienced stick-up men in 1927.[3] So was Wilbur Underhill.[4] At that time all three were associated with the Kimes brothers, safecrackers who later turned to bank robbery.[5] Fults would stage a number of burglaries with Thompson before switching to auto theft on a full-time basis.[6]

Hardluck also introduced Fults to a fellow who ran an auto parts junkyard. The junk man offered Fults $350 for each late model Ford or Chevrolet he could bring in. Fults hitched a ride to Oklahoma City and returned with a brand new Model T that evening.

"Nice going, kid," laughed the junk man, counting out the cash. "You oughta get real rich if you keep it up." One night, however, Fults and another boy were on their way back from Oklahoma City with another stolen car when the Shawnee County sheriff spotted them.

The sheriff's old car lost ground quickly, but Fults's accomplice took a corner too fast. The car overturned, throwing both boys free. Miraculously uninjured, they scrambled to their feet and dashed across the limestone prairie. Fults heard gunshots. Something struck his right arm. He knew he'd been hit, but he kept running.

At Hardluck's gallery Fults's arm was treated by a physician who kept a closed mouth for the right price. A tight-lipped doctor was a fugitive's most valuable asset. Fults had to pay several hundred dollars, but the doctor saved his arm and his life.

As soon as his arm had healed sufficiently, Fults returned to Oklahoma City. At one of his favorite Ford dealerships he picked out a fine looking Model T and climbed in. Suddenly a heavy hand was on his shoulder.

"Hey kid, where are you goin'?" said a city detective. Fults turned toward the sound of the voice. The barrel of a .44 was all he saw.

"Put that hogleg away. I'll come quietly," said the boy. Within days he was back at the reformatory in Texas.

After losing his freedom, Fults tried to stay out of trouble. He joined the school football team and started attending optional Sunday church services. One Sunday Fults asked his friend Johnny if he wanted to go

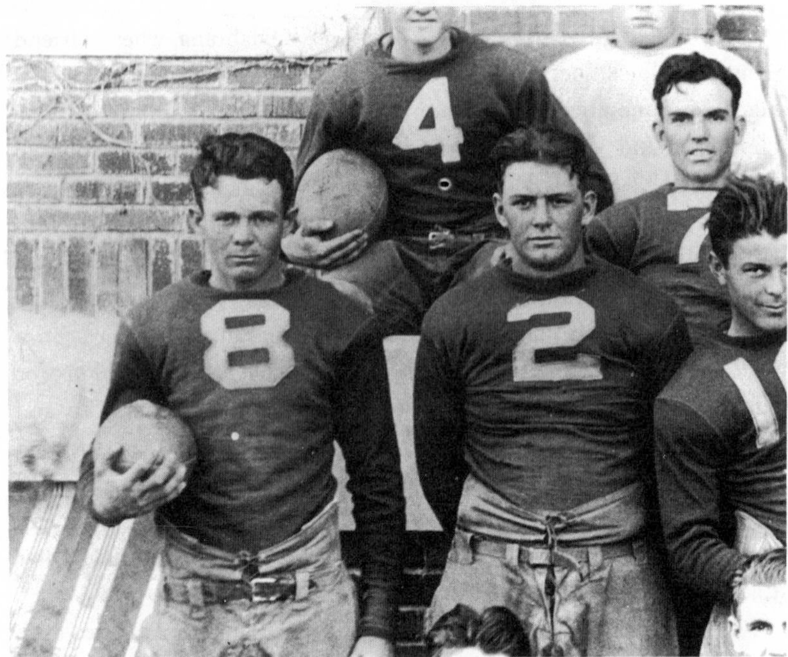

Ralph Fults, number 8 and Johnny, number 2, on the football squad of the Texas State Juvenile Training School at Gatesville. Fults once tried to secure a seat for Johnny in the reformatory chapel. Johnny later become part of the Lake Dallas Gang and was with Clyde Barrow and Ted Rogers the night John N. Bucher was killed. (Courtesy of the Fults family.)

to church with him. Johnny said yes.

Fults agreed to save a place for Johnny. Before the service, from the wings of the chapel the chaplain saw Fults lean over to the next boy and ask him to hold a seat for Johnny.

After church Fults was grabbed by the arm and dragged toward a shed reserved for the administration of corporal punishment.[7] In the scuffle he could see the other boy, the one he had spoken to in church, being dragged behind him. They were both shoved into the dark shed and forced to remove their clothes.

Fults was startled when the two-hundred-pound camp commander kicked the door open with the toe of his boot and charged into the room.[8]

"O.K., tough punk," he said, "Back here less than two months and already in trouble."

The commander unrolled a thick leather strap, called "the bat," and started crimping the edges.

"The chaplain seen you little bastards talking in church," he said. "I'll teach you not to do that again."

The other boy was first. Twenty lashes came and went with no indication the commander was going to let up. Above the screaming and crying, Fults could hear the sound of leather slapping across bare flesh. After thirty-two lashes, the boy's back was a bloody mess. Now it was Fults's turn.

He was thrown over the bench and held down by five guards. Fults could see the commander in the corner of his eye. He saw him toss the first strap aside and reach for another. It had been soaked in linseed oil,[9] making the leather thick and heavy.

The first few lashes found Fults's naked haunches. An eternity passed. Again and again the oil-soaked strap tore into his flesh. Each blow sent blinding waves of pain throughout his body. He tried to keep a steady count—35, 36, 37. He faded in and out of consciousness. He wanted to die. He very nearly got his wish.

Those on the parade grounds listened to the screams. Finally, the commander threw the bat down and left the shed. Fults lay in a state of delirium. Blood was everywhere. He could not move.[10]

Three boys from the dormitory were summoned to carry Fults to his bunk. One of them took a soft sponge and daubed cool water on his cuts. Fults had never hated anyone before. But now he hated the chaplain and the commander. He wanted their deaths. He wanted to kill them both. If they were examples of Christian civilization, then he wanted no part of it. Such a life was meaningless. The game was over. "Slim Jim" was dead.

It was three months before Fults could lie on his back again. Nevertheless, he was expected to be on the job the day after the beating. Before dawn he was helped out of his bunk and guided to the parade grounds. In the fields he worked without a shirt because the fabric stuck to his wounds. A sunburn resulted.

Three months later Fults and Johnny escaped in an old four-cylinder Chevrolet truck parked in the reformatory garage.[11] Speeding past a startled guard at the front gate, the escapees turned their vehicle onto Valley Mills Road. It was a steep grade, and the truck began losing power. Soon smoke poured from beneath the hood. The truck finally died halfway up the hill.

The boys heard the sound of snarling hound dogs. The mounted posse was on the trail. Grabbing a couple of pick handles for protection, the escapees ran through a nearby mesquite thicket. Briars and prickly pear needles tore their clothes, and soon the boys were entangled in the underbrush. Before long a dozen or more large dogs cut them off. They were trapped.

After a few minutes the posse rode up. Shouting men armed with shotguns, revolvers, and carbines closed in. The dogs were loud and angry. Everyone was out of breath and filled with the heat of pursuit.

A horseman moved in close to Fults. Fults responded with his pick handle, trying to break the guard's leg with the first swing. The horseman retreated. The dogs charged, and a roar went out from the pack as they lunged forward. Fults and Johnny killed the first two dogs to reach them.[12] The other animals halted. The leader of the posse signaled to a fellow horseman to fetch his bullwhip. In a matter of minutes he was stinging the boys about the face, forcing them to the ground while the rest of the posse closed in and chained them together.[13] Fults watched as the dog sergeant surveyed his dead and injured animals.

"Guess every dog has his day," Fults said sarcastically. Suddenly a blow across the back of his head sent him crashing to the ground. The next day Fults found himself in the commander's office.

"Fults," said the commander, "you're the worst kid we've ever had here at Gatesville. We think your ready for a diploma. You've just graduated to the 'pen'."

"Well, Captain," said Fults, "I don't think I'm old enough for the pen."

"No, but by god you're damn mean enough for it," he said, banging his fist on the desk. "Tomorrow you're walkin' out of this here front gate. We want you to get the hell out and stay out," he screamed. "Maybe we can't put you in the pen but I guarantee you'll put yourself there faster than hell. Now get out."[14]

The following morning, the boy picked up his release papers, packed his belongings, and stepped through the main gate. He could not believe he was being kicked out of a reform school.

Unable to find work, Fults drifted in and out of illegal card games in McKinney. The link to these games was the City Cafe, on Tennessee Street. Located in the shadow of the county courthouse, and only a block from the jail, it was favored by underworld figures and honest citizens alike. Bootleggers would take their calls across the street in the domino parlor and later would meet buyers in the cafe. Nearly everyone, including local authorities,[15] knew about the transactions, but few cared. It was a sign of the times.

It was 1929, and although an optimistic America hoped that perhaps its new president, Herbert Hoover, could stabilize the already crumbling rural economy, it was too late for the farmers of North Texas. Hoover's Farm Relief Bill of 1929 did little to squelch the prohibitive costs of production.[16] Feed and machinery had become luxuries. Ranchers destroyed their livestock rather than watch the animals starve to death. One Denton County farmer lost his house, his barn, and two-hundred acres of choice land because of a $110 mortgage.[17] Some farmers tried to slug it out, barely breaking even. Others packed up for Dallas.

By contrast, Dallas was a virtual boom town in 1929. In ten years its population had nearly doubled.[18] Industry was thriving, and the southwest was flocking to its doors.

Upward mobility may have been an American byword of the early 1920s, but the city of Dallas was founded much earlier on the concept. In 1841, when John Neely Bryan arrived on the rolling plains above the Trinity River, he envisioned a colossal real estate venture.[19] Before long other entrepreneurs and land developers joined him.[20] From that point on, jobs, trade, and cash flooded the area. It was the latter commodity that most interested Fults. In April 1929 he joined the rural exodus to the city.

Fults located Johnny and another reform school friend named Fuzz. Together they began stealing boxcar loads of cigarettes from a freight yard south of downtown and selling them to a grocer from Greenville,

Texas. However, when the grocer was caught selling the stolen merchandise, he named Fults, the only one of the three he knew, in exchange for clemency.

At the close of Fults's trial, the judge offered a cryptic warning: "Change your ways, boy, or prepare yourself for the feel of those three jolts of electricity they give you down in Huntsville. At the rate you're going, you'll be sent to the chair or hanged before you're 21."[21]

Fults was sentenced to two years in the Texas State Penitentiary. The judge initially tried to send the eighteen-year-old back to the Texas reformatory, but the institution refused to have him. The commander there had been right. Six weeks after leaving the reformatory, Ralph Fults indeed graduated.

Escape from the Hole

As a youngster growing up in McKinney, Fults would join the large crowds that gathered at the train depot whenever a load of prisoners bound for the penitentiary happened to pass through town. The tough-looking convicts were not their object of interest, however; they were curious about the lone figure standing guard. His name was Bud Russell. The people would gaze in awe as he disembarked from the train, lined his men up on the platform, often as many as eighty at a time,[1] and led them in chains down the street to the county jail. In later years he transferred all of his prisoners by truck, but initially such work was accomplished by rail. He spoke few words, made no fast moves, and never allowed an escape. Fults thought Russell was the meanest-looking man he had ever seen.

Fults never dreamed that one day he would wind up on the business end of Russell's chain. Following the youngster's conviction, however, that possibility became reality. Two days after the close of his trial, Fults became one of the 115,000 faceless men and women to be transferred to the penitentiary during Russell's long career.[2]

Russell's reputation was enormous. A delicate balance of fear and respect followed him wherever he went. The prisoners knew that in the event of an attempted escape, gunplay could be expected. Russell would never lay down his weapons. "You're just about forty years too late if you think you're tougher than me," he often said.[3] He would die before giving up a prisoner.

Once, in Houston, Russell emptied his shotgun into the face of an unarmed bystander.[4] The victim, apparently breaking from a crowd of curious onlookers to greet his brother, died on the spot. Thinking an escape attempt was underway, Russell, shot first and asked questions later.

Over the years at least two folk songs were written about Russell—tales of "Uncle Bud" and the boys he kept "working on his farm."[5]

Russell's transport truck had a sinister look about it. The rear of the oversized frame was encased in heavy black boiler plate and wire mesh. During cold or rainy weather canvas flaps were lowered over the mesh to afford some protection. To the rear, narrow double doors, twice bolted and secured with Yale padlocks, sealed the convicts in. Mirrors were placed throughout the cab so that the guard could observe the prisoners from different angles. Mud-grip tires and heavy-duty springs supported the massive weight. A high-performance engine carried the load at peak speeds. Due to the considerable reputation of its designer, Bud Russell's pride and joy was soon tagged "the one-way wagon" by its convict passengers. Wherever they went, "Uncle Bud" and his "one-way wagon" drew crowds.[6]

On the morning of Fults's journey to "the walls" the alley behind the Dallas County Jail contained just such a crowd. Fults mingled with the other county prisoners. He could feel the eyes of the transfer agent penetrating the group, sizing up each convict. In his dark glasses, suit, and Stetson hat, he looked every bit as menacing as Fults remembered. A blue steel .44 and a double-barrelled shotgun served to reinforce the image.

Before a prisoner was allowed into the alley, a younger man took him aside, wrapped a short length of chain around his neck, and locked it to a longer chain. This prevented escapes by linking each convict to the others.

Fults was the last to be chained. In the process he was able to get a good look at Russell's young assistant. It turned out to be Roy Russell, Bud's son. Roy was a gaunt young man in his late twenties. Taller than his father, Roy stood six feet, two inches tall, but he possessed many of the elder Russell's traits—silence, reservation, and a sense of fair play. Nevertheless, many remember him as being much tougher than his father.[7]

"Inside," Roy commanded, motioning toward the black transport.

By 1929 the Texas Prison System was considered one of the most notorious of southern agencies—overcrowded, disorganized, and brutal.[8] Rumors of overzealous guards and long hours in the fields made the reformatory at Gatesville seem like a country picnic. As the transport approached Huntsville's fringes, Fults viewed the prison's notorious walls for the first time. What he saw was the aging facade of a penitentiary started before the Civil War and enlarged as the need arose, subject to the availability of funds. Meant to house no more than twelve-hundred prisoners, it had nearly one and one-half times that amount stuffed into it by the time Fults arrived.[9] Each cell held up to four men. There was no running water, and buckets took the place of toilets. Prisoners also slept in the corridors or out in the yard—wherever a blanket could be thrown.

The East Building, started in 1843, was originally nothing more than a one-story row of open-air cells, like cages in a zoo. Within its walls Kiowa chieftain Satanta and John Wesley Hardin had been held. By 1900, however, the East Building had been enclosed and expanded to three levels.[10] The South Building, completed in 1919, radiated from the East Building at a ninety-degree angle, making one large L-shaped cell block. South Building had an extra row of seven cells. That was 7 Level—Death Row.

The addition of the South Building had done little to relieve the crowded, filthy conditions. Rats roamed freely through garbage stacked in the yard. The rotting, three-story, frame hospital was so outdated and infested with insects that it was virtually uninhabitable. Fire prevention was nonexistent.[11]

"Nothing could be worse than this," Fults thought, gazing at the filthy main prison upon his June 16 arrival. He was wrong. Eastham Farm, his final destination, would be worse. Encompassing thirteen thousand acres of boggy Trinity River bottom land forty miles northeast of Huntsville, Eastham was at the time actually two separate farms sharing a common

Ralph Fults, age nineteen, Walls Unit, Huntsville, Texas, 1930. (Courtesy of the Texas Prison Archives, Texas Department of Criminal Justice, Institutional Division [TDCJ-ID].)

woodland. Fults was assigned to Camp 1, the older of the two.

From the moment Fults first set foot on Eastham soil, he knew it was no reform school. Reserved for incorrigibles, Eastham was aptly termed "the bloody 'ham."[12] The presence of a large graveyard attested to the effectiveness of the bonuses paid for each escapee brought back dead or alive. Piles of garbage lay in stagnant pools of raw sewage not far from the main building. The sight compelled a visiting member of the prison board to remark that "the slave camps of olden times could not have been more unsanitary."[13]

The main building, constructed of reinforced steel and concrete, was dark and purely functional. The structure faced south and utilized a central, two-story, rectangular core from which a pair of large, one-story halls radiated, producing a T-shaped floor plan. The west wing housed the dormitory where prisoners slept on two- and three-tiered cast-iron bunks. Once a year the men removed their mattresses while a crew of trustees applied blow torches to the bed frames. It was the only efficient method of killing the millions of insects that infested the building. Along the back wall stood a row of open toilets and showers. The aging, inferior plumbing invariably backed up, leaving pools of raw sewage in the yard.

Two rows of iron bars were anchored in the floor and ceiling along the length of the dormitory, separating the bunks from the open, barred windows by about four feet. The effect was to create a space within a space, affording greater security.

Disturbances often flared in the bunk area. Convict trustees called "building tenders" usually handled any problem. If the disturbance continued, an armed guard posted outside the bars would take his weapon, aim high, and fire a few rounds over the prisoners' heads. If the trouble persisted, the guard would lower the muzzle and shoot indiscriminately into the crowd. The west wall bore pock-marks of holes blasted out by those bullets.[14]

The east wing housed the kitchen, dining, laundry, and utility areas. In addition, a small, brick bakery had been added to the northeast corner of the hall. Its positioning would later become a strategic factor for Fults.

The ground floor of the building's rectangular midsection housed Eastham's administrative offices, while a barracks, supplied for the farm's many live-in guards, occupied the second floor. Reached by means of interior and exterior stairways, the barracks overlooked the prison yard as well as the tar-and-gravel roofs of the two single-story halls.

Lights were out at 9:00 P.M. sharp. However, beneath the prisoner's bunks a row of low-wattage bulbs glowed eerily all night. An armed guard kept an eye out for feet on the floor. If a prisoner had to use the bathroom at some point during the evening, he was expected to call out to the guard beforehand.

Two building tenders were positioned inside the bunk area. Each of these men may have carried a blackjack, a knife, or a glove mounted with razor blades called a "tough nut." They were often a little too anxious to use these weapons.

The farm manager, later fired for incompetency,[15] approached Fults and the other new arrivals. He wasted no time in demonstrating his authority.

"What are you here for, boy?" he asked one of the prisoners. "Armed

Eastham Camp 1, 1994. (Photo by John Neal Phillips.)

robbery," the man said. Without warning, the manager struck the convict across the face with a cane he was carrying. The man tumbled to his knees.

"I just want to let you bastards know that when addressing me, you begin and end your statement with 'Captain, Sir'," said the warden. "You're here to be punished, not rehabilitated. Any of you caught breaking the rules will wind up over in that graveyard. Understood?"

"Yes, Captain, Sir," the prisoners answered.

"Good," said the manager. "Now grab them tools and get your butts out in them fields, pronto!"

An 1871 ruling had established that any convicted felon in the state of Texas was to be considered "a slave of the state . . . civiliter mortuus . . . a dead man."[16] In the fields of Eastham this ruling was taken quite literally. A shotgun ring, six guards armed with Browning Long Tom shotguns, surrounded each work squad. Beyond the shotgun ring, a series of strategically placed horsemen lined the perimeter of the field. The horsemen, referred to as highriders, were noted marksmen, each carrying a Winchester 30–30. Should a prisoner break past the shotgun ring, it was the job of the highriders to prevent his escape.[17]

Fults found the penitentiary an excellent training ground for crime.

Two notorious brothers from Amarillo openly outlined the tricks of their bank-robbing trade to the eager eighteen-year-old. Henry Methvin, nicknamed "Scarneck" because of an old ax wound in back of his head, also spoke of armed robbery, as did Joe Palmer, a convicted killer from San Antonio. Cupping a hand over their mouths, as if to support the ever-present cigarette dangling from their lips, the inmates masked their conversations. On the inside, everyone smoked.

Occupying the bunk across the isle from Fults was a gangland refugee named Eddie. Eddie was a small, wiry fellow, standing about five feet tall. Originally from Chicago, he was, at least until February 14, 1929, directly connected to the Capone mob. The heat of the St. Valentine's Day Massacre had prompted him to leave town fast. He drifted to Texas where he was arrested and convicted of armed robbery. His share of a few dollars netted him a ten-year sentence.

In soft, methodical tones, Eddie related stories of Chicago, rival gangs, and the northern underworld. Fults listened with enthusiasm. He suspected that Eddie was planning an escape. One night, as Fults rolled onto his mattress, he noticed that Eddie's bunk was empty.

"Where's Eddie?" asked Fults of a fellow prisoner.

"The hole," whispered the prisoner.

"Solitary! How come?" asked Fults.

The prisoner glanced over to Fults. "He wanted to go in the hole," he said. "You wanna get outta here, too?"

Fults sat up in his bunk, "You know I do."

"Well, get yourself tossed in the hole as quick as you can."

"How?"

"Just refuse to work that cotton—you'll get kicked around a bit, but you'll also get thrown in solitary faster'n hell."

The word *solitary* was actually a misnomer. Located at the end of a narrow hallway, between the dining hall and the administrative offices, the small, one-room cell often held many prisoners. A heavy iron door that opened to the hall served as the cell's only entrance. An armed guard stood at the opposite end of the hall. Because of the persistent stench of urine, the inmates dubbed it "the piss-hole," or just "the hole."[18]

The following morning, after Fults refused to leave his bunk, the

Eastham Camp 1 solitary, 1994. In 1929 Fults and three others became the only inmates ever to escape from there. (Photo by John Neal Phillips.)

guards shaved his head, undressed and whipped him, and tossed him into the tiny room. When he hit the concrete floor, a muslin night shirt was tossed to him.

"What the hell are you doing here?" asked Eddie.

"I'm going over with you guys," answered Ralph. "What's the plan?"

"You'll see," said Eddie.[19]

That evening a tray of hot food arrived from the kitchen. Eddie eased his hand under the tray and retrieved a set of hacksaw blades.

"My favorite dish," he said.

Immediately, the men began cutting one of the steel bars securing the cell's only window, a small opening situated ten feet above their heads. Balancing on a cell mate's shoulders to reach the bars, each of the four men involved took a turn at the window. As daybreak approached, soap was pressed into the incomplete cut and smeared with grease to conceal its presence.

By the fourth night the job was complete. Severed only at the base, the bar was then worked loose in the mortar above and returned to its original position. The men decided that the escape would take place the following evening, April 8, 1930.[20]

It was past midnight when Eddie scrambled on to Fults's shoulders, snatched the bar from the loosened mortar, and disappeared through the window. Fults quickly followed, landing feet-first on the cool, rough surface of the concrete stairway outside. Eddie was already on the landing, directly in front of the second-story entrance to the guards' barracks. Crawling on his hands and knees, Fults soon joined him. From the landing it was just a matter of stepping onto the darkened roof of the dining hall and running to the bakery annex at the northeast corner of the building, a distance of eighty feet.

Once there, Eddie tied three or four blankets together and lowered them over the edge of the roof into a darkened corner of the building. A nearby electric generator created enough noise to cover any unexpected sounds caused by the descent from the roof. Once on the ground, the men tore their blankets into strips and fashioned protective coverings for their feet and legs. Then the quartet began crawling toward the woods. Immediately to his right Fults could see the shadowy silhouettes of the northern picket guards, casually chatting. Everything was quiet until suddenly, without warning, the dogs in the kennels erupted into a frenzy of snarling and barking.[21] Fults lay still. It was the thing he had feared most. Slowly raising his head, he looked toward the guards. Surprisingly, they seemed unconcerned. Occasionally they turned toward the kennels but otherwise gave no indication of alarm. Still, Fults expected a copper-jacketed slug to tear through his brain at any moment. He started moving again and eventually reached the woods. He rose to his feet and started running, the others close behind.

The underbrush soon shredded the pieces of torn blanket he had wrapped around his bare feet. Thorns, nettles, and pine cones cut him badly. The others were being cut as well.

"Hey, we're leaving a trail of real blood for them hounds," Fults shouted, laughing. No one cared. They were free. A mile from the prison yard Fults and the others happened upon the Missouri-Kansas-Texas railway tracks. Inside a nearby shed was a motorized car used by railroad crews to inspect the tracks. The four men pushed the car onto the main track and cranked it up. Facing east, they expected to accelerate toward the distant town of Trinity, but instead, the car took off in reverse.

"Hey," Fults shouted, "stop this thing—we're on our way back to Eastham!"

Eddie hit the brakes. Laughing aloud, the fugitives grabbed the corners of the car, picked it up, and turned it around. Within minutes they were rolling toward Trinity.

In town, as Eastham guards and sheriff's deputies searched the surrounding countryside, the escapees concealed themselves in the loft of a Baptist church. They traded their nightgowns for new clothes stolen from a nearby store, and they dined on raw ham and jelly, the only items the escapees were able to locate in the darkened store. On the evening of the third day, the fugitives split up and slipped quietly out of town.

In the freight yard Fults and Eddie spotted a line of box cars sitting on a side track. At first they thought about hopping in, but a railroad crew had been using the boxcars for shelter. Several families were crammed into each space. It was a strange sight. The fugitives decided to cross the bridge and wait for the next freight train to pass.

A night watchman was posted at the bridge. The two convicts hid in a ditch, watching the guard. They expected trouble and wanted to see if he was alone. When they cautiously rose out of the ditch, the watchman showed no alarm. He smiled and offered the strangers a sandwich. Fults and Eddie accepted.

The watchman turned out to be a Mexican-American who despised prison guards. His brother, a prisoner at the Retrieve Farm, near Houston, had been beaten and tortured by the Retrieve guards because he was Hispanic.[22] Laying his rifle down, the watchman dug around in his pockets until he produced a handful of silver change. "Take this," he said, extending his hand. "Take this, an' get away from Texas fast." The two fugitives took the money and the advice.

In southern Illinois Fults and Eddie committed a series of burglaries, using a small hotel in East St. Louis as a hideout. Well known in East St. Louis, Eddie had connections to Dinty Colbeck and the notorious Egan's Rats.[23] Still, the two outlaws never relaxed. Rival gangs roamed freely, and the police couldn't be trusted to take bribes or even to honor a bribe once it was accepted.

One time while crossing the bridge between East St. Louis and St. Louis, Fults spotted two detectives making random checks of pedestrians. It was too late to turn back. Both bandits had pistols in their belts, as well as a great deal of cash.

The detectives stopped them both. Fults was separated from Eddie and marched a few yards away. The officer began firing questions, but Fults was convincing, answering each query directly. From the corner of his eye he could see that Eddie was getting nervous. Fults started inching his hand toward his gun.

"Hey, what's that in your pocket, boy?" asked the detective, pointing to the box of .38 caliber shells.

"Just some medicine," Fults replied, moving his hand closer to his pistol. "I've been sick. My doctor over in East St. Louis gave it to me."

The detective stared at Fults for a long time. A shootout seemed inevitable. Eddie watched for a signal. Neither outlaw wanted another prison stretch. Each was prepared to die if necessary.

Suddenly the detective turned to his partner. "These boys are OK," he shouted.

The other detective nodded and waved the two young bandits on. Fults lowered his gun hand, glanced at Eddie, and began breathing again. He and Eddie resumed their walk to St. Louis, later deciding to split up. Eddie went home to Chicago. Fults hopped a train to the west coast.[24]

Los Angeles was depressing. Fults trusted no one as he drifted from card game to card game, trying to make ends meet. The California dream, that of runaway prosperity, was about as real as a Hollywood movie.

On a lark, he took a streetcar to the palatial private residence of President Herbert Hoover. Fults gazed at the glittering chandeliers, the rosewood furniture, the marble fireplaces. "Times are sure tough for old Hoover," he thought sarcastically.

In the valley, not far from where he stood, Fults had seen whole families—their clothes tattered, their bodies malnourished—working the fields and orchards. He thought about the homeless people he had seen in St. Louis and Kansas City. Then he looked at the president's home. He left in disgust. Within a week he was back in St. Louis, breaking into a large hardware store. Upstairs, on a thick rug in front of the safe, Fults carefully assembled his safe cracking tools. He drew a .45 automatic, cocked the hammer, and placed it alongside the tools. Soon he had removed the heavy outer door of the safe and located the strong box within. A punch would be needed to break the lock. He backed out of the safe and started to grope for the tool. Unexpectedly, a large shoe appeared, pinning his hand to the floor with a painful crunch. Fults looked up. The shoe belonged to a St. Louis city detective.

"How'd you know I was in here?" Fults asked.

Without saying a word, the officer lifted the small rug in front of the safe. A buzzer had been planted beneath it. Fults had tripped the burglar alarm himself.

Fults was handcuffed and taken to police headquarters for interrogation. Three days later he was Texas bound, chained at the neck in the rear of Bud Russell's one-way wagon.

Clyde and the "Bloody 'Ham"

En route to the penitentiary, during the layover in the Waco, Texas jail, Fults offered his own three-piece suit to another prisoner in exchange for the man's striped prison uniform. Fults knew that the man was supposed to appear in court the following day. He also knew that a suit would look better to a judge than stripes. However, on the morning after the exchange, September 18, 1930, Bud Russell noticed the switch. He was not amused.

"What's with the stripes, kid?" Russell said, pressing the full weight of his body against Fults. Fults looked into Russell's sunglasses. "I traded my suit with a guy going before the judge," he answered.

The lawman glowered at Fults.

"You'll be getting yourself some stripes soon enough, what with you being an escapee. Now, what's the idea?"

Fults looked straight ahead.

"How would you feel about having to face a judge in stripes?" he asked quietly.

Russell remained silent, staring intently at Fults. He stared at him for a long time. Finally he stepped aside. Fults boarded the transport and sat down. He leaned against the mesh siding and watched the other prisoners settle around him. Before long the truck was on the road,

Roy and "Uncle Bud" Russell and their "One Way Wagon," in the lower yard of the Walls Unit, Huntsville, Texas, 1934. Ralph Fults and Clyde Barrow first met in the rear of this prison transport, where they were chained together at the neck. (Courtesy of Robert H. Russell.)

speeding toward Huntsville and the walls.

In Madisonville the truck stopped for gas. A crowd gathered, staring at the prisoners.

"Y'all take a good look now, they'll be feedin' us animals soon," a convict shouted. The other prisoners started laughing.

Momentarily Bud Russell pushed his way through the crowd and walked up to the back of the wagon with two bottles of soda pop. He leaned against the back door and handed one of the sodas to Fults.

"I've been thinking," he said. "I reckon that was alright, you giving that guy your suit. I guess I'd feel pretty low, having to go before a judge dressed in prison stripes. That was OK."[1]

Fults took a drink from the bottle and nodded appreciatively to Russell. Without another word the old man finished his soda and returned to the cab of his truck. Not long after that, one of the other prisoners started quizzing Fults about Eastham. He was small and looked much younger than he actually was. His name was Clyde Barrow.

Scandals and mismanagement plagued the Texas Prison System in the years following World War I, raging to a political head in 1929. The public outcry for prison reform brought every state official up for air. Published press releases took on an air of opportunism as politicians groped for a personal piece of the action. Committee after committee convened, inspected the prisons, and reported to the governor. Testimony revealed widespread graft and corruption involving high prison officials.[2]

Land had been purchased at inflated prices, vendors were selling rancid meat to the farms, and medical care was virtually nonexistent. Moreover, by the mid-1920s brutality was epidemic, and rumors of "spot killings" disguised as escape attempts were too numerous to ignore. The public was outraged.[3]

The prison board responded by voting to strictly enforce the existing rules regulating public and private correspondence with inmates. Henceforth, all contact with the press would be handled through the general manager of the Texas prison system.[4]

Following an investigation in 1925, W. H. Meade was appointed general manager. Deeply disturbed by the brutality at hand, he eventually terminated every guard suspected of inmate harassment. Whippings had to be cleared by Meade, and only the most severe disciplinary cases were considered. Although many guards continued to circumvent Meade's instructions, the number of incidents of brutality had dropped considerably by the time Fults first arrived at Eastham in 1929.

Funds appropriated for prison improvements were forever tangled in a web of bureaucracy. Newspaper editorials branded the prison system "a disgrace," citing the many escapes and poor living conditions as examples. Although great strides had been made to curb brutality, nearly every other aspect of the system was crumbling.

By 1929 the prison system, "in the red" since 1918, was still losing money. A great many inmates lay idle through lack of supervision, and escapes became commonplace. On June 19 of that year forty-four men simply walked away from the Clemens farm.[5] Twelve weeks later eighteen men tunnelled their way out of the Wynne Farm, termed "the tuberculosis farm" by state investigator Mrs. J. E. King because of the horrible conditions she found there.[6] Convicts roamed the streets of Huntsville,[7] and Ralph Fults escaped from solitary confinement at Eastham. The newspapers were filled with stories of reported escapes, each report followed by much political rhetoric.

One state representative, a man named R. L. Kincaid, sponsored a bill providing for the involuntary sterilization of all inmates housed in Texas institutions.[8] Although favorably received, the bill was never passed.

On November 5, 1929, General Manager W. H. Meade suddenly resigned. He blamed the immense bureaucracy and "politics of the job"[9] as reasons for his departure. Lee Simmons of Sherman, was appointed as Meade's successor, but he declined to serve. During the next four months a massive, but fruitless search was conducted for a new general manager. Under pressure from Governor Moody, the prison board again offered the job to Simmons. He reconsidered, and on March 25, 1930, Lee Simmons assumed control of the prison system. The brief oath, administered by Board Chairman W. A. Paddock, was punctuated with the curious statement:

"Here it is. . . . Do the best you can with it."[10]

Simmons's first official move was to evaluate the massive problem of escapes and overcrowding. He fired the warden of the main unit and all but two of the farm managers. The priority was, ". . . hold the prisoners."[11]

To quell escapes, Simmons announced that each prison boss would be held personally responsible for any future breaks. The pressure was on, and many guards previously fired by Meade for brutality were rehired. Simmons spoke against inmate harassment and brutality but reinstated at least one farm manager who had been fired by his predecessor for vicious behavior. Simmons also fought against attempts to outlaw "the bat," the oil-soaked strap used on Fults and others at the Texas reformatory and throughout the prison system. Simmons likened its use to that of spurs on an uncooperative horse.[12]

Simmons then revealed his plan for stepping up farm production, to bring the prison system within the realm of self-sufficiency.[13] The previous year, 1929, Simmons had toured several southern prisons, each having the reputation of self-sufficiency. The breakneck pace of the host penitentiaries impressed the future general manager. Arkansas even used human plough teams. Texas never adopted such a plan, but an increased workload was immediately put into effect. Fults, Barrow, and the others began joking about the "eight hour days—eight in the morning, eight in the evening."

Each farm was expected to increase its production substantially. Inmates who did not keep up with the pace were beaten down and thrown back into service. If they continued to lag, the guards rode them harder. Some prisoners died.

Inside the main prison Fults and Barrow were housed in the South Building, or simply "the jail," as the prisoners called it. It served as a staging area for inmates awaiting their turn on 7 Level, Death Row, or those destined for transfer to one of the farms.

At one point Fults decided to get rid of his conspicuously striped uniform. A prisoner in the laundry supplied him with a plain white uniform. However, officials soon discovered his deception. They whipped him and sent him off for his first encounter with new General Manager Lee Simmons. Simmons, a small, thin man, sat behind a big mahogany desk. The new warden of the Huntsville unit, W. W. Waid, was seated to his right.

"Mr. Fults," Simmons said, "you were found parading around here without your stripes. Well, you're not to take it upon yourself to do as you please. I run the show around here, not you."

The guards hustled Fults out of the office, handcuffed him, and stood him on a pickle barrel. This punishment, called "ridin' the barrel," was, and still is, notorious. First the legs go to sleep; then the handcuffs start digging into the prisoner's wrists. For most of the afternoon Fults fought a losing battle. He tried shifting his weight from one foot to the other; it worked for awhile, but near the end of the day he lost his balance and tumbled into the assistant warden's rose garden. The official bolted from his office and cursed Fults, sprawled across a bed of thorns. Fults was heaved aboard the barrel and forced to remain there throughout the night and most of the following day.

A few days after the barrel incident Fults heard that he and Clyde were being sent to Eastham Prison Farm, Camp 2. Physically, Camp 2 was quite different from its sister colony. Only a small percentage of the farm was wooded. Large open fields of cotton and corn surrounded the main compound. Escape, whether by day or night, was virtually impossible without outside assistance. There was too much risk involved in crossing those open fields.

The main building was constructed entirely of wood. The floor plan was similar to that of the stone structure at Camp 1. One difference was the absence of "the hole," or solitary. In its place a sheet metal "sweat box" stood outside in the sweltering Texas sun. Shut up in it, an inmate virtually baked alive.

Upon arriving at Camp 2, Fults and Barrow stepped from the transport and assembled with the other prisoners before a large stack of farm tools. To the right a half-dozen handcuffed convicts stood atop narrow oak barrels. Nearby a pair of thin arms groped through the tiny air vents of the sweat box. Another man, stripped to the waist, was tied to a tree; his back bore the marks of a railroad trace chain. The scenes were deliberate, calculated for the benefit of new arrivals. The message was clear: prison would be a place so vile as to make any veteran of its confines dread the consequences should he ever break the law of Eastham.

After several minutes the farm manager stepped forward. Fults did not recognize him. Indeed, he had been the manager of another farm before being fired for bad behavior in 1929. Lee Simmons reinstated him and assigned him to Eastham on May 19, 1930.[14] The manager approached the group, singled out one of the prisoners, and slashed him across the face with a cane walking stick. The convict fell, bleeding. It was the same show Fults had seen the year before, just different players.

"Now, the rest of you shitheads get your asses out in them fields," said the manager. "And I mean run out there! We ain't having no goddamned walking at this camp."

Fults and Barrow started running toward the appointed field, perhaps two miles in the distance. "What the hell did that damned warden have to hit that guy for?" Barrow asked between breaths.

"'Tune up'," Fults answered. "They call it a 'tune up'.[15] It's psychological."

"They'd better not try that crap with me," Clyde said. "I might just come around here someday, after I get out, and kill some of these bastards."

Fults said nothing, having heard such talk before. He was not yet familiar with the single-minded determination that drove Clyde Barrow.

Once they were in the fields, the prisoners had little time to think. The work was fast and furious. When noon rolled around, Fults and Barrow dined on dry cornbread and a cup of water. They stood in their cotton row, ate as quickly as possible, and returned to hoeing. No one was allowed more than a five- or ten-minute lunch break. The farm management assessed the time in relation to how long it took an inmate to consume a single piece of cornbread.

With the ever-present weapons of the shotgun ring bearing against them, Fults and Barrow finished out the day. They then joined the other field hands, sprinting in single file to the camp compound for supper and sleep. That night, as Fults settled stiffly into his bunk, a trusty came over to him.

"They've drawn straws to see who gets you," he whispered, without looking at Fults. Fults nodded.

The guards had drawn lots to see who would have the pleasure of beating Fults for having escaped. It was a tradition at Eastham, and Fults knew it. Guards did not like escapees. Unless an escapee could be killed, or captured for the reward, he was useless—except for vengeance.

The next day Fults and Barrow were assigned to the woodpile. A six-man shotgun ring surrounded the pair as they worked. Two mounted riders sat about a hundred yards to either side.

The work was backbreaking. After a few hours of heaving a double-bladed ax, Fults and Barrow felt like lying down for a week. To take their minds off the work, they talked quietly. The two young convicts discovered they had a lot in common. Both were from large families, and each exhibited a fascination for westerns—Fults sharing Barrow's fantasy of reliving the adventurous exploits of Cole Younger, Jesse James, and Billy the Kid.

Barrow spoke at length about a girl named Bonnie. He also talked quietly about his large, extended family, focusing often on his mother and his older brother, Buck. Clyde looked up to Buck.[16]

Fults and Barrow continued relating stories between swings of the ax. They shared the same cynical sense of humor, laughing and making light of their situation. Fults began to like Clyde a lot.

"Hey, white trash," shouted one of the six or seven guards standing nearby. Neither Clyde nor Fults looked up. "You—white trash in the stripes," the guard said. "I think you're a son-of-a-bitch."

"Oh yeh?" Fults said. "Well I think you're a son-of-a-bitch too!"

Two guards rushed Fults, pistols and chains drawn. The others held their weapons on Clyde. One man grabbed Fults by the hair and threw him to the ground. Someone sank the toe of a boot deep into his ribs and raked the barrel of a pistol across his face. Gasping for air, Fults felt himself being pulled to his feet by both men. The pistol sliced deeper into his face. Blood streamed from the top of his head, matting his hair. Before long Fults could hardly see, so badly swollen were his eyes. Again and again Fults felt the barrel and butt of the .44 dig into his flesh. Finally he sank to the ground in a daze.

"You gonna give us some crap, you little bastard?" the guard shouted as he jerked Fults's head back. "How about it? You gonna run again?"

Fults made no response.

"Oh! 'Sulled' up on us, eh?" said the guard as he raised his revolver one last time and brought it down on Fults's head. Numbness gripped the boy's body as he faded into a state of semiconsciousness.[17]

Through bloodied eyes Fults could barely see Clyde standing about ten feet away. He was squared off like a gunfighter, ready to draw a nonexistent six-shooter. Both hands were clenched in tight fists. The knuckles of his hands were turning white. His face was taut and flushed with anger.

"Hey, what's the matter with you, kid?" yelled one of the guards, "You want some of this too?"

Barrow made no reply. He glowered menacingly at the guard who had beaten Fults, refusing to respond.

"You better back off, punk," said the guard.

Clyde stood fast, leaning forward, head thrust out, looking as if the muscles of his neck would burst. All eyes and weapons were fixed on him, but no one made a move. Suddenly the spell was broken. One of the guards holstered his revolver and turned away. Soon the others did the same. Clyde moved toward Fults and helped him by the arm to the woodpile.

Fults was impressed by Barrow's show of loyalty. It took a lot of nerve to call that much attention to himself. He had risked his own life and, in doing so, had saved Fults from being beaten to death.[18]

That night in the dormitory, Clyde was still angry. "They ain't supposed to be doing that kind of thing," he said. "It's just not right. . . . Them guards were too yellow to face you one on one—they had to hold you down. I know we gotta serve out our time, but we shouldn't have to duck every time a guard walks by."

Fults lay in his bunk on the lower berth, staring at the mattress above him. "Yeh, but there ain't nothing you can do," he said, "They're holding all the cards."

"There's plenty we can do," said Clyde, "We can get the hell out of here, round up a gang, and raid this crummy place. I'd like to shoot all these damned guards and turn everybody loose."

Fults was stunned by the tone of Barrow's voice. There could be no question of his seriousness.

"Yeh," Fults reasoned, "but first we've got to get out of here. Those hooligans hold all the cards, and they do just what they please."

"But we ain't going to be in the joint forever," said Clyde. "We should work as a team."

Clyde was serious. He was deeply disturbed by the pistol whipping; his conduct on the woodpile had shown that. The sincerity of his concern for the brutality he had witnessed intrigued Fults. It was as if the beating had been inflicted on Clyde personally.

"We'd have to work in teams and coordinate our movements," Fults said.

Clyde's face lit up, "I know some guys in West Dallas we could use."

"I know a couple of guys with contacts in Denton and Amarillo," said Fults.

"So do I," added Clyde.

Fults closed his eyes. The more he thought about Clyde's scheme, the more he liked it.

"Think about it," Fults said. "An army could lay up in those trees near Camp 1 and spring a whole squad of prisoners before anybody knew what was going down."

Clyde nodded. Within minutes the lights were out. The murmur of conversation soon dwindled to the low drone of snoring men. Fults lay awake in the shadowy light, thinking about his new partnership. He had never known anyone quite like Clyde Barrow. Quiet and introspective, he exhibited a moodiness matched only by an unusually sensitive nature. He loved to laugh and joke around, but somewhere beneath the surface lurked an extremely volatile personality. Nevertheless, his manner was that of genuine concern—almost idealistic.

For his part, Fults felt good about Clyde's plan. Neither he nor Clyde could foresee the pain and suffering that would result from their prison merger. Like many who resort to crime and violence in the face of personal humiliation,[19] they viewed themselves as the spearhead of a noble cause, in the tradition of Robin Hood or Jesse James—headstrong thoughts for two children of an ever-darkening era.

Clyde Barrow was born on March 24, 1909, near the north-central Texas town of Telico.[20] The fifth of seven children, he spent most of his early life fighting for floor space in the family's three-room shack. Despite numerous references to the contrary, only seven children were born to the elder Barrows.[21]

His father, Henry T. Barrow, was a tall, hard-working tenant farmer who had migrated to Texas from Florida around 1890.[22] Described as exceedingly quiet, Henry Barrow worked hard to provide what he could for his growing family. Most mornings found him trudging out to the fields well before dawn. It would be dark before he returned. Carefully picking his way across a floor full of sleeping children, he would finish a plate of potatoes and greens, then tumble into bed.

For Cumie, Clyde's mother, life was a matter consumed with children, household chores, and the rigors of farm work. A tiny woman with precise and angular features, she stood just under five feet tall and weighed less than one-hundred pounds.

Each day after tending to the farm animals, she often joined her husband in the fields. By late afternoon she was back at the house preparing supper. Her day ended no sooner than her husband's.

At an early age Clyde, like Fults, developed a strong sense of identification with certain cowboy movie stars and nineteenth-century outlaws. He often spoke of growing up to be like Jesse James or one of the many characters portrayed by actor William S. Hart. When he was older, Clyde joined his other brothers and sisters in the fields. He learned to hoe and pick cotton as well as care for livestock. He attended school rather irregularly, cutting class as often as possible.

Like many Texas farmers after World War I, the Barrows grew increasingly pessimistic about the future of agriculture. The future looked bleak, and both Henry and Cumie were beginning to feel as old as they looked. They dreamed of moving to Dallas and starting a small business of some kind. Their eldest son, Jack, and two of their daughters were already living there, so Cumie and Henry packed their few possessions and moved the rest of the family to the city in 1922.[23]

From the early 1920s Dallas attracted a great many tired and disillusioned workers like Henry Barrow. By the end of that decade the influx was so great that whole families were camping under city bridges,[24] waiting for jobs and housing to become available. Most of these people were so poor that even after finding work they could not afford much more than a small shack in West Dallas.

For those seeking social prestige, West Dallas was not the place to call home. Long referred to as "the bog" because of its location along the Trinity River flood plain, it was neither a part of Dallas nor an independently incorporated city. Consequently, until the community was annexed to Dallas proper in 1952, a great many homes in West Dallas were without the benefit of water, gas, or electric service.[25] West Dallas has always remained an embarrassment to the city's general citizenry.

Life in "the bog" was stoic, at best. Small frame homes and shotgun houses lined the gravel streets. Many businesses took advantage of the low rent and set up shop along the rail line. Refinery Castings, Simms Oil Refinery, and Trinity-Portland Cement helped employ the many job-seekers moving into the area.

Pavement was scarce; even Eagle Ford Road, the main thoroughfare, was unpaved.[26] Frequent flooding from the nearby Trinity River undermined roadwork of any kind. Following the massive flood of 1908, a levy was constructed between downtown Dallas and the river's east bank, but many years would pass before anything substantial was done to protect the west side.[27] A gummy mixture of mud and water often covered much of the settlement.

The Barrows lived for a time in the campgrounds beneath the Houston Street viaduct and in West Dallas before Henry build a three-room house near the Texas and pacific railroad tracks.[28] Henry supported the family by selling scrap metal to the many foundries in West Dallas. He traversed the city in a horse-drawn cart, collecting whatever he could find.[29] Then–Dallas County Deputy Sheriff Bill Decker, later sheriff, said his earliest memory of Clyde and his older brother Buck was when he arrested them for stealing brass from a West Dallas company. They probably did it for the old man, though certainly without his knowledge.[30]

Henry Barrow's childhood ambition was to own a fast horse, but the poor old animal pulling his wagon was a far cry from that. One day a car struck his cart and killed the horse. Barrow hired an attorney and won a suit against the driver. He took the proceeds, moved his house to a vacant lot already owned by one of his daughters, and built a combination service station-convenience store on the front of it. The location was 1620 Eagle Ford Road, and the new business was called the Star Service Station. Two pumps issued red or white gas. Cold Nehi sodas and fresh snacks were just inside the door.

Clyde attended Sidney Lanier High School for a very short time after his arrival in Dallas. He soon quit, moved in with his sister Nell, and went to work for the Brown Cracker and Candy Company for one dollar an hour.[31] Like Fults, Clyde was not interested in school. But unlike Fults, he loved music, particularly jazz. Clyde bought an alto saxophone and had his brother-in-law, a professional jazz musician, teach him how to play. Barrow apparently learned to play quite well and went on to learn how to play one or two other instruments, including the guitar.[32]

It has been charged that most of Clyde's initial trouble with the law began with his brother, Buck.[33] In truth, Buck often took the blame for Clyde's early crimes.[34] Actually, a number of factors would contribute to the younger Barrow's criminal development, not the least of which was

West Dallas itself. Its reputation was such that, in the eyes of the local authorities, simply residing there was sufficient cause to suspect criminal activity.[35]

Clyde's situation was further complicated by an incident occurring in 1926, when he was seventeen. He had quit the his old job and gone to work for Proctor & Gamble, working fifty hours a week. He later took a higher paying job with A & K Auto Top Works, but not before he had fallen in love with a Forest Avenue High School girl named Eleanor. The teenaged couple hoped to marry. Then came the trip to Broddus.

Tucked away in the dense East Texas forests, not far from the historic city of San Augustine, is the town of Broddus. Eleanor had relatives living there. Late in the fall of 1926, after a fight with Clyde, she decided to pay them a visit. Barrow followed her in a rented car—without telling the rental agency he was leaving town. He invited Eleanor's mother to accompany him, hoping she could help him smooth things over with her daughter.

Meanwhile, the Dallas car rental agents were furiously looking for their automobile. They called Clyde's mother, and she told them of the trip to Broddus. Before long the local sheriff's deputies arrived at the home of Eleanor's relatives, looking for Clyde and the car. Instead of talking to the deputies, Clyde ran out the back door and hid in a corn field. The sheriff retrieved the car and left.[36] Afterward, Clyde went back to the house.

The following day the sheriff returned. Clyde hid in the attic—Eleanor passing notes to him as the sheriff searched the house.[37] Eventually, the lawman left, never to return.

Eleanor's mother was shocked by the sudden turn of events. This was a new side to Clyde Barrow, and she did not like what she saw. Although Eleanor was willing to accept Clyde, her mother insisted that the engagement be terminated.

A few days after the incident Barrow thumbed a ride back to Dallas, where he was arrested for auto theft. The date was December 3, 1926. However, the rental agency was so happy to recover the automobile that they dropped all charges against Clyde. He had to be released.

The first thing Barrow did was rush over to Eleanor's house and try to rectify matters. Her parents, however, considered the subject closed. They rejected his apologies and informed him that he was no longer welcome in their home.

One of Eleanor's friends recalled seeing Barrow pacing up and down the street, hoping to catch a glimpse of the girl:

"[Clyde] was just a kid then, and very much in love with Eleanor. After the ordeal with the rent car, he was fired from his job because the police kept picking him up. Whenever a car was stolen, or a house was burglarized, the police would drag him downtown. Of course he was never charged with anything, but they'd beat him up and try to make him confess to things he'd never done.

"Now, I don't agree with the horrible things Clyde later did—the robbery and killing—but I still say that if the Dallas police had left that boy alone we wouldn't be talking about him today."[38]

Later, Clyde and Eleanor started meeting in secret. They eventually eloped, but Barrow kept hedging about actually getting married, and Eleanor returned to Dallas.[39]

Shortly thereafter a young burglar named Frank began paying regular visits to Clyde.[40] Deceptively handsome and well groomed, Frank first met Barrow in the city jail. Soon the two of them were disappearing overnight. Suddenly Clyde was making a lot of cash. He made several purchases and even took a girlfriend, Gladys, to Mexico for a holiday, sending hastily written postcards to his mother, detailing the fun he was having. Eventually Clyde stopped looking for steady work and moved in with Frank. Both boys, though unemployed, were living leisurely lives. Besides cracking safes, they were also stealing cars for an interstate auto-theft ring. Clyde's mother would later blame young women like Gladys, and later Bonnie, for her son's criminal activities, citing their need for cash, gifts, and good times.[41]

On October 29, 1929, Clyde, Buck, and fellow named Sidney burglarized a Denton, Texas, filling station. Instead of opening the safe on the premises, however, they loaded it in their stolen car and proceeded slowly through town. A few blocks away the occupants of a police squad car noticed the fleeing vehicle and decided to pursue it. Clyde tried to take a corner too fast and slammed into a light pole. The force of the crash threw everyone out of the car. Clyde took off on foot, Buck and the others hot on his heels. Shots rang out and Buck screamed. Clyde crawled under a vacant house and hid there all night.[42]

Buck was badly wounded, shot through both legs. He and Sidney were arrested. By the end of the year they were both convicted of burglary and sentenced to the penitentiary. Buck started a five-year term on January 14, 1930.

Not long after Buck's conviction, Clyde went to the home of Clarence Clay, who lived just a short distance from the Barrow house.[43] Clay's daughter had been involved in an accident, and Clyde wanted to look in on her. A young woman was also visiting Clay's daughter. The new girl was cute, just under five feet tall. A stylish arrangement of reddish-blonde hair accented the deep blue of her eyes. Clyde may have seen her waiting tables at Marco's Cafe: her name was Bonnie Parker. Clyde immediately fell for her.

Bonnie, unlike Eleanor, was a West Dallasite. Nevertheless, she was a popular student in high school, exhibited great scholastic ability, and graduated with honors. But a failed marriage to an abusive young man left her with a poor self-image and nothing to look forward to but dull, low-paying jobs and no future. Disillusioned, exhausted at the end of each day, she was ready for a fast-moving wild card like Clyde Barrow.

Clyde found Bonnie bright and refreshing. She made jokes about nearly everything, including herself. More importantly, she never questioned Clyde's past. They began seeing each other regularly. By the end of the month friends rarely saw one without the other.

During the second week of February 1930 Barrow was awakened at Bonnie's house and arrested. He was taken to Denton and charged with burglary. He was held there less than a week. Although Buck had drawn a five-year term for the gas station burglary, the evidence against Clyde was insufficient to bring a conviction. On March 2 he was transferred to Waco, where the evidence was strong enough to bring a guilty plea on two counts of burglary and five counts of auto theft.[44] On March 3 Bonnie moved to Waco to be with Clyde when he was sentenced. Barrow's mother also made the journey.

Clyde was assessed a two-year sentence on each of seven counts—a total of fourteen years. The judge, however, decided to allow each two-year term to run concurrently, thus cutting the sentence from fourteen years to two. It was a lucky break for Clyde, but he never saw it that way. A fellow prisoner told him about a pistol hidden in his mother's house. Barrow drew a map and persuaded Bonnie to go to the house, locate the gun, and smuggle it into the jail. "You're the sweetest baby in the world to me," Barrow wrote on the map.[45] Bonnie was scared to death of firearms, but her passion for Clyde far outweighed her fear. She nervously accomplished the task, slipping past the jailer with the loaded weapon concealed between her breasts. It was Bonnie's first active involvement in a crime.[46]

On March 11, as darkness fell, Clyde and his friend were ready. The jailer was delivering several dinner trays to the run around when Clyde jammed the pistol in his face. Taking the keys, Clyde locked the jailer up. As the prisoners made a dash for the front door, a third escapee joined them.

The three friends caught a ride north, slipping into West Dallas late that evening. Clyde quickly located a couple of boys who were willing to drive back to Waco and pick up Bonnie. Two days later they returned empty-handed. Clyde could not wait any longer. When he got to Illinois he sent a telegram to Bonnie. Perhaps she could join him when things cooled off. Things never cooled. On March 18 Clyde was arrested in Ohio. Within a few days he was back in Texas.

The Waco judge who had presided over Clyde's case was not impressed with his armed escape. He ordered Clyde to serve his string of two-year sentences consecutively rather than concurrently. Suddenly Clyde was staring at fourteen years in prison—all for a few days of freedom.

On March 4, because of severe overcrowding, the prison board placed a moratorium on the induction of new inmates. Each county was ordered to hold all Huntsville-bound prisoners until the state could relieve the terrible conditions of the penitentiary.[47] Clyde was more than a little apprehensive about prison life. His letters to Bonnie confirm this. He had no doubt heard about the horrible things uncovered during Governor Moody's January tour of the main prison at Huntsville. In the governor's own words the standard of living was "not fit for a dog."[48]

On April 12 General Manager Lee Simmons lifted the March 4 moratorium. Forty convicts held in various parts of the state were to be sent to Huntsville on April 21. Clyde Barrow's name was on the list.

Throughout the spring and summer of 1930 Barrow was housed inside the walls at Huntsville. On more than one occasion he was transferred to some Texas town on a bench warrant to face new charges. In each instance there was insufficient evidence to bring an indictment, and the charges were dropped.[49]

Knowing that he was about to be transferred to Eastham, Barrow started quizzing his fellow inmates about the conditions there. On his last trip out on the bench warrant, ironically to Waco, Barrow was told about Ralph Fults. Someone pointed him out in the Waco jail. He was trading his suit for another convict's striped prison uniform. The following day, September 18, while en route to Huntsville in the back of Uncle Bud's transport, Barrow spoke with the young outlaw. He would later watch angrily as two Eastham guards held him down while a third beat him with the butt of a .44 revolver.

Not long after the pistol whipping, the farm manager paid Fults an unexpected visit. Ignoring the raw spots still visible on the convict's head and face, the warden drew a chair up to the triple-tiered bunk. A guard and two building tenders stood nearby.

"Fults," he said, "I hope you ain't thinking of trying to run out on us again."

Fults met the warden's eyes with a contemptuous glint.

"Don't clam up on me, boy," said the warden.

"I'm not going anywhere," said Fults. "I got all the comforts of home, right here."

"That's what I like to hear," said the warden. "You ain't got but a couple of years on you. If you stay clean you might live to see them front gates. But if you run again, I'll kill you."

Fults made no response.

Following a brief moment of eye contact, the warden started to rise out of his chair. Glancing over to the adjoining bunk, he noticed Clyde reading a Jesse James paperback.

"I wouldn't be buddying up too much if I was you, fellas," he added.

"Some of the boys might begin thinking you got ideas."

A moment of silence passed. Clyde turned the page without looking up. The warden summoned his men and departed.

It was not long before the meaning of the warden's statement became perfectly clear. Fearing another escape, the guards attempted to isolate Fults. Two men had already been whipped for talking to him, but Clyde continued to fraternize. In doing so, he was asking for trouble.

It was picking time on the farms, a time when inmates hauled oversized cloth bags over their shoulders and ripped wads of fiber from the mature cotton plants in the fields. The hard, nutlike husk splits open when the cotton is ripe. Fingers grow raw from grabbing the splintered husks.

Fults and Barrow had worked cotton before. They knew the tricks. However, because Clyde was thought to be a city boy, the guards may have hoped he would lag behind, giving them a reason to run him down. They did not know that he had been raised on a farm.

One of the guards, still remembering the standoff at the woodpile, grew impatient. From high atop his horse he watched as Fults and Barrow worked a nearby cotton row. It was midafternoon. Fults straightened up for a few seconds to wipe the perspiration from his brow. He was about to reach for another handful of cotton when he heard the muffled clatter of horses hooves bearing down hard. A mounted guard was charging at Clyde. He was going to ride him down. Before Fults could call out, Clyde whirled around in the path of the oncoming horse. Side-stepping to the left, he grabbed the reins and turned the horse around. The animal reared slightly, then settled to a dead stop. As the dust cleared, the guard thrust the barrel of his shotgun in Barrow's face. Clyde refused to release the horse. Seething with anger, he stood fast, looking beyond the gun barrel into the guard's eyes. Fults was sure Barrow had breathed his last. However, for some reason the guard did nothing. He probably could not risk killing Clyde in full view of the other convicts. The attempt to run him down was only meant to frighten him. It did not work.[50]

Clyde eventually let the reins fall from his hands and slowly backed away. The guard released the hammer of his weapon, took up the reins, and rode back to his post. Not a word had been spoken. Barrow picked up his bag and returned to the cotton row.

In an effort to increase the farm's productivity, Eastham officials stepped up the work schedule. Whippings increased, and those who failed to keep up started disappearing. The pace became so brutal that many desperate inmates deliberately injured themselves or simply ended their misery by feigning an escape, letting the shotgun ring or highriders kill them.

Self-mutilation was the most popular means of escape from the almost certain death in the fields. Severe wounds nearly always meant a trip to the walls at Huntsville—away from the Eastham personnel. Practically nothing short of a full amputation was considered serious enough to warrant such action. Injured convicts were often bandaged and pressed back into service the same day. Loss of limb was the only assurance of a ticket inside. In a single week at Eastham Barrow and Fults witnessed fourteen amputations. Some inmates injected kerosene or dirty water into their legs to induce infections.

In the fall of 1930 Fults and Barrow heard about a Houston newspaperman who was writing exposés of brutal prison practices. He was Harry McCormick, crime reporter for the *Houston Press*. He was one of the few writers in Texas who would touch the subject. Prison authorities screened all outgoing information.[51] Press statements were carefully worded, and inmate letters were censored. McCormick started having information smuggled out of the walls by way of the prison chaplain, Father Hugh Finnegan, a fellow Houstonian. Many inmates at Eastham started funneling stories to McCormick, Fults and Barrow included.

A rumor was being circulated that a Houston bank robber named "Two-Gun" Stillman was going to be killed at Eastham. A noted trouble maker, he may have been suspected of leaking information to McCormick. The rumor was further substantiated by the sudden appearance of a guard known only as "Boss Killer." Part of a specialized group, "Boss Killer"'s sole function was enforcement, by whatever means necessary. A note was smuggled to McCormick, but it was already too late. The following day, "Boss Killer" and another guard pulled Stillman from his squad and marched him behind a nearby hill. Barrow and Fults heard two shots. The guards later returned, saying that Stillman had pulled a gun and tried to escape. He was dead.[52]

Later that year a convict informant was discovered at Camp 2. Strongly suspecting his involvement in the Stillman spot killing, Fults wanted to eliminate this man. One day Fults and Barrow were about to fell a large pine tree when they spotted the informant. He was taking it easy only a few yards from where they were working. After watching him for quite some time, the two convicts started cutting a wedge on the informer's side of the tree. The tree was beginning to sway when a guard stepped over to chat with the informant. Fults and Barrow held up, faking a few cuts on another part of the trunk. As the guard turned to walk down the line, they let the giant tree fall.

"Timmmberrr," they yelled. The man was buried beneath a tangle of branches.

Someone started shouting. The guard ran over to pull the injured man free. All the hair on the back of his head had been torn away and his neck appeared to be broken.

"He's dead," the guard announced, rolling the man's head around. "Busted his neck." Eyeing Fults, he added, "It must have been an accident because I heard you call out. He just wasn't paying no attention."

Fults, Barrow, and a couple of the other inmates laid the body in the back of a flatbed truck. As they turned away from the truck a low moan caught their attention. To everyone's surprise the informant was sitting up, complaining about a pounding headache. He was treated for a mild concussion and transferred to another farm.

A week later Barrow and Fults were cleaning a felled tree when two guards walked up and led Clyde away. He never returned. That evening Fults noticed Barrow's bunk had been stripped. His personal effects, too, had disappeared. Later it was learned that Clyde had been transferred to Eastham's Camp 1, the site of Fults's escape. The transfer was deliberate; the Eastham authorities were evidently still worrying about the friendship between Fults and Barrow. However, moving Clyde did nothing but give him a first-hand look at the camp he would one day raid. Moreover, he and Fults were still able to meet occasionally when their work details mingled in the woods between the two camps. It was during one of these encounters that Fults heard the details of Clyde's first killing.

A vicious building tender named "Big Ed" had been preying on Barrow, beating him and sodomizing him repeatedly. Well over six feet tall and weighing more than two-hundred pounds, Ed was remembered by Fults as brutish, overbearing, and dangerous.

Another building tender, named Aubrey, was at odds with "Big Ed." He told Barrow to lure Ed, alone, to the dormitory toilets and kill him. Aubrey promised to move in and take the blame, making it look like a knife fight between two building tenders. Aubrey was already serving a life term as a habitual criminal. He knew that the killing of another inmate would mean very little, if anything, to prison officials. He also knew of the plans to raid Eastham and wanted to be included. Besides, Aubrey hated "Big Ed" too, but he had no stomach for killing. He could see that Barrow did.

In the short span of a year Eastham had, in Ralph Fults's words, transformed Clyde Barrow "from a schoolboy to rattlesnake." He had become the incarnation of cynicism and pent-up hatred.[53] Sadly, he was not unlike other young men marked for rehabilitation but schooled in brutality. Something was terribly wrong with the system, and many of the convicts, recognizing this, reacted negatively. Clyde rejected authority, equating it with the injustice he saw around him. He would later combat such authority with the same vindictiveness that flared during the "Big Ed" affair.

Clyde found a short length of pipe and concealed it in the leg of his trousers. As soon as he stepped in from the fields, Clyde baited the hook by walking toward the toilets after the other prisoners had finished there. Seizing any opportunity to catch a victim alone, "Big Ed" closed in while Clyde was pretending to urinate. With Aubrey looking on, Barrow suddenly spun around to face Ed, who stood near a large concrete column, smiling at the small convict. Without a word, Clyde lunged forward, weapon in hand. "Big Ed" never felt a thing. He crumpled to the concrete floor in a bloody heap, a piece of his skull torn away.

Aubrey quickly pulled his knife, cut himself on the abdomen, and sank the blade deep into the dead man's ribs. By the time the guard on duty was able to pick his way through the gathering crowd, Barrow had returned to his bunk. The guard took one look at Aubrey, then examined "Big Ed," lying face up near the commodes.

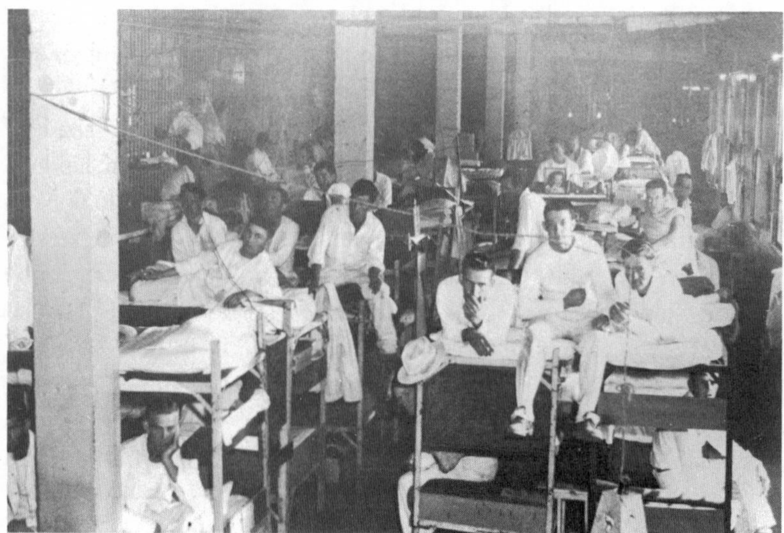

Eastham Camp 1 dormitory, 1930. Clyde Barrow killed his first man behind the furthest column. (Courtesy of the Texas Prison Archives, Texas Department of Criminal Justice, Institutional Division [TDCJ-ID].)

He merely shook his head and turned away. The incident was never investigated. Everyone knew of Ed's belligerent nature, and his passing was not mourned. The building tender's massive head wound went unnoticed. No one cared.[54]

Sometime in December 1931 Clyde received word that his brother Buck, who had escaped from the farm twenty-one months earlier, was thinking of giving himself up, mostly at the urging of his mother and his wife.[55] Because of the wounds Buck had received in Denton, it was not likely that he would be sent to one of the farms. Indeed, Warden Waid was so pleased with Buck Barrow's decision to voluntarily return to prison that he assigned him to light duty inside the walls at Huntsville.[56] It had been more than two years since Clyde last saw his brother, and he wanted desperately to be with him. He began plotting to get himself transferred to Huntsville. Only one road led from Eastham to the walls—hospitalization. Clyde found an inmate who was willing to cut him with an axe. On January 27, 1932, he was admitted to the main infirmary in

Huntsville with two toes of his left foot completely severed. The brothers were thus reunited.[57]

At the time of Clyde's injury Ralph Fults was back home in McKinney—a pardon signed by Governor Ross Sterling in his pocket. Fults knew that Barrow's chances of having his sentence reduced were growing with each passing day. Barrow's mother was about to petition the Texas Supreme Court on her son's behalf. When Fults was released on August 26, 1931, he decided to go home and wait for Clyde.

Fults felt like a sore thumb in McKinney. He could sense the nervous eyes following him as he walked the streets. Home was not much better. His parents tried to make him feel comfortable, but he was restless, edgy. He barely knew his brother and younger sisters. They had been mere babies when he had left home seven years earlier. Now they were teenagers who were being chided at school because of their older brother's criminal record. Consequently, family relations were strained.

Job offerings were scarce in 1931, especially for an ex-con. Fults relied on his ability as a gambler, parlaying a little cash into a nice bundle, at least enough to live on.

When he was not sitting in on a dice game, Fults was down at the City Cafe, on Tennessee Street, drinking coffee, scanning the Dallas dailies, looking for Clyde's name. In those days lists of convicts scheduled for release were published in the papers. So far, Clyde's name had not appeared.

Each afternoon as he walked home from the cafe, Fults would cut through the alley between Tennessee and Kentucky, behind the old county jail. It was shortly after the new year, late January 1932, and icy gusts whipped around the downtown buildings like blasts from a shotgun. As he approached the jail, Fults thought he heard someone call out his name. He noticed a pair of arms poking through the bars of a ground level window, motioning to him. It turned out to be a fellow he and Clyde had known at Eastham Camp 2.

"What's up?" asked Fults.

"This kid in here knows Clyde," the prisoner said.

"Who is it?" Fults inquired.

"Come here, kid," the inmate said to someone behind him.

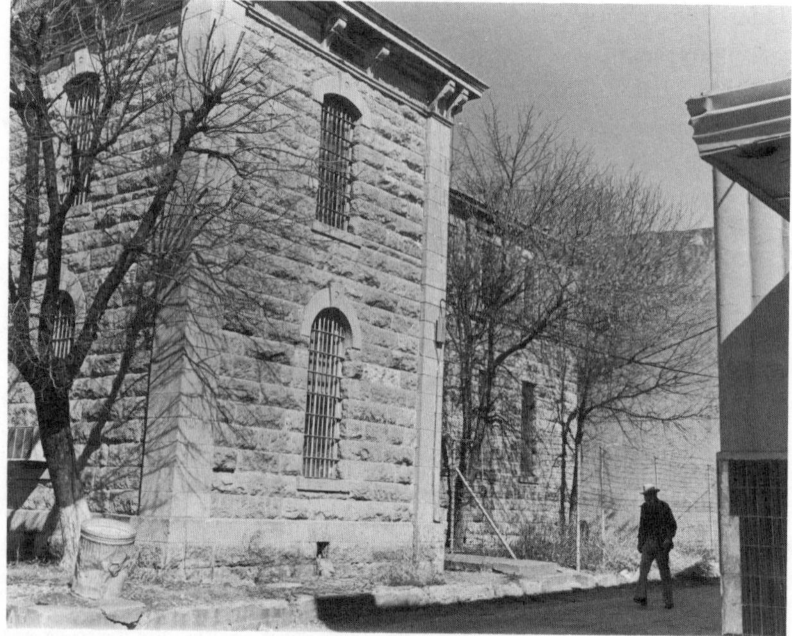

Ralph Fults, 1982. Fults walks beside the McKinney Jail (Collin County Prison) just as he did in January, 1932, when an inmate called to him from a ground floor cell and introduced him to Raymond Hamilton. (Photo by John Neal Phillips.)

Suddenly another face appeared in the window.

"This here's Ray Hamilton," said the inmate. "He's OK"

Fults looked the boy over. He was small, like Clyde, with blonde hair and deep-set blue eyes. At age eighteen he had already chalked up several auto thefts and was awaiting arraignment on just such a charge.

"Where do you know Clyde from?" Fults asked.

"We grew up together in West Dallas," answered Hamilton, grinning proudly.

Without saying a word Fults strolled around to the front of the jail and asked to see Hamilton.

"Hamilton," he yelled. "Somebody to see you."

Ray leaned against the iron door of the runaround. His face, smooth and fair, revealed a glint of childish irresponsibility. The two men started making small talk until the jailer disappeared into his office. Without actually saying so, Hamilton began hinting around that he wanted to get out. Fults understood perfectly.

"I'll drop off a few magazines," he said, turning to leave.

That evening, Fults took a detective thriller and opened the binding with a razor. He slid three or four cold-steel hacksaw blades into the spine and resealed the flap. The following morning Fults handed a stack of magazines to a female accomplice who had agreed to deliver them to Ray. Included in the stack was Fults's personalized collection of detective stories.

Jimmy Beldon, at the time a thirty-three-year-old McKinney deputy sheriff, recalled that Ray suddenly began chattering a lot—joking, scamming, bumming cigarettes.[58] He was covering the sound of the blades dragging across the chilled steel bars of his cell. He worked steadily through the night, finishing shortly before daybreak, January 27, 1932.

Raymond Hamilton, 1932. (Courtesy of the Dallas Public Library, Texas/Dallas History Archives Division.)

Back at the City Cafe, Fults had just pulled a chair up to his favorite table when the cook, who had been delivering breakfast to the prisoners at the jail, burst through the front door with the news of Hamilton's escape. Within seconds the cafe was buzzing with talk and speculation. Fults ordered a plate of fried eggs and buried his face in a newspaper. An item of particular interest caught his eye. Conditional pardons were being issued to several Dallas area convicts, effective February 2. Clyde Barrow's name topped the list.

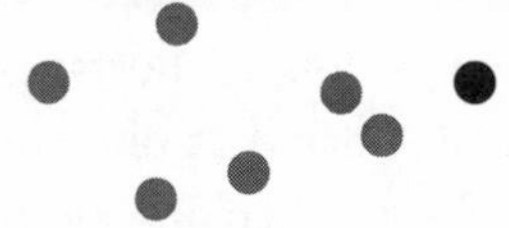

The Lake Dallas Gang

It was midnight, March 25, 1932.[1] Three shadowy forms had concealed themselves near the railroad tracks behind the Simms Oil Refinery, at 2435 Eagle Ford Road in Dallas. One of the men carried a heavy leather satchel laden with tools. The others carried firearms.

The tallest of the group took a pair of bolt cutters from the bag and applied the jaws to the cyclone fence enclosing the refinery. Within minutes he had cut a sizable hole in the fence. He crawled through, and his companions quickly followed.

A refinery hand was working nearby.

"Stay here, kid," whispered the tall intruder, producing an automatic pistol. The kid nodded, clutching his satchel. The third man, weapon already drawn, joined his lean accomplice in the task of detaining the Simms employee.

"Keep your mouth shut and your hands at your sides," they ordered, shoving a pair of pistols in the man's ribs.

Cautiously the man turned to face his assailants. Ralph Fults and Clyde Barrow returned his gaze. Raymond Hamilton, lugging the satchel of tools,[2] hurried up from the shadows.

"Let's go," said Barrow motioning toward the main office. Along the way Fults rounded up two more members of the oil company's graveyard shift. A fourth man, the night manager, was taken captive inside the main office.

While Clyde kept an eye on the hostages, Fults made a preliminary examination of the safe situated at one end of the office. Selecting a mallet and a punch, Fults started chipping away at the tumblers. No one spoke. An unseasonably warm wind rattled across the office windows. Ten minutes later the door of the big safe swung open. Eagerly, Fults poked his head inside the vault.

"Empty," he mumbled.

"What?" said Clyde.

"The damned thing's empty," Fults snapped angrily.

The bandits had been told a large payroll would be waiting for them. Inexplicably, it had been removed earlier in the evening.

The four Simms employees were bound and gagged. Without another word Barrow, Fults, and Hamilton disappeared through the office door, retraced their steps through the hole in the back fence, and sped away in a 1932 Chrysler.

"I don't think our boy Scotty knew what the hell he was talking about," said Raymond from the back seat. Clyde and Fults made no response, silently watching the side streets for strange cars.

Scotty was the Simms employee who had first told Clyde about the possibility of making a big haul at the refinery. Friday was payday, and the wages, drawn from the bank each Thursday and held overnight in the company safe, were always distributed in cash. Either Scotty had been mistaken about the money, or someone tipped the refinery. Fults and Barrow were beginning to think there was not much future in such petty operations. They needed to make a lot of money to buy weapons and recruit men for the raid against Eastham, and time was at a premium.

It had been nearly two months since Clyde Barrow's release from prison. A lot had happened in that short span of time. After learning of Barrow's February 2 pardon, Ralph Fults took the interurban train from McKinney to Dallas. Not far from Southern Methodist University Fults stole a Buick and drove it through town, crossing the Lamar Street bridge into West Dallas.

He had never been to West Dallas. What he found was a community of muddy, rutted streets and substandard housing. Unpainted shacks, tin sheds, lean-tos, and tents lined Eagle Ford Road. Many houses, their windows smashed and doors ripped away, were nevertheless inhabited. Families were camped beneath bridges and railroad trestles.[3] Rusted automobile bodies clogged the vacant lots, and the nearby industrial section poisoned the air with smoke and noxious fumes.[4]

Several blocks from the river Fults pulled up to a frame gas station with two pumps beneath a low canopy. East Texas "white" gas was selling for twelve cents a gallon. Advertisements for Nehi and Dr. Pepper adorned the outer walls. On one of the canopy joists seven hand-painted letters—BARROWS—greeted the station's customers. Clyde's parents had moved their house to Eagle Ford Road and added the filling station while he was in prison.[5]

A grey-haired man dressed in denim overalls sat beneath the canopy. An Atwater-Kent radio set, situated in a nearby window, was tuned to the local news on KRLD.

"Howdy," said Fults, raising an index finger to the brim of his Stetson.

"Howdy," replied the old man in a reserved tone.

Star Service Station, West Dallas, 1934. Just inside the door to the right, Clyde told his mother he would never be taken alive. (Courtesy of the Dallas Public Library, Texas/Dallas History Archives Division, Hayes Collection.)

"Are you Mr. Barrow?" inquired Fults.

"That's right, son," replied Barrow.

"I'm Ralph Fults, from McKinney. I done time with Clyde."

Barrow's expression suddenly changed. "Clyde's been expecting you to drop by," he said. "Come on in. He'll be back from work soon." Fults was puzzled. He had no idea he'd find Clyde working an honest job.[6] Frankly, he refused to believe it, thinking Barrow was putting on a show for his mother. Later, he would come to think the show was for Bonnie's mother instead.[7]

Fults accepted Henry Barrow's offer, stepping through the door that led to the living quarters in back of the station. Clyde's father was a big, rather handsome man with gentle eyes and a soft speaking voice. The house and its furnishings were simple but comfortable. In the hallway a frail, diminutive woman with slightly greying hair and stooped shoulders offered Fults a friendly smile. It was Clyde's mother.

"Clyde won't be long," she said. "Go on in and warm yourself by the fire."

Fults stepped into the next room. Three young people were seated around a woodburning stove. L. C. and Marie, Clyde's younger brother and sister, were only teenagers then. They idolized their older brother—so daring and clever he seemed.

"Two cons is enough for this family," Clyde often said to the youngsters whenever they asked to ride with him. "We don't need no more."

Later, however, L. C. took many trips with Clyde. Clyde also smuggled bootleg liquor from East Texas and Louisiana for L. C., who sold it in Dallas.

Seated across from Clyde's little brother was an attractive young woman with dark, brooding looks. Her features were petite and angular, her cheekbones high, her eyes piercing. It was Clyde's sister-in-law, Blanche—Buck's wife.

"Clyde told me all about you," she said revealing a slight Oklahoma accent. "Buck and I visited him a couple of times down there at Eastham." Unbeknownst to Fults, Blanche also knew about the plan to raid Eastham.[8]

Fults looked around the house. There was one bedroom and only

Dallas, 1925. The bridge in the foreground is the Houston Street Viaduct where Henry Barrow's horse-drawn cart was struck by a motorist. A free campground once existed beneath the bridge. There W. D. Jones first met Clyde Barrow. (Courtesy of the Dallas Public Library, Texas/Dallas History Archives Division.)

one bed in this tiny place. Almost every inch of remaining space was taken by neatly arranged pallets and handmade blankets, apparently to accommodate the many people living there. There appeared to be no indoor plumbing.

Suddenly footsteps thundered across the wooden porch. The door jiggled open, and Clyde stepped into the room. He looked troubled.

"You showed up just in time," he said to Fults. Mrs. Barrow then entered the room, and Clyde gave her a hug.

"Mama," Clyde said. "McCrary let me go."

"What for?" she asked.

"Them 'laws' kept coming into the shop and dragging me downtown," he said, " 'on suspicion'[9] they called it. Hah! Suspicion of what?"

His face was taut with rage, the way he looked at the woodpile the day Fults was pistol whipped.

"They got no reason," he added. "It's just because I'm a con and my name's Barrow. McCrary says 'I know you ain't doing nothing wrong, but all them cops hanging around is making business even worse than it already is.' "

"Mama, I'm never gonna work again," said Clyde, "and I'll never stand arrest, either. I'm not ever going back to that Eastham hell hole. I'll die first! I swear it, they're going to have to kill me."[10]

Barrow went into another room to get one of Buck's guns. Fults followed. A shiny brass saxophone was lying on the bed.

"You play this thing?" asked Fults.

"A little," answered Clyde.

"You better not lose that gun," Blanche warned. "Buck'll skin you alive."[11]

On March 25, 1932, Fults and Barrow staged their first holdup. It was the failed Simms Oil Refinery robbery—a failure they had dragged Raymond Hamilton into. Hamilton, hiding in West Dallas since his escape from the McKinney jail, had wanted nothing to do with the armed robbery. He preferred selling hot cars to one of the many scrap yards lining West Commerce.

"There's no money in that," said Fults.

"I'm doing OK" said Hamilton. "I got money."

"Not like you'll have if you come with us," replied Fults. "And no middle man," he added, thinking of the grocer who had fingered him in that Dallas boxcar burglary in 1929.

"Yeh," added Barrow. "Scotty's been after me to knock over Simms Oil. That would be a nice haul, but we need a third man."

Hamilton thought it over. "OK," he said, reluctantly. "But just this once."

To Fults, Ray seemed loud and overly talkative, quite unlike the introspective Clyde Barrow. But Barrow thought he would be a strong, reliable recruit for the raid on Eastham, and Fults really had no reason to think otherwise.

Raymond Hamilton was born in a tent on the banks of the Deep Fork River, near Schulter, Oklahoma.[12] The date was May 21, 1913.[13] He was two years old before his family was able to move into a house.

Sometime after 1918 Ray's father completely abandoned the family, disappearing without a trace.[14] In 1920 he turned up in West Dallas. He sent for his wife and family and moved them into one of the more livable houses there. Raymond was enrolled in school but, like Barrow and Fults, found it boring and irrelevant. In 1922 his father vanished again, thus reducing the family's standard of living to well below the poverty level. Selling newspapers for a few extra pennies became Ray's idea of education.[15] The juvenile authorities, however, thought otherwise. Time after time he found himself facing charges of truancy. Soon he was being picked up habitually, usually for vagrancy, sometimes for truancy, often for no reason at all.

Hamilton made friends with an older boy whose family lived across a vacant lot from his house.[16] Clyde Barrow had a lot in common with Ray—farming background, small stature, large family. And both boys shared an exceptional popularity with the local authorities, or "laws" as

West Dallas in the Great Depression, 1934. (Courtesy of the Dallas Public Library, Texas/Dallas History Archives Division, Hayes Collection.)

they were called.

In September 1931 Hamilton was charged with his first solid crime—grand theft auto. He was told that if he were to plead guilty to the charge, he would receive a three-year suspended sentence.[17] He chose that option, walking away from the courthouse a free man.

Hamilton's freedom was short-lived. Five months later he was again arrested for auto theft, this time in McKinney. On January 27, 1932,[18] as he awaited trial, Ray cut his way to freedom, aided by the hacksaw blades Ralph Fults had smuggled to him in the binding of a magazine.

After the break Hamilton hid out in West Dallas. Nearly two months later Barrow and Fults rolled up in the alley behind his house, convincing him to join them in the ill-fated Simms Oil Refinery hold up. Hamilton must have been harboring second thoughts about his big-talking friends as they pulled away from the refinery empty-handed.

While passing through the nearby town of Arlington minutes after the Simms fiasco, Barrow, Fults, and Hamilton developed car trouble. The back seat was full of tools and weapons, and the eastern sky was getting brighter by the minute. They had to switch cars before some local officer arrived. The only fresh car in sight was a luxurious, late-model Pierce Arrow.

Raymond pulled the wires from beneath the dash of the grand touring car and started the engine. Sliding over on the seat, he then drew a cigarette to his lips and pulled from his shirt pocket a large kitchen match, striking it on the dash.

"Hey!" shouted Clyde, climbing behind the wheel. "Don't be scratching up my car."

Raymond turned toward Clyde, unlit cigarette dangling from his open mouth.

"If someone sees you tearing up the dash, they'll know we don't own this thing," Barrow said. Fults burst into laughter. The idea that anyone would think a trio of misfits like themselves could possibly own such a car struck him as ludicrous. They abandoned the Pierce Arrow and stole a Ford.

Barrow, Fults, and Hamilton began staging a series of small safe jobs, the most successful of which occurred along Greenville Avenue, in Dallas. A pair of local policemen actually stood guard in front of the businesses while they were being raided, taking a share of the money afterward.[19]

"I think it's time we graduate to banks," Fults said.

"Wait a minute," said Raymond. "Payrolls are OK, but banks . . . well, banks are a bit too much for me."

"Look, Ray," said Clyde. "Me and Ralph have this deal going down, the one we started in prison. We need a lot of cash to get a raid like that off the ground. We'd love to have you throw in with us, but we need to get the ball rolling right now. What's it gonna be?" Reluctantly, Hamilton decided to stick it out.

In 1932, five thousand U.S. banks closed.[20] Almost every town that Barrow, Fults, and Hamilton passed through had its own boarded-up monument to financial mismanagement.

In Okabena, Minnesota, the outlaws discovered what looked like the perfect bank—situated on the main square, with plenty of roads leading out of the area. However, when they started to explore the roads and rehearse an escape plan, they found too much snow and ice on the ground to make the job feasible.[21] With Fults at the wheel, the would-be Minnesota bank robbers headed south toward Lawrence, Kansas, a town they'd noticed the day before. It was more than 350 miles away, but the Texans decided to drive straight through.

Sometime after dark Fults began to get drowsy. He glanced at his companions. Both were sound asleep. "I'll try to make it to some all-night diner and tank up on coffee," he thought to himself. Suddenly the car started vibrating furiously, rocking up and down as it thundered through an open field. "I'm awake. I'm awake!" shouted Fults. Barrow and Hamilton opened their eyes just in time to see an endless line of young Iowa corn stalks crashing beneath the running boards. "You're in a cornfield, Ralph," laughed Clyde. "You sleepy or something?"

"I'll take over for awhile," said Ray.

Fults crawled into the back seat while Ray maneuvered through the corn rows in search of the highway. Before long, the night riders were on their way south, the rhythm of the road lulling Fults fast to sleep. Within minutes, however, he felt himself being jostled about. A series of bumps, followed by the screeching sound of barbed wire dragging across the body of the car, snatched him rudely from sleep.

"I'm awake!" announced Ray. "I'm awake."

"Too late," said Clyde, "we're in another damned cornfield—let me drive."

Barrow slid behind the wheel, backed through the demolished barbed wire fence, and drove onto the highway. Soon, the car was hurtling along at high speed—Barrow's foot buried in the accelerator. Fults felt his eyes closing. He was falling back to sleep. Suddenly, a sharp jolt wrenched him from yet another comfortable position. The familiar sound of snapping wire and crashing stalks of corn told him they'd driven into their third cornfield of the evening.

"I'm awake, I'm awake!" exclaimed Clyde excitedly. The car rocked to a sudden stop more than a hundred feet from the road. Considering the speed at which Clyde usually drove, it's a wonder the car had not overturned, killing everyone inside. The three men decided they had seen enough cornfields for one night. Concealing themselves in a nearby clump of trees, the weary travelers stretched out beneath the stars for a bit of rest.

In Lawrence the three men checked into the old Eldridge Hotel. There they spent the remainder of the first day observing the First National Bank at the corner of Eighth and Massachusetts. The bank was active, which bothered Fults and Barrow. A large crowd might prove hard to handle. Fults decided to take a closer look by changing a ten-dollar bill at the teller's cage.

In 1932 bank robbery was on the increase. Many banks began stationing armed security agents in cage-like balconies above the lobby. However, on that day Fults could see no such installation, just a lone guard leaning placidly against the front door jam. The many customers still posed a problem.

The following morning at 8:45 A.M. the bandits noticed the bank president stroll quietly up the street and let himself into the building. For nearly ten minutes he was alone inside. Eventually the other employees began to arrive. The next morning the same thing happened. Barrow, Fults, and Hamilton knew what to do.

"Let's do it tomorrow," said Barrow. Fults and Hamilton nodded in agreement.

At 8:45 A.M. the following morning the bank president came strolling up the sidewalk, just as he had done the previous two mornings. Barrow and Fults stepped from their car, adjusted the sawed-off shotguns beneath their overcoats, and crossed the square to meet the unsuspecting banker. Hamilton waited in the car. Just as they walked up to their intended victim, the two bandits spotted a man and a woman approaching from the opposite direction. They were bank employees. There was little time to lose. Fults walked over to them. Barrow approached the president.

"This is a stick up," said Clyde. "Don't raise your hands and don't try nothing funny." The startled man fumbled with the keys for a few seconds before calming down enough to turn the latch on the front door. "We ain't going to hurt nobody," Barrow added, following Fults and the three victims into the empty bank "We just want the money."

Fults, .45 in one hand, shotgun in the other, stood guard while Barrow accompanied the president to the main vault. The outlaw soon reappeared, hauling two large sacks of currency. While the rest of the bank's employees were being hustled into the vault, Fults stepped over to the window and motioned for Raymond to bring the car around.

The bank robbers never looked back. Speeding from town, they switched to a backup car without incident. If a posse was ever organized, the bandits saw no evidence of it. They did not even see the bank guard. Nothing stood in their way as they fled east across two state lines.

In a small hotel room in East St. Louis, Illinois, Fults counted the money.

"Well?" Clyde inquired.

"Yeh," asked Ray, eagerly, "how much?"

"Thirty-three big ones!" replied Fults.

"Huh?" asked Clyde.

"Thirty-three thousand dollars." Fults said. "Thirty-three and some change."[22]

"Are you sure?" asked Barrow.

"Hell, yes," Fults answered. "Here, count it for yourself."

"No, that's all right," said Barrow. "I believe you. . . . I mean, I just can't believe we got so much."

Raymond stood in silence, mouth wide open. He had never even dreamed that so much money existed. For a kid whose family could barely afford shoes, his cut of thirty-three thousand dollars must have seemed like all the cash in the world.

"When's our next job?" he asked.

"What's that?" asked Clyde.

"Let's take another bank right away," said Raymond, excitedly.

"Hey!" said Fults with a smile. "I thought you didn't think much of the bank-robbing trade."

In nearby Dupo, Fults located the pawn shop owner who'd sold a pair of pistols to him and Eddie two years earlier. Through him a meeting was arranged with an underworld figure who dealt in heavy weapons. Both Fults and Barrow wanted to increase their firepower before making an attempt at organizing the raid against Eastham. Ray went along for the ride.

The dealer didn't have much to offer. The Texans looked through an odd assortment of .45 caliber automatic pistols, some shotguns, and Thompson .45 caliber submachine guns. The Thompsons, featuring drum clips, were cumbersome, inaccurate, and notorious for jamming.[23]

Fults and Barrow did not like the selection, but it was better than nothing. They bought the weapons and a few bulletproof vests and started to leave. The time had come to finalize the plans to raid Eastham.

Hamilton laughed. "Are you guys really serious about that prison farm bull?"

Barrow and Fults nodded.

"I don't care about no cons on no prison farm," Ray said. "If that's your game, just count me out." Hamilton grabbed his share of the bank money and took off.

Fults merely shrugged. Only an ex-con could understand the plan to raid Eastham, someone who had felt a trace chain slam into his body, or watched a fellow prisoner disappear behind some hill, never to return. Barrow was angry, though. "I hope the little rat chokes on that wad of money," he said.[24]

Clyde Barrow, 1933. Fults commented that Barrow looked angry in this picture. (Courtesy of Cecil Mayes.)

Barrow and Fults returned to Texas. They often visited West Dallas. Using what they called "the back door," variously, U.S. 80 through Arcadia Park, or the old Coppel road through the Trinity River bottoms, they would drive up to the Star Service Station just long enough to gas up and touch base with the family. Invariably Mr. Barrow would be seated beneath the canopy, listening to his radio. Whenever police bulletins were broadcast, he would relay the information to the two outlaws. It often helped them avoid trouble.

During one of these visits Fults first met Bonnie Parker. She was working at a downtown Dallas restaurant at the time. Everyone called it "the courthouse cafe," but that was not its real name.[25] She had just finished her shift and had dropped by the filling station for a visit when Barrow and Fults drove up. Her eyes brightened when Clyde walked through the door. Smiling broadly, he introduced her to Fults.

Next to Mrs. Barrow, Bonnie was the tiniest woman Fults had ever seen. She was attractive, with milky-smooth skin and deep blue eyes. Her reddish-blonde hair was bobbed in the style of Marion Davies or Myrna Loy, popular actresses of the day. The look accentuated her outgoing manner.

"Could you give me a ride out to Mama's?" she asked Clyde. Barrow gladly agreed to the request.

Bonnie lived with her mother at 2430 Douglass, just north of downtown Dallas. Her sister, brother, and sister-in-law also shared the house. Fults cannot recall ever being invited inside the house. Mrs. Parker did not particularly approve of her daughter's association with ex-cons.[26]

After seeing Bonnie safely home, Fults and Barrow drove to Denton, one of Clyde's favorite haunts. With Hamilton out of the picture, new recruits were needed—reliable ones. Denton was a good place to start

Bonnie Parker, 1926. (Courtesy of of the Dallas Public Library, Texas/Dallas History Archives Division.)

looking. There, they met with a fellow named Jack. Jack was an old friend of both Clyde and Buck, especially Buck. His underworld contacts made him an attractive recruit for the Eastham raid. He was also acquainted with Johnny and Fuzz, the two boys Fults had known first at the state school at Gatesville and had later joined in the theft of a boxcar-load of cigarettes in Dallas. Clyde knew them as well. Jack said they were both in Denton. Later, in the back room of a house on Railroad Avenue, Clyde, Ralph and Jack met Johnny and Fuzz. They were also introduced to another man, Ted Rogers. Ted bore a striking physical resemblance to Raymond Hamilton—small, blond, and very young. Emotionally, however, there was no similarity. Ted was cool, quiet, and extremely dangerous.

Barrow and Fults outlined the planned raid on Eastham. The group would go in at night, take the four picket guards hostage at Camp 1, and storm the second story barracks while its guards slept. If the raiders acted fast enough, they could get the drop on the entire guard force and presumably release every single convict at the camp.

Clyde wanted the gang divided into at least two independent squads. Should one of the squads run into trouble, the other would be free to help. The idea was well received.

Fults suddenly noticed how much taller he was than the others. "I can see right now I'm in the wrong line of work, fellas," said Fults. "I just know we're going to get cornered someday and the cops are going to point at me and say 'shoot the big one'." Everyone laughed, but in two future gun battles, one involving Barrow and another involving Hamilton, the statement would prove prophetic.[27]

Someone mentioned the two banks on the southwest corner of Denton's main square. Because of the success of the Barrow-Fults-Hamilton robbery in Lawrence, Kansas, the others wanted to make their own attempt at bank robbery. The six men decided to rob both Denton banks at the same time.

At twenty minutes to nine on the morning of April 11, 1932, two Buick sedans rolled through Denton's square, turned east on Hickory (between the two banks), and came to a stop just beyond Austin Avenue.

Fults stepped from his car and took a slow walk around the old courthouse. Wagons and automobiles rattled slowly past one another. Nearly every parking place was taken. People were milling around on the sidewalks, waiting for the shops to open. Gripping a sawed-off shotgun beneath his overcoat, Fults returned to the waiting cars.

"Looks good," he said. "What time is it?"

"Ten till," someone answered.

"I think I'll make one more pass around the square," said Fults. Fults walked in front of the R. C. Scripture Building and examined a line of cars on the north side of the square. Something caught his eye—a small detail. Every car parked on the square was parked facing in, except one.

Fults crossed the street and approached the odd car. It was a brand new Chrysler, but it looked heavier than most Chryslers—armor-plated. Two men sat in the front seat. Fults took a closer look. He had seen them both before. Their names were Tom Hickman and M. T. Gonzuales. They were Texas Rangers. Fults walked slowly back to the rendezvous point.

"Hickman and Gonzuales are on the square," he said. "Something's up."

Clyde and the others agreed that the raid should be called off. It was a wise decision. Gonzuales, whose reputation for working alone had earned him the nickname of "Lone Wolf," was particularly dangerous.[28] Because of his impressive skill as a marksman, confrontations with him were consistently one-sided. In fact, both Rangers were exceptional shots, able to fire from the hip and strike objects as small as silver dollars from across the street.[29] Although outnumbered, the Rangers certainly would have given the young bandits a disastrous run for their money.

The gang abandoned the bank-robbery scheme and drove to a hideout on the shores of nearby Lake Dallas.[30] Even though Clyde had given away most of his share of the Kansas bank money,[31] there was still enough left between him and Fults to finance the raid on Eastham. Robbing the two Denton banks was not a necessity.

At the Lake Dallas hide out the six men tested the new weapons from Dupo, Illinois. Fults draped the bulletproof vests across a barbed wire fence. He and the others drew .45 automatic pistols and opened fire. Within seconds the vests lay in shreds, absolutely useless. They were left to rot on the fence.

Many of the guns turned out to be defective as well. Barrow and Fults both knew they had been cheated. They never bought another weapon again. They resorted to stealing them from gun shops and military posts.

"Maybe we ought to get a couple of more guys to go with us to Eastham," one of the gang members suggested. The others agreed. Barrow and Fults decided to drive to Amarillo, in the Texas Panhandle, to locate two brothers they had known at Eastham.

Before they left Barrow and Fults were approached by a youngster named Red. Red was a friend of Jack's. He had always wanted to run around with Barrow, and he convinced the outlaw to take him along to Amarillo, emphasizing his request by pulling a .44 revolver from his belt.

"I hope some cop tries to stop us," he said. "I'd like to part his hair with this thing."

That evening in Amarillo the three men tried in vain to locate the brothers. All night long they cruised the streets. At sunrise, April 14, the trio decided to start back to Denton.

In the town of Electra, Texas, thirty miles west of Wichita Falls, their car stalled in front of a produce warehouse.[32] A. F. McCormick,[33] city oil and gas agent, watched the strangers with great interest from the offices of the Magnolia Gas Company, directly across the street. Having read about the many exploits of Charles "Pretty Boy" Floyd,[34] and fearing an impending bank robbery, he quickly telephoned the police. At 9 A.M., Police Chief James T. Taylor answered the call, catching a ride to the ice house with J. C. Harris, head of the city water department. Along the way Taylor and Harris spotted the youths in question walking toward town.[35] Fults noticed the approaching vehicle. When it slowed to a stop, he and Clyde casually spread apart. Red, dumbfounded, stood still. Chief Taylor, seated on the passenger side of Harris's car, leaned forward.

"What seems to be the problem, boys?" he asked.

"Our car went dead on us," answered Fults, passing a glance to Clyde.

"Where are y'all boys from?" inquired the Chief.

"Wichita Falls," answered Fults, as Clyde moved around to the driver's side of the car.

"Well," said Taylor, producing a pair of handcuffs, "I'm afraid I'm going to have to take y'all in and check you out."

While Fults and Red were raising their hands, Clyde slipped around behind the car and eased up next to Harris, still seated behind the wheel of his car. When Barrow was in position, Fults dropped his right hand to his belt and whipped out a .45 automatic. Clyde instantly jabbed the barrels of two pistols in Harris's startled face. Red stood with his mouth wide open, frozen in place, hands still raised. The police chief started motioning with his left hand.

"Oh, that's OK," he said, "You boys can go on."

"Nothing doing," said Fults, reaching through the window to relieve Taylor of his service revolver. "We've got to take you, now."

At that moment a green Chevrolet coach rolled to a stop not more than twenty feet away. A man emerged from the driver's side. It was A. F. McCormick, the oil and gas agent who had called the police chief. Thinking Chief Taylor had everything under control, McCormick crossed the street to join in the arrest.[36] It didn't take long before he realized the folly of his move.

"Get back in that car," shouted Fults, aiming Taylor's service revolver toward the Chevy, "in the back seat."

McCormick complied without a word, Fults rushing over to join him. Barrow pulled Harris from the first car, ordering him and Chief Taylor over to McCormick's Chevy.

"Up front," said Clyde, climbing behind the wheel of the car, "next to me."

Fults started looking around for Red.

"He done took off," said Clyde, adjusting his pair of tortoise-rimmed sunglasses. Sure enough, Fults could see Red running in the distance. "Big talker." Later it was revealed that Red was the one who had tipped the Texas Rangers about the plan to rob both Denton banks.[37]

Clyde put the Chevrolet in gear and pulled away from the shoulder of the road. Cruising slowly through Elektra, he turned south at the junction. On the way out of town Barrow and Fults spoke freely with their captives, apologizing for the inconvenience.[38] Eight miles southeast of town, the three prisoners were freed not far from the Lazy J ranch. Fults held on to Taylor's revolver. "We'll take good care of this," he said.[39] A mile down the road Barrow turned east. He and Fults planned to back track north through Oklahoma, then turn south to McKinney. Not much further along, however, near Fowlkes the Chevy ran out of gas.[40]

W. N. Owens, a rural mail carrier, was about to overtake the stalled vehicle when the two outlaws leaped onto the running boards of his car and pressed automatic pistols against his neck.[41] Fults ordered Owens to pull over, which he did without hesitation.

The hijackers acted fast. After wiping the Chevy clean of fingerprints, they hopped into the mailman's car and raced off with their fourth kidnap victim of the morning. Barrow performed as if he'd personally designed the roads he turned down, his ever-present dark glasses shielding his eyes from the dust and glare. Several hours were spent winding through the foothills north of Wichita Falls.[42] By late afternoon the hijacked mail car was approaching the Randlett Toll Bridge, spanning the Red River on the Texas-Oklahoma border. Two bridgekeepers were posted in the small shack adjacent to the road. A simple sign, dangling low across the road, greeted the travelers: RANDLETT BRIDGE–Pay Toll.

Clyde let his foot off the gas and started to slow down. One of the bridgekeepers stepped from the shack and watched the approaching car.

"Don't stop," said Fults. "Bust that chain in two."

Barrow shifted to second gear and gave it the gas. The bridgekeeper retreated to the shack and shouted as the car passed. The chain snapped with a loud crash. Both bridge keepers then emerged from the shack with pistols drawn, firing several rounds at the fleeing auto.[43] Not one bullet found its mark.

Owens, blindfolded during much of the trip, later spoke of the casual ease with which his captors executed their flight into Oklahoma.[44] Barrow spoke often with Owens. Fults, seated in the rear, said nothing. Because of this, Owens grew nervous. He was certain that Fults meant to kill him. Shortly after crossing the toll bridge, Clyde stopped the car and waited with Owens while Fults climbed a telephone pole to cut the wires.

"You'll probably read in the papers about our deaths any day now," said Barrow.[45]

"I'm scared," Owens said.

"Don't worry," said Clyde.

"No," replied Owens, looking toward Fults, "I'm afraid of him. I think he means to kill me and take my car."

"Him?" asked Barrow. "He ain't going to do nothing."

Clyde got out of the car and met Fults at the base of the telephone pole. "Talk to this guy," he said. "He's nervous about you being so quiet." Fults approached Owens with a smile. "We're not going to hurt you, mister," he said. "We just need to use your car for awhile. My dad's a mailman. I couldn't hurt no mailman." The conversation seemed to pacify the frightened man.

Fifteen miles south of Fletcher, Oklahoma, the outlaws and their captive heard a radio report that a roadblock had been organized in town. Under the cover of darkness Clyde bypassed Fletcher, using a series of farm-to-market roads lacing the town's perimeter. Ten miles northeast of Fletcher, on the main road to Oklahoma City, Barrow pulled over.

"We better let you out here," said Fults. "You ought to be able to catch a ride into Fletcher from here."

"What about my car?" inquired Owens.

"We'll leave it in plain sight," said Clyde.

"It'll be found in a day or so."

"You guys would be doing me a big favor if you just burned it up," said Owens.

"Burn it?" asked Fults.

"Yeh," said Owens. "That way the government'll have to buy me a new one."

"OK," said Clyde. "We'll burn your car for you."

Back in Denton, Barrow and Fults rejoined the other members of the Lake Dallas gang. Following a brief discussion, the group decided to move on Eastham without the brothers from Amarillo.

"Clyde and me will go to Tyler Monday night and pick out a couple of big, fast cars," said Fults.

Jack mentioned a hardware store in Celina, northwest of McKinney, that stocked a wide selection of rifles and shotguns.

"Them guys in the joint are going to want some guns," he said. "Them

Illinois guns ain't worth a damn."

"We'll take Celina the same night you two go to Tyler," he said. "We'll meet next Tuesday, down on Lake Dallas."

"Agreed," said Fults. The others nodded. Later that evening Fults and Barrow drove to Dallas to see Bonnie. They asked if she would mind going to Eastham with them on the following day. They needed someone to pass a message to Aubrey, outlining the latest developments of the impending raid. Bonnie was all too happy to oblige—anything to be near Clyde. The two outlaws agreed to pick her up early the next morning.

It was noon, April 17. Bonnie, Clyde, and Ralph turned west from Trinity, Texas, onto the dirt road leading to Eastham. One mile from the camp's main building the two men got out of the car and let Bonnie drive on alone. She would pose as Aubrey's cousin, supposedly taking advantage of a beautiful Sunday afternoon to pay her wayward relative a family visit. Barrow and Fults waited in the woods a hundred feet from the road.

"Do you think we'll have any trouble getting them cars tomorrow night?" asked Clyde.

"No," said Fults.

"Do you think Bonnie can come along?" Barrow asked.

"I don't see why not," answered Fults.

After a few minutes a truckload of guards rolled by. Fults and Barrow recognized a couple of the faces in the group. They watched with great interest as the truck disappeared down the road. Shortly thereafter Bonnie drove up. She was all smiles. Aubrey understood the message and promised to pass the word to Joe Palmer and Henry Methvin.

It would be well past dark before Fults, Clyde, and Bonnie returned to Dallas. With the promise of returning for her on the following evening, the two men dropped Bonnie at her mother's house and started back to Denton by way of Dallas's "back door." Not long after turning onto West Davis, outbound, a police car began following them. The officers, staked out on a West Dallas side street, recognized Barrow as he passed.

Already traveling at a high rate of speed, Clyde was able to get a tremendous lead. He was trying to make it to the edge of Chalk Hill, where West Davis begins a steep grade toward Arcadia Park. By the time he and Fults began their descent, the squad car was three or four city blocks behind them.

Just beyond the crest of the hill Barrow cut the lights, hit the brakes, and turned the wheel hard to the left. The car spun completely around, sliding across the center line and into the opposite lane. Clyde then shifted to second, switched on the lights, and topped the hill just as the police car roared past, speeding in the opposite direction with red lights blazing and sirens screaming.

Fults was riveted to his seat. He'd been around a lot of cars and witnessed some fancy driving in his day, but that was the fastest turn-around he'd ever seen. Clyde's hours of driving practice had paid off.[46] The outlaws crossed the Trinity River bridge at Eagle Ford, west of Cement City. The police were long gone.

After the incident it was decided that Clyde should avoid Dallas for a while. The following evening, April 18, 1932, Fults dropped Barrow near the Buckner Home for Boys, on Samuel Road ten miles east of town, and drove on alone to pick up Bonnie.

Bonnie was in a good mood that evening, bubbly and talkative. As she and Fults proceeded east through town to pick up Clyde, she spoke of her family and how she hated serving lunches to the politicians and businessmen downtown. She also disliked the lawmen who frequented the cafe. "Laws" she called them, imitating Clyde's West Dallas slang. "They made him what he is today," she said. "He used to be a nice boy.[47] Now he's just an ex-con without a job. This town's good at keeping boys like him down," she added, gazing at the fresh new office buildings downtown and thinking of the wealth they represented. "Why even try?"

Bonnie was articulate, thoughtful, and witty. Fults liked her a lot, but he could never understand her attraction to the outlaw life. She hated guns[48] and rarely participated directly in any crime.[49] She had been immensely popular in school, and remained so throughout her years as a waitress in three downtown area restaurants.[50] There was hardly a businessman, county official, or lawman that didn't know and like her.[51] Despite her ability with people, however, Bonnie felt somehow shut out, inferior.

"I'm just a loser—like Clyde," she confided to Fults. "Folks like us haven't got a chance."

Bonnie was born to Emma and Charles Parker on October 1, 1910, in Rowena, Texas (near San Angelo). The second of three children, she does not appear to have had a remarkable early life, certainly nothing to indicate a penchant for crime.

At an early age Bonnie discovered that by entertaining her admirers she could hold their attention indefinitely. Songs, recitations, and impromptu dances soon filled the Parker household. Bonnie's love of dramatics would remain a part of her throughout her life.

When Bonnie was four years old, her father, a bricklayer by trade, suddenly died.[52] The event is significant for two reasons. It served to catalyze a strong family bond and precipitated, for better or worse, the single most important event of Bonnie's life—her move from West Texas to the rural reaches of far West Dallas and her subsequent introduction to Clyde Barrow.

In 1914 Mrs. Parker and her three young children arrived at 2908 Eagle Ford Road, the home of Bonnie's maternal grandparents, Frank and Mary Krause. Although Bonnie's new home was located in a rural setting, a small town called Cement City and several industries stood nearby. The air was often thick with the smell of petroleum and smoldering coke. Oil refineries and foundries lined Eagle Ford Road, just east of Frank Krause's property. A mile and a half to the southwest, beyond a low ridge, white smoke belched skyward from the Trinity-Portland Cement Company stacks. Across an open field, several hundred yards to the northeast, lay the bleached white monuments of the fifty-eight-year-old Fishtrap Cemetery, last remnants of the LaReunion settlers, the first European residents of what would later become West Dallas.[53]

Cement City, like most of West Dallas, was a tough industrial district. Along a dusty little thoroughfare called Chalk Hill Road, lived African Americans to one side, whites to the other. Cement City was actually nothing more than an unincorporated neighborhood, a company community serving the needs of the many Trinity-Portland Cement Company employees.[54] Adults as well as children learned little more than how to survive. Few avoided trouble. Most fought their way through life.

Bonnie married young. she was only fifteen when she fell in love with her high school flame, Roy Thornton. Thornton, like Bonnie, was just a youngster, but children grew up fast in West Dallas. Already well acquainted with local hoodlums like Raymond Hamilton and the Barrow brothers, Roy was headed striaght for trouble when he and Bonnie were married on September 25, 1926.[55]

On August 9, 1927, he vanished for ten days. When he came back home, he offered no explanation for his absence. He then began abusing Bonnie and drinking heavily. On October 1 Roy disappeared again. Nineteen days later he stepped through the front door smiling, acting as if nothing had happened. Bonnie, though, was growing tired of her husband's unexplained hiatuses. By the evening of December 5, when it was becoming painfully apparent that he had left for the third time, she decided she was through with Roy Thornton.[56] She would never see him again. Nevertheless, Bonnie never sought a divorce and continued

Bonnie Parker and her husband Roy Thornton, 1926. (Courtesy of the Dallas Public Library, Texas/Dallas History Archives Division.)

to wear the ring Thornton had given her on the day she was married. She was still wearing it when they pulled her body from the wreckage of a bullet-riddled car, six and one-half years later.[57]

In January 1928 Bonnie took a job at Hargraves Cafe, at 3308 Swiss Avenue. The steady work seemed to alleviate her loneliness and sense of failure. She enjoyed talking and carrying on with the cafe regulars. Her ready smile and energetic personality quickly established her popularity.

Located in a small semicircular building, Hargraves no doubt drew a lot of its business from nearby Baylor Medical College. The employees of Yates Laundry, too, frequented the cafe. Yates, for years one of Dallas's largest and finest laundries, was situated in two large buildings on Floyd Street, directly behind Hargraves. The back door of the cafe faced the laundry.

Because the laundry workers were not allowed to leave their stations except during the noon hour, they had developed a system with which to obtain snacks and sandwiches. At Bonnie's suggestion, whenever the Yates people needed something from across the street, they'd go to their front door and whistle. Bonnie would appear at the cafe's back door, run across the street, and take everyone's order.[58]

If it happened to be slow in the cafe, Bonnie would stay a while and chat with the laundry women. They liked her a lot. She reminded them of a "delicate china doll,"[59] small, almost fragile, with a round, petite face and creamy porcelain complexion. Moreover, her appearance was typically fresh and clean, something the Yates personnel always noticed in a person.[60]

Sometime in the spring of 1929 Bonnie was offered a job at a downtown restaurant known as Marco's, at 702 Main. Just two blocks from the Dallas County Courthouse, Marco's attracted a different sort of clientele. Lawyers, judges, and businessmen drifted in and out at a regular rate.[61] City police, deputy sheriffs, and postal employees also patronized the little cafe. However, Marco's was forced to close in November 1929.[62] Less than a month after the great stock market crash, the young waitress found herself among the growing ranks of the unemployed.

In January 1930 Bonnie began hiring out as a housekeeper or babysitter or anything she could get. Toward the end of the second week in

January she moved into the West Dallas home of Clarence Clay. Clay's daughter had broken her arm. Bonnie was to help her keep house and cook while her arm healed.

Shortly after Bonnie moved into the house, a visitor dropped by—a young man. His family lived just a few blocks away. A dimpled smile punctuated his introduction to Bonnie. His name was Clyde Barrow.[63]

From the moment they first met, Bonnie and Clyde were strongly attracted to each other. In fact, when Barrow was later arrested on burglary charges (February 1930, at Bonnie's place), he had known her less than three weeks. Apparently, though, it was plenty of time to fall in love. Bonnie, in particular, became obsessed with thoughts of Clyde.[64] It didn't matter what he had done; she was prepared to follow him all the way to the penitentiary if necessary.

Her undying loyalty was put to the test on March 11, 1930, when

Bonnie Parker, 1933. (Courtesy of Trey Ford.)

she smuggled a loaded revolver to Clyde in the Waco jail.[65] Afterward Bonnie rejoined her cousin Mary in the foyer of the McLennan County jail. Shaking uncontrollably, the two women returned to Mary's house in Waco and waited for Clyde to make his break. All night they waited—not a word from Barrow. The following morning when Bonnie read about the escape, she was crushed. She was convinced that Barrow had merely used her to his own ends and had no intention of picking her up after the break as was planned.

After dark two men walked up to the door and started pounding. "Laws," Mary and Bonnie thought to themselves, gazing nervously at the figures on the front porch. Finally the strangers turned away, but they did not leave. They sat down on the curb across the street, staring blankly at Mary's darkened house. The women were petrified.[66] Finally, however, the mysterious visitors drove away. Bonnie hitched a ride back to Dallas, arriving sometime on the thirteenth of March. Disgusted with Clyde Barrow, for the next day or so she moped around her mother's house. Then she received a telegram from Nokomis, Illinois, and her attitude improved. Clyde had dropped her a line to tell her about the two boys he had sent back to Waco to pick her up. They had waited in front of Mary's house until well past midnight but saw no one. Barrow promised to send for her when he got resettled up north. He never got the chance. In Middleton, Ohio, he was picked up and returned to Texas. A few months later he was chopping wood next to Ralph Fults at Eastham's Camp 2.

Upon his February 2, 1932, parole, Clyde hurried to Bonnie's side. When she saw him hobbling up to her front door on a pair of penitentiary-issue crutches, she melted. It was as if he'd never been away.

Bonnie's mother was skeptical. She saw a change in Barrow. He seemed cynical, bitter.[67] However, when he took his old job back at United Glass and Mirror, she decided to give him another chance.[68] Even when she discovered that he had been laid off, she didn't intervene. Perhaps she was hoping that Barrow would find another job and settle down. She could not have known of his vow to die rather than contribute to a society that seemed intent on keeping an ex-con from earning an honest wage. Even if she had known, it is doubtful that Mrs. Parker could have convinced her daughter to abandon him. Bonnie's loyalty was absolute. Time and again it was tested, sometimes severely. Always she returned to him, eventually at the cost of her own life.

Ralph and Bonnie continued east on Samuel Road, stopping long enough to retrieve Clyde from a cafe near the Buckner Home for Boys. En route to Tyler the trio made a quick stop in the town of Kaufman, thirty miles southeast of Dallas. Low on ammunition, Fults bought two boxes of shells at a hardware store on the square. Rejoining Clyde and Bonnie, he commented on the array of rifles and shotguns for sale inside.

"Maybe we oughta bust in there on our way back from Tyler—just in case them other guys come up dry in Celina," he said.

"OK," said Clyde.

In Tyler the two men found unattended autos nearly everywhere. They took their time, looking for a pair of really nice cars—big enough to

Bonnie Parker, 1933. (Courtesy of L. J. Hinton.)

accommodate the many passengers they hoped to have following the Eastham raid.

Fults selected a brand new Buick. Clyde chose a plush Chrysler. On the way back to Kaufman they worked on the engines. Soon the two cars were able to travel over the gravel roads at speeds in excess of 90 miles per hour.

At midnight the freshly stolen vehicles cruised quietly into Kaufman. With headlights extinguished, Clyde, Bonnie, and Fults coasted to a stop behind the hardware store they had visited earlier in the evening. The sudden appearance of two sleek cars on the deserted square aroused the curiosity of night watchman Tom Jones.[69] He crossed the square. Fults was preoccupied with the padlock on the rear door of the shop, but Barrow was continually scanning the darkness for movement. From the corner of his eye he saw something flicker. Jones rounded the corner, chrome revolver drawn. Barrow whirled and fired. Jones dove behind the Chrysler and returned the fire. Bonnie, still inside the car, crouched nervously on the floor board. Lead screaming past his ears, Barrow ran toward Jones, hoping to pin him down, but he lost the watchman in the shadows. Seconds later, the evening quiet was again shattered by the clanging of a fire bell.

"We'd better get going," shouted Fults. "That watchman's going to have the whole town out here in a minute."

Indeed, a few people had already gathered on the square. The two cars containing Fults, Barrow, and Parker, roared past them, turning north on Highway 40 toward Dallas. As soon as he had rounded the curve, Fults saw Clyde's brake lights blink on. The reason became immediately clear. Two heavy road graders had been pulled across the highway. Several armed men stood nearby.

Barrow spun the Buick around in the middle of the road, slinging gravel through the air. Fults followed suit, reentering Kaufman at high speed. The small group of sleepy town folk, still assembled on the square, watched mutely as the big cars careened through their town for a second time. The maneuver proved futile. Several hundred yards southeast of town another road block was visible. Once again the fugitives reversed their direction and backtracked to Kaufman. The people on the square must have thought they were dreaming. They stared in disbelief as the bandits looked for an escape route. Still in the lead, Bonnie and Clyde turned east on a thoroughfare called County Road (now Farm-to-Market 1391), with Fults close behind. Not a soul stood in the way of their flight. It looked as if they were home free. Then it started raining.

Kaufman County soil is laced with a heavy clay, dense and black. In dry weather a shovel will snap before penetrating the surface. After a good rain, however, the ground is transformed into a queasy gumbo that sticks like glue to everything it touches.

The road had nearly disappeared in the sudden deluge. Before long, Fults's Buick was at a virtual standstill, mired in the sludge. Clyde circled back to pick him up. Two-hundred yards down the road, however, the Chrysler sank to the running boards. The luckless fugitives bailed out of the car and hiked across an open pasture to a small farm house nearby. It was well past 1:00 A.M. when Clyde started pounding on the front door of the darkened house. When the farmer, a man named Rogers,[70] poked his head outside, Fults grabbed him.

"We need your car—fast," he announced threateningly.

"Huh? What the—" mumbled Rogers.

"Give me the keys to your car, mister," demanded Fults, jabbing the barrel of his pistol in the man's stomach.

A quizzical look came over Rogers's face. "I don't have no car," he said, staring at the gun. "But I've got mules."

Bonnie, Clyde, and Ralph peered through the darkness toward the corral. Two mules were standing in the drizzle, just beyond the gate.

"We'll take them," said Clyde.

Barrow mounted the first mule. Fults cupped his hands around Bonnie's tiny waist and lifted her up behind Clyde. She was so light she fairly floated through the air. Fults then pulled himself astride the second animal. Suddenly he felt himself being heaved high into the air and thrown, head first, into the mud. Fults pulled himself to his feet and wiped a mask of damp earth from his face. The mule stared at him.

"You OK?" shouted Clyde.

"Damn," said Fults, retrieving his pistol from the mire. "To think I used to break wild mules in Gatesville."[71] His second attempt at mounting the beast was accomplished with no trouble. Soon the bareback riders disappeared south through a rain-soaked mesquite grove.

In the tiny hamlet of Kemp, a few miles south of Rogers's farm, the fugitives stopped in front of the home of Dr. Scarsdale, the local physician.[72] Trading their mules for the automobile parked in Scarsdale's driveway, the trio made their way back to Highway 40 and turned southeast toward Athens.

Not more than a mile from Kemp, however, Scarsdale's car ran out of gas. Daybreak was drawing dangerously near. A posse would surely be organized when Scarsdale woke up and discovered a pair of surly mules standing where his car had been parked.

"We've got to get off this road," said Fults, climbing from the car.

With Clyde and Bonnie close behind, Fults forged a path through the thick underbrush of vines and briars. Shortly after sunrise the countryside was filled with armed men literally beating the bushes for the bandits. The posse, comprised mainly of local farmers, were recruited in Kemp by City Marshall Knute Barnes.[73] Junior Legg arrived in Kemp early on the morning of April 19. The first thing he saw was Barnes detaining a couple of strangers. "Bend over," he commanded. "Let's see if you've been riding mules." Dutifully, the startled out-of-towners acquiesced. Finding no traces of damp, brown hair on the backsides of the men's trousers, Marshall Barnes released the pair.

"I need men to comb the countryside," he shouted. "We got some car thieves hemmed up between here and Mabank. It'll take everyone in town to flush them." Only sixteen at the time and looking for adventure, Junior Legg tagged along.

"I was just a farm boy," said Legg. "There wasn't any work because of the rain, so I was looking for something to do. And so was everyone else around Kemp."[74]

Huddled near a grove of mesquite trees, the fugitive youths were growing apprehensive. They lay flat on the rain-soaked ground as four or five members of the posse passed within ten feet of their hiding place. Groups of shouting men were thrashing the bushes on all sides.

At 5:00 P.M. the trio decided to try crossing the main road. A nearby country store, it was thought, might yield an automobile with which to escape. Five-hundred yards to the south, on a high hill overlooking the road, the occupants of a small farmhouse witnessed the crossing. Having been forewarned of the presence of outlaws on foot, the farmers telephoned for help. Within minutes a horde of vehicles and horsemen descended.

Fults dove into the heavily vegetated banks of Cedar Creek, taking a .38 slug in the ankle. Barrow and Parker followed. Several shots rang out. Clods of dirt exploded along the edge of the ditch. Barrow raised up and emptied a clip over the heads of his pursuers. Fults did the same. White as a sheet, Bonnie hugged the ground.

A thick cloud of black gunsmoke soon blanketed the ground. Bullets ricocheted overhead, slamming into the bushes and trees nearby. Several members of the posse kept roaming into the line of fire, apparently unaware of the outlaws' position. Fults and Clyde could have shot any number of them but chose to fire at random over their heads,[75] hoping to scare them off.

One particularly large man named "Boss" Ballard positioned himself behind the three bandits. A young sapling was all that he used as cover. Fifty percent of the man's great bulk protruded well past either side of the little tree.[76]

The gunmen in the ravine could have easily picked the buttons off the big fellow's overalls. They simply ignored him, concentrating on the fusillade pouring in from the front. It was a grave mistake. Ballard braced his pistol and drew a bead. Instantly, a copper jacketed .3220 slug ripped through Fults's left arm just above the elbow, pinning him to the embankment.

When Bonnie turned to Fults and saw blood gushing from his limp arm, transforming the ivy and dewberry vines to a sickening maroon, she nearly passed out. Clyde helped Fults tie a piece of his shirt around the wound, then turned to empty another clip into the woods.

"I'm gonna make a run for it," he said. "If I make it, I'll get the others and come back for you both."

Barrow jumped to his feet and ran toward a distant line of bushes. A pair of deputies, stationed behind two trees, stood in his path. Inexplicably, not a shot was exchanged as Clyde sprinted between the lawmen. By chance, both men had been caught in the act of reloading their weapons. They didn't even notice the outlaw disappearing into the scrub brush behind them.[77] Barrow never looked back.

Seeing that Clyde was safe, Fults turned to Bonnie. She looked pale. Her dress had been ripped to shreds, her shoes lost somewhere in the mud. "You'd best give yourself up," he said to her. "You're going to get yourself killed in this damned creek. It's almost dark. I'll try to slip away and rejoin Clyde," he answered. "They ain't got nothing on you. Reload my gun and get the hell out of here, before you get your head blown off." Bonnie nodded, taking Fults's weapon. The outlaw watched her tiny hands push the thick .45 caliber shells into the clip.

"Tell them I crawled away," he added. "Say you don't know where I went." Bonnie forced the loaded clip into the automatic.

"Cock it for me," Fults said, pointing to the housing above the main chamber. Bonnie knew nothing about guns and had to be coached by Fults every step of the way.

"Tell them we kidnapped you. Tell them anything you like."

Bonnie handed the loaded pistol to Fults, took a deep breath, and pulled herself over the embankment.

"I got her!" someone shouted. "I got her!"

Fults strained to hear the ensuing conversation.

"Where's the other one?" sounded a gruff voice.

"I don't . . . know," answered Bonnie, faintly.

Fults was so involved in what Bonnie was saying, that he failed to notice what was going on behind him. A shotgun-wielding farmer had crawled up to the edge of the ditch on his hands and knees.

"Just hold it right there," commanded the voice from behind. Fults turned slowly. A pair of black, gaping barrels was all he saw.

"Get them hands up," shouted the farmer. Fults lifted his right hand over his head.

"Get that other one up," demanded the gunman, motioning with his weapon.

"Ain't no way, mister," Fults explained. "I can't even move it."

The man lowered his shotgun and peered through the dusky light at his captive. Fults's face was racked with pain—his arm, shattered and bloody.

"I got this one!" called the farmer, scrambling to his feet. "Hey, over here. . . . I got the boy!"

Who Pulled the Trigger in Hillsboro?

Sometime after dark Clyde slipped into Kemp. The distant echo of random gunfire erupting from the creek bed two miles away had ceased. Barrow knew then that Fults and Bonnie had been captured, perhaps even killed.[1] Sliding behind the wheel of an unguarded Magnolia gas truck, he sped away, later switching to a shiny new Ford V-8. Unarmed and exhausted, he drove to West Dallas to tell Blanche and L. C. about the gun battle and then pressed on to Lake Dallas in search of Jack and the others.

Back at Cedar Creek Fults and Bonnie were engulfed by a flood of local citizens. The whole town of Kemp had turned out for a look at the pair of desperadoes.

"Why, that's 'Pretty Boy' Floyd!" exclaimed a deputy, watching excitedly as Fults was pulled from the ditch. "I once seen him up in Oklahoma."

Fults, clutching his bloody, swollen arm, was led past the crowd of onlookers to a nearby grocery store to await the arrival of Sheriff Barnes. Bonnie walked at his side. Both seemed cool, reserved, and quite unconcerned by their arrest.[2] Later, the sheriff transferred the prisoners to Kemp and locked them in the tiny, one room jail a block south of town.

The small one-room jail in Kemp, Texas, where Bonnie Parker and Ralph Fults were detained following their capture on April 19, 1932. (Photo by John Neal Phillips.)

"You ain't going to put that little girl in the same cell with that boy, are you?" cried a distraught woman.

"Ain't going to make no difference," said Sheriff Barnes. "Them two done spent all night and most of the day in the woods together." Laughter filled the air.

"Boss" Ballard was trying to make the most of having been the one who shot Fults in the arm. "I could have picked the buttons off them overalls of yours," said Fults as he tumbled in a painful heap on the dirt floor of the jail. "Hell, I was shooting over all of y'all's heads, just trying to scare y'all off."[3]

Bonnie examined the many pairs of eyes that peered through each of the cell's two small windows. Outside, thirty armed men surrounded the boxlike structure. Torches bathed the scene in an eerie light.

"You'd better get a doctor down here," shouted Bonnie, angrily. "This boy's in pain."[4]

A physician stepped forward. It was Dr. Scarsdale, the man whose car Parker, Barrow, and Fults had stolen.

"You kids come through town, stealing cars and getting yourselves shot up," said the doctor, "and then you expect me to patch you up. Well, I won't do it. . . . I just won't do it."

"Hey, Doc?" said Fults. "You didn't, by any chance, take that Hippocratic oath, now did you?" Scarsdale turned red with anger and stormed away. Fults's shattered left arm would remain unattended until the following morning, April 20, when Sheriff Barnes moved his prisoners to the more substantial county jail at Kaufman. The arm was finally treated twelve hours after the shooting.

Later in the day voices began filtering up from the first floor, followed by footsteps in the stairwell.

"Somebody here to see you," the old jailer announced, mounting the landing. Blanche and L. C. were behind him.

"Clyde's gone to Denton to fetch them other fellows," L. C. said as soon as the jailer left. "It won't be long now. Where're they keeping Bonnie?"

"Downstairs," Fults replied. "They ain't got nothing on her—I told the DA I'd take the rap if they'd let her go. He told me they probably wouldn't be charging her with nothing anyway—I don't know why they're still holding her." Blanche and L. C. hurried downstairs to see Bonnie. Fults settled back to wait for Clyde. His wait would be a long one.

Arriving at Lake Dallas, Clyde located Ted and Johnny. Jack and Fuzz, however, had dropped out of sight. Moreover, there had been a delay in the Celina raid, originally planned to coincide with Fults's and Barrow's April 18 trip to Tyler. As a result, no additional guns had been obtained. Clyde had to act fast.

At 11:45 P.M. on April 20 Clyde accompanied Ted and Johnny to Celina. There was no time to wait for Jack and Fuzz.

"What can I do for you boys?" inquired night watchman Floyd Perkins, intercepting the strangers on the main square of Celina.

"We're looking for the home of my cousin," said Barrow, stalling for time.[5]

"Who would your cousin be?" asked the watchman, unaware that Ted was moving around behind him. Barrow made mention of a name he had seen on a mailbox outside of town. Before the watchman could respond, however, Ted slugged him with the butt of a .44 revolver.

Celina Mayor F. M. Francis then emerged from the town hall. "Turn around and start walking," Ted ordered, pistol in hand. The mayor obediently trudged toward the train yard two blocks east of town.[6] He was forced into an empty Frisco boxcar along with the semiconscious night watchman.[7] The door was secured.

Back on the square, however, the trio of belligerent, gun-wielding strangers surprised another pair of Celina citizens.[8] They, too, were quickly hustled to the sidetracked Frisco car and forced inside, next to Perkins and Francis. Once again, the big door was pulled shut and locked.

The raiders then started prying the lock from the rear door of what they thought was the hardware store. Inside, however, instead of guns and items of hardware the intruders found only medicine, peroxide, and sterilized cotton. In the darkness of the alley they had somehow confused the doors—breaking into the pharmacy by mistake. Without disturbing a thing,[9] the outlaws backed out of the building and tried the next door. The back wall of the second store was lined with rifles and shotguns. Each burglar took a load of weapons out to the car and returned for a case of ammunition. Suddenly the town's fire bell started clanging.

A boy had spotted the suspicious-looking group and sounded the alarm.[10] Deputy Sheriff "Dutch" Stelzer ran from his office just as the bandits' black Ford V-8 was pulling away. The deputy hopped in his parked sedan, but it would prove a useless move. Clyde Barrow had the keys to the deputy's car in his pocket.[11] The officer watched helplessly as the burglars' Ford drove south at high speed.[12]

At the Lake Dallas hideout Ted and Johnny spent most of the following day camouflaging a homemade tin shed with branches and scrub brush. Clyde started cleaning and modifying the stolen weapons, later concealing several hundred rounds of ammunition in an inner tube.[13] By late afternoon Fuzz and Jack still had not shown up. Clyde, Ted, and Johnny decided to test the firearms while they waited. The repeated shooting roused the suspicion of a farmer who was working less than a mile away.[14] Denton County Sheriff G. C. Cockrell was notified, and a posse was quickly assembled.[15]

At 5:00 P.M. Clyde thought he heard muffled voices nearby. Peering through the forest, he spotted the sheriff and two other men talking and pointing. Alerting the others, Barrow stuffed a .45 in his belt, grabbed a shotgun, and slipped silently into the thicket, Johnny and Ted close behind.[16] Sheriff Cockrell never saw them.

The lawmen soon stumbled across the abandoned shed and its cache of weapons. While they were examining the booty, a lone auto approached.[17] Cockrell and his men crouched beside the narrow logging road. When the vehicle moved into range, the lawmen leaped from their hiding places. Jack and Fuzz were arrested without a fight.[18] The investigation appeared complete—but there was more. A group of Celina citizens had traveled to Denton to retrieve their stolen merchandise. However, they could not identify one of the pistols, a fancy chrome .44 with monogrammed pearl grips.[19] It looked very much like a lawman's service revolver.

Recalling that such a gun had been taken from one of the Electra kidnap victims just seven days before, Sheriff Cockrell notified the Wichita County Sheriff's Department. Cockrell then traced the ownership of the two cars recovered on Lake Dallas. One, the Buick, was found to have been stolen from a Ft. Worth residence the week before. The Ford V-8, on the other hand, proved to be of particular interest to the sheriff. It had been reported stolen from a Kaufman County man named Mays on April 19, the same night that a desperado was shot and captured less than two miles from Mays's home.

It was clear to Sheriff Cockrell that the Lake Dallas hideout had been the focal point of some kind of organized gang. Moreover, it appeared that the Electra kidnapping, the shootout in Kemp, and the Celina hijacking were somehow linked.[20] Despite his findings, however, Cockrell would never understand the full extent of the apparent conspiracy, nor would he realize the part he had played in postponing a desperate raid on a remote prison farm nearly two-hundred miles away.

Jack and Fuzz were transferred to McKinney to face burglary charges.[21] On April 24 the four Electra officials who had been kidnapped ten days earlier by Fults and Barrow arrived in Denton. They were accompanied by two special agents from the U.S. Bureau of Investigation. Police Chief James Taylor promptly identified the unidentified chrome revolver as his own, thus confirming Sheriff Cockrell's theory.[22] The next stop was Kaufman, where the men from Electra identified Fults.[23]

Fults was transferred to Wichita Falls,[24] to face indictment for kidnapping. En route he was taken to the McKinney jail. The sight of Jack and Fuzz took Fults by surprise. He kept his feelings to himself, though. Further down the aisle another familiar face loomed out of the shadows. It was Red, the big-talking boy who had deserted Fults and Barrow in Electra.

"You know him?" demanded one of the Justice Department agents.

Fults stared intently at the nervous youth, studying the curly red hair and pale, freckled skin. "Never seen him before in my life," he replied. Without another word, Fults was led outside to the waiting car and rushed to Wichita Falls.

The following day Blanche and Clyde drove to Kaufman with the idea of raiding the jail there and freeing Ralph Fults. They discovered, however, that he had already been transferred. They discussed helping Bonnie escape but realized she would probably be released anyway and decided not to risk it. They returned to West Dallas to find out where Fults was being held.[25]

During his stay in Wichita Falls, Fults shared a third-story cell block with a dangerous killer named Hilton Bybee. Bybee was already facing a life term for the shooting death of a Breckenridge, Texas, lawman and had just been sentenced to die in the electric chair for the murder of an East Paducah, Texas, man.[26]

Desperate and determined, Bybee somehow obtained a number of hacksaw blades. Many of the cell's bars were already rusty and worn from previous escape attempts,[27] and the killer decided to take full advantage of their weakness. He invited Fults to join him in the break. Fults gladly accepted.

The next day, during an exercise period, a prisoner from the first floor moved up beside Fults. " 'Butch' was asking about you yesterday," he said under his breath. "Parked himself in the alley near my window—says he's been thinking about you. . . . going to give you a hand, real soon." Butch was an alias often used by Clyde. "Tell him I'm OK," said Fults. "I've already got a deal in the works." The prisoner nodded and returned to his cell.

On the evening of May 10 Bybee succeeded in removing one of the bars of his cell. Pulling himself into the runaround, he climbed on top of the cage-like cell block. After a few minutes jailer Sid Johnson made a routine appearance on the third floor. When Johnson stepped up to Fults's cell, Bybee dove on top of him, grabbing the deputy's pistol and knocking him unconscious. Bybee took the jailer's keys from his belt and let Fults out of his cell. Just as the two criminals were about to reach the bottom of the stairs, Deputy Sheriff Pat Allen happened to step through the door. Bybee raised his weapon and pulled the trigger. Nothing happened. Again he tried to squeeze off a shot; still nothing. By then Allen had drawn his weapon, and the two escapees knew they could go no further.[28]

Bybee was disarmed and dragged into a first floor office. Fults was led back to his cell. He later found out why Bybee's pistol had failed to fire: The jailer had removed the powder from each shell, apparently anticipating such an incident. Deputy Allen owed his life to the precautionary move.

Bybee was moved to the Tarrant County Jail, in Fort Worth. His lawyers were able to keep his case on appeal for quite some time, eventually overturning his death sentence. Bybee was sent to Eastham Camp 1 later that year.

On May 11, 1932, Fults was convicted of armed robbery and assessed a ten-year term.[29] On the twenty-ninth Bud Russell transported him to Huntsville. Immediately upon his arrival Fults began hearing about the involvement of Clyde, Ted, and Johnny in a nasty killing in Hillsboro, sixty miles south of Dallas.[30]

Toward the end of April the three remaining Lake Dallas fugitives were running desperately low on funds. Barrow, who had given most of the cash from the Lawrence, Kansas, bank robbery to friends and relatives along the Trinity River bottom,[31] was beginning to feel the pinch. He remembered he used to run around with a boy whose family owned a jewelry store in Hillsboro.[32] Clyde, Ted, and Johnny decided to check it out.

J. N. Bucher, the sixty-five-year-old proprietor, greeted the youths as they browsed through the displays. Besides selling jewelry, Bucher repaired watches, pumped gas, and stocked a variety of sundry odds and ends, including a couple of guitars and a knife, the latter of which Johnny bought. Mrs. Bucher recognized Clyde, but he and his two companions decided to rob the store anyway.[33]

Sometime after ten o'clock in the evening of April 30, Ted and Johnny walked up to Bucher's store. Clyde opted to wait nearby in the getaway car. Johnny started beating on the door of the shop, trying to wake the old man, under the pretext of needing a guitar string. Momentarily the disgruntled shopkeeper arrived downstairs to attend to his late night customers.[34]

"It'll be twenty-five cents for the string," said Bucher, fishing through a box of Gibson guitar parts. Johnny handed the merchant a ten, knowing he would have to open the safe to make change. Apparently Bucher did not have the combination to the small Mosler safe because he called his wife downstairs to open it.[35] Momentarily she handed the alleged musician $9.75 in change and turned to close the safe. Ted pulled a .45 and leveled it on Bucher. Unexpectedly, however, the old jeweler stepped over to the safe and reached for his own gun.[36] Ted's weapon discharged, bathing the darkened store in a blinding, split-second flash of orange light.[37]

Mrs. Bucher wheeled around. Her husband was stumbling over the safe, gasping for air, a gaping bullet wound in his chest. Undaunted, the woman went for her husband's pistol.[38] Ted lunged forward and wrenched it from her hands. "Get away from that safe," he shouted, pushing her over to Johnny.

The gunman proceeded to search the safe, retrieving forty dollars in cash and approximately fifteen-hundred dollars in jewelry.[39] Johnny finally released his grip on Mrs. Bucher and followed Ted through the front door. Just beyond the gas pumps, Clyde waited, the getaway car's

V-8 engine idling fast.

"That old man went for a damned gun," Ted stated excitedly. "I had to plug him."

"Damn!" said Barrow. "Now we're in for it."[40]

On August 7, 1932, Ralph Fults was taken from his cell in Huntsville, loaded into the rear of Bud Russell's van, and transferred to Kaufman, Texas.[41] There he would be tried for armed robbery and auto theft. He was not surprised to find that Bonnie no longer occupied her first floor cell.

On June 17, 1932, she appeared before the Kaufman County Grand Jury. As planned, she claimed she was a kidnap victim at the time of her arrest and had no knowledge of the identities of the two boys involved in the Kemp shootout. Bonnie was therefore excused from the courtroom and subsequently released from jail.[42] Fults had already offered to plead guilty if the woman was set free. Upon being indicted, he stuck by his word, pleading guilty on all counts and taking a fifteen-year sentence. Before long he was back in Huntsville.

Inside the walls Fults struck up a friendship with Clyde's older brother, Buck Barrow. Standing five feet, five inches tall and weighing only one-hundred ten pounds, he was even smaller than Clyde, but to Fults he was more gregarious and easy-going. He exhibited none of the bitterness that marked the personality of his younger brother. Others, however, dispute this opinion.[43] Nevertheless, Buck was one of a handful of people Fults could trust on the inside.

Some sources have said Buck blamed himself for the way Clyde turned out,[44] but Fults never heard him make such a statement. Buck spoke instead about his own escapades in burglary, often in the company of Clyde.

Once, in Atlanta, Georgia, the police surrounded Buck, Clyde, and two other men in a garage they were burglarizing. Somehow Clyde managed to slip through the cordon of officers, but the others remained trapped inside. While the police were seizing the two Barrow accomplices, Buck squeezed between the engine and fire wall of a big delivery truck, pulling the hood down over his head. The arresting officers, never dreaming that anyone could fit in such a tight place, left the scene with their two suspects. As soon as the coast was clear, Barrow vacated his greasy hideaway and rejoined his brother. The unrepentant pair robbed another Atlanta establishment and escaped to Texas.

Fults recalled that Clyde often spoke of freeing a couple of his buddies from a chain gang in Georgia. In fact, he talked of doing it right after the Eastham raid. Fults always wondered how Clyde came to be involved with a couple of Georgia cons. His conversations with Buck answered many questions. It was through him that Fults found out about Clyde's reunion with Raymond Hamilton.

After parting company with Fults and Barrow, Hamilton discovered he had been linked to the attempted hijacking of the Simms Oil Refinery.[45] He was forced to abandon a brand new car containing all of his clothes and the remainder of his share of the money from Lawrence, Kansas, to a group of officers who had organized a road block near Wichita Falls. Hamilton barely escaped on foot. "I'll never again pay cash for a car I can just as easily steal," he would later say.[46] Hamilton then relocated to Bay City, Michigan, arriving on April 12, 1932.[47] There he took a construction job, working side by side with his father until the end of July, when he was laid off. Hoping the police had forgotten about him in Texas, Hamilton returned home. Instead of a family reunion, however, he found a price on his head.[48]

Mrs. J. N. Bucher, wife of the slain Hillsboro merchant, had identified Hamilton as her husband's killer. Indeed, Raymond could have easily passed for Ted Rogers, the real killer.[49] Moreover, Hamilton was a well-known associate of Clyde Barrow, whereas only a handful of persons knew of Barrow's dealings with Rogers. Thus faced with a murder charge, Raymond took to crime with a vengeance, starting with the July 29, 1932, stickup of the Interurban Station in Grand Prairie,[50] eighteen miles west of Dallas.

Early the next morning Hamilton met with Bonnie, Clyde, and a fellow named Ross.[51] Barrow wanted to rob the M. Nuehoff Brothers Packing Company, north of Dallas. In fact, he was planning to pull the job the following Monday, Nuehoff's payday. Ross would drive the getaway car, but a third man was still needed—someone to go inside the plant with Barrow. Bonnie, who had secretly rejoined Clyde two weeks after her release from the Kaufman jail, still took no active part in Barrow's robberies. She would wait for Clyde at the Star Service Station.

It was shortly past four o'clock on the hot afternoon of August 1, 1932. Joe and Henry Nuehoff were busy billing invoices in the rear of the main office. They had just returned from the bank with a $440 company payroll. Monday was payday.[52] Elsie Wullschleger, twenty-four-year-old Nuehoff Company clerk, stood counting the payroll at a tall desk near the front of the office. She had just finished dividing the money into neat piles of tens, fives, and ones when two young men entered the building. "May I help you?" she asked, peering through a pair of round spectacles.[53] Clyde Barrow and Raymond Hamilton jerked pistols from under their rough khaki shirts and strode past.[54]

"Mr. Joe," she called timidly. "Mr. Henry."

The Nuehoffs stirred.

"All right," said Barrow, "this is a hold up."

The brothers turned to see what all the commotion was about. When they saw the guns, they started to raise their hands.

"Get them hands down," Barrow commanded.[55]

Hamilton then reached inside his shirt and produced a large grocery bag. While he was scooping up the loot, Barrow noticed a large antique safe standing in the far corner.[56]

"What about that safe, there," asked Barrow.

"There's nothing in that old thing," they answered.[57]

Clyde stepped over and removed one of the boxes from the safe. Something jingled inside. It sounded like silver coins sliding across the bottom of the container.

"You lying sons of bitches," he said. "You told me there ain't no more money—now what the hell's this?"[58]

"We just keep a little change in there for stamps," said Joe. "Here," he added, reaching into his pocket, "I'll open that for you."

"Shut up," shouted Clyde, leveling his .45 at Joe Nuehoff's face. "I'll kill you if you don't stop moving around like that."[59]

"Don't shoot," said Joe. "I was just reaching for my keys."

Barrow took the keys and opened the box. When he saw the handful of nickels and dimes, he hurled the box against the wall. Satisfied that no more money was stashed in the office, Barrow and Hamilton backed slowly through the front door, jumped off the end of the loading dock, and disappeared into the parking lot.

Easily eluding all pursuers, Clyde, Raymond, and Ross retrieved Bonnie from the Barrow gas station and drove on to a hideout in Grand Prairie.[60] Five days later Bonnie asked Clyde to drop her off in Dallas for a few days. She wanted to visit her mother.

When Bonnie left home in the latter part of June 1932, two weeks after her release from the Kaufman County jail, she told her family she had been hired as a waitress at a Wichita Falls restaurant.[61] In truth, Bonnie did leave for Wichita Falls, but not to seek employment. She and Clyde checked into a motor court on the edge of town, living the quiet life of a vacationing couple until the end of July.

To disguise the fact she had been with Clyde all those weeks, Bonnie was delivered to the Barrow residence. From there she took a cab to her mother's house.[62] In the interim Barrow, Hamilton, and Ross decided to take a ride to Oklahoma, arriving in the foothills west of the Kiamichi Mountains late Friday evening, August 5, 1932.

They had apparently acquired a friend or a hitchhiker along the way, because by the time they rolled through Stringtown, eight miles north of Atoka, there were four men riding in the stolen V-8.[63] On the way out of town Ross noticed an outdoor dance in progress and persuaded Clyde to pull over. He and the unknown fourth man wanted to see if they could pick up a hip flask of moonshine,[64] knowing that such functions nearly always attracted bootleggers. The last thing Clyde and Raymond wanted to do was dance, and they cared even less about drinking,[65] but they were happy to wait in the car while their companions ventured over to the lantern-lit dance platform for a brief fling. After a few minutes, however, the two outlaws decided to look for a fresh car to steal in the parking lot.

Atoka County Sheriff C. G. Maxwell and Undersheriff Eugene C. Moore noticed the pair moving from car to car and decided to investigate. With their guns holstered, the lawmen approached the parking lot,[66] apparently expecting to find nothing more than a couple of school kids. A volley of gunfire erupted. Moore was killed instantly, as a wall of lead ripped through his chest and skull. The force of another half dozen .45 caliber slugs slammed Maxwell to the ground, his left arm and leg shattered.[67]

Frightened dancers began diving from the dance floor. Someone screamed. Barrow and Hamilton made a dash for their own V-8. Stringtown Deputy Chip Miller drew his weapon and fired several rounds.[68] Sheriff Maxwell, using his good right hand, also fired, to no avail. The killers roared past the crowd in a cloud of dust, disappearing east toward Antlers. Ross and the fourth man slipped away on foot, taking separate routes in their flight from the area.[69]

Twenty-one hours after the Stringtown killing, a strange car pulled up in front of 2430 Douglass. Bonnie and her grandmother were sitting on the front porch, taking advantage of an early evening breeze. Bonnie recognized the man behind the wheel as one of Clyde's buddies and ran out to the street. Momentarily returning to the porch, Bonnie told her grandmother she had found a ride back to Wichita Falls and her alleged job. To avoid the growing posse of Texas and Oklahoma lawmen, Clyde, Raymond, and Bonnie headed west, to New Mexico. Bonnie's aunt lived on a farm two miles from Carlsbad. It would be the perfect place to hide—perfect except for the fact that New Mexico was, at that time, undergoing a massive cleanup of intrastate auto thefts. A Roswell newspaper had just reported the presence of a large "ring" operating out of southeastern New Mexico, and Carlsbad authorities were on the alert for strange cars and unusual license plates.[70]

It was Sunday morning, August 14. While Bonnie's Aunt gathered garden vegetables for a planned family feast, Clyde and Raymond assembled all the necessary ingredients for homemade ice cream, later driving into Carlsbad for a block of ice.[71] Their vehicle drew the attention of Chief Deputy Sheriff Joe Johns. Barrow's V-8 matched the description of a car reported stolen from a nearby motor court. Cautiously following the outlaws back to the home of Bonnie's aunt, Johns closed in. At 9:00 A.M. the deputy rapped lightly on the front door of the farmhouse. Bonnie appeared.

"Whose Ford is this?" Johns inquired.

"Oh, that belongs to one of the boys," replied Bonnie, sweetly.

"They're dressing right now—I'll send them out in a minute."[72] Her response, momentarily placating the lawman, was actually a predetermined signal designed to alert those in the house. Clyde and Raymond began searching frantically for some kind of weapon. Their pistols and sawed-off shotguns were locked up in the trunk of the car, out of sight. Bonnie's relatives were still unaware of their guests' criminal backgrounds, and any display of firearms would have certainly raised questions.[73]

Clyde finally located a shotgun tucked away in one of the closets. By then Deputy Johns had started looking at the V-8, tugging at the locked trunk latch. Seconds later Barrow and Hamilton burst from the rear door, whirling to face the lawman. "Stick 'em up," shouted Clyde, jabbing his 16-gauge at Johns. The deputy took one look at the youthful-looking Barrow and went for his side-arm. Clyde fired a blast of bird shot over Johns's head, a pellet or two knocking his hat to the ground.[74] Johns let his service revolver fall to the dirt. Hamilton rushed over to retrieve the discarded weapon.

"Jump in," he said, motioning to Johns.

Bonnie ran from the house and hopped in the front seat. Johns climbed in back. Hamilton, pistol in hand, squeezed in beside him. Barrow, as always, took the wheel. Bonnie's aunt was still in the garden when the gunfire and shouting began. Before she could get up to the house, the car containing her niece was already speeding away.

City police and members of the Eddy County Sheriff's Department soon converged on the farm, followed shortly by a crowd of curious onlookers. Someone was overheard talking about the deputy's hat being shot from his head. Soon, word was out that "Johns's head was shot off."[75] Local newspapers and radio stations soon picked up the false report. When a pair of truck drivers discovered the decapitated body of a hitchhiker near the summit of Texas's Guadalupe Mountain range, the corpse was instantly identified as that of Deputy Johns.[76] Bonnie, Clyde, and Raymond never heard the reports. Nor did Johns. Barrow guided the Ford at high speed swiftly back to Texas.

Twelve hours later a road-weary Johns found himself gazing at the twinkling lights of San Antonio.[77] There the outlaws cruised around in search of a fresh car to steal. Johns noted the relative ease with which

Barrow crisscrossed the city.[78] He seemed to know the area well. By daybreak, however, a suitable replacement vehicle had not been located. Barrow abandoned the search.

Fifteen miles outside of San Antonio, on the Vance-Jackson road, Deputy Johns was freed. Without sleep, Clyde, Raymond, and Bonnie continued on to Victoria, 114 miles southeast of San Antonio. There Raymond stole a Ford V-8 and followed Bonnie and Clyde northeast, eventually picking up old Highway 90, apparently en route to Houston.

Just west of Wharton, a pair of local deputies concealed themselves along the highway near the Colorado River.[79] One officer covered the old bridge while the other, flashlight in hand, crouched in a ditch about a hundred feet from the west bank of the river. As the cars approached, the first lawman was to make positive identification and signal his partner at the far end of the bridge. The second lawman would then block the east side of the bridge with his car, trapping the outlaws over the river.

Clyde, always wary of potentially dangerous situations, was paying particular attention to the rapidly approaching expanse of bridge. Beside the road, a light suddenly blinked on. Barrow slammed on the brakes, cut the wheels hard to the left, and shifted to second.

The V-8 coupe skidded into the oncoming lane, spun around, and sped off in the opposite direction,[80] past Hamilton's eastbound sedan. By the time Ray was able to react, he was nearly to the bridge. Bullets whizzed through the air as Hamilton repeated Clyde's maneuver. To the deputies' consternation, the bandits' vehicles melted rapidly into the darkness, headlights extinguished.

After so many near misses, Hamilton decided to part company with his friends and cool off for awhile at his father's place in Bay City, Michigan. Barrow, too, was anxious to vacate the Southwest, and he offered to drop Ray at his dad's front door. Clyde and Bonnie planned to drift through the Great Lakes states, sightseeing.

Following the Stringtown shootout and the kidnapping of Deputy Joe Johns, alleged sightings of Bonnie and Clyde began pouring into Dallas from all over the country. Soon scores of unsolved crimes were being attributed to them. Some of the charges were justified. Most were not. Sometimes other criminals imitated Parker and Barrow in hopes of casting suspicion away from themselves.[81] It often worked. It was the price of notoriety. Barrow usually acknowledged his crimes to his mother, including the murders.[82] He and Bonnie were too close to their families to hide such things. However, as false reports surfaced, the fugitives were just as quick to discount them. Such was the case with the Howard Hall killing.

On Tuesday evening, October 11, Homer Glaze and Howard Hall were preparing to close their small Sherman, Texas, grocery store. A lone man stepped through the door. He was small, fair-complected, approximately twenty to twenty-five years old.[83] Quietly collecting a small bottle of milk and a package of meat, the stranger stepped up to the cash register, dollar bill in hand. Hall rang the sale and turned to issue change to his customer. The barrel of a large caliber pistol was all he saw. Without a word the young bandit reached into the cash drawer and pulled out about fifty dollars. Hall tried to grab the man's arm but missed. A vicious blow to the head knocked the grocer to the floor. He was then kicked several times and jerked to his feet.

The assailant grabbed Homer Glaze, shoved him toward Hall, and started pushing both men toward the door. Hall turned suddenly and made a desperate play for the gun. Four shots rang out, and, just as suddenly, Hall lay dead, three slugs in his body. The gunman quickly leveled his smoking weapon on a horrified Homer Glaze and pulled the trigger. Glaze heard the firing pin crash into the metal casing of the cartridge but nothing happened. The gun had misfired. The killer darted into the street and sped away in a waiting sedan, occupied by two unidentified men.[84]

Sources placing Barrow in Sherman on October 11, 1932, often describe Hall attacking him with a butcher knife, which did not happen. Some sources mention the presence of a woman, while others describe male accomplices waiting in the car. Inconsistencies such as these damage the credibility of these sources and make it easier to accept Clyde Barrow's own assertion that he never staged a robbery in Sherman; especially since he readily admitted his other crimes.

Toward the end of October 1932 a burned-out car found abandoned in East Collin County was finally traced to Electra kidnap victim W. N.

Owens. Because of this, it was thought that Owens's assailants could somehow be linked to the disappearance of a Ford V-8 belonging to a Farmersville man named Blair.[86] Occurring early on the morning of April 15, the theft came less than sixteen hours after the Electra incident, making Ralph Fults a prime suspect. On November 5 Fults was again loaded into Bud Russell's truck and readied for the trip north, this time to McKinney, where he would stand trial for auto theft.

"Boy, you're gonna wear my truck out," said Bud, applying a second padlock to the transport's rear door. Five hours later Fults was peering through the bars of a McKinney cell, examining the dozen or more faces in the runaround.

Fults was already well acquainted with many of his fellow prisoners, especially Ted Rogers, the fair-haired boy leaning against the far wall. Rogers had been picked up on an unrelated charge shortly after the Hillsboro affair. Slowly linked to a number of other crimes, he, like Fults, began a slow judicial odyssey around the state. It was by purest coincidence that he and Fults wound up in McKinney together.

"Any word from 'Butch'?" asked Ted, meaning Clyde.

"Not a thing since May, when I was in Wichita Falls," said Fults. "He's getting pretty darned hot."

Ted nodded. "How about Johnny?" Fults inquired. "Dunno," Ted answered. "He kind of dropped out of sight. I don't think anybody's seen or heard from him since April or May."

Twelve days later Fults was sentenced to five years for stealing the Farmersville car.

On December 19 a visitor arrived in the foyer of the McKinney jail. "Fults," called the jailer, "your cousin's here to see you." Fults slid from his bunk and shuffled over to the door. He could see the petite young woman standing only a few feet away, a red tam draped low across her forehead. It was Bonnie. Fults had not seen her since the Kemp shooting. Her presence in the McKinney jail could have meant but one thing: The rumors that she had rejoined Clyde were true. Barrow was probably parked in the alley.[87] Bonnie handed Fults a pack of Camel cigarettes.

"Everything's in here," she said, indicating a note was stuffed between the cigarettes. "We're taking you and Ted out of here today."

"Too late," said Fults. "They keep the keys over at the courthouse. They don't ever fetch them except to feed us, and we done had supper. You'll have to catch them at breakfast."

Bonnie nodded and turned to leave. Fults pocketed the Camels and returned to his cell. With visions of a clean escape dancing in his head, Fults stretched out on his bunk. At 4:00 A.M. however, the sound of muffled voices and shuffling feet echoed through the old jail. Fults opened his eyes. Suddenly the door of the runaround burst open, revealing the hulking figure of Bud Russell, ten-gallon hat firmly fixed atop his head, 12-gauge in hand.

"We come by early to give you boys a ride to the walls," said Russell, eyeing Fults and Rogers, the latter having been convicted of armed robbery a few days earlier.

"Grab your shirts, and let's move out."

It was a tough break. With chains dangling from their necks, the two convicts stared intently from the rear of the transport, hoping to spot a black Ford bearing down on them in the distance. It was a futile thought. Uncle Bud's three-hour lead would be next to impossible to beat, even for Clyde Barrow. Their only hope lay in the possibility of a stopover in Corsicana.

Neither Fults nor Rogers spoke. Each man knew that Clyde would have to kill Bud Russell to get to them. Certainly Clyde knew it. There could be no doubt about it. The old man would never lay down his weapons. He had made it perfectly clear on more than one occasion.[88]

In Corsicana Bud and his son Roy pulled up behind the old county jail. A deputy stepped outside to greet the transfer agent. Even though he had no prisoners to pick up, it looked as if Russell might have been thinking about spending the night. After a few minutes with the deputy, however, Uncle Bud started stretching his big arms. "I'm feeling pretty good," he said, "think we'll just drive on in to Huntsville."

On Christmas Eve, 1932, Bonnie and Clyde drove into West Dallas, where they hoped to meet Clyde's mother and little sister, Marie. Just ahead of them on Eagle Ford Road they spotted old man Henry Barrow's jalopy. Clyde's younger brother, L. C., was at the wheel. Riding with him was a sixteen-year-old boy named William Daniel Jones (sometimes known as "Deacon," "Dub," or W. D.). The two boys had been to a Christmas dance and were in the process of polishing off a pint of bootleg whiskey.[89] Clyde turned in behind his father's car and signaled for L. C. to pull over.

Jones waited in the car while L. C. got out to talk to his brother. After a few minutes the younger Barrow returned. "Clyde wants to talk to you," he said, sliding behind the wheel. Jones quickly joined Bonnie and Clyde in their car, maneuvering past an arsenal of guns to get situated in the back seat.

"We're here to see Momma and Marie," Barrow said. "You stay with us while L. C. gets them."

Jones sat in the shadows. The two fugitives were seated before him, their backs turned. Not another word was spoken. Before long, L. C. returned with Cumie Barrow and Marie. Christmas gifts were exchanged. After the visit Barrow asked Jones to accompany him and Bonnie Parker to East Texas. "We been driving a long ways," he said. "We need someone to keep watch while we get some rest."[90]

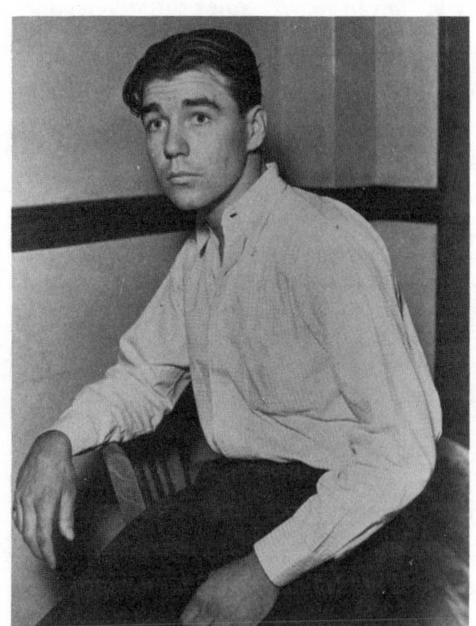

William Daniel Jones, 1933. He was also known as "W. D.," "Dub," and "Deacon." (Courtesy of the Dallas Public Library, Texas/Dallas History Archives Division, Hayes Collection.)

Although he would later view it as the biggest mistake of his life, Jones jumped at the chance to ride with Bonnie and Clyde, boyishly flattered by the request. He had known Clyde since childhood.[91] He looked up to him. For the killer to place his life in the hands of a poor West Dallas kid seemed an incredible gesture of trust. Jones was practically speechless.

At two o'clock on Christmas morning Bonnie, Clyde, and W. D. checked into a small tourist court outside of Temple, Texas. Parker and Barrow fell onto the bed, exhausted. Jones pulled a small pallet over to the window and stretched out.[92] The group slept late, rising shortly before noon. The kid changed two worn tires on the Ford coupe and climbed in the back seat.[93] A cold Texas wind whipped through the cab as Bonnie joined Clyde in the front seat. Barrow drove to town and stopped on a side street one or two blocks from a small pharmacy. Even though it was Christmas Day, the drug store was nevertheless open for business.

"Follow me while I get us some spending money," said Barrow, handing Jones an old .41 caliber revolver.[94] W. D. stepped around the corner with Clyde but waited in front of the little store. Momentarily Barrow emerged empty handed.[95]

"Come on," Barrow said tersely, "get in here." Jones timidly accompanied Clyde inside the pharmacy. The two would-be robbers stood around for a few minutes but saw no one. W. D. got the jitters and ran outside.

"You yellow punk," Barrow said, chasing the kid outside.

"I want to go home," cried Jones, walking swiftly from the drug store.

"You want to go home?" Barrow asked, pointing to a Model A parked on the street. "Well climb in that car and take yourself back to Dallas."[96]

Jones eyed the car, keys dangling in the ignition. Dutifully the boy pulled himself behind the wheel to try his hand at pinching a car. But it was a cold day, and Jones had trouble getting the engine to turn over.[97] Barrow grew impatient.

Meanwhile, Mrs. Doyle Johnson happened to see Clyde, wearing a dark overcoat and tan hat, climb into her brand new family car. Another man, similarly dressed, was already sliding over on the front seat.

"Those men are taking the car," she cried to her husband.[98]

Salesman Doyle Johnson took one look at the robbery in progress and ran outside, where two of his in-laws already stood shouting at the thieves. Barrow, who had taken over for W. D., got the Ford started just as Johnson leaped to the running board.

"Get back, man, or I'll kill you," hollered Clyde.[99] Johnson scrutinized the little man behind the wheel of his car, reached past the window curtains, and began choking Clyde with his bare hands.

"Stop," Barrow said, "or I'll kill you!"[100]

Ignoring the second warning, Johnson tightened his grip on Barrow's throat. Suddenly an earsplitting explosion filled the air. Johnson reeled backward and spun to the pavement. He had been shot in the neck.[101]

Barrow drove away from the curb and turned north, stopping just two blocks from the shooting. Bonnie, at the wheel of the V-8 coupe, pulled alongside. Wasting no time, Clyde and W. D. transferred from Johnson's car to the faster V-8.[102] A mile or two from town Barrow pulled over. "Boy," he said, handing Jones a pair of pliers, "shinny up that pole and cut them phone wires. We don't want no calls ahead."[103] The following day, December 26, 1932, Doyle Johnson died, leaving behind his young wife and infant son. He was only 26.[104]

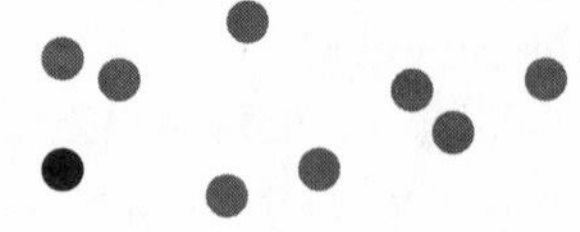

Money from Joplin

1933 was a pivotal year in American history. It began with a great surge of public optimism. The general elections of the previous fall had brought about many changes in America's federal, state, and local governments. To the financially beleaguered populace, a fresh sense of political rebirth prevailed.

Democrat Franklin Delano Roosevelt, the brash, energetic governor of New York, had easily outdistanced seven other presidential candidates to carry the federal election.[1] Moreover, with a Senate majority of nearly two to one and a House majority of three to one, Roosevelt's party had achieved an unprecedented shift in legislative power.

Texas, too, saw many changes. Governor Ross Sterling, the man who had pardoned both Ralph Fults and Clyde Barrow, was replaced by Miriam Ferguson, a woman whose concern for the welfare of Texas's state prisoners remains both legendary and controversial.

On January 1, 1933, Dallas introduced a host of new city and county officials, many unseating firmly entrenched incumbents. The courthouse experienced the biggest turnover, with fifty seats changing hands.[2] In addition, a new sheriff was sworn in, Richard Allen "Smoot" Schmid.

"Smoot" Schmid, the owner of a Dallas bicycle shop, seemed an unlikely candidate for sheriff. Large and ponderous, sporting a size thirteen shoe, Schmid gave the appearance of being too friendly and outgoing to fit the bill as a lawman. However, his tough views concerning budget and crime won him the vote. Six days into his new administration, though, a complex series of events would bring him face to face with the cold realities of the latter—crime. Unknown to anyone at the time, Schmid's deputies were on a collision course with Clyde Barrow.

On December 29, 1932, the Home Bank of Grapevine, Texas, in northeast Tarrant County, was robbed of $2,850.00.[3] Although a twenty year-old suspect named Les was quickly apprehended, a second man avoided capture by posing as a member of the posse.[4] Nevertheless, it did not take long for Tarrant County officials to link Les to a West Dallas outlaw named Odell.

Shortly after the first of the year a member of the Tarrant County District Attorney's office contacted Dallas's new sheriff, "Smoot" Schmid. After briefing Schmid on the nature of his findings, the Tarrant County official suggested that Odell might soon rendezvous at the West Dallas home of one of Raymond Hamilton's sisters, Lillian McBride. The two lawmen decided to lay a trap for Odell.

On the afternoon of January 6, 1933, Dallas County Deputy Sheriff Ed Castor visited the McBride house at 507 County Avenue.[5] Castor asked a few questions and left.[6] At 11:00 P.M. that evening more officers returned. Tarrant County Assistant District Attorney W. T. Evans, accompanied by Special Ranger J. F. Van Noy and Fort Worth deputies Dusty Rhodes and Malcolm Davis, met Dallas Deputy Sheriff Fred Bradberry and another officer in front of the house. Instead of Mrs. McBride, however, they found another Hamilton sister, eighteen-year-old Maggie Fairris.

Seating himself on the divan near the front window, Bradberry chatted quietly with Mrs. Fairris, trying to extract information. Rhodes and Van Noy looked on. Malcolm Davis and W. T. Evans stepped to the rear of the house and waited on the back porch.[7]

Time passed slowly. After a few minutes Maggie got up to tuck the children into bed. She seemed jittery. Bradberry ordered her to turn out all the lights. She complied but insisted that a small red light situated in the window next to Bradberry be left on for the children. The deputy agreed to the request.[8]

At midnight, a coupe[9] cruised slowly past the house. Seconds later it reappeared, slowing as if to stop, then picking up speed as it rounded the corner. Bradberry grew suspicious of the red light and had it turned off. The car made one more pass, then stopped, motor running, lights extinguished.

A small, lean man dressed in a black overcoat and tan hat emerged from the driver's side of the coupe. It was a cold, dark night. Bradberry could not tell if the figure mounting the front steps was really Odell or merely a curious neighbor, checking on young Maggie.

"Open the door," Bradberry told the frightened woman. She gripped the knob, nervously pulling it toward her with a sudden jerk. "Don't shoot," she cried, standing in the gaping doorway. "Think of my babies."[10]

Standing less than ten feet away, Clyde Barrow responded by opening his coat and leveling a 16-gauge, sawed-off shotgun at the window where Bradberry sat. A single blast of .00 buckshot ripped through the sash, showering the front room with splintered glass. The four lawmen in the house dove to the bare wooden floor.

Barrow, smoking shotgun still raised, started backing away from the porch. He noticed a spent shell had jammed his weapon.[11] Suddenly, a pair of figures appeared on his left. Davis and Evans, aroused by the gunfire, had run around to the front of the house.

"Get back," shouted Clyde, prying the spent shell from his shotgun. "Don't come any closer."[12]

Running ahead of Evans, Davis paid no heed. "Don't come any closer," Clyde repeated, whirling to face the deputy.

Still Davis advanced.

Barrow fired a single shot at point-blank range. The impact threw Davis across the porch steps with nine pellets of .00 buckshot in his heart.[13] Evans dove behind a fence just as a second blast hurtled past his ears.

Clyde ran around to the side of the McBride house and down the alley. A young boy awakened by the sound of gunfire watched sleepily as Barrow ran past his window and turned left at the alley.

Bradberry pulled himself off the floor and ran outside. Two blocks south, the coupe was making a right turn onto Eagle Ford Road, kicking gravel high into the air. Sprawled face down across the porch steps, Malcolm Davis bled profusely from a massive chest wound. Bradberry lifted the stricken deputy in his arms and carried him to his car. Four or five bystanders gathered nearby as Davis was placed on the rear seat.

Suddenly Van Noy appeared. Apparently thinking he had trapped the gunmen, the ranger drew his pistol, squared off, and to the horror of those looking on, fired two shots into Bradberry's car.[14] West Dallas residents, Ted Shupback and W. V. Strait dropped to the ground as the bullets ripped through the cab and whistled past their faces. Miraculously, no one was hit.

The mortally wounded Davis was then rushed to Methodist Hospital, but it was too late. The fifty-two-year-old lawman had already succumbed to his wounds.

Despite Odell's prior threats to fight to the death if cornered, the investigating officers correctly deduced that only one man in all of Texas could have faced a house full of detectives, gunned down a seasoned veteran like Davis, and disappeared without a trace—Clyde Barrow.

"If we'd known Barrow was coming," a sheriff's department spokesman later said, "we'd have been better prepared."[15] But why had Barrow chosen that night to visit Lillian McBride? The key to the mystery was sixty-five miles away in Hillsboro, where nineteen-year-old Raymond Hamilton was being held for a murder he did not commit.

After parting company with Bonnie and Clyde on September 1, 1932, Hamilton stayed with his father in Bay City, Michigan.[16] However, by the first week in October he was back on the dusty streets of West Dallas, searching for a fast buck. On October 8, 1932, Hamilton scrounged a gun, stole a car, and drove to the sleepy town of Cedar Hill,[17] just south of Dallas. There, he robbed the First State Bank of $1,401.[18]

On November 9 Ray and a friend named Gene O'Dare[19] strolled into the Carmen State Bank, in LaGrange, Texas, and robbed it of $1,061. O'Dare returned to his young wife in Wichita Falls. Hamilton slipped into West Dallas.

At ten o'clock on the morning of November 25 a bright yellow Studebaker[20] stopped in front of the First State Bank, in Cedar Hill.

Barrow-Fults-Hamilton Sites in Texas, 1925–1935

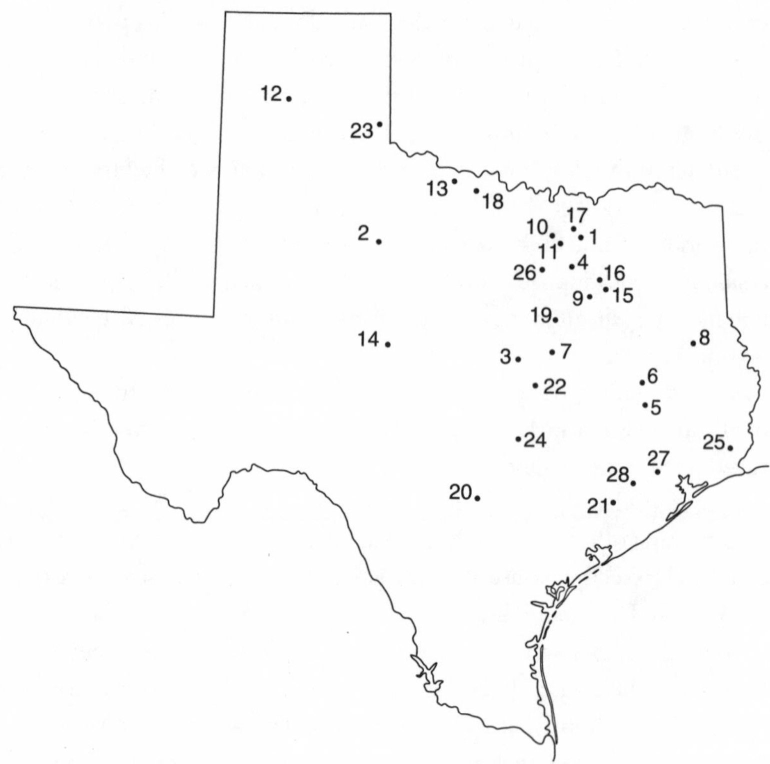

Listed in order of appearance in the text:

1. McKinney, Fults's hometown
2. Aspermont, Fults's jailbreak
3. Texas Juvenile Training School, Gatesville
4. Dallas
5. Texas State Penitentiary, "the walls," Huntsville
6. Eastham Prison Farm
7. Waco, Clyde Barrow's jailbreak
8. Nacogdoches, Clyde Barrow's relatives and hideout
9. Telico, Clyde Barrow's birthplace
10. Denton, arrest of Buck Barrow, hometown of some Lake Dallas gang members
11. Lake Dallas, Lake Dallas Gang's hideout
12. Amarillo, home base for a number of Midwestern outlaws
13. Electra, Barrow-Fults abduction of four city officials
14. Rowena, Bonnie Parker's birthplace
15. Kemp, Fults-Parker arrest
16. Kaufman, Fults-Parker held there after arrest
17. Celina, midnight raid by Clyde Barrow
18. Wichita Falls, Fults-Bybee escape attempt
19. Hillsboro, Bucher murder
20. San Antonio, release of Johns
21. Wharton, attempted roadblock of Barrow-Parker-Hamilton
22. Temple, Johnson murder
23. Wellington, Barrow-Parker-Jones car wreck
24. Austin
25. Beaumont, Fults-Hamilton armory raid
26. Fort Worth, Raymond Hamilton capture
27. Houston, Fults-Hamilton "kidnap" of McCormick
28. Central Prison Farm, Fults and "Boss Killer"

Assistant cashier R. H. Carrell was opening the morning mail and chatting with a customer when the car rolled up. Carrell could not believe his eyes. There, walking into the lobby, was the same boy who had robbed the bank a month earlier—and this time he had a friend with him, an unemployed youth named Les.[21] This same boy would later help Odell rob the Home Bank of Grapevine, leading to the County Avenue shoot out.

"Say! I know you," announced Carrell, "you were the fellow who stuck us up before."

"Yeh, sure," replied Hamilton. "Hurry it up. We don't want to be as long with this job as we were with the other one." Hamilton and Les swept $1,802.02 into a sack and ran outside to the waiting Studebaker.[22] In Ft. Worth the outlaws split up. Hamilton located Gene O'Dare, his accomplice in the Carmen State Bank robbery, and convinced him to go to Bay City, Michigan. Upon their arrival, the bandits began buying expensive clothes and living it up.

On the evening of December 6, 1932, Ray and Gene were to meet a pair of young ladies at a local skating rink.[23] Arriving early, the two outlaws donned their skates and entered the rink. Suddenly a group of Michigan state police surrounded the pair. O'Dare pulled a .38 but was knocked to the ice by one of the officers. Hamilton, though armed, chose not to fight. Wearing a pair of skates, he could do little else.

On Wednesday evening, December 14, Hamilton and O'Dare arrived in Dallas. For several days the dapper prisoners, likened by reporters to "furnishing store manikins,"[24] were viewed by witnesses from three states. O'Dare was eventually transferred to LaGrange and charged with one count of robbery by firearms, at the time a capital offense.[25] Hamilton remained in Dallas, facing four counts of robbery by firearms.

By Christmas Eve, as Bonnie and Clyde arrived in West Dallas for a holiday visit, charges of auto theft, kidnapping, and murder were still pending against Hamilton. There was little Barrow could for his friend as long as Ray remained locked up in Dallas. However, as soon as it became known that he had been transferred to Hillsboro to be arraigned for the murder of J. N. Bucher,[26] the picture suddenly changed.

Clyde Barrow conspired with Raymond Hamilton's older brother

Floyd and Lillian McBride to smuggle several hacksaw blades into the Hillsboro jail, agreeing to retrieve Ray as soon as he had managed to cut his way to freedom. Hamilton's sister later delivered a small radio to the accused killer just hours before Barrow's visit to 507 County Avenue.[27] The date was January 6, 1933.

Sometime after sundown, Bonnie, Clyde, and W. D. Jones drove up to Lillian McBride's house to see if the radio and its cargo of hacksaw blades had been delivered to Ray. Barrow spoke with Maggie Fairris. She told him that he had just missed Lillian and that a sheriff's deputy had paid her a visit that afternoon. Barrow decided to try again at midnight, arranging for Maggie to leave a red light in the window should the sheriff's men return.[28] Bonnie, Clyde, and W. D. then drove to the nearby Star Service Station and stopped just long enough for Clyde to look in on his family.[29] Minutes later, the fugitives were speeding west on Eagle Ford Road.

At midnight Parker, Barrow, and Jones returned to West Dallas. Lillian McBride's house looked abandoned as Clyde turned onto County Avenue. He was just about to stop when he spotted the red light in the window. He down-shifted to first and turned the corner. On the second pass the light went out. Barrow circled the block one more time and stopped.[30]

He must have known something was amiss as he stepped warily from the car with a sawed-off shotgun concealed beneath his black overcoat. With the engine idling smoothly in neutral, he stepped onto the sparse lawn and approached the house. Bonnie was peering through the window on the passenger side of the car. Jones sat comfortably in the back seat.[31]

Suddenly, a woman's voice cut through the night, followed by a gunshot exploding in front of the house and the sound of shattering glass. Bonnie slid behind the wheel of the car and put it in gear. Jones scrambled to the edge of his seat, waving a pistol around. Another gunshot resounded, then another. Jones began firing wildly toward the house.

"Stop it," Bonnie screamed. "You're likely to hit Clyde."[32]

Barrow ran through the McBride's backyard and down the alley. Bonnie released the clutch and took off, sliding around the corner as she turned west onto Eagle Ford Road.

Chief of Detectives Bill Decker, of the Dallas County Sheriff's Department, right, plays the part of Clyde Barrow in an official reenactment of the January 6, 1933, gunfight at 507 County Avenue, Dallas. Fort Worth Deputy Sheriff Malcolm Davis was killed in the fray. (Courtesy of the Dallas Public Library, Texas/Dallas History Archives Division, Hayes Collection.)

To her right she saw a figure darting through the shadows. She stopped the car. Clyde jumped in and took the wheel.[33] The Chevrolet leaped forward. Barrow cranked a stolen police siren furiously as the car roared past the Star Service Station.

Fourteen year-old Marie Barrow happened to be on Eagle Ford Road at that time, riding the bicycle her brother Clyde had given her. She had just left the home of her friend Audrey Hamilton, yet another one of Raymond's sisters, when she saw Bonnie, Clyde, and W. D. speed past. Her brother was cranking furiously on a police siren bolted to the dash of the car. She had not heard the shots and did not find out until later what it all meant.[34]

By morning the fugitives were in northeastern Oklahoma. They robbed a filling station of eight or nine dollars, promising to pay the owner back if he did not report the crime.[35]

In Springfield, Missouri, as the three fugitives approached a bridge at high speed, motorcycle patrolman Thomas Persell drew alongside. "Pull over," Persell shouted.

"Just a minute, sir," Clyde said, smiling politely.[36]

"Stop right here, now," the lawman snapped.

"Just a minute, sir," Barrow said again, making no attempt to stop. He did not want to get trapped on a bridge. After reaching the opposite bank, Clyde turned up a side street and applied the brakes. The officer was very angry as he stepped over to the driver's side of the car. "Where's the fire?" he yelled at Clyde.

"Right here," Barrow replied, raising his 16-gauge shotgun through the open window of the car. "Get out and unharness him, boy," he said to Jones. The youth disarmed the lawman and forced him into the back seat.[37] Leaving the patrolman's motorcycle behind, the kidnappers sped north. One-hundred and fifty miles away the car died when a generator failed.

"Boy, you're going to have to go get another battery," Clyde told W. D. "Take this John Law with you."

Persell and Jones trudged together toward town, pliers and wrenches in hand. Upon their return, the kid commented on the officer's helpfulness, saying that Persell had shared equally in the task of lugging the heavy, acid-laden apparatus back to Clyde and Bonnie.

Barrow was impressed. He gave Persell a few dollars and turned him loose on the spot.[38] The puzzled officer watched in disbelief as the three youths drove away. Several days later the three outlaws returned to the Oklahoma gas station they had robbed earlier. Barrow gave the astonished owner a hundred dollars for not reporting the theft.[39]

In Dallas, amid reports that the killing of Malcolm Davis would hasten the "clean up" of West Dallas,[40] "Smoot" Schmid and his men were finding it difficult to extract information from the impoverished residents along the Trinity River bottom. Despite the fact that many of the five-hundred or so inhabitants of "the bog" were related to either Barrow or Hamilton, it did not take long for the sheriff to find out what Clyde had been doing with much of his stolen money. He was giving it to needy friends and relatives, partly to quell talk, but mostly because the people were unemployed and desperate.[41] Barrow also purchased the vacant lot next to the Star Service Station for his parents. Before long the newspapers had picked up the story, describing Barrow and his companions as "modern 'Robin Hoods' "[42] and "phantom fugitives."[43]

Raymond Hamilton, the object of Barrow's special Dallas visit, had little time to use the hacksaw blades passed to him in Hillsboro. On January 8 he was found sawing the bars of his cell, his sister's radio covering the sound. Ray was immediately transferred to the Dallas County Jail.

On January 25 Hamilton sat through a pair of whirlwind trials in Judge Nolan G. Williams's Court. For the October 8 robbery of the First State Bank of Cedar Hill Hamilton was assessed a thirty-year sentence.[44] Later that same day, following testimony from Joe and Henry Neuhoff,

Bonnie's favorite picture of her and Clyde, 1933. (Courtesy of L. J. Hinton.)

as well as Elsie Wullschleger, Hamilton was given an additional twenty-five years for the August 1, 1932, robbery of the Nuehoff Meat Packing Company.

Through both trials Hamilton sat stoically, pleading not guilty but offering no defense. Of the outlaw, Henry Neuhoff observed: "He never said a word. He just sat there, expressionless, all dressed up like he was ready to go to work at a bank."[45]

By mid-March Hamilton was back in Hillsboro, the place he most dreaded. One of the first witnesses to be called in the Bucher murder trial was Martha Bucher. She testified that she had never actually seen her husband's murder. Her back was turned when the gun went off. However, she was convinced that Hamilton was the triggerman, based on acoustics. She thought the sound of the gunshot came from "Raymond's side of the room."[46]

Hamilton's attorney called a witness to the stand, who testified that he and Raymond Hamilton had travelled to Michigan in mid-April 1932, remaining there until the end of July. Hamilton's mother later corroborated the story. Regardless, on March 18, 1933, Hamilton was convicted of the murder of John N. Bucher. The jury, however, had a lot of trouble deliberating Hamilton's sentence. For two days they argued. Should Hamilton live or die? A crowd of interested spectators, including Sheriff C. G. Maxwell, of Atoka County, Oklahoma, waited as the jury deliberated.[47]

In Huntsville a small group of inmates were paying particular attention to the court proceedings. Although Ralph Fults had heard rumors of Ted Roger's involvement in the Bucher killing, Rogers himself had never discussed it. One day, during an exercise period in the prison yard, Fults and Jack were talking with Buck Barrow when Rogers strolled up. "If Hamilton gets the chair," he said, "I'll tell them I did it. I'll tell them I killed Bucher."

Rogers would never let anyone die in his place. As it turned out, though, Ray was in no immediate danger. On March 20 the Hillsboro jury was declared irrevocably deadlocked.[48] There would have to be a new trial.

Two days later Buck Barrow was granted a full pardon by Governor Miriam Ferguson. Many of Buck's friends knew he would try to contact his brother, Clyde.[49] "Don't get in that car with Clyde," Fults warned. "If you do, you're a goner."

Two weeks later Fults received a crisp twenty-dollar bill tucked neatly inside an envelope bearing a Joplin, Missouri, postmark, in payment of a gambling debt. He knew then that Buck and Clyde were conducting more than a friendly family reunion.

Shortly after leaving prison, Buck began talking to Blanche about a rendezvous with Clyde. He was not enthusiastic about such a visit,[50] but to family and friends he intimated a sense of responsibility for the way his little brother had turned out. He felt compelled to locate Clyde and somehow convince him to give himself up—to "get straight with the law."[51]

Nearly everyone in West Dallas told Buck his quest would be futile. Even Blanche was skeptical. Nevertheless, contrary to false reports that she wept bitterly on the day of their departure, Blanche was willing to make the trip. She was never an unwilling or unwitting accomplice. Although often portrayed as such, Blanche was far from it, accompanying Buck on a number of robberies staged in 1930 and 1931 when Clyde was still in prison.[52] Besides, though she never really liked Bonnie,[53] Blanche thought it would be nice to drive to Missouri and at least see Clyde again.

On March 29 Blanche and Buck purchased a Marmon sedan[54] and left for Missouri. Not far from Joplin Buck and Clyde were reunited. It had been fourteen months since they had last seen one another, and the meeting was a happy one.[55]

In the company of the ever-present W. D. Jones, the two couples drove to nearby Joplin. There, they rented a rather nice garage apartment on thirty-fourth Street, near the intersection of Oak Ridge. The area was called Freeman Grove. For Barrow's purposes it was the ideal place to settle down. Constructed of stone, with its living quarters situated above a two-car garage, the apartment afforded an unobstructed view of the sparse neighborhood.

Each morning Bonnie would call Snodgrass's Grocery Store, located a few blocks away, and order the day's provisions. A young delivery boy named Herman Biggs would arrive shortly thereafter, carrying an arm-load of groceries. He always tried to peek into the kitchen, but a young

Blanche and Buck Barrow, 1933. (Courtesy of Ken M. Holmes, Jr.)

woman invariably met him on the stairs before he had gone too far.[56]

Once in a while the couples would venture into Snodgrass's on their own. Clyde Snodgrass remembered them as "very nice customers," often laughing and carrying on "just like ordinary people."[57]

However, by then Clyde, Buck, and W. D. were roaming at night, raiding small businesses in the surrounding communities, including the Neosho Milling Company in nearby Newton County.[58] Someone tipped the state police that a roadster similar to the one used in Neosho was parked in the Barrow garage.[59] State Troopers G. B. Kahler and W. E. Grammer contacted Newton County Constable Wes Harryman and accompanied him to Neosho, where a liquor search warrant was obtained. Their investigation had led Kahler and Grammer to believe the occupants of the house on thirty-fourth street were, among other things, bootleggers.[60] Driving back to Joplin, the three lawmen rendezvoused with City Detective Tom DeGraff and Motor Detective Harry

McGinnis, proceeding south on Main Street to Freeman Grove.

It was late afternoon, April 13, 1933, and all was quiet in the apartment on thirty-fourth Street. Bonnie, dressed in a nightgown and house shoes, sat at the kitchen table working on revisions to "Suicide Sal," the poem she had begun in the Kaufman County jail.[61] Blanche sat alone at another table playing solitaire, her dog "Snow Ball"[62] asleep at her feet. The two women said nothing to one another. Friction between them was mounting by the second.[63] Buck was behind the house washing the Marmon. He and Blanche were planning to return to Dallas the following day. Clyde and W. D. were in the garage.

"Let's go scouting," Clyde said, opening the doors. Barrow then steered the roadster onto thirty-fourth, turning east. Before he and Jones reached Main, however, Clyde noted the car was handling poorly. He turned around and drove straight home. Buck met them at the garage door. Pulling inside, Clyde discovered a flat tire on the roadster. While he and Jones discussed what to do next, Buck started to close the door.[64] At that instant Tom DeGraff, Detective McGinnis, and Constable Harryman drove up, parking directly in front of the west door of the two-car garage. State troopers Kahler and Grammer drove slowly past the driveway, stopping on thirty-fourth, just west of the apartment. "Laws," Buck shouted. Clyde and W. D. grabbed shotguns.[65]

Wes Harryman had seen someone at the garage door[66] and jumped, gun drawn, from the car before it stopped.[67] Harryman lunged for the door, apparently hoping to reach it before it could be closed. Clyde and W. D. opened fire.[68] The constable fell to the ground, fired one round and then died. McGinnis leaped from the car and actually managed to jab his weapon through the still-open garage door before being struck by a volley of shotgun blasts that severed one of his arms. Incredibly, he managed to squeeze off three shots before slipping into unconsciousness. He died several hours later.[69]

Buck hurried upstairs to help Bonnie and Blanche. At first the two women were unsure what was going on. A few days before, Clyde had accidentally discharged a Browning automatic rifle (BAR) inside the apartment. They thought it had happened again.[70] They quickly realized, however, the police were outside.

One of the bullets from McGinnis's gun hit Jones in the side. He went upstairs, passing Buck, who was on his way back to the garage. Buck took Jones's shotgun and rejoined Clyde.[71] DeGraff dove from his parked car and ran for cover toward the house next door. There he surprised troopers Kahler and Grammer, who were taking cover at the southeast corner of the house. Thinking DeGraff was one of the gunmen from the garage apartment, they whirled and very nearly shot him.[72]

"Leave everything," Jones screamed to Bonnie and Blanche as he arrived upstairs, clutching himself painfully. "Y'all get down in the car. Get in the back, on the floor board."[73] Apparently both Jones and Parker then fired several rounds at DeGraff as he ran to the house next door. Grammer reportedly saw "a woman and a younger man" firing from the front windows of the garage apartment not long after another woman had emerged from the front door and started walking down thirty-fourth Street, away from the scene. Indeed, as we shall see, Blanche did go outside, which would have left Bonnie and Jones upstairs. Other sources too, including the unpublished memoirs of Cumie Barrow, mention Bonnie firing from an upstairs window. However, Blanche said both she and Bonnie arrived downstairs at the same time, and Jones has stated he never saw Bonnie shoot a gun. Moreover, Trooper Grammer failed to mention the shooting from upstairs at either of the coroner's inquests.[74]

Nevertheless, at some point Jones and both women arrived downstairs. Bonnie tumbled into the V-8 sedan while Clyde, Blanche, and the wounded W. D. Jones opened the garage doors. Bullets were slamming into the walls. Buck was grazed slightly, and a ricocheting bullet lodged in Clyde's chest, just under the skin. Neither brother was seriously hurt.[75]

Clyde then stepped calmly through the garage doors and crouched near the west corner of the apartment. Seeing Kahler, he drew a bead on the officer and emptied a charge of buckshot in his direction, blasting a huge hole in the wall of the house next door. Kahler had one shot left. He stood up and started to fire, but he tripped over a piece of bailing wire. Thinking that he hit the trooper, Clyde turned to Jones. "Where's the other fellow?" he asked. Just then, Kahler fired the last shot in his revolver. Clyde ducked, which made Kahler think he had wounded the outlaw.[76]

Paying no heed, Barrow, Blanche, and W. D. Jones tried to move DeGraff's car, which was parked in front of their Ford V-8. They could not release the hand break, so they retreated inside the garage.[77] Blanche then noticed her little dog was missing. She had trained it to run to the V-8 on command,[78] but for some reason "Snow Ball" had darted outside and disappeared down the street. Blanche decided to follow,[79] stepping outside and calmly walking past an astonished Trooper Grammer, calling for her dog.

The notion that Blanche ran from the scene in a screaming fit of terror, clutching a fist full of playing cards, has not been substantiated. Those who knew her well said she would have never done such a thing. Indeed, Blanche herself said she would have never left Buck. This would be substantiated by her actions three months later in Platte City, Missouri, and Dexfield Park, Iowa.[80]

Back inside the garage, Clyde decided to shove the police car into the street with the nose of the Ford.

Photograph by Blanche Barrow of the house in Joplin, Missouri. The *X*'s were added by Blanche to indicate the location of the two officers who died during the bloody April 13, 1933, gunfight. (Courtesy of Ken M. Holmes, Jr.)

"Let's move that guy out of the way," he shouted, meaning Harryman, who had fallen in front of the door between the outlaws' Ford and DeGraff's car.[81]

"I'll do it," Buck said.[82]

Grammer and DeGraff fired several shots as Buck lifted Harryman's limp body and dragged him clear of the door.[83] Clyde revved the big V-8 engine. Buck climbed in next to him, sinking low in the seat. Bonnie and W. D. were already on the floorboard in back.

Easing the hood of the sedan through the doors, Clyde felt the chrome bumper of his car mash against the police vehicle. Then, with a sudden lurch, he sent the abandoned car careening wildly down the short driveway and out into the rutted, unpaved street. Its rear wheels crashed over the opposite curb.[84] Wasting not a second, Barrow sped past the dead and dying lawmen, driving madly through a hail of gunfire as he turned east on thirty-fourth. A block from the house Clyde stopped to pick up Blanche, who was looking for her dog in the weeds of a vacant lot. Her search was useless. The dog was gone.[85]

Without sleep, Barrow drove straight through to Amarillo, Texas,[86] a distance of 450 miles. Jones was convinced that two bullets were lodged somewhere inside his body. Clyde took an elm branch, wrapped it in gauze, and poured alcohol over it. He then pushed the apparatus through the ghastly hole in W. D.'s side.[87] When the stick popped out of a second hole in Jones's back, it was clear that the shot was clean and would eventually heal.

Back in Joplin, police were trying to pick up the pieces. The house in Freeman Grove revealed a great deal of information concerning the identities of those responsible for the deaths of Harryman and McGinnis. Buck's Marmon was found nearby. The roadster and an arsenal of weapons, including a bloodstained 16 gauge shotgun, were found in the garage. However, the biggest find was made upstairs. Besides an unfinished game of solitaire, a guitar,[88] and several handwritten pages of original poetry, police investigators found Blanche's purse. Inside, it they discovered Buck's pardon papers, signed by Texas Governor Miriam Ferguson, and a marriage license issued to Marvin I. Barrow and Blanche Caldwell. Nearby, a camera and one or two rolls of exposed Kodak film were also discovered.[89]

The film was rushed to a local photographer for processing. Within hours several clear photos of the outlaws were being wired to every major newspaper and law enforcement agency in the country. The snapshots nearly resulted in the inadvertent arrest of one of Clyde Barrow's previous victims.

Three and a half weeks earlier, just days before Buck's pardon, Bonnie, Clyde, and W. D. were on their way from Texarkana to Dallas. In Marshall, Texas, Barrow spotted a new Ford V-8 parked in a driveway. Jones got out and quickly started the car, preceding his friends to the outskirts of town. Somewhere along a dusty back road between Marshall and Dallas, Bonnie and Clyde transferred their belongings to the new car. One of the items was a box camera they had borrowed from Blanche,[90] a shutterbug who was rarely without a camera.[91]

For the next several minutes the trio took pictures of each other mugging with great armloads of weapons. Clyde and W. D. each took cigars from a box they had found in the stolen car and lit them, posing proudly like prosperous bankers. At one point, Bonnie decided to parody her male companions, snatching Jones's cigar.[92] Propping her left foot on the bumper of the new car, she poked the stogie between her teeth and drew Missouri lawman Thomas Persell's big double-action service revolver across her out-thrust hips. The resulting image would become one of the most famous American photographs of the twentieth century, and one that Bonnie Parker would never live down. She despised the picture. Her name is still synonymous with that of a "cigar-smoking gun moll."[93] In reality, of course, she never smoked cigars and rarely handled guns. The snapshot was a joke. Her image was a media fabrication.

Apart from the sensational appeal of Bonnie's pose, a tiny detail caught the attention of the Joplin investigators. There, captured in the lower right-hand corner of the photograph, was a clear view of the license plate of the getaway car used by the killers of Harryman and McGinnis. A quick check revealed the vehicle's owner to be a Marshall, Texas insurance salesman named Roseborough. Fortunately for him, however, he had reported the car stolen three weeks earlier. It would be more than a month before it was finally located, abandoned in Oklahoma. The bipod of a Browning automatic rifle was bolted to the dash.[94]

Puzzled by the growing number of murders attributed to Clyde, Ralph Fults relayed a message to Clyde and Buck through underworld connections, asking why so many people were dying.

"They think we're just school kids," Clyde replied. "They won't 'go up' for us. They don't think we're serious when we show them our guns. I guess because we're so small."

One week later Barrow again made headlines. It was early afternoon, Thursday, April 27, when Clyde drove up to a rooming house in Ruston, Louisiana. W. D. Jones got out of the V-8 and strode over to a black Chevrolet coach parked out front. The keys were in the ignition. Jones jumped in and started it up.

The owner of the car, thirty-five-year-old mortician H. D. Darby, happened to emerge from the rooming house as Jones was driving off. With a scream of alarm, Darby ran across the lawn and leaped onto the running board of his car.[95] By then Jones was going too fast and Darby decided to abandon the tactic, diving to the sidewalk with a crash. Sophie Stone, a twenty-seven-year-old home-economics instructor, witnessed the theft from the window of her high school classroom directly across the street.[96] She offered Darby the use of her own car. He gladly accepted.

In the company of Miss Stone, Darby took the wheel, driving north, toward Dubach. Eighteen miles northwest of Ruston, a Ford V-8 sedan rolled up.

"Have you seen a Chevrolet pass this way?" the driver called out.

Darby got out and walked back to the mud-streaked car. "Yes, I have," he answered.

"Why were you following that car?" the driver asked.

"Because it's my car," Darby answered.

Suddenly, the driver's expression changed. Like a wildcat, he burst from the sedan, drew a .45 caliber automatic, and grabbed the Ruston man by the collar, pulling him inside the Ford.[97] A small woman jumped from the front seat and ran over to the passenger side of Miss Stone's car, grabbing the frightened young teacher by the arm. "Come on," she said, "you're coming with us."[98]

Darby and Stone were forced into the front seat of the sedan, squeezing in between the angry driver and his tiny female companion. Clyde Barrow, at the wheel, fumed. Darby and Stone had unwittingly forced him to abandon the idea of robbing a Ruston bank that afternoon.[99] He had also lost track of Jones in the process.

Clyde grumbled as he turned down a gravel road toward the town of Bernice. Barrow never used a main highway, traveling, instead, over a complex network of back roads. Sophie Stone watched the speedometer incessantly. Often, the needle swept past ninety miles per hour.[100] Over caliche and gravel the sedan roared, slinging white mud high into the air.

More than once the V-8 rumbled over a series of deep ruts, throwing a number of BAR clips from the glove box. Without reducing speed, Barrow reached across Darby and Stone, retrieved the clips, and laid them in the abducted woman's lap. "Here," he snapped, "hold these things."[101]

Bonnie was intrigued by the captives. She asked them questions and conversed freely. When she discovered that Darby was a mortician by trade, she laughed.

"I know we're going to get it sooner or later," she said with a grin. "I know you would enjoy embalming us. Promise us you will."[102]

Six miles from Waldo, Arkansas, Barrow stopped the car. Bonnie opened the door and stepped to the gravel road, motioning for Darby and Stone to get out, which they did. The big Ford started to pull away. Then suddenly, the car skidded to a stop. Barrow put it in reverse and started to back up. Darby and Stone must have thought they had breathed their last. But instead of a shower of bullets, a five-dollar bill sailed through Bonnie's window and floated to the side of the road.[103]

In Waldo Blanche and Buck stole a fresh car for themselves and took off for Oklahoma.[104] Bonnie and Clyde spent the remainder of that day searching the Arkansas backroads for W. D. Jones. Six weeks would pass before they found him.[105]

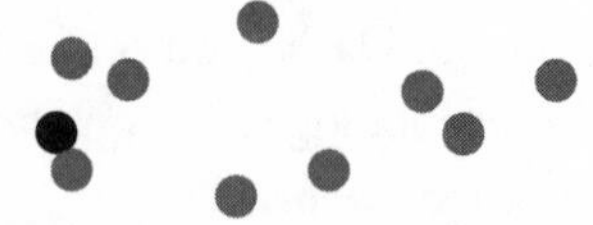

"They Think We're Just School Kids"

The Midwest was still reeling from the shock of the terrible Joplin murders and the Ruston kidnap incident when another Texas terror, Raymond Hamilton, was transferred to LaGrange, Texas, to stand trial for the robbery of the Carmen State Bank. Hamilton's accomplice, Gene O'Dare, had already been sentenced to ninety-nine years for his part in the same robbery,[1] and not much hope was held for Ray. On May 5, 1933, Hamilton too was convicted of the crime and quickly assessed a ninety-nine year sentence.[2]

Three weeks later Ray was back in Hillsboro to stand trial a second time for the slaying of John Bucher.[3] On June 2 the jury found Hamilton guilty of the murder and sentenced him to ninety-nine years in prison. In Huntsville Ted Rogers, who had renewed his pledge to step forward should Hamilton be sentenced to death, showed no emotion upon hearing the verdict.[4]

Seven days later Bonnie and Clyde arrived in Dallas. On Denton Road, between Bachman Dam and the Five Point Dancehall,[5] they spotted W. D. Jones. "Come on, boy," Barrow called out. "We're going up the country."[6] For the remainder of the day and for most of that night Barrow guided the V-8 coupe through a maze of back roads, working his way to the Texas Panhandle.

The following evening, June 10, seven miles north of Wellington, Texas, the gleaming new sedan was pushing seventy miles per hour as it sped over the seldom-used farm road. It was well past dark, and already Clyde had traversed hundreds of miles of Panhandle back roads, en route to Erick, Oklahoma, and a scheduled meeting with Buck and Blanche. Bonnie sat to Clyde's right. W. D. Jones was asleep in the back.[7]

Suddenly the road disappeared. A bridge was out—possibly swept away by a flood. For a terrifying split second, the car was airborne, sailing into the dry wash of the Salt Fork River. After rolling twice, it landed upside down in the damp sand. Clyde, thrown clear, momentarily regained consciousness and crawled back to the overturned auto. Amid the gentle gurgle of leaking fuel, he heard W. D. and Bonnie stirring within. Jones pulled himself from the back seat while Clyde worked to free Bonnie. The boy started gathering weapons. He was about to hide them in a nearby clump of weeds when a spark ignited the puddles of gasoline collecting inside the cab. Flames shot high into the night air as Barrow and Jones worked frantically to beat the fire to Bonnie, but it was too late. Fire engulfed the trapped woman's right leg and started licking about her face. She screamed, begging Clyde to kill her.[8] Barrow paid no heed, beating back the flames as he tugged on the burning auto.

Two farmers, Steve Pritchard and Lonzo Carter, suddenly arrived. With the extra help Clyde finally pulled Bonnie from the twisted wreckage. However, by then she had been severely burned. At first Barrow failed to recognize the seriousness of her injuries. It was not until Pritchard and Carter carried the young woman to their farmhouse that he saw her leg and arm.[9]

"She needs a doctor," said Pritchard's wife, applying a homemade salve to Bonnie's charred limbs and blistered face. "No," said Bonnie and Clyde in unison.[10]

"We can't afford that," Barrow added. "Try and do what you can."

"I can't do much more than this," said Mrs. Pritchard,[11] wistfully. Slowly coming to understand Bonnie's predicament, Barrow paced out to the front porch and stared blankly at the distant glow of his burning car. Seconds later he returned to Bonnie's side, referring to her as "sis" and "honey" as he stroked her singed hair.[12] After a few minutes Barrow left the house to retrieve the cache of weapons gathered by Jones just prior to the outbreak of the fire. In the interim a suspicious Lonzo Carter managed to slip away from W. D. Jones.

"Where'd the other guy go?" asked Jones, suddenly aware of Carter's disappearance.

"I don't know," said Pritchard. "He's probably out back."[13]

At that moment the local sheriff was turning up Pritchard's dirt drive. Jones decided he and Bonnie should hide themselves in the yard outside. With the semiconscious Bonnie cradled in his arms, he stepped through the kitchen door into the cover of darkness.

Clyde hurried up to the house from the river bottom, his arms loaded with automatic weapons. He met Bonnie and W. D. in the bushes surrounding the house. Tossing a BAR to Jones, he turned toward the house.

"Everyone get on the floor," Barrow called out.[14]

Collingsworth County Sheriff George Corry and Wellington City Marshall Paul Hardy emerged from their car. At first the officers thought they had a trio of drunk kids cornered on the front lawn.[15] Before either man knew it, though, they were looking at a pair of rifles.

"Raise your hands," Clyde shouted. Corry and Hardy were quickly disarmed and bound together with their own handcuffs. Barrow was curt with the captured cops, shoving them over to Corry's car. "Get in back," he ordered. Clyde then lifted Bonnie out of the bushes and carried her to the car.[16]

"You hold her easy," he told the lawmen, placing Bonnie across their laps. "Don't make her hurt any more than she's got to."[17]

Inside the house Steve Pritchard's daughter-in-law decided to reach up and latch the kitchen door. Standing outside, Jones thought she was reaching for a gun, and he fired a shot through the screen, wounding the young woman in the hand.[18]

Jones then climbed in the car next to Clyde, who took the wheel. At 11:30 P.M. Corry's car rolled down the drive and turned north toward Shamrock.

Now Barrow became less abrasive, almost friendly. He was impressed with the way Bonnie was being treated by the two cops. They cradled her gently, holding her head and stroking her face, talking to her softly, soothing her moans and suffering. At three o'clock Barrow stopped the car near a long bridge outside of Erick, Oklahoma. He gave the horn a short blast, then waited in the darkness. A few minutes passed before a horn sounded from the opposite end of the bridge. Soon Buck Barrow came running up. Clyde got out of the car and pulled Corry and Hardy from the rear seat.

"Take the car across," he told Jones.

"Are we going to kill these men?" Buck asked.

"No," Clyde replied, a painful smile wrinkling his singed face. "I've been with them so long, I'm beginning to like them. Just tie them to a tree and come on across."[19]

Buck led the two lawmen, still handcuffed, toward a stand of trees lining the river bank. He cut a strand of rusted barbed wire from an old fence line and looped it around his victims, tying it off to a stout gum tree. Rejoining Clyde and the others, Buck said he had used barbed wire to restrain Corry and Hardy.

"You didn't have to do that," he said tersely.[20]

Taking the wheel of Buck's V-8 convertible, Clyde transported his outlaw family northeast across the state of Oklahoma. After a brief stay in Pratt, Kansas, the fugitives moved to the Twin Cities Tourist Camp in Ft. Smith, Arkansas.[21] There Blanche rented a double cabin from the proprietors while Clyde drove into town to find a doctor. Explaining that his wife had been burned by an exploding oil stove, Barrow coaxed Dr. Walter Eberle back to the courts.

"This woman needs to be hospitalized!" decreed Eberle as he cleaned and dressed the wounds. "Either that, or a full-time nurse must be employed."[22]

Barrow hired a nurse. In her pain and agony, Bonnie cried continually for her mother. An intensely distraught Clyde fed her, adjusted her pillows, and even carried her to the bathroom.[23] By the nineteenth she had shown no improvement. She was most severely injured at the knee, and the extensive damage to her tendons made it impossible for her to straighten her leg.[24] Barrow called another physician. The second doctor held little hope for her survival. Clyde jumped in the convertible and drove to Dallas. Bonnie's mother wanted Clyde to take her to Arkansas, but he refused to consider the idea. Instead, he reluctantly asked Bonnie's little sister, Billie, to make the trip.[25]

For the next six days Billie nursed her injured sister.[26] Her presence seemed to make a difference, although it took a while before Bonnie recognized her sister. Clyde, of course, never left for more than a few minutes. Blanche, too, was a great help. Miraculously, Bonnie began to respond.

To finance the high cost of Bonnie's medical treatments, Buck and W. D. began staging robberies in the Ft. Smith area. On June 23 they held up Brown Grocery in Fayetteville. En route to Ft. Smith, not far from the town of Alma, Buck was rounding a bend at top speed. Suddenly he spotted a slow-moving vehicle directly in front of him. Unable to maneuver around the motorist, Buck hit the brakes, skidding headlong into the rear of the nearly stalled automobile.[27]

The force of the impact threw W. D. against the dash and tossed Buck across the steering wheel. When Jones regained consciousness, he spotted Arkansas auto mechanic Webber Wilson, the irate driver of the first car, approaching with a rock in each hand. Buck kicked open the door and leveled a 16-gauge shotgun in Wilson's face.[28] W. D. jumped out of the other side of the car with that old .41 caliber pistol Clyde had given him in Temple, Texas. Wilson dropped both rocks, let out a scream, and ran across a nearby field.

At that moment Alma City Marshall H. D. Humphrey and Deputy A. M. Salyers happened to drive by. They had been cruising the Fayetteville road in hopes of intercepting the Piggly-Wiggly bandits. Slowing down to observe the wreck, the officers saw Wilson, whom they knew, throw his hands into the air and run away from the scene in terror.[29] Gliding to a stop, Humphrey and Salyers got out of their car, drew their weapons, and started walking back toward the two disabled vehicles.

Humphrey took one last step and was blown into the ditch by a blast of buckshot. Salyers fired his weapon in the direction of the wrecked cars and retreated to the front porch of a farmhouse two-hundred feet away. Reloading his revolver, the lawman proceeded to harry the gunmen with an amazing show of marksmanship. Buck ran to the police car and tried to start it. Bullets whizzed through the cab. On the highway W. D. Jones stood in the open, searching for a small gold ring he had dropped on the pavement.

"Get that cop's gun and come on," Buck shouted.[30] Jones located his ring, retrieved Humphrey's weapon, and darted toward the car. Salyers drew a bead and fired. The shot sailed through the open door, sliced off the tips of two of Jones's fingers, and slammed into the steering column, shattering the horn button.

"My god!" cried Jones, clutching his bloody fingers. "That guy can shoot!"[31]

Buck finally got the officer's car started and, evading Salyers's frightfully accurate gunfire, steered north toward Fayetteville. Not far down the road they turned west, then south, commandeering another car and driving to the top of Mt. Vista, overlooking the towns of Van Buren and Ft. Smith.[32] There they ditched the second car and walked back to the tourist courts via a railroad trestle across the Arkansas River.[33]

On Monday, June 26, as newspaper headlines announced the death of H. D. Humphrey, Clyde and his entourage cautiously entered Sherman, Texas. There Billie was handed a sum of money and helped aboard the Interurban train to Dallas. Clyde then turned the car north and proceeded to Great Bend, Kansas, 450 miles away. The group rented two rooms at a tourist court and settled down to nurse the slowly improving Bonnie Parker.

One night Clyde drove to Oklahoma with Buck and W. D., where they raided the National Guard armory at Enid. The three men loaded five Browning automatic rifles, forty-six Colt .45 automatics, and ten-thousand rounds of ammunition into their sedan. There were so many guns in the car that the men could hardly find a place to sit.[34]

While in Enid, the trio also stole a physician's car for the medical bag inside. From there they drove to the home of "Pretty Boy" Floyd, in Salisaw, Oklahoma, to see if a safe house could be secured for the duration of Bonnie's convalescence. Floyd wasn't there, but his family agreed to have him forward a coded letter to the Barrows in West Dallas, telling Clyde where and when he could meet him. Floyd apparently sent the letter, but Barrow received it too late. Many months would pass before the outlaws finally met. By then a safe house was no longer needed, and the visit was purely social.[35]

Returning to Great Bend, Clyde took one of the Browning automatic rifles and cut off the barrel and stock so that he could drive with the weapon in his lap.[36] He then paid a construction worker to weld three of the twenty-shot clips together, creating a sixty-shot banana clip. Barrow tagged the monstrous creation his "scattergun," and practiced with it as often as possible.[37]

On July 18 the five fugitives relocated to Platte City, Missouri, checking into a small motor court at the junction of Highways 71 and 59, six miles south of town.

The courts, facing southwest, consisted of two small brick cabins joined together by a pair of one-car garages. In addition to their stout construction, Clyde liked the cabins because of their rather isolated position,[38] affording little opportunity for nosey neighbors to peek through a carelessly opened door or wind-blown shade.

Several yards to the south stood the Red Crown Tavern,[39] which housed a cafe, a ballroom, and the motel office. Buck and W. D. sank low in their seats as Clyde drove up to the tavern.[40] Blanche got out and went inside to inquire about the cabins. Manager Neal Houser watched the young woman as she paid in advance with silver, no bills. This mildly interested Houser, who decided to keep an eye on the strangers.[41]

Bonnie, Clyde, and W. D. moved into the room on the northwest side, on the left as one faces the court. Buck and Blanche took possession of the southeast cabin, on the extreme right. From the Red Crown Tavern, Houser and his nephew, William R. Searles, watched the strangers settle in their rooms. Because W. D. stayed out of sight much of the time, it was thought that only two couples occupied the little cabins.

Houser and Searles were not the only ones interested in the new arrivals. Kermit Crawford and his sister Lois were co-managers of a little place called Slim's Castle, a combination grocery store/filling station standing catty-corner to the Red Crown Tavern. Kermit, whose fiancée worked as a waitress at the Red Crown, watched with a measure of amusement as the mysterious strangers crossed back and forth between the two rooms that night with the lights of the tavern illuminating them as they trekked from door to door.[42]

The idea that he might be observing some of the most dangerous killers in the Midwest never crossed Crawford's mind. The people he saw looked like "school kids taking a couple of days off to shack up and have a good time."[43]

The following day, July 19, Blanche and Buck stepped into the Red Crown Cafe for lunch. Kermit's fiancée, Mildred Anderson, waited on them, finding the couple quiet and very polite.[44] Again they paid with small change. A set of scales stood nearby the cash register. Jones, who often kidded Blanche about her weight despite her lean appearance, picked her up and put her on the scales. He and Blanche and Buck were laughing loudly when they spotted Sheriff Holt Coffey watching them.[45] They finished paying for their lunches and left.

Later Blanche drove into town to purchase bandages and medicine for Bonnie. Her request for hypodermic syringes and atropine sulphate concerned the druggist, who contacted Sheriff Coffey.[46] Coffey had been alerted by Texas, Oklahoma, and Arkansas authorities to be on the lookout for strangers seeking medical supplies. Soon Coffey began to suspect that the Red Crown was playing host to the Barrow brothers. The sheriff contacted Captain William Baxter of the Missouri Highway Patrol. Baxter called for reinforcements from nearby Kansas City, asking for an armored car as well.[47]

At 6:00 P.M. on July 19 the officers began assembling at the Red Crown Tavern. Because of the great number of customers on hand that evening, it was decided to wait until closing time, 11:00 P.M., to approach the cabins.

From across the street Kermit and Lois Crawford watched anxiously as the police gathered. By ten o'clock, the tavern was packed with a cross-section of cafe regulars, dancers, and police officers. Thirty minutes later a lone figure emerged from the northwest cabin of the motor courts. Neatly dressed and clean-cut, the teenager strolled casually across the highway and entered Slim's Castle.[48]

The boy ordered five sandwiches and five sodas to go. By chance he happened to look through the front window, toward the Red Crown Tavern. Without another word, he fished out enough small change to cover the tab, gathered his purchases, and left, glancing again and again toward the tavern. It was 11:00 P.M.[49]

Back at the Red Crown, as lights were being extinguished and weapons drawn, several of the patrons decided to linger. William R. Searles and a few of his buddies crowded into a cramped men's room facing the cabins.[50] Clarence Coffey, the sheriff's sixteen-year-old son, joined a small group of thrill-seekers in the kitchen.[51] The Crawfords decided to watch the arrest from the driveway of Slim's Castle. They were soon joined by Kermit's fiancée, Mildred.[52]

At 11:30 P.M. Sheriff Coffey led the small army of heavily armed officers toward the courts. The yard lights had been extinguished. With bulletproof vests, hand-held shields, and Thompson .45 caliber submachine guns, the officers formed a semi-circle in front of the darkened cabins. The armored car was driven up to the garages, blocking both doors.[53]

Sheriff Coffey walked up to the southeast cabin and rapped vigorously on the door. Blanche was rinsing out a few articles of clothing for Bonnie.[54]

"Yes?" she called out. "Who is it?"

"I need to talk to the boys," the sheriff said.

"Just a minute," Blanche replied, uttering the predetermined words of warning.[55]

"Let us get dressed."

With his back facing the northwest cabin, Coffey relaxed and waited—a near fatal mistake. Clyde rolled out of bed, jerked his "scattergun" from between the mattress and box spring, and turned to Jones.

"That's the law," he said, cocking the weapon. "Get the car started."[56]

W. D. ran into the garage. Clyde opened the front door just enough to look into the yard. He spotted the armored car parked directly in front of him. Beyond that, he could barely see Coffey, facing Buck's door. Unable to get a clear shot from that position, Clyde ran into the garage, jumped on the rear bumper of the Ford, and peered through one of the three small windows that lined the top of the garage door. The sheriff stood not more than ten feet away. Barrow raised the deadly BAR, took aim, and fired a short burst through the door, splintering the wooden panels and glass panes.[57] Coffey spun around and crashed to the dirt, a bullet grazing his neck. Dropping his own gun and shield, the sheriff scrambled to his feet and ran back to the tavern, the other officers covering his retreat with a roar of gunfire.

Clyde darted inside the cabin and fired a massive salvo from each of the three windows—north, south, and west. Long shafts of flame spewed through the shades as lawmen in all directions dove for cover.[58] Barrow opened the front door and emptied the contents of his homemade banana clip into the armored car, each one of the steel-jacketed slugs passing right through the vehicle.

Deputy George Highfill, the driver of the car, suddenly felt a hot, stinging pain in his legs. Looking down, he saw blood pouring from both knees. He put the vehicle in reverse and started to back up. Suddenly, a wild shot struck the horn, causing it to blow furiously. Another slug slammed into one of the headlights, casting its beam skyward.[59] Relentlessly the driver continued backing his machine out of the line of fire, eventually pulling up behind the tavern. By then a thunderous blast of police gunfire was peppering the facade of the motel.

A burst of automatic weapons fire raked across the road, several of the bullets passing within a few feet of Mildred Anderson and the Crawfords.[60] Kermit escorted his sister and his fiancée safely inside the store, then ran up to the roof to watch the rest of the battle.

Inside the Red Crown Tavern William R. Searles and his friends dropped to the floor of the tiny men's room.[61] In the kitchen Clarence Coffey and a waitress sought refuge behind a large cast iron stove.[62] A volley of automatic weapons fire cut across the exterior wall of the kitchen, blowing out glass and chunks of red brick. One of the armor-piercing shells penetrated the brick wall, passed through the cast iron stove, and struck young Coffey, breaking his arm.[63]

Inside the garage Jones quickly started the car while Bonnie, though still suffering from the severity of her burns, managed to pull a few things together and drag herself into the garage unassisted.[64] Buck and Blanche decided to make a break for the garage. Instantly a fusillade of bullets began splattering the walls behind them. Seconds later a .45 caliber slug ripped through Barrow's left temple, tumbling along the

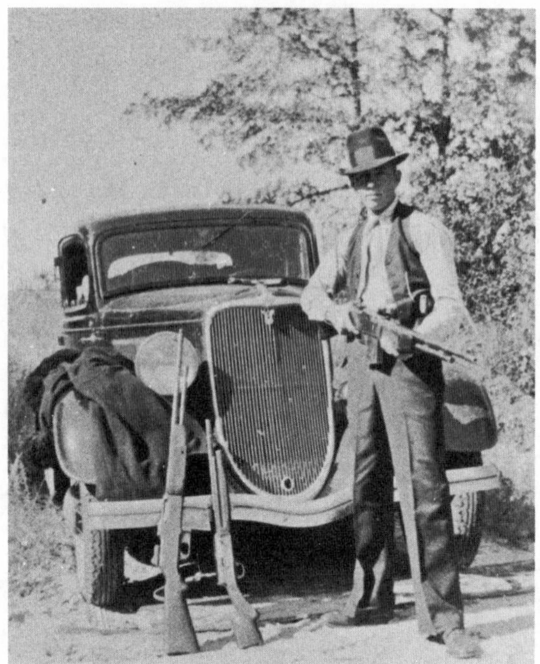

Clyde Barrow holding a Browning automatic rifle. Stolen from National Guard armories, BARs could fire a twenty-shot clip loaded with armor-piercing ammunition in under three seconds. Barrow ripped an armored car to shreds in Platte City, Missouri, with such a weapon. (Courtesy of Marie Barrow.)

interior circumference of his cranium before exiting on the opposite side of his forehead. The force of the blow sent the bandit reeling backwards, his weapon firing wildly in the air.[65] Surprisingly, however, the shot failed to kill Buck. In fact, he was still conscious, though gravely wounded and thoroughly dazed.

Blanche clutched her husband and helped him to his feet, bullets zinging past her face. She began screaming[66] above the sound of the gunfire, calling for Clyde to open the garage door. Barrow lowered his weapon and raised the bullet-riddled door. The first thing he saw was Blanche, with Buck sinking in her arms. Clyde stepped into the line of fire and helped his horribly wounded brother into the garage, burning his right hand when he accidently grabbed the hot barrel of Buck's BAR.[67] They then placed Buck in the back seat of the car, and W. D. and Blanche climbed in beside him.

Bullets crashed into the rear of the Ford as Barrow backed out of the garage. Bursting glass filled the cab with jagged projectiles, a large sliver striking Blanche's left eye. Seconds later a bullet fragment struck her in the forehead.[68] Then, inexplicably, the shooting stopped. Barrow turned the car around, cut across the yard, and drove through a nearby ditch to the open highway beyond, traveling north with headlights extinguished.[69]

Kermit Crawford hurried down from the safety of his rooftop perch and walked swiftly over to the cabins. There he and a number of other curiosity seekers sifted through the many items left behind by the gunmen. In addition to some makeup and several pieces of women's clothing, five empty soda bottles stood mutely beside an equal number of uneaten sandwiches.[70] Elsewhere in the room lay a pair of Browning automatic rifles, three sawed-off shotguns, four Colt .45 automatics, and H. D. Humphrey's service revolver.

A medical bag containing hypodermic syringes, atropine sulphate, and morphine sulfate gave rise to the theory that the Barrow gang was composed largely of drug users—a rumor that persists to this day.[71] The drugs, of course, were being administered to Bonnie, who was still recovering from the burns she received five weeks earlier.

Late on the afternoon of Thursday, July 20, Clyde and his seriously injured band of fugitives rolled through the town of Dexter, Iowa, 180 miles north of Platte City. A few miles north of town, near the remains of an abandoned amusement park called Dexfield, Clyde turned left onto a seldom-used access road known to some area residents as Lover's Lane.[72] The narrow, overgrown road wound past a number of small farm plots and lease properties. Several hundred yards from the highway Barrow left the road and drove through the dense underbrush until arriving in a small clearing several yards from Lovers Lane.[73] There he stopped the car.

Makeshift beds were constructed for Bonnie and Buck. Blanche stayed with her husband constantly—talking to him, easing his agony. Clyde made several trips to Dexter for food and medicine[74] but the appearance of the Platte City getaway car posed a problem. Using mud to conceal the dozen or more large bullet holes in its body helped, but Barrow knew he would have to get another car soon. There had not been enough rain in the area that summer to justify so much mud. Barrow and Jones drove north to Perry, where they stole another late model V-8.[75] The Platte City car was kept as a backup. The Perry car would be used for errands.

At noon on July 21 John Love was hard at work in his shoe shop, located in the rear of a clothing store. Suddenly a stranger appeared. He spoke with a heavy Texas accent and had a slight limp to his gait. It was Clyde.

"Got any white shirts that'll fit me?" Barrow asked with a broad, dimpled grin.

"Hi ya, Bud," Love replied. "I figure you for about a fourteen?"

"Yes sir," Clyde answered. "Got any black shoes that'll fit me?"

"Well," replied Love, viewing the young man with a cobbler's instinct, "I figure you for a size six."[76]

Love retreated to the stock room and located a suitable pair of Oxfords. Upon his return, though, he found the stranger's manner had changed. He seemed edgy, curt, his eyes searching the shoe repairman's face.

Barrow pushed a wad of money toward Love, grabbed the shirts and shoes, and hurried out to his car without waiting to have the items wrapped. Love was bewildered. Thinking the stranger had been offended by some abnormality in his appearance, he stepped to the mirror. But he found nothing out of the ordinary. Hair neatly combed, no stains blemishing his crisp white shirt. The pocket drooped a little, but only from the weight of his deputy sheriff's badge, barely visible to anyone who cared to look.[77]

At Blohm's Meat Market, a combination grocery store and restaurant not far from the shoe shop, Clyde stopped again. From inside the restaurant Wilma Blohm watched as the young man emerged from the driver's side of the car and entered the market. He was clean and neatly attired.[78] An attractive and petite young woman with light colored hair waited outside.

"Would it be possible, ma'am, to order five dinners to go?" asked the newcomer in a quiet, courteous manner.

"Why, yes," answered Mrs. Blohm, thinking the customer a guest of some nearby friend or relative. "You probably won't be needing plates and silverware," she added. "I'll just put everything in one big bowl."

"Uh, no ma'am," Clyde said quickly. "I want the china and silverware. I promise I'll bring it all back."[79]

Mrs. Blohm, struck by the stranger's boyish good looks, nodded agreeably and began preparing the five dinners. In the interim her husband loaded a large block of ice onto the bumper of the V-8, just as Clyde had requested. Barrow then stepped across the street to Pohle's Pharmacy for medical supplies, making a large purchase of gauze, alcohol, and burn salve.

The nature and quantity of Clyde's order alarmed the drugstore clerk, a friend of Wilma Blohm's. Later, the merchants discussed the strange young man and his mysterious companion. They agreed something was rather odd about them.

"For God's sake don't tell anyone," said Wilma Blohm's husband nervously.[80]

On Saturday and again on Sunday the strange young customer returned to the restaurant. Each time he ordered the same thing—five dinners and a block of ice. He would then cross the street to Pohle's Pharmacy, pick up more alcohol and gauze, and disappear northward, with an affectionate Bonnie at his side. Through it all, Wilma Blohm never lost a single plate or piece of silverware to Clyde Barrow.

Lying in Dexfield Park, Buck grew steadily worse. His brain was swelling, and more than once Blanche pressed her fingers against the hole in his head to prevent tissue from oozing out. Clyde made several attempts to obtain some form of pain-killer for his brother, but aspirin was the strongest thing he could get.[81] By Sunday afternoon Buck was fading fast. Apparently he was still conscious[82] and could eat some of the food Clyde was bringing out from Blohm's, but he was growing weaker by the minute. Despite this, Clyde went ahead and made his regular daily visit to Dexter, leaving Jones to look after Buck and Blanche. As always, Bonnie went along. On this particular day, a man named Henry Nye happened to take his weekly Sunday walk through the heavily forested area just beyond the southeast corner of old Dexfield Park.

Barrow-Fults-Hamilton Sites in the United States, 1925–1935

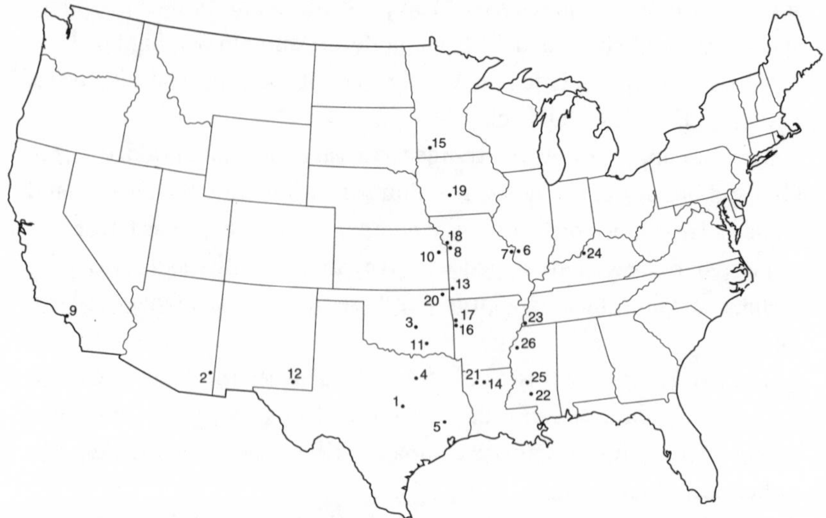

Listed in order of appearance in the text:

1. Texas Juvenile Training School, Gatesville, Texas
2. Duncan, Arizona, Fults's jailbreak
3. Seminole, Oklahoma, Fults's hideout
4. Dallas, Texas
5. Eastham Prison Farm, Texas
6. East St. Louis, Illinois, Fults's hideout
7. St. Louis, Missouri, Fults's hideout
8. Kansas City, Missouri, Fults observes squalid conditions at local "Hoovertown"
9. Los Angeles, California, Fults's hideout
10. Lawrence, Kansas, first bank robbery, Barrow-Fults-Hamilton
11. Stringtown, Oklahoma, Moore murder
12. Carlsbad, New Mexico, Johns abduction
13. Joplin, Missouri, Harryman and McGinnis murders
14. Ruston, Louisiana, Stone-Darby abduction
15. Okabena, Minnesota, Barrow-Fults-Hamilton visit/Barrow brothers bank robbery
16. Ft. Smith, Arkansas, Barrow-Parker hideout
17. Alma, Arkansas, Humphrey murder
18. Platte City, Missouri, gunfight
19. Dexfield Park, Iowa, gunfight, capture of Blanche and Buck Barrow
20. Commerce, Oklahoma, Campbell murder
21. Gibsland, Louisiana, ambush of Bonnie and Clyde
22. Prentis, Mississippi, Fults-Hamilton bank robbery
23. Memphis, Tennessee, Fults-Hamilton split
24. Louisville, Kentucky, Fults's hideout
25. Jackson, Mississippi, Fults in jail prior to trial
26. Mississippi State Penitentiary, Parchman, Mississippi

Through the branches of the trees, Nye spotted the top of a 1933 Ford V-8. "Just some campers," he thought to himself. But then he looked down. There on the ground before him was a partially burned road map and a discarded shirt, caked with dried blood.[83]

Nye hurried back to his farmhouse to telephone John Love, the shoe repairman who was also leader of the local vigilante group. Love had already received two similar calls from a couple of Nye's neighbors. He decided to meet Nye on Lover's Lane and take a look for himself. He did not like what he found.

Love promptly contacted Sheriff Clint Knee, in Adel. "Could be the Barrow gang," the sheriff said. "They're dangerous killers. I'd better come right over."[84]

Arriving in Dexter, Knee began interviewing a number of local citizens and shopkeepers in hopes of identifying the polite young southerner who had been frequenting the town for the past three days. Wilma Blohm was among those questioned. "Well," began Mrs. Blohm, "he's not overly friendly, but he's quiet, courteous, and very nice looking."[85]

The officers stared blankly at the woman. "Oh yes," she added, "he walks with a slight limp and has a little scar, down his nose." "Oh, well," said Knee, emphatically, "that's Clyde Barrow."

Reinforcements were requested from Des Moines and other nearby communities, but only a handful of officers responded. Two men from the Iowa State Department, "Rags" Riley and Bill Arthur, arrived, as did a number of Des Moines citizens. By nightfall, less than a dozen lawmen and scores of sightseers had converged on Dexter.

Jesse Ross, an employee of Blohm's market, could not wait to get off work. Like many others, he planned to join the all-night vigil at the park. He was not about to miss a thing when the posse made its move at daybreak. Then, unexpectedly, Clyde Barrow walked into the market with five sets of dishes and silverware in hand. Setting the utensils on the counter, he turned to young Ross and ordered a few items for breakfast. Barrow, apparently in a hurry, paid for the order, grabbed only one of the two sacks, and started for the door.

"Hey, there," Ross hollered.

Clyde whirled around and instinctively plunged his free hand into the pocket of his blazer.[86]

"Uh, you forgot your weiners," Ross said, nervously offering the second sack. Barrow relaxed and walked over to Ross. Thanking him, he took his package of weiners and departed.[87]

Not long after Barrow left town, the officers and curiosity seekers converged on Dexfield Park. Every road was covered. John Love was posted at the Lover's Lane entrance.[88] Sheriff Knee, "Rags" Riley, Bill Arthur, and three other men waited near the outlaws' camp. A group from Redfield, Iowa, spread out along the main road northeast of the park, while Everett Place, editor of the *Dexter Sentinel*, and Deputy Evan Burger took up positions near the decaying archway[89] that once marked Dexfield Park's northernmost entrance. A bridge spanning the South Racoon River stood nearby.

As the night progressed, an estimated one hundred spectators began traipsing into the woods behind the lawmen, spilling into a clearing adjacent to the Barrow encampment. Some brought dates. There was a lot of drinking.[90] Through it all, Clyde and W. D. serviced the cars, changing tires and tuning the engines. Then they cleaned and loaded all their weapons.[91] At 5:15 A.M., July 24, it was already light enough for them to see out across the dew-soaked pasture. Barrow sat down beside Bonnie on a seat cushion he had pulled from the Platte City car. Blanche attended to Buck, who had asked for a glass of water.[92] W. D. started roasting some of the weiners Clyde had nearly forgotten the day before at Blohm's Meat Market.[93]

Clyde and Bonnie happened to glance up from the campfire. Through the misty light of dawn they spotted six gray figures walking toward them in the clearing. Barrow shouted a warning to the rest of the camp and reached for his "scattergun."

Apparently aiming high to scare off the intruders,[94] Clyde sent the contents of his sixty-shot clip spraying through the tangle of branches above the lawmen. Limbs two and three inches thick began crashing on top of the posse. A ricocheting bullet burned across "Rags" Riley's scalp, stunning him momentarily.[95] The other officers scattered, firing their weapons toward the camp as they ran.

One hundred yards away John Love dropped to the ground as bark and chunks of wood tumbled down the back of his neck and into his shirt.[96] Everywhere, officers and spectators alike were frantically seeking cover, caught completely off guard by the firepower of the strangers camping in the park.

W. D. had just dropped the skillet and straightened up when a stray buckshot pellet slammed into his chest, knocking him to the ground. Clyde started yelling for everyone to get into the Perry car. Jones got to his feet and stumbled around to the driver's side of the car. Before he could get in, however, a second shotgun blast struck him. Bloodied but not seriously hurt, he pulled himself behind the wheel. The boy was so frightened that he couldn't get the Ford started.

Clyde walked over to the car, fired two more clips and jerked W. D. from behind the wheel.[97] In a matter of seconds, he was revving the engine and shifting to reverse.

Bonnie, who had not walked well in six weeks, limped to the aid of Blanche and Buck. Together they reached the car just as Clyde was getting it started. Jones crawled in the back seat. With a sudden lurch the V-8 started backing away from the six officers, crashing over bushes and briars en route to the narrow access road above the camp. Clyde then put it in first and took off. Soon, however, the outlaws encountered another squad of deputies. Barrow threw it in reverse.

The deputies raised their weapons. Clyde was just about to get the car turned around when a bullet cut into his shoulder. Losing his grip on the wheel, he accidentally backed over a tree stump.[98] Jones jumped out and tried to pry the car loose, but it would not budge.

"I'm checking out," Jones said.[99]

Clyde decided to do the same. "Everybody out of the car," he shouted. "Pile out—for God's sake, pile out."

The group ran toward the camp, hoping to grab the Platte City car. The posse, however, beat them to the punch, wrecking the vehicle with a wall of lead. Sixty-four slugs found their mark,[100] cracking the engine block, blowing out the windows, and destroying the tires.

Clyde herded everyone northeast through the woods. Buck fell to the ground. W. D. then reeled and fell against a tree, a shot glancing off his forehead. A shotgun blast splattered Bonnie, two of the pellets drilling deep into her abdomen.[101]

Jones gathered Bonnie in his arms and continued northeast down a narrow ravine. Blanche was trying to raise Buck to his feet. Clyde hurried over to help her. "Take Blanche and run for it," Buck whispered repeatedly. "I'm done for."[102]

Clyde paid no attention to the statement. He dragged his wounded brother and half-blind sister-in-law through the dense underbrush. Before long the group encountered a fence row stretching the length of the park's east side. Without stopping to rest, Barrow turned everyone north, following a heavily wooded fence line to the top of a long, steep hill. They had moved fast, arriving on a high embankment above the South Racoon River within minutes of abandoning their cars.[103] Buck could go no further.

"Take Blanche," he said. "I can't make it."

Blanche, of course, refused to leave. Clyde went to the edge of the embankment and spotted the bridge a quarter of a mile to the west. "I'm going after a car," he said. "Hide here. They'll never find you in these thickets."

Barrow then took the BAR, cocked his .45, and disappeared through the brush. W. D. and Bonnie crawled into the bushes nearby. Buck and Blanche dragged themselves toward the remains of the old baseball diamond, overgrown with vines and tall grass.

When Clyde stepped from the woods, he could see Deputy Evan Burger and E. A. Place leaning against Dexfield's old archway, several yards from the bridge. The two possemen noticed Barrow at the same time and opened fire. Clyde jumped behind a large tree and started shouting: "Hey, don't shoot. I'm a state man."[104]

Burger and Place took the bait, lowering their weapons. Before they had time to respond to Barrow's false statement, though, a salvo of rifle fire raked across their position. Because of his wounded arm, however, Clyde could not steady the weapon, and the shots went wild. Deputy Burger, an expert marksman, got the outlaw in his sights and fired only two shots, knocking the Browning from Clyde's hands and grazing his cheek. Barrow drew a .45, fired his last clip toward the lawmen, and stumbled off through a briar patch.

Back on the embankment, Bonnie and W. D. were huddled together. They had heard the shots and were convinced that Clyde had been killed.[105] Then several minutes later the leaves rustled nearby, and Clyde appeared, soaked in blood and crawling on all fours.

"You OK?" he asked Bonnie.

She nodded, wrapping her arms around his neck.

"They've got the bridge blocked," Clyde said to Jones. "Can you help Bonnie cross the river? We'll have to swim for it."

The river turned a sickening, muddy pink as Bonnie, Clyde, and W. D. slipped into the water. Jones, carrying Bonnie on his back, dogpaddled to the opposite bank, Clyde close behind. Reaching the river's north bank, Jones placed Bonnie on a patch of soft grass and sat down on a log.[106] Clyde drew his empty .45 and turned toward a distant barn. It was 5:45 A.M.

Just outside the barn eighteen-year-old Marvelle Feller was preparing to feed his father's cattle. The animals were skittish, apparently frightened by all the commotion erupting across the river in Dexfield Park. Gradually the stock grew more and more nervous. With eyes wide open, they searched the landscape, snorting and moving erratically from side to side. Then Marvelle's German Shepherd started growling and baring his teeth, the hair on the back of his neck bristling. Suddenly, the dog ran toward the cornfield, snarling furiously. The reason became immediately apparent. Just beyond the barbed wire fence, amidst the stalks of corn, a small, ragged-looking young man stood. His clothes were soaking wet and streaked with mud. The sleeve of his shirt was red with blood. A pistol was clutched in his hand.

"Call this dog off," yelled Clyde, raising the empty weapon. "Call him off or I'll kill him."[107] Marvelle rushed down to the fence line and snatched the angry dog by the collar.

"Y'all get down here," Clyde called out to Marvelle's father and Uncle Walt, both of whom were standing near the barn. They hurried over to the fence. Barrow, a nasty, bloody gash on the side of his face, placed his fingers to his lips, whistled, and waited. Momentarily a young boy appeared, carrying a tiny, blood-soaked woman. Wet and muddy, she wore nothing but a thin, tattered nightgown. It was apparent she had been shot twice in the abdomen.[108]

"Help me get her over the fence," Barrow ordered. Marvelle's father stepped forward and took Bonnie in his arms. As soon as he had lifted her over the barbed wire, he started to put her down, thinking she could walk on her own. Her body fell limp, nearly crashing to the ground. Feller grabbed the woman and looked quickly toward Clyde.

"Oh no," said Barrow anxiously. "You'll have to carry her. She's too weak. Let her put her arms around your neck." Barrow then waved his pistol in the direction of the barn. "OK," he said, "let's go."[109]

A woman and young girl emerged from the farmhouse. It was Marvelle's mother and little sister.

"They've got a bunch of outlaws cornered in the park," Mrs. Feller said excitedly, "so be on the lookout for—."[110]

Suddenly, the woman noticed the bloody, battered strangers. Stopping, she grabbed her daughter by the hand and started running back to the house.

"You'd better stop her—quiet her down," warned Barrow. "We ain't going to hurt you folks. We just need a car. The 'laws' are shooting the devil out of us. Can you help us out?"[111]

There were three automobiles on the premises, only one of which was operable—a blue 1929 Plymouth. The other two were up on blocks—byproducts of the Depression.

"OK, back it out," Clyde demanded, pointing to the garage. Through bleary eyes, Clyde watched Marvelle back the four-year-old Plymouth out of the garage. To him, it looked like a limousine. Marvelle got out and helped his father place Bonnie in the back seat, taking her by the arms and lifting her frail body through the door. W. D. got in next to her. Clyde then crawled behind the wheel, closed the door, and laid his pistol on the seat. Unfamiliar with the workings of that model Plymouth, Barrow stared blankly at the dash.

"OK," he said to Marvelle, "how's this thing work?"

Marvelle jumped to the running board, poked his head through the window, and reached across Clyde to demonstrate the gear sequence. For a split second, he thought about grabbing the weapon and overpowering the weakened bandit.[112] One look at the nasty-looking gun, however, changed his mind. Fifty years later he would find out the pistol was not loaded.

"You ain't going to shoot us in the back while we're driving off, are you?" Barrow asked.

"Heck no, mister," Marvelle's father answered. "We've only got one shotgun shell and it's in the house." Barrow shifted to first and pulled away from the Feller home.[113]

Still in Dexfield Park, Blanche and Buck hovered behind the trunk of a large tree that had been felled near the old baseball field. The progress of the posse had been slowed considerably by the reluctance of the men to charge haphazardly through the dense underbrush. The vicious and desperate nature of the men and women they pursued made for brittle nerves. The officers cautiously picked their way north, slowly moving from tree to tree. It was midmorning before they reached the ball field. A member of the posse spotted the tree and suggested that it would be a good place to hide.[114]

Despite his wounds, Buck was able to reload his weapon and ready himself for the approaching lawmen. He then pulled himself on top of Blanche to shield her.[115] She slid out from beneath him and tried to shield him instead. Buck was struggling to shield Blanche again when she suddenly stood up and faced the posse.

"Stop—for God's sake, stop," Blanche said. "You've already killed him."

The officers closed in. "Make him raise his hands," said one deputy.

"He can't," Blanche said. "You've killed him."[116]

As the lawmen brought the outlaws into Dexter, more than a thousand people surged through the streets, hoping to catch a glimpse of Blanche and Buck as they arrived at Dr. K. M. Chapler's office for treatment. Chapler and his wife, Elinor, found Blanche bruised, badly cut, and quite uncooperative. Her eye had been seriously injured by pieces of glass in Platte City, and a bullet fragment was still lodged in her scalp. The wounds were cleaned and bandaged. Buck remained calm and pleasant, chatting informally with Chapler and several others present. With brain tissue protruding from the massive Platte City wound,[117] Barrow spoke of his family and of the events leading up to his capture. He freely admitted to his involvement in the Joplin shootout as well as in the killing of Arkansas constable Henry Humphrey.

"I done that," he admitted weakly. "Clyde wasn't even there."[118]

"Where are you wanted by the law?" Chapler asked.

The capture of Blanche and Buck Barrow, Dexfield Park, Iowa, July 23, 1933. Blanche's dramatic reaction was actually caused by the photographer who snapped this picture. When he raised his camera, Blanche, blinded in one eye in the Platte City gunfight, thought the photographer had a gun and was about to shoot her husband. (Courtesy of the *Des Moines Register*.)

"Wherever I've been," Barrow answered.

In a few minutes, Blanche was taken outside and placed in Sheriff Knee's car. She was to be transferred to the county seat. Before reaching the car, her escort stopped long enough to pose for photographers, smiling broadly as he held the outlaw woman firmly by her handcuffed wrists. His expression suddenly changed, however, when a friend pointed out that Clyde might someday see the pictures and hunt him down.[119] The officer quickly pulled Blanche over to the sheriff's car and pushed her through the open door. She would never see her husband again.

On Dr. Chapler's recommendation Buck was transferred to King's Daughters Hospital in Perry. Immediately upon arriving, Barrow underwent surgery. Nevertheless, with a sustained temperature of 105 degrees and a pulse rate fluctuating between 120 and 160, he was not expected to survive.[120]

Two days later, on July 26, Buck's mother and younger brother, L. C., arrived in Perry. They were accompanied by Bonnie's mother and sister. Under heavy guard, they began their bedside vigil with Buck. Apparently he was quite lucid on that Wednesday. However, his condition quickly deteriorated. He began confusing L. C. with Clyde and thought Billie was Blanche, calling to them as if they were still together in Dexfield Park.[121] Opiates were being administered to Buck on a regular basis. Notwithstanding, on at least two different occasions (and possibly more) stimulants were injected into his system in an attempt to draw him back to reality. This was done primarily for the purpose of interrogating the accused killer. At one point, Deputy Sheriff A. M. Salyer, whose partner had been killed in the Alma, Arkansas, gunfight, approached the dying man's bed.

"Do you remember me, Buck?" asked Salyer.

"I sure do," answered Barrow. "You're damned lucky to be alive. We was shooting to kill both of you guys that day."[122]

Afterward, hour by hour, Buck faded. By Friday pneumonia had developed, resulting, in part, from an operation performed to remove a piece of buckshot from his chest. Finally, at 2:00 P.M. on Saturday, July 29, Marvin Ivan "Buck" Barrow was pronounced dead. He was thirty years old.

While Buck was being lowered into a rocky West Dallas grave overlooking Ft. Worth Avenue, Bonnie, Clyde, and W. D. were camped along a deserted midwestern stream, nursing their considerable wounds. They were virtual invalids for weeks.[123] Eventually, though, Clyde's arm healed enough for him to drive. Bonnie, too, improved, although the calf of her right leg had drawn up tight against her thigh—indicative of damaged ligaments. But the pain had subsided.

Zigzagging through Kansas, Missouri, and Colorado, the Dexfield survivors slowly resumed their criminal activities—robbing grocery stores, filling stations, and occasionally, factory paymasters. On August 20, 1933, they raided a National Guard armory in Plattsville, Illinois, stealing three Browning automatic rifles, a box of Colt .45 automatic pistols, and several thousand rounds of ammunition.[124]

One night near Clarksdale, Mississippi, Barrow sent Jones to steal a fresh car. "Fill it with 'red'," Clyde ordered, handing the boy some change. "We'll meet you on the other side of town."[125]

The meeting never took place. Jones pocketed the cash and caught a bus for Texas.[126] He was through with Bonnie and Clyde.

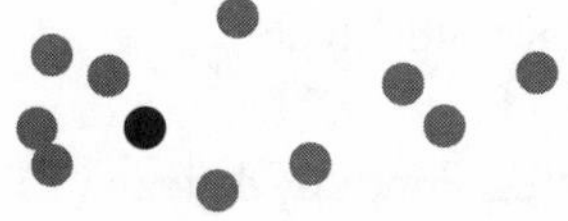

The Raid

For Texas authorities, the crowning achievement of that bloody summer of 1933 was the transferral to the penitentiary of twenty-year-old Raymond Hamilton—an event very nearly foiled by the young bank robber. On Sunday, July 22, the day before his friends' debacle at Dexfield, Hamilton was surprised, in his cell on the sixth floor mezzanine level of the Dallas County jail, while he was tying strips of cloth to a large pile of bed sheets. Nearby, lay the severed bars of an exterior window. Raymond had come within minutes of lowering himself to the deserted alley below.[1] On August 8, under heavy guard, the securely manacled bank robber was placed in Bud Russell's transport and whisked south to Huntsville.[2] By nightfall he was moving among a number of former acquaintances, including Ralph Fults.

Well over a year had transpired since Fults had last seen Raymond Hamilton. So much had happened in those many months, and yet Ray appeared to have changed very little. Fults was working on the woodpile that day, hacking kindling with a one-man saw. Sudden laughter erupted. Looking up from a chunk of oak, Fults spotted Raymond.

"Hey, Ralph," Ray shouted from across the yard, "don't worry none. Clyde'll be coming to fetch us real soon." Fults turned away. He wanted to crawl beneath one of the buildings and hide. Surely every guard in the compound heard the remark, but, strangely, none of them paid much attention to Hamilton. Still, he strutted around the prison, bragging about his friends Bonnie and Clyde.

"They can't hold me for long," he told more than one group of convicts. "Clyde'll be coming along any day now." Two weeks later Hamilton was transferred to Eastham Camp 1.

Among the newsmen milling about in anticipation of the arrival of the notorious Raymond Hamilton was Harry McCormick, the chain-smoking reporter from the *Houston Press*. Earlier, he had written stories of brutality and corruption based on information smuggled to him by the prison chaplain and various inmates. McCormick was fascinated by the boy who had been assessed a total sentence of 263 years.[3] Ray, anticipating this, smiled broadly as he jumped from the rear of Russell's transport, chains rattling about his neck. He seemed to thrive on all the attention.[4]

"Say, this joint's a pushover," he said. "Why, I'll be out of here in just a few weeks. There ain't no prison can hold me, not while I got Clyde Barrow to help me out on the lam."[5]

Despite Hamilton's blatant remarks, Texas prison officials refused to take notice, remaining confident in their ability to break any man's spirit. Clyde Barrow, on the other hand, was no doubt concerned about the indiscreet rantings of his former running-mate. Nothing would have pleased him more than to drive down to Eastham and carry out the raid he and Ralph Fults had planned three years earlier, but Barrow knew that Ray's persistent talk would lead to nothing but trouble.[6]

Bonnie and Clyde had not slept indoors since July 19, the night of the Platte City gunfight. They were living in cars and camping beside small lakes and streams.[7] Clyde often abandoned roads altogether, driving cross-country through open fields and dense forests.[8] In that way, towns were completely avoided. Because of this, many believed the fugitives had indeed succumbed to their horrible wounds. Finally, however, in late August, after six weeks of hushed rumors and official speculation, Bonnie and Clyde appeared in a remote area of Dallas's Chalk Hill escarpment, overlooking the converging lines of Eagle Ford Road and the Trinity River.[9] There a rendezvous with friends and family was carried out.

Both fugitives looked ragged, Bonnie in particular. Underweight and pale, she appeared much older than twenty-two. Clyde, his arm still stiff from the wound he had sustained in the Dexfield fight, lifted Bonnie out of the car and carried her to a blanket he had spread on the hot limestone terrain.[10] She was still unable to straighten her right leg because of the damage to her tendons resulting from the Wellington crash. Never again would she walk or even stand without the assistance of a cane or another person.

Their physical appearance notwithstanding, Bonnie and Clyde were in good spirits, merely happy to have survived long enough to see their friends and loved ones again. From that time until their deaths nine months later, Bonnie and Clyde visited the Dallas area on a regular basis. They often drove right up to the Star Service Station to tell Clyde's mother the time and location of the next meeting."[11]

At one of these meetings, which almost always took place at dusk,[12] L. C. tried to show his older brother how to ride a motorcycle. L. C. was an expert biker, but Clyde, a master behind the wheel of a car, could not get used to operating both throttle and brakes while balancing on two wheels. He stalled the motor and fell over repeatedly. Finally, though, he was able to get going, zooming off down a dirt road at high speed. But when he did not return, L. C. began to worry. Then a gun went off in the distance. L. C., Cumie, Marie, and Bonnie jumped in one of the cars and drove in the direction of the gunshot. They soon found Barrow pinned under L. C.'s motorcycle in the middle of the road. He had fired a shot from his Colt .45 automatic, hoping that his family would hear it and rescue him.[13]

Clyde's movements were difficult to predict, even for his own relatives. He purposely waited until the last minute to tell his family where to meet him. Even then he could be expected to change the plan. Only once did Barrow agree to meet a second time at the same precise location. On November 21, 1933, when he and Bonnie arrived for the celebration of his mother's birthday, Barrow had no gift. But he promised to give her one the following evening at the same time and place. This enabled the Dallas County Sheriff's Department, with the help of an informant, to organize an ambush.

Bonnie and Clyde behind the car they would abandon on November 22, 1933. (Courtesy of the Dallas Public Library, Texas/Dallas History Archives Division.)

The site chosen for the meeting was typical of Clyde Barrow—it was a lonely, seldom-used stretch of freshly graded road northwest of Irving, Texas, near the tiny farming village of Sowers. Eventually, the two-hundred-foot right-of-way would be paved and designated Texas State Highway 183, but in 1933, it was a primitive, unfinished road known locally as Highway 15, or the North Ft. Worth Pike.

Fourteen miles from downtown Dallas, where Esters Road crosses "the Pike," a high hill rises above the terrain. It commands an impressive view of northwestern Dallas County and overlooks a great deal of neighboring Tarrant County.[14] It was on this hill, not far from the intersection, that Barrow intended to meet his family.

The informant, someone close to both Bonnie and Clyde,[15] told the sheriff's men where Barrow was expected to stop his car. A few minutes before sundown on November 22, 1933, two county vehicles pulled up to the location and then drove away, proceeding along the gravel-topped right-of-way for another half mile. After concealing the automobiles, Dallas County Sheriff "Smoot" Schmid, along with deputies Bob Alcorn, Ted Hinton, and Ed Castor, hiked back to the spot, crawled through a barbed wire fence and ducked down in a ditch on the property of dairyman Charlie Stovall. They were approximately seventy-five feet from the road.[16]

Schmid and Hinton each carried a Thompson .45 caliber submachine gun. Ed Castor packed a .351 "bullhead" repeating rifle, and Alcorn, in hopes of matching the firepower of Clyde Barrow, had borrowed a Browning automatic rifle.[17]

Between 6:00 and 6:30 a lone car topped the far hill a mile east of Stovall's farm. Traveling west at a leisurely pace, the vehicle passed the concealed officers, turned around, and stopped less than 150 yards from the junction of Esters Road and the North Ft. Worth Pike.[18] Now facing east, toward Dallas, the car was one of two Schmid and his men expected to see that evening. Behind the wheel was Clyde's soon-to-be brother-in-law, Joe Bill. According to plan, he had picked up his fiancée Marie, as well as L. C. Barrow, Billie Mace, Emma Parker, and Cumie Barrow, and had driven them to the prescribed meeting place, stopping directly in front of the lawmen.[19]

At 6:45 P.M., the early evening tranquility was again broken, this time by the intense, high whine of a distant automobile traveling at an incredible rate of speed. The roar of the engine grew louder as it approached rapidly from the north, thundering over gravel-topped Esters Road. Schmid and his men cocked their weapons and peered west through the dusky light. In their hearts the county men held no illusions as to the identity of the driver of the car. No one but Clyde Barrow would dare navigate such a road at high speed.

Seconds later a shaft of light spewed from Esters Road, followed shortly by the car, a black 1933 Ford V-8. The headlights of another car, traveling further down the line, silhouetted the two-door sedan as it idled in the middle of the right of way.[20]

"How do you feel about it, honey?" he asked Bonnie. "It seems phoney tonight."[21] Bonnie shrugged her shoulders. Against his better judgement, Barrow turned east onto the dirt surface of the North Ft. Worth

Pike and began to accelerate toward the parked car. He had just shifted to third gear when something beside the road caught his eye, something bright, said to have been a tin can.[22]

"I don't feel good about stopping," he said, rolling past the parked car. Quickly shifting to second gear, Barrow pressed the gas pedal to the floor. At that instant, three shafts of flame erupted from the ditch seventy-five feet away, accompanied by a thundering explosion of sound.[23] A stream of bullets slammed into the driver's side of the Ford, stitching the wheel well, door, and hood with a pattern of large, gaping holes. Bursting panes of glass showered the cab. Chunks of the steering wheel crumbled in Barrow's hands and fell to the floorboard. Lengths of shredded material dangled from the ceiling of the car.

Within seconds Barrow had accelerated to well over sixty miles per hour, weaving down the road on three flat tires. Joe Bill turned his own car around and sped west, away from the gunfire and Bonnie and Clyde. Amid repeated commands to get down, fifteen-year-old Marie Barrow, in the back seat of her fiancé's car, watched Clyde's coupe moving away in the opposite direction.

"He's made it over the hill, Momma," she cried. "They're all right."[24]

Four miles south of the attempted ambush, near the entrance to Hensley Field on Highway 80, Barrow spotted a 1932 Ford coupe traveling west in the oncoming lane. The outlaw turned his car in front of the Ford. Thomas R. James, behind the wheel, slid sideways into a shallow ditch.[25] Barrow jumped from his car and ran over to James, shotgun in hand. "Get out of there," he shouted.[26]

Stunned, James and his companion, Paul Reich, failed to respond. Clyde placed the stubby barrel of his 16-gauge shotgun against the closed windowpane of James's car, aimed high, and pulled the trigger. The shot filled the cab with shredded glass and thick, black smoke, ripping James's hat from his head and tearing a jagged hole in the roof of the coupe. James and Reich jumped out of the car, their faces cut and their hands held high. Bonnie hurried to Barrow's aid—a pronounced limp to her stride. Barrow thought his victims were lawmen, which accounts for his viciousness.

"Let's go," Clyde said. The desperate couple then got into the com-

The car Bonnie and Clyde abandoned following the attempted ambush of November 22, 1933. (Courtesy of the Dallas Public Library, Texas/Dallas History Archives Division, Hayes Collection.)

mandeered vehicle and prepared to make their escape. As Clyde slid behind the wheel, however, a puzzled look came over his face. The coupe, a four cylinder model, was unlike the cars he had grown accustomed to driving. In the darkness he failed to locate the ignition switch. "OK," he asked, "where's the key?"

"You're so smart," retorted James, wiping a trickle of blood from his forehead, "find it yourself."[27] Barrow found the ignition on his own. James and Reich then watched as their coupe was driven away.

Almost immediately Sheriff Schmid fell under a crush of public ridicule. On the street newsboys waved their papers and called out: "Read all about it. Sheriff escapes from Clyde Barrow."[28] To alleviate his position, Schmid, the supreme politician, produced an unexpected witness. Inviting newsmen into his office, he pulled out a document entitled:

"Voluntary Statement #B–71," a twenty-eight page deposition dated November 18, 1933, and signed by a hitherto unknown West Dallas teenager named W. D. Jones.

After leaving Clyde and Bonnie, Jones had caught a bus back to Texas, where he took a job picking cotton on a farm near Houston. Somehow, Dallas County Deputy Sheriff Bob Alcorn found out and nabbed the fast-shooting teenager. On November 18, 1933, Jones outlined the activities of the Barrow gang from December 24, 1932, through the middle of August 1933. The statement, sketchy in some areas, amazingly detailed in others, established the facts behind four murders already attributed to Clyde and his companions during those months. However, the revelation of Barrow's involvement in the December 25, 1932, shooting death of Doyle Johnson came as a complete surprise and embarrassment to Texas authorities.[29]

Another man had been charged with the crime earlier in the year. In fact, his case had already gone to trial. Despite rather convincing testimony placing him in the Johnson car on that freezing cold Christmas morning, the jury could not reach a verdict and was declared deadlocked.[30] A new trial was being scheduled when the true identity of Doyle Johnson's killer was learned.[31]

Schmid took Jones's statement and used it to satiate a ravenous press. Then on November 25, 1933, he paraded the boy before the reporters. The following morning numerous photographs of the wide-eyed youth appeared in the local papers, accompanied by excerpts from "Voluntary Statement #B–71," much of which was misquoted.[32] But it did the trick. Schmid was off the hook.

Meanwhile, after commandeering Thomas R. James's 1932 coupe, Parker and Barrow sped north toward Oklahoma. On a country road not far from the state line the fugitives rolled up to a gate. A freezing rain enveloped the landscape. Chilled water poured incessantly through the mangled hole in the shotgunned roof of the car.

Barrow got out to open the gate but lost his equilibrium and tumbled to the sloppy earth. He tried to get up but could not. Floundering on his hands and knees, he managed to crawl up to the rain-drenched fence and drag the gate across the gummy road.[33] Bonnie, seeing Barrow's condition, got out, took one step, and fell headlong into the frozen muck.

"We must be hit somewhere," said Barrow as he and Bonnie hoisted one another into the cab. "I can't walk!"

"I can't either," said Bonnie, "but I can't feel any pain either."

"Me either," Barrow said.[34]

At a filling station later that evening, Bonnie finally located the source of the couple's increased weakness. Spotting a trickle of blood on the floorboard of the new coupe, she traced it to a pair of clean bullet wounds passing through each of her knees. Clyde searched his own legs, quickly discovering two similar wounds. Bullets from Alcorn's BAR had found their mark, ripping through the legs of both fugitives.

From an Oklahoma doctor well known to the midwestern underworld Parker and Barrow received medical treatment.[35] After six days of food and rest the duo returned to the road.

It has been suggested that Clyde Barrow was so angry about the attempted ambush at Sowers that he plotted to kill both Sheriff Schmid and the informant. One source states that Clyde's older sister, Nell, actually talked Barrow out of killing the two. But according to other members of the Barrow family, Nell never saw her brother after he went to prison. Indeed, this is substantiated by the fact that Nell was never charged with harboring, a fate that befell many others in her family.

Floyd Hamilton said he was the one who talked Clyde Barrow out of killing Schmid and the informant. However, Marie Barrow maintains that no such exchange took place. Although Clyde had a strong idea who tipped off the sheriff, Marie said he was not angry enough to avenge the betrayal.[36]

As soon as it became known that Bonnie and Clyde were back in Texas, Raymond Hamilton began trying to get Barrow to resurrect his plan to raid Eastham Camp 1.[37] Hamilton wanted to include the original operatives—Joe Palmer, Henry Methvin, and Aubrey—but Hilton Bybee, the killer who had tried to escape from the Wichita County Jail with Ralph Fults, was to be added to the list at Fults's request. A fifth man, James Mullens, was brought into the picture by Ray.

Mullens was an eight-time loser who was just about to finish a twenty-one-year sentence for robbery. The forty-eight-year-old convict was also well known to both Ralph Fults and Clyde Barrow as a drug addict—unpredictable and wholly unreliable. Nevertheless, because Mullens was due for release, Raymond promised him a thousand dollars if he could locate Clyde and arrange to have a number of weapons planted in the prison farm compound.[38]

On Friday evening, January 12, 1934, after wandering around West Dallas for the better part of two days, James Mullens finally located Floyd Hamilton's house, hoping to contact Barrow through him.

After introducing himself as Jimmy LaMont, the decrepit ex-con accompanied Hamilton to a deserted road near Irving, ten miles west of Dallas. After several minutes' wait, a black V-8 drew alongside Hamilton's car. Bonnie and Clyde were inside, staring intently at the man seated next to Floyd. No doubt Barrow was wondering what was going on when he finally recognized the shriveled-up addict transferring from Floyd's car to his own. Mullens was just about the last person on earth he wanted to see. For the next several minutes Barrow sat in stony silence as Mullens and Hamilton outlined the plan.[39]

"Ray wants you to plant at least two .45s in a drainage ditch culvert about seventy-five feet from Eastham's main building," Floyd said. "Aubrey will fetch the guns and bring them inside."[40]

Barrow said nothing, playing with the safety catch on his Browning automatic rifle. He already knew the plan, having collaborated with Ralph Fults on its design nearly three years earlier. He also knew it would work. However, three things bothered him: Ray's big mouth, the memory of Hamilton's refusal to help with the raid in 1932, and James Mullens.

"Raymond's doing time for you," Floyd added.

Clyde said nothing. Every time he looked at Mullens, wheezing in the back seat, he grew angrier. "OK," the killer said. "I'll help you out, but I want Mullens to plant the guns himself."[41] Barrow, convinced that Mullens was setting a trap for him, wanted no part of the deal unless the addict was willing to take a front row in the action.

Mullens stiffened up. "I'm not doing that alone," he said, turning to Floyd. "You're coming with me!"[42] Reluctantly, Hamilton agreed.

Two hours before dawn on Sunday, January 14, Bonnie and Clyde delivered Floyd Hamilton and a trembling James Mullens to a point

Calhoun Ferry Road bridge, near Eastham, 1994. On January 16, 1934, the getaway car was parked to the left of the bridge. Bonnie remained in the car, ready to blow the horn, while Clyde and James Mullens hiked up the creek beyond the bridge and waited for Eastham's prison work crews to arrive. (Photo by John Neal Phillips.)

less than a mile from the main prison compound of Eastham Camp 1. Floyd and Mullens emerged from the car carrying a bound rubber inner tube. Inside the tube were a pair of army-issue Colt .45 automatics. After traversing the thick pine forest between the road and the Camp 1 compound, the two men quickly placed the inner tube beneath the culvert[43] near the woodpile and exited through the brightly lit prison yard, crawling on their hands and knees to the main road, beyond which Bonnie and Clyde waited.[44] Floyd Hamilton was driven back to Dallas. Mullens was forced to stay with Parker and Barrow.

At 6:00 A.M. on January 16, 1934, a black Ford V-8 coupe slipped quietly through the blanket of dense fog rising from the nearby Trinity River.[45] With lights extinguished, the Ford turned southwest from the Trinity-Weldon Road onto the Calhoun Ferry Road, eventually gliding to a stop just beyond a narrow bridge. Barrow and Mullens stepped into the damp morning air with loaded BARs tucked under their arms. Turning their collars to the knife-like chill of the breeze, the men tramped through a nearby clump of trees, hugging the banks of a narrow, muddy creek. Beyond the creek, a stark, wet field loomed, its opposite end shrouded in a damp, filmy haze. Barrow and Mullens waited.

At 7:00 A.M. Barrow detected movement beyond the dull outline of several large brush piles. The ghost-like images of a line of prisoners slowly materialized in the distance. The white denim of their prison uniforms glowed with an eerie radiance. Darker forms, bearing weapons, accompanied the line. Beyond them, spread out along the fog-covered timberline, a handful of mounted guards loomed. Barrow and Mullens cocked their weapons and crouched in the gully. Soon the field was covered with prison work crews, each preparing to clear the land for the spring planting.

Guard Olan Bozeman had already noticed something amiss. Raymond Hamilton had moved from his own squad and joined Palmer, Methvin, and Bybee in another group.[46] The guard chose not to take any action, however, until the squad had moved into the field. He then called for a mounted guard to hold a gun on the offender so that he could be whipped with a trace chain, something Hamilton had counted on.[47] At that point his squad was less than a hundred feet from the creek where Barrow and Mullens were hidden.

Major Joseph Crowson, who had reportedly beaten Joe Palmer repeatedly in the past, answered Bozeman's call. While Bozeman conversed with the twenty-four-year-old Crowson, Palmer strolled up as if to ask a question. He turned to Crowson, leveled his weapon, and fired a single round into the guard's stomach,[48] knocking him from the horse. Bozeman dropped the barrel of his shotgun and pulled the trigger. Joe ducked just as a charge of buckshot sailed past his head, a lone pellet creasing his temple. Palmer fired two shots, tearing the shotgun from the guard's hands and wounding him in the hip.[49]

Raymond fired one shot, then the clip popped from its housing and tumbled to the sloshy ground.[50] Virtually disarmed, Hamilton watched helplessly as Joe fought it out alone, felling the two guards in a matter of seconds. Barrow and Mullens then reared up and fired a volley above the heads of the startled men in the field. While guards and prisoners alike were diving on their stomachs, Hamilton, Palmer, Methvin, and Bybee ran for the gully and the road beyond. Waiting in the getaway car, Bonnie sounded the horn, using it as a beacon for the fleeing men.[51] Three guards started running as fast as they could in the opposite direction, leaving their squads unguarded.[52] Taking advantage of this, J. B. French, two squads down from Bozeman's, slipped quietly into the forest and made his way to the Trinity River on foot. He was recaptured the following day without ever meeting the men responsible for his brief taste of freedom.

"Nobody but Raymond and Palmer can get in the car," Mullens called out, as the group scrambled up to the waiting V-8. "Everybody else go back."

"Shut your damned mouth, Mullens," Clyde snapped. "This is my car. I'm handling this. Three of you can ride back there; guess four of us can make it up here."[53] As the distant whine of prison sirens filled the otherwise calm morning air, Barrow shifted to first and sped away. Three and a half years after its conception, the Eastham raid, though modified and scaled down was at last a reality.

Roadblocks sprang up in nearly every town between Crockett and Dallas, but Barrow outflanked them all by leaving the road and driving cross-country through farm after farm. Barrow, it seemed, could not be stopped. Reaching Hillsboro, Clyde stopped for gas. The attendant spoke excitedly as he serviced the getaway vehicle.

"Did you hear about Raymond Hamilton escaping from prison?" he asked.

"No," replied Barrow, "really?"

"Yeh!" exclaimed the attendant. "Clyde and Bonnie just walked right into the dining room this morning and took Ray out while everybody was eating!"[54]

As they fled from Texas, the outlaws switched vehicles often. Inside one car, stolen in Fayetteville, Arkansas, Bonnie found a pair of dolls hanging from the dash. When Barrow stopped for gas outside of Joplin, Bonnie spotted two little girls playing near the pumps. She called them over to the car and gave them each a doll.[55]

From Joplin the caravan continued on to Iowa, passing within a few miles of Dexfield Park as they sped toward Rembrandt, in the far northwest corner of the state. Palmer, Methvin, and Bybee had previously agreed to help Raymond raise the one thousand dollars owed to James Mullens by robbing a bank as soon after the break as possible.

Joe Palmer, who suffered from asthma, bleeding ulcers, and possibly tuberculosis, was very ill when the bandits rolled into town. Too weak to sit up or even participate in the robbery, he slept on the floorboard in the back seat of the car while Raymond and Bybee went inside the bank. Despite this, Barrow insisted that Joe be given an equal share of the thirty-eight-hundred-dollar haul. Bybee and Methvin readily agreed to the idea, but Raymond objected. Clyde was nevertheless adamant, and Hamilton finally had to give in.[56]

Shortly after the Rembrandt heist Bybee struck out on his own. On January 30, however, he was recaptured in Amarillo, Texas, and whisked back to Eastham. The remaining members of the so-called Barrow gang drove to Houston. There Joe Palmer gave a large sum of money to a local attorney for the purpose of literally buying a parole for an Eastham building tender named Wade. Palmer held a grudge against Wade, a vicious trustee who, like the building tender Clyde had killed, delighted in the torture and beating of his fellow inmates. His treachery had resulted in many severe whippings for Palmer. Joe meant to even the score, but that would come later.[57]

Thirty miles north of Marshall, Wade was shot to death and left in the woods.[58] Palmer drew a map and mailed it to Harry McCormick. The attached note read, "One of the [Texas] prison system's worst rats could be found [there]."

From Houston, Barrow, Palmer, and the others drove north. Ray began complaining that things would be much better if he were running the show. Palmer, whose condition had worsened, was in no mood for one of Ray's soliloquies. Palmer despised Hamilton. He knew him to be an informant at Eastham.[59]

"Punk blabber-mouth braggart," Palmer suddenly said to Ray, staring at him.[60] Ray turned red but he did not reply. Palmer pulled the covers over his head and tried to rest. Minutes later Hamilton drew a pistol, as if to shoot the sleeping Joe Palmer. Barrow, apparently expecting such a move, reached in the back seat and slapped Ray across the face.[61]

In the scuffle Clyde missed a curve in the road and drove straight into a ditch, breaking one of the car's wheels. He had to steal another vehicle to replace the wrecked machine. In Joplin, Barrow pulled up to the Conner Hotel and let Palmer out of the car. Joe was feeling worse and did not think he could stand another minute of Raymond Hamilton. With a promise to return in four to six weeks, Barrow and the others departed.

Shortly thereafter Hamilton decided to bring a friend of his own into the group. True to form, his choice of companions proved questionable. Even Ray's brother did not think much of Mary O'Dare, characterizing her as a "prostitute" and "gold digger" with enough makeup caked on her face "to grow a crop."[62] Her first husband, Gene O'Dare, was serving ninety-nine years for his part in the Carmen State Bank robbery. Barrow took one look at the newcomer and cringed—making his displeasure clear enough by snubbing the nineteen-year-old girl whenever possible. Bonnie and Henry also resented Mary, calling her "washerwoman" to her face.[63] They had good reason. She once tried to persuade Bonnie to give Clyde knockout drops, steal his money, and leave him stranded.[64] She even suggested killing Clyde while he slept and collecting the reward. Moreover, according to a letter from Barrow to Hamilton, Mary was strongly suspected of trying to slip away from the group and arrange an ambush. Apparently because of Bonnie's insistence that she always accompany Mary during any absences from the gang, the plan was thwarted. In turn, Parker, Barrow, and Methvin discussed killing Mary O'Dare.[65]

Ironically, over the years many incidents involving Mary have been incorrectly attributed to either Bonnie or Blanche—adding fuel to the already unquenchable fires of folklore surrounding the two. Bonnie's supposed promiscuity was actually one of Mary's traits. Whenever Raymond Hamilton was away, she would invariably throw herself at the next available man.

In addition, a scene from a popular 1967 movie depicts a rift between Buck and Clyde over the division of stolen money, a rift supposedly instigated by Blanche. The movie also implies that Blanche vindictively

Gene and Mary O'Dare, 1932. Gene robbed banks with Raymond Hamilton. Mary became Hamilton's lover. Clyde Barrow despised Mary, calling her "washerwoman." (Courtesy of Cecil Mayes.)

aided in the ambush of Bonnie and Clyde. In reality, there was never an altercation between the Barrow brothers, and, rather than aid her captors, in Iowa Blanche actually impeded the investigation by volunteering false and misleading information concerning the identity of W. D. Jones and the whereabouts of Bonnie and Clyde. Finally, as we shall see, it was Mary O'Dare, not Blanche, who demanded a share of stolen money and later offered information leading to the arrest of her lover, Raymond Hamilton. Regardless, for the time being Mary stuck like glue to the group, adding momentum to the ever-widening division between Barrow and Hamilton.

On Tuesday, February 20, Clyde and Ray were able to put their differences aside long enough to raid the National Guard Armory at Ranger, Texas, where they loaded a large quantity of Browning automatic rifles, Colt .45 automatic pistols, and ammunition into the rear of their stolen V-8. On Tuesday morning, February 27, a Chevy sedan and Ford V-8 were seen moving at a leisurely pace along the old Wilmer-Seagoville Road in far south Dallas County. One mile west of the Trinity River bridge, between Gravel Slough and Cottonwood Creek, the cars pulled over. Bonnie got behind the wheel of the new Ford while Mary stretched out on the back seat for a snooze. Clyde and Ray joined Henry in the Chevrolet sedan for the short run into Lancaster, sixteen miles south of Dallas.[66]

At 11:50 A.M. Methvin drove up to the side entrance of the R. P. Henry and Sons Bank, standing one block east of the main square. Clyde, wearing a light grey Stetson hat, stepped to the sidewalk to survey the noon-hour scene. He had a tiny sawed-off shotgun concealed beneath his brown-and-grey-checked overcoat.[67] Ray, bareheaded, quickly joined him on the pavement. He had a blue steel revolver tucked neatly in the pocket of his fine grey coat.[68] It was a cold, blustery day, and the outlaws turned their collars against the chill wind as they stepped around to the front of the bank. Ollie Worley, a laborer for the WPA, was inside the bank cashing his twenty-seven-dollar government paycheck when he noticed a nicely dressed pair of young men step briskly through the low, swinging doors that led behind the teller's cage.

"Bank examiners," he thought to himself, watching cashier L. L. Henry snap two tens, two ones, and a five from the cash drawer. Without a word, Clyde Barrow reached past the cashier and snatched Worley's money with his left hand. The laborer looked first to Barrow, then to Hamilton, who casually pulled a large, blue-steel revolver from the pocket of his overcoat. The frightened man thought it was the biggest gun he had ever seen, an endless length of barrel emerging from Raymond's pocket.[69]

"OK," Barrow said quietly, "everybody get on the floor." Four of the five persons present responded immediately, sinking to the cold tile floor without resistance. Apparently, however, E. D. Brooks, an elderly gentleman of considerable financial means, failed to understand what was taking place.[70]

"What?" he asked. "What are we doing?"

"We have to get on the floor, Mr. Brooks," said Worley.

The old man remained standing.

"Say, old man," snapped Barrow, "you'd better get down."

"What are those two young men doing back there?" Brooks asked, oblivious to Clyde's command.

"Please, Mr. Brooks," L. L. Henry cried, "please get down."

"Get down?" asked Brooks.

"Yes, Mr. Brooks . . . get down on the floor."

"Why should I get on the floor?" he asked.

At that point, Worley reached up and grabbed Brooks by the collar, pulling him to the floor.

"Hey!" Brooks protested.

"Get down here," Worley said.

"How come?" Brooks inquired.

"It's a robbery!" answered Worley.

"What robbery?" asked Brooks. "Is somebody being robbed?"[71]

The old man was still mumbling as Raymond picked up all the money behind the cashier's cage and stuffed it into a large paper sack. He then motioned for L. L. Henry to open the safe, which he did. Hamilton disappeared inside the vault while Barrow kept a silent vigil over the captives sprawled on the floor. The muffled sound of the old man's voice occasionally echoed through the lobby. Seconds later Hamilton stepped from the vault, his sack bulging with currency.

"Open that door," commanded Barrow, pointing to the side entrance. Henry grabbed his keys and unlocked the door. As the two gunmen started to leave, Clyde turned to Worley. The bandit still had the laborer's twenty-seven dollars clutched in his left hand.

"You worked like hell for this, didn't you?" Barrow asked quietly.

Worley looked up and nodded. "Yes sir," he answered, "digging ditches along Pleasant Run Road."

"Here," the bandit replied, handing Worley the cash. "We don't want your money. We just want the bank's."[72]

A grateful Ollie Worley accepted the money from Clyde Barrow's hand. He gazed in disbelief as the vicious outlaw stepped calmly through the side door where Raymond Hamilton and an unidentified third man waited in a big black Chevy.

"Now, what was them nice fellers doing behind the counter?" asked

Barrow-Fults-Hamilton Sites in the Dallas-Fort Worth Area, 1925–1935

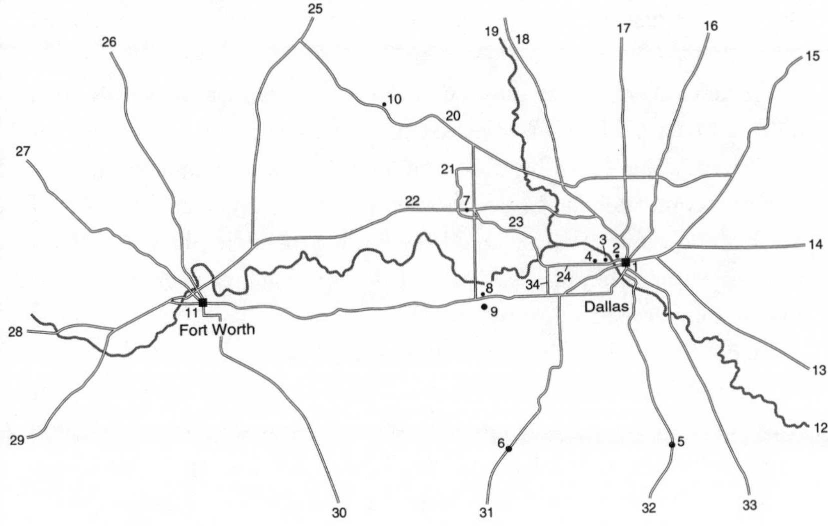

Redrawn from 1930 map, courtesy of the Dallas Public Library, Texas/Dallas History Department.

1. Downtown Dallas
2. Nuehoff Meat Packing Plant
3. 507 County Avenue, West Dallas, Davis murder
4. Star Service Station, West Dallas
5. Lancaster, Barrow-Hamilton-Methvin bank robbery
6. Cedar Hill, Hamilton bank robberies
7. Sowers, attempted ambush of Bonnie and Clyde
8. Car hijacking following Sowers ambush
9. Hensley Field
10. Grapevine, Wheeler, and Murphy murders
11. East Belknap train yard, Fort Worth, Hamilton capture
12. Trinity River
13. Highway 40, to Kaufman
14. U.S. 80 East (Samuell Road)
15. Garland Road, to Farmersville
16. U.S. 75 North, to McKinney
17. Preston Road, to Celina
18. Denton Road
19. Elm Fork of the Trinity River
20. Northwest Highway, to Grapevine
21. Esters Road
22. State Highway 15 (North Fort Worth Pike)
23. Irving Road
24. Eagle Ford Road, West Dallas
25. To Denton
26. To Decatur
27. Jacksboro Road
28. U.S. 80 West
29. Stephenville Road
30. To Mansfield
31. To Cleburne
32. To Austin
33. U.S. 75 South to Houston
34. Chalk Hill Road, Cement City

old Mr. Brooks as Worley and Henry helped him to his feet. No one bothered to answer.

Roy Worley, one of Ollie Worley's cousins, happened to be hauling a load of gravel from Hutchins to Cedar Hill that day. Like his cousin, Roy was enrolled in the WPA, transporting road materials for five dollars a day. He had just turned west onto Pleasant Run Road when he spotted a brand new Chevrolet racing toward him from Lancaster.

Worley pulled over to the side of the road as the Chevrolet rounded a distant curve. The car's wheels slanted at a forty-five degree angle as the "knee action" assembly absorbed the full force of a high-speed turn. A split second later the Chevy zoomed past the gravel truck in a blur of black and chrome. Worley could see but one man clearly, so brief was the encounter. A blond youth, sat in front, his fine gray overcoat caught in a momentary shaft of sunlight.

"School kids," Roy thought to himself.[73]

The theft had netted Barrow and Hamilton $4,176, according to at least three sources.[74] After making the switch to the Ford sedan, the outlaws drove to the Oklahoma line. Raymond, seated in the back with Mary and the guns, wanted to start dividing the loot. Barrow agreed. Hamilton went to work, splitting the money into three equal parts.

"What about me?" asked Mary.

"You get nothing," snapped Barrow.

Raymond slid a handful of cash onto Mary's lap. Clyde, who had been watching everything carefully in the rear-view mirror, was enraged. He pulled over and searched Hamilton, finding an extra six-hundred dollars on him.

"Ditch Mary right now, or get out," Barrow snapped.[75]

Ray took Mary and left.[76]

Barrow said nothing. He could not have been more pleased. He was finally rid of the hated "washerwoman."

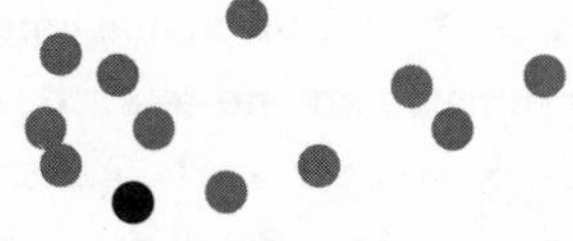

Death in the Morning

Initial reports of the raid at Eastham spread like wildfire through the corridors of Huntsville's main prison unit. Rumors grew, greatly embellished with inflated accounts of those left maimed and murdered in Clyde Barrow's rampage. Ralph Fults recalled hearing that a dozen or more guards were thought to have been killed, with many others injured. Tales that Bonnie and Clyde had driven straight into Eastham's main compound, weapons blazing, were rampant. However, as the morning progressed, the true story began to surface, and Ralph began to recognize some of the details of the raid he had helped to plan so long ago.

For some unknown reason Aubrey failed to get away from the barracks in time to join in the escape. However, when it was learned that Raymond, Henry, Joe, and Bybee had disappeared into the foggy morning, Fults smiled quietly.

The delivery of Raymond Hamilton from the toughest, most inaccessible prison farm in the state caught General Manager Lee Simmons, and indeed everyone connected with the Texas prison system, by complete surprise. The newspapers soon filled with speculation as to why a confirmed incorrigible like Hamilton could be exposed to the temptation of executing such an escape. Soon legislative wrath exploded, fueled by the immense publicity generated by the very mention of Clyde

Barrow's name.[1]

Simmons was profoundly embarrassed. Upon taking office, he had vowed to keep politics out of prison management. The events of that foggy winter morning signaled an end to such tactics, bringing the full weight of state government to bear on the general manager's shoulders. Moreover, fewer than twenty-four hours after the prison break matters were further complicated by the death of Major Crowson, the Eastham guard who had ridden straight into the muzzle of Joe Palmer's gun. Simmons quickly reacted to the overall situation by firing the three guards who had deserted their squads in the face of Barrow's challenge,[2] thereby appeasing the growling legislative body in Austin. He then turned his considerable energies to the task of "resettling accounts"[3] with Raymond Hamilton, Joe Palmer, and, in particular, Clyde Barrow.

On February 1, Simmons drove to Austin to meet with a retired Texas Ranger named Frank Hamer.[4] He delivered to Hamer a commission in the Highway Patrol and told him to eliminate Bonnie and Clyde. On February 10, Hamer took to the road, using Dallas as his base of operation. Within nine days the ex-ranger had reason to believe one of Clyde Barrow's trusted friends was ready to sell out,[5] something Barrow had long suspected would happen.[6]

"I know somebody'll be putting me on the spot soon," Clyde said on more than one occasion. "I can't see living much longer." On March 10, 1934, during a family gathering at a cemetery near Lancaster, Texas, Barrow tried in vain to convince Bonnie to give herself up and thus avoid the same fate that awaited him. Bonnie refused to consider the idea. "When my time comes," she said, "I want to be with you."

Several days later Raymond Hamilton returned to Texas. On March 19 he and his brother Floyd robbed the Grand Prairie State Bank of $1543.74.[7] On March 31 Raymond, accompanied by Mary O'Dare, stole $1867.74 from the State National Bank of West, Texas.[8] Minutes after the West robbery, the bandits' getaway car slid into a muddy embankment. Mary and Ray were thrown against the dash and windshield. Hamilton broke his nose. O'Dare was cut about the face. When a passing motorist, Mrs. Cam Gunter, stopped to help, Ray pulled a gun. He and Mary forced their way into Gunter's car and made her accompany them on an all-night drive through East Texas, arriving in Houston the next morning.

"I'm going to find us a new car to steal," Ray announced, turning to his captive. "When I get one, we'll let you go."[9]

Hamilton then handed the young woman a sum of money. "I'm sorry about messing up your car. Maybe this'll cover expenses."[10]

The trio then drove around for quite some time before spotting a suitable getaway car—a new Ford V-8 parked in a driveway. Ray casually stepped up to the unattended sedan. Soon it and Ray were both gone, the bright yellow wheels of the car catching a shaft of morning sunlight as they rounded the corner.

Mary had Mrs. Gunter follow Hamilton for several blocks. O'Dare's hand gripped a small .32 caliber blue steel revolver. Suddenly, just as both vehicles rolled up to a stop sign, Mary jumped from the Gunter car, ran up to the freshly stolen V-8, and climbed in next to Ray. Hamilton then turned the corner and sped past a row of white frame houses. Mrs. Gunter sat on the corner, numb with relief. Though intrigued by her captors, she was nonetheless glad to be rid of the pair. It was 9:30 A.M. on April 1, 1934, Easter Sunday.[11]

While newspapers across the state were speculating about the identity of Raymond Hamilton's red-headed accomplice, some saying it was Bonnie Parker,[12] the real Bonnie Parker was playing with a pet rabbit on an unpaved side road overlooking Texas State Highway 114,[13] five and a half miles northwest of Grapevine. She had been there since 10:30 A.M., waiting with Clyde Barrow and Henry Methvin for a number of relatives and friends, including, amazingly, Raymond Hamilton and Mary O'Dare, to arrive for an Easter visit.[14] The rabbit was to be a gift for Bonnie's mother.

Joe Palmer, who rejoined the group shortly after Raymond's exit, had earlier thumbed a ride to Dallas to alert the Barrows and Parkers as to the location of the meeting.[15] Palmer went to Emma Parker's house at 232 Eighth Street, but he found no one home. He then dropped in on the Barrows but found only old Henry, diligently attending to his customers at the Star Service Station. Palmer decided to wait.

North of Grapevine, Bonnie, Clyde, and Henry also waited, basking in the sunny spring weather. The rabbit hopped leisurely beside the road, munching blades of grass and playing quietly. Methvin sat alone. Barrow was stretched out on the back seat of the car.[16]

At approximately half past three in the afternoon, Bonnie happened to look toward the highway. Three highway patrolmen were cruising slowly past the entrance to the dirt road, traveling northwest on 114. They took a long look at the black V-8 with canary yellow wheels and then split up. Two of the officers, E. B. Wheeler and H. D. Murphy, made a wide circle on their motorcycles, as if to turn around. The third patrolman, Polk Ivy, continued on toward Roanoke.[17]

Bonnie collected the rabbit and walked casually back to the car to wake Clyde. Barrow rubbed his eyes and peered through the windshield at the two approaching lawmen. With a sawed-off shotgun concealed behind him, he slipped from the back seat and took up a position behind the open car door. Methvin, already aware of the officers, gripped a Browning automatic rifle.

"Let's take them," said Clyde as the cyclists drew within twenty-five feet of the car. Barrow, remembering the days of Ralph Fults and W. D. Jones, meant to catch the unsuspecting officers off guard and take them hostage. Methvin, however, thought otherwise. Misunderstanding the command, he raised his weapon.[18]

Out on the highway Mr. and Mrs. Fred Giggal of Dallas were taking advantage of the beautiful day to roam the countryside by car. They had been following three highway patrolmen for several miles when they noticed two of them break away and turn up a side road. Amid jokes about getting pulled over on such a nice Easter day, the Giggals passed the dirt road. They caught a brief glimpse of the motorcycles moving slowly toward a big black car with yellow wheels. Then they heard a succession of loud explosions. Thinking at first the sounds were merely backfires, the Giggals drove on. Not far down the road, however, they decided to turn around and take a look.[19]

Grapevine farmer William Schieffer, whose property adjoined the unpaved side road, was standing on the front porch of his house quite a distance from the car when the explosions shattered the country silence. He had seen the highway patrolmen approach the black Ford with the yellow wheels. Unlike the Giggals, however, he knew instantly the sounds were not backfires.

E. B. Wheeler, twenty-six, was in front of his twenty-two-year-old partner, H. D. Murphy. It was obvious to Clyde that neither lawman sensed any danger—their side arms were plainly holstered. When Wheeler drew within ten feet of the car, Barrow started to leap into view and get the drop on both officers. To his surprise, however, Methvin opened fire, striking Wheeler in the chest with a line of steel-jacketed slugs.

Murphy, serving his first day in the patrol force, watched in horror as the four-year veteran fell bloodied and lifeless from the seat of his bike. Bringing his motorcycle to a halt, the lone officer dismounted, fished two shotgun shells from his pocket, and started to reach for the sawed-off shotgun strapped to the rear fender of his machine.[20] At first hesitant, Barrow saw that the patrolman intended to fight and raised his weapon, squeezing off three rounds. When the smoke cleared, both lawmen were lying in the dirt.

The Giggals managed to get turned around just as the shooting stopped. The couple strained to see through a line of trees as they approached the intersection. They spotted two armed men standing over the dead and dying motorcycle patrolmen. Easing up to the entrance of the dirt road, the Dallasites then saw "the taller of the two men," Henry Methvin, fire several shots into the limp, prostrate body of H. D. Murphy. The "smaller man," Clyde Barrow, noticed the Giggals and started walking rapidly toward the car; the tall man followed close behind. Fred Giggal quickly turned his vehicle around and sped away.[21]

News of the slayings cast a sense of gloom over an otherwise beautiful Easter Sunday. An outcry of public rage and indignation followed the police announcement that a set of fingerprints, lifted from a whiskey bottle found at the scene of the shooting, were tentatively identified as Clyde Barrow's. In fact, only a thumbprint was found, and it was later identified by Tarrant County Bertillon experts as belonging to Henry Methvin.[22] Regardless, headlines and editorials carried one theme: "Get Clyde Barrow." Sheriff Schmid would say, "[Barrow] is not a man; he's an animal. . . . [H]e sleeps in the open like a coyote."[23]

Clyde Barrow, left, and Henry Methvin, "the taller of two men," as described by two eyewitnesses to the 1934 Grapevine killings. (Courtesy Marie Barrow.)

Others referred to Barrow as "eel-like."

L. G. Phares, superintendent of the Highway Patrol, posted a thousand dollar reward for "the dead bodies of the Grapevine slayers."[24] Governor Ferguson backed the offer with an additional five-hundred dollars for each killer brought in "dead or alive." As events continued to unfold, the media began to focus its attention on lawmen and lawmakers alike, charging the courts with too much leniency and the police with ineffectiveness.[25] The Texas Rangers were cited as virtually "destroyed by politics . . . a $100,000 waste of the taxpayer's money." One political cartoon appearing in the *Dallas Evening Journal* on April 3 depicts a lawman named "Two-Gun Tex." He is sitting up in bed with a quizzical look on his face. Beneath his mattress hide a jumbled mass of bank robbers and murderers, their machine guns jutting out in all directions. "Two-Gun Tex" is scratching his head and wondering aloud, "Seems to me, I keep forgetting something I should do!"[26]

Following the killing of Wheeler and Murphy, the outlaw trio drove north, presumably to find Joe Palmer, who immediately fled Dallas. At 2:30 A.M. on April 6, they arrived in the industrial mining district of northeastern Oklahoma. The area, one of Clyde's favorites, was rugged, sparsely populated and not far from two neighboring states. Just south of Commerce the Barrow gang turned west from Highway 66 and crossed the railroad tracks. Approximately a quarter of a mile down the road, between the Lost Trail Mine and the Crab Apple Mine, Clyde turned the V-8 around and pulled over.[27] For the rest of the night the three travelers took turns watching the road and sleeping.

Between nine and ten in the morning, thirty-five-year-old Commerce City Marshall Percy Boyd received a complaint that a car full of drunks was parked outside of town.[28] Drunks were sometimes unruly, so Boyd contacted Constable Cal Campbell, and together the two men drove out to the mining district just west of Highway 66. Barrow was still half asleep when he noticed the suspicious-looking city car crossing the railroad tracks. He cranked the big V-8 engine and let it idle quietly as the car approached.

Boyd and Campbell, expecting to find a group of party-goers merely sleeping off a heavy night, eased up in front of the strange Ford sedan and casually stepped from their car. They had walked about ten feet when the V-8 suddenly took off in reverse. The lawmen watched the car back away at high speed.[29]

Barrow hoped to get far enough down the road to turn around and escape to the west. One hundred yards down the line, however, he momentarily lost control of the wheel and veered into a muddy ditch—the rear wheels sinking up to the rims. Seeing this, Campbell and Boyd hurried back to their own vehicle.

Clyde grabbed a BAR, cocked it, and jumped from the sedan. Campbell and Boyd were just about to get in their car when Barrow began firing a few rounds above their heads, hoping to scare the country cops into surrendering. Both lawmen responded by drawing their weapons and returning the fire. Barrow lowered the muzzle and fired again. Boyd was grazed on the head and knocked down. Campbell continued firing.

Methvin, who was sound asleep when the action commenced, took the remaining rifle, tumbled out of the car, and blazed away at the sixty-three year-old man. Campbell toppled to the ground, a massive hole in his midsection.[30]

"Bring them up," said Clyde, turning to Henry.

Methvin hurried over to the stricken lawmen and made a quick examination of their condition. Campbell was not moving; a thick puddle of blood collected beneath him. Methvin stepped over to Boyd, who was moaning and beginning to stir.

"Get up and come with me," Henry ordered, poking the barrel of his BAR in the marshall's face. Boyd pulled himself to his feet and raised his hands.

"Hurry up," snapped Henry. "We are going to take you with us."[31]

Methvin then escorted the dazed prisoner back to the V-8. By then Clyde had commandeered another car and a rope from a nearby farmhouse and was trying to pull his own vehicle from the ditch. Bonnie, bright red dress glowing in the morning sun, sat behind the wheel of the sedan while Clyde pulled the thick rope with the second car. Methvin stood guard while Boyd got down in the ditch and tried to push the trapped vehicle to dry ground. At that moment a man named Jack Boydson crossed the railroad tracks, heading west. Seeing Campbell lying in the middle of the road, Boydson put his car in reverse and tried to back away from the scene. Before he could do so, however, Barrow bailed out of the commandeered car and ran over to him. Methvin followed.

"Get out of there and help us get this car out of that ditch," commanded Clyde. The terrified man did exactly as he was told, joining Boyd in the mud. Barrow returned to the second car and made another attempt to liberate the faster, more durable Ford. But the rope gave way. Frustrated, Clyde decided to try and push the car out of the ditch. He and Methvin stood in the road and flagged down seven or eight vehicles, forcing the bewildered occupants to lend a hand.

"Boys," Barrow announced, "one good man has already been killed, and if you don't obey orders, others are liable to be."[32]

Soon the area was ringed with local residents and employees from the neighboring mines. Aroused by the gunshots and shouting in the road, the people stood just out of range, observing the drama unfolding before them. For several minutes the dozen or so men pushed and tugged on the bandits' car, but to no avail. The rear wheels merely buried themselves deeper in the muck. Clyde was just about to give up. Just as he decided to take one of the other vehicles that clogged the road, a truck happened along. The two gun-wielding desperadoes motioned for driver, Charley Dodson, to pull over.

"You got a chain?" Clyde called out. Dodson nodded. "Hook it up to this car, here, and pull it out of the ditch," Barrow ordered.

Dodson got out, looped one end of a trace chain around the bumper of the V-8, and tied the other end to the frame of his truck. To Clyde's relief the Ford rolled easily from the shallow ravine.

"Get in back," said Clyde to Boyd.

The wounded marshall climbed in, and Methvin moved in beside him. Barrow waited for Bonnie to slide over to the passenger side, then took the wheel. There were so many cars and people in the road that it was difficult for the killer to get the sedan turned around. Finally, with the help of his reluctant road crew Barrow managed to turn west and drive away.[33]

At first Boyd was unable to identify his captors. For quite some time he sat in silence, looking first at Clyde and at the great arsenal strewn about the car, then at Bonnie. He asked Methvin if the couple in the front seat were Bonnie and Clyde. Methvin nodded. Boyd then decided that Methvin was Raymond Hamilton.[34] He started talking to the fugitives, in particular to Bonnie. Strangely, as the day progressed, he developed a fondness for her. Her reaction was reciprocal. Soon even Clyde warmed up to the officer, treating and bandaging his head wound and replacing his bloodied shirt with a fresh one. Barrow was impressed by the lawman's demeanor. He would later say that Boyd displayed "more real guts" than anyone he had ever met. Of Barrow the officer said, "He is the coolest operator I ever saw."[35]

In Ft. Scott, Kansas, Clyde pulled up to a country store. It was well after dark, and everyone in the car was hungry. Methvin went inside and ordered four hot dinners. While he waited, a paper filled with headlines about the Oklahoma battle caught his eye. He took the plate dinners, grabbed a copy of the paper, and hurried back to the car. Clyde scanned the paper.

"I'm sorry about shooting the old man," he said, handing the paper to Boyd.[36] He would say no more. Eight miles north of town Clyde stopped the car.

"OK," he said, turning to Boyd, "we'll let you out here." The marshall opened the door and stepped to the pavement.

"Now, you wait till we get over that hill, there, before you take off," Barrow added, passing Boyd a ten-dollar bill. "We usually tie them up, but I know you'll do as you're told. Now, take this for the bus and be sure to see a doctor."[37] Boyd nodded.

"Bonnie," he asked. "What do you want me to tell the press?"

"Tell them I don't smoke cigars!" she answered.[38]

Barrow released the clutch and took off. In less than a minute the taillights of the car were disappearing beyond a distant hill, the rumble of the engine fading into the night.

Bonnie and Clyde had been using an abandoned farmhouse, ten miles south of Gibsland, Louisiana, as a hideout. According to historian Carroll Y. Rich, the house had been the boyhood home of a man named Otis Cole.[39] No one had lived in the rambling, four-bedroom bungalow in four years, but much of the furniture still remained. Despite this, the solid pier-and-beam structure, with its typically rural "dog-walk" and corrugated tin roof, was seldom if ever visited. Consequently, the property appealed to the outlaws. There they could swim, fish, and roam the peaceful forests together, well hidden from the probing eyes of curious neighbors.

Rich maintains that Otis Cole never consented to the occupation of his parents' house. However, many others, including the Barrow family, Ted Hinton, and Billie Parker have all said that Clyde Barrow, posing as an independent logger, purchased the Cole place.[40] Regardless of ownership, it was well known that the small, well-dressed strangers in Bienville Parish were not a young lumberjack and his wife, but, in fact, were Bonnie and Clyde.[41]

Following Percy Boyd's release, Bonnie and Clyde returned to their north Louisiana hideout. After a few days rest they were back on the road. In Memphis, Tennessee, Bonnie bought a new suit for Joe Palmer,[42] who was still separated from the group in the wake of the Grapevine killings. She planned to give it to him the next time they met. Clyde bought a brand new service revolver for Percy Boyd, whose weapon had been lost during his abduction.[43] How Barrow planned to deliver the gun is not known, but one way or another he was going to save the lawman the added expense of having to replace his property.

Back on the road, Barrow's thoughts began to focus rather angrily on Raymond Hamilton and the nationwide publication of a letter from Hamilton to his lawyer, A. S. Baskett, disavowing any allegiance to Barrow. Hamilton had written:

Dear Mr. Baskett,

I am sending you a bill for the hotel I was staying in at the time of that killing in Commerce, Oklahoma. I haven't been with Clyde and

Bonnie and Clyde, 1934. A picture they never saw, from unprocessed film recovered after their deaths. (Courtesy of Ken M. Holmes, Jr.)

Bonnie since the Lancaster bank robbery. I'm sending you $100 and want this put before public and proved right away. I'm sending you more money just as soon as I find out you are doing what I ask. I'm putting also my fingerprint on this bill. I'm also leaving a letter at this hotel for you. You can call for it. My fingerprint will be there when you call for it. You know I try to keep my promise. I want you to let the public and the whole world know I am not with Clyde Barrow, and don't go his speed. I'm a lone man and intend to stay that way. I wrote Mrs. M. A. Ferguson but I guess it was in vain. I was in Houston the night of April 4 and have been here (New Orleans) ever since April fifth.

Yours truly,
Raymond Hamilton[44]

"The rat," said Barrow, as he read the newspaper headlines. "He's just trying to cover his own butt. I'm going to kill him." Barrow spent weeks searching for Hamilton. He meant to find him and shoot him down.

Once while driving in central Texas, Barrow thought he saw his former companion approaching in the distance. He stopped his car and got out, a Browning automatic rifle raised to his shoulder. At the last second he realized the occupant of the other car was not Hamilton. He lowered his weapon and let the car pass.[45] Barrow did not know it, but he would never get the chance to face Raymond Hamilton.

Broke, ragged, and sunburned, Hamilton had been riding the suspension cables of a boxcar for nearly two weeks. He had parted company with Mary O'Dare in New Orleans to minimize detection. Along the way the bandit became chummy with a Wichita Falls hobo named Teddy.[46] Somehow, Ray convinced him to assist in the daylight robbery of the First National Bank in Lewisville, thirty miles north of Dallas. At 2:45 P.M. on April 25 Hamilton and Teddy drove up to the front door of the bank in a stolen car. Dressed in a dirty, wrinkled shirt, Raymond stepped to the sidewalk and moved quickly inside. Teddy waited with the car.

"Something for you?" asked assistant cashier, E. R. Walter, greeting the fair-haired boy with a pleasant smile. Raymond raised a .45, stuck it through the cage, and pointed it toward Walter's heart.[47]

"Shut up and get back there," he replied in a soft voice. Bank president M. H. Milliken whirled around in his swivel chair and faced the bandit.

"It's just a holdup," Raymond said, walking around behind the teller's cage. "Now, both of you get on the floor." Walter and Milliken, their hands raised, sank to the floor while the shabby looking gunman rifled through the cash drawers.

"Any more money in the vault?" he asked quietly.

"Yes," answered Milliken, "but it's on a time lock."

"Ain't that a mess?" scoffed Raymond. "That's the trouble with Texas, all the banks are on time locks!"[48] He turned and ran briskly from the building.

Speeding east through Gunter and turning north on Highway 75 near McKinney, Raymond and Teddy made exceptional time. A few well placed phone calls, however, resulted in a massive roadblock just north of Howe.[49] Grayson County Deputy Sheriff Roy McDaniel then decided to patrol the road between Howe and Van Alstyne, where Hamilton's blue Chevy coach was last seen. In the company of Deputy Collier Yuery and Dr. John T. Nall, McDaniel proceeded south on Highway 75.

Still traveling north, Hamilton spotted Deputy McDaniel racing toward him in the southbound lane. Before McDaniel knew it, the outlaw car had zoomed past. The deputy spun his vehicle around and gave chase, topping eighty miles per hour as he raced through Howe.[50] Suddenly Hamilton spotted the roadblock north of town. Mashing the brake pedal and cutting his wheels hard to the left, Hamilton executed a 180-degree turn in the middle of the road. However, McDaniel was not about to let Ray pass him a second time. As the approaching car drew within range, the deputy swerved in front of it, forcing the oncoming vehicle to the side of the road.

Dr. Nall jumped from the car and got the drop on Ray with one of those unpredictable Thompson submachine guns. Hamilton and Teddy both emerged from the Chevy with their hands held high.

"I suppose you know who you've got," said the haggard fugitive.

"Raymond. . . ?" Nall asked.

"You damned right!" the bandit said. "Raymond Hamilton!"[51]

"Smoot" Schmid rushed to Sherman, the Grayson County seat, to secure Hamilton's extradition to Dallas. But Lee Simmons, in a statement from his Huntsville office, made it clear that he would fight Hamilton's transferral to any county that could not guarantee a rapid assessment of the death penalty.[52] District Attorney Robert Hurt of Dallas County, assured the general manager that his office had an airtight case in the Grand Prairie bank robbery and would indeed seek the death sentence. At the time, Texas law provided for the maximum penalty in cases involving firearms.

At 3:00 A.M. the following day, while Teddy, a completely dumbfounded accomplice, was being arraigned in Denton County, Ray was transferred to the Dallas County jail. Taking advantage of the crowds of spectators and reporters, the publicity-wise "Smoot" Schmid held an informal press conference in his office. Ray looked terrible—weary and ragged—not at all the dapper, "gentleman bandit" heralded by the news media. Nevertheless, he seemed in amazingly good spirits, almost jovial.

"It's not so bad being back in the old county jail," he said.[53]

"Is it true that you and Clyde hate each other?" a reporter asked.

"No," said the outlaw. "We split up because I had some business elsewhere. . . . We always intended to get together again."

"What do you think about Mary getting caught in Amarillo?" a voice called out. Ray's expression changed.

"She's a sweet girl," he said faintly, not knowing of the part she had played in his capture.

"I guess I got her in trouble. I guess I got my whole family in trouble."[54]

The following afternoon Ray was reunited with his brother, Floyd, who had been picked up two weeks earlier as an accomplice in the raid on Eastham. He was also a prime suspect in the Grand Prairie bank robbery. In the basement of the county jail the brothers were made to pose for photographers, shaking hands like a pair of old college buddies.[55] Neither had much to say.

Not long before Raymond's capture, Bonnie, Clyde, and Henry finally located Joe Palmer, who was hiding in Joplin, Missouri. He had gone directly there from Dallas as soon as he heard the news of the Grapevine murders. Palmer accompanied the trio to the farm in Louisiana. Clyde gave Joe two pistols, one of which had been taken in the Ranger, Texas, armory burglary. He and the others then went down to the creek bottom behind the house for some target practice. Even Bonnie squeezed off a few rounds, amazing Palmer with her steady hand,[56] much improved since the time she accidentally shot herself in the foot near Martinsville, Texas, on the farm of one of Clyde's uncles.[57]

On April 25 the quartet heard the news about Hamilton's arrest. Clyde told Joe he wanted to kill Raymond after reading the many published accounts of his famous letter from New Orleans.

"I ought to write my own letter," he said. On the morning of April 27 he did, dropping the envelope in a Memphis, Tennessee, mailbox that same day. Forty-eight hours later, on the afternoon of April 29, the Barrow troupe was cruising the streets of Topeka, Kansas, in search of a new car.[58] At 2107 Gable Street, the home of Jesse and Ruth Warren, Clyde spotted a beautiful new, cordoba gray, Ford V-8 Deluxe parked in the driveway. Barely six weeks old, with its contoured trunk and wire wheels the four-door luxury sedan was too nice to pass up. Unknown to anyone at the time, the new Ford was destined to become the very last vehicle used by Clyde Barrow and Bonnie Parker.[59]

On April 30 Clyde's letter to Raymond Hamilton arrived at the Dallas County jail. All correspondences addressed to county inmates were routinely screened and in many cases were shown to the sheriff. As "Smoot" Schmid scanned the neatly arranged lines of the text, he knew there could be no doubt of its authenticity. No doubt penned by Bonnie, the sarcastic tone and dark intent of the letter, filled with references to incidents known only to a handful of persons at the time, could only have come from Clyde.

Barrow mentioned Raymond Hamilton's attempt to shoot Joe Palmer and the rift over the Lancaster bank money. He also characterized Hamilton as being "too yellow to fight" during a gun battle in the Ozark Mountains.[60] Barrow said Hamilton "cowered on the floorboard, afraid of being shot." He then took a few jabs at Mary O'Dare, saying she would have turned them all in to the authorities had she not been so closely supervised by Bonnie Parker. Barrow closed the bitter letter by suggesting to Hamilton that he talk his way out of the electric chair, or perhaps "write a few more letters . . . at least it will gain you some publicity."[61]

Although this letter is no doubt genuine, a number of other correspondences attributed to Barrow also appeared at the same time. One, a particularly vulgar piece of drivel mailed to Ft. Worth newspaperman Amon Carter, is filled with graphic sexual references and bears no resemblance to anything Clyde Barrow would have written. Another addressed to auto manufacturer Henry Ford is a short, rather laconic endorsement of the V-8. Although sounding like Clyde, members of the Barrow family have stated the handwriting is not his, adding that he would have never signed his name, Clyde Champion Barrow.[62]

One of the most famous of the alleged Barrow communiques is a note typed on a discarded leaf of Western Union stationery. The text of the note, addressed to Dallas Assistant District Attorney Winter King, appeared in most Texas newspapers. Despite the presence of a thumbprint, supposedly identified as Clyde Barrow's, the letter is generally considered a fake.[63]

On May 3 Clyde, Joe, and Henry robbed an Everly, Iowa, bank of $2800. Bonnie, as always, waited outside of town with the backup car.

Clyde Barrow, left, Bonnie Parker, and Joe Palmer, 1934. (Courtesy of Ken M. Holmes, Jr.)

After the job Clyde favored settling down in Louisiana, but Joe opposed the idea, preferring to take his share of the bank roll back to the Conner Hotel in Joplin.[64]

"Come on," pleaded Clyde. "We'll do some fishin' down on Black Lake [or Bass Lake]. We'll probably jump in and swim around a little."[65]

"Naw," said Joe, firmly. "Why don't y'all come up north with me? Maybe go to that World's Fair in Chicago!"[66] Barrow cared little for the World's Fair. After leaving Palmer on the outskirts of Joplin, Clyde mailed a short letter to his mother, telling her of his intention to hide out in Louisiana for a while.

On May 6 Bonnie and Clyde made a quick trip to Dallas,[67] arriving that evening on a gravel road four miles east of town. While Clyde entertained his folks, Bonnie started thumbing through a stack of snapshots.

She selected a photograph of herself and Clyde. They are pictured on a dirt road between Dallas and Marshall, a 1933 Ford V-8 parked directly behind them.[68] The chrome grille of the car gleams in the bright sun. Clyde, grinning broadly, is lifting Bonnie with one arm, raising her above him, her hands resting gently on his shoulders. Her face is bright, smiling.

"I like this one," she told her mother.[69]

On Wednesday, May 9, the trial of Raymond Hamilton got underway in Judge Noland Williams's court, Dallas County. Although soundly convicting the outlaw for his part in the March 19 robbery in Grand Prairie, the jury could not agree on the severity of the sentence; they were evidently swayed by the twenty-year-old bank robber's youthful manner. The jury was eventually declared irrevocably deadlocked and dismissed.[70]

Rather than try the case a second time, the authorities transferred Hamilton to Denton, where another "guaranteed" death penalty awaited his arrival. The resulting court appearance, however, was only slightly more successful. On May 19, after pleading guilty to participating in the Lewisville hijacking, Hamilton was given a ninety-nine year sentence.[71] This probably displeased Lee Simmons.

On May 9, while Raymond Hamilton was facing Judge Williams, Clyde Barrow arrived beside the Star Service Station less than two miles away. Barrow needed to see his mother, but only old Henry trudged up to the car. "Your Momma's visiting up the road," he told his son. Clyde asked his father to meet him near the railroad tracks at midnight, which the old man did. He watched as his son opened a large suitcase and pulled out a document of some kind. There was also a very large quantity of cash in the suitcase.

"I'm going to sign these for you and Momma," Clyde said, producing a pen. But the pen would not write. He searched the car for another pen but found none. "I'll have to come back," he told his father, returning the papers to the suitcase.[72] Clyde drove off. It would be his last trip to Dallas.

Throughout the country alleged sightings of Bonnie and Clyde were being reported. Dallas journalist Larry Grove recalled that on one afternoon in May 1934 the managers of three businesses each claimed they had just been robbed by Bonnie and Clyde—one was in east Texas, another was in San Angelo in far West Texas, and the third was in Indiana.

In Oklahoma two men and a woman were stalking squirrels when the local sheriff arrested them, thinking he had cornered Clyde, Bonnie, and Henry. A pair of Texas Rangers were pulled over no less than six times when, in the company of their red-headed female stenographer, they tried to drive from Austin to Dallas for the purpose of eliciting testimony in an unrelated case.[73] A Dallas-based jewelry store offered one-thousand dollars to Clyde Barrow, Bonnie Parker, and John Dillinger if they could find a single flaw in any of their "certified perfect diamonds."[74] It was a great gimmick, but not all news items were as light-hearted. Many citizens still vividly recall the numerous radio bulletins broadcast during the spring of 1934: "Remain indoors until further notice. Keep windows and doors securely latched. Bonnie and Clyde are at large!"[75] The Southwest was gripped with fear.

On May 21 Bonnie, Clyde, and Henry turned down the narrow dirt path leading to the Cole farmhouse in Louisiana.[76] Clyde only planned to spend a few hours there, so he did not think it strange when Henry left for awhile with his parents. Bonnie and Clyde, more than most people, understood the value of keeping in touch with one's family.

Later that same day the threesome drove away. In Shreveport, forty-five miles to the west, Barrow stopped in front of the Majestic Cafe and sent Methvin in for a few sandwiches.[77] While they waited, so the story goes,[78] Bonnie and Clyde spotted a squad car cruising slowly past. Methvin, seated at the counter inside, had his back to the street and either failed to notice or chose to ignore, the events unfolding behind him.

Unable to risk being spotted by the Shreveport policemen, Clyde sped away. As soon as Barrow was out of sight, Methvin calmly rose from his stool and stepped to the door. Moving out to the sidewalk, he glanced both ways, then strolled off down the street, leaving the sandwiches and drinks on the counter.

In the event of just such an occurrence, Bonnie and Clyde, by prior agreement, were to rendezvous with Henry as soon as possible at the Cole place. For some reason, however, the outlaw couple took longer than expected to circle back to Bienville Parish,[79] evidently spending the twenty-second travelling the back roads of Arkansas and southern Missouri.

At 8:00 A.M. on May 23, 1934, the flashy, gray V-8 pulled up in front of Canfield's Cafe, in Gibsland, ten miles northeast of the Cole farmhouse.[80] Bonnie, wearing a bright red dress with matching shoes and hat, waited as Clyde, dressed in a silk suit, blue western-style shirt, and tie, got out to open her door. Together, the dapper couple mounted the sidewalk and disappeared into the little restaurant for a breakfast of fresh donuts and coffee. Afterward they ordered two sandwiches to go and returned to the car. Clyde removed his shoes, as he often did when driving. Backing into the street, he turned south, sliding the barrel of a 12–gauge sawed-off shotgun between his left leg and the car door as he proceeded through town. A 20-gauge shotgun rested, muzzle up, against his right leg.[81]

Upon reaching the picturesque little settlement of Mount Lebanon, four miles from Gibsland, Barrow veered to the right at the only intersection and continued southwest on what was known locally as the Ringgold Road. As usual, Barrow had his foot buried in the floorboard when he rounded that bend eight miles south of Gibsland. He noticed a familiar Model A logging truck parked at the crest of a long, low grade in the distance. Clyde immediately identified the open-cab vehicle as belonging to Ivy Methvin, Henry's father.[82] Barrow had purchased the truck for Methvin, who used it to haul timber for sale. It was also used as a reason for Barrow's presence in the parish. He was supposed to be working for Methvin as a logger. Few of the area's residents believed the story, though.[83]

Removing his foot from the gas pedal, Barrow let the automobile coast approximately five hundred yards, gliding effortlessly toward a shallow valley at the base of two small hills. Methvin's truck was on top of the first hill, oddly facing north in the southbound lane.[84] It had been jacked up, its left front wheel removed and placed haphazardly in the middle of the gravel road. Old man Methvin stood nearby, eyeing the approaching Ford.

Easing into the passing lane, Barrow drew alongside the stricken truck and applied the brakes, shotguns still in place on either side of his legs. Bonnie took one last bite of her sandwich and placed it on the magazine she had in her lap.[85] A nickel-plated Colt .45 automatic lay beneath the magazine, cocked and ready to hand to Clyde should the need arise.

Looking to his right, past Bonnie, Barrow examined the apparently disabled truck in the road and greeted Henry's father. Suddenly, the old man clutched his abdomen and excused himself, rushing to the edge of the woods as if to vomit. Puzzled, Clyde straightened up and glanced down the road. A northbound pulp wood truck was very slowly topping the second hill less than a quarter of a mile away. Realizing he was blocking the lane, Barrow depressed the clutch, shifted to first, and started to pull out of the workmen's way. By chance Bonnie happened to look over to Clyde and in doing so spotted a man rising from behind a brush pile in the woods to her immediate left, not more than twenty feet from the car. Suddenly a gun flashed and five more men appeared from behind the pile, each drawing weapons to their shoulders.[86]

Bonnie screamed.[87] Two shots rang out. Then a thick grouping of well-placed slugs slammed into the driver's side of the V-8, ripping through both steel walls of the front door and stitching the windshield with a tight grouping of deadly holes. The first two shots hit Barrow in the head. Another shot sheared the triggering mechanism of Clyde's 12-gauge as it lay unused at his left side. Twenty to twenty-seven other slugs hacked through Barrow's body, his foot slipped from the clutch pedal as eight of the missiles snapped his spinal cord.[88]

The car began to wobble uncontrollably down the road. Bonnie's ninety-pound frame was then shredded by at least twenty-eight shots, her red hat sailed into the rear seat as a lone bullet exited through the top of her skull. Two bullets crashed into the left side of her face, shattered her jaw, and crushed her teeth. Another tore several fingers from her right hand.[89]

In a matter of seconds the six gunmen had emptied their weapons into the car; then they grabbed shotguns and blasted away with buckshot at the slowly moving vehicle. Two of the men suddenly discarded their smoldering weapons, drew .45s, leaped into the road, and chased behind the car, firing round after round into its trunk.[90] Alcorn called out for everyone to stop shooting, but no one heard him.[91] Finally, the once-gleaming Ford sedan, stolen in Topeka, Kansas, from Jesse and Ruth Warren, rolled to a stop against an embankment on the south side of the road, approximately a hundred yards from the officer's position. The force of the jolt tossed the bodies forward. Clyde's head drooped lifelessly through the chipped and broken rim of the V-8's big steering wheel.[92] Bonnie slumped against the door on the passenger side of the car, her own head slipping between her knees as if she were trying to recover from a fainting spell. But of course she was not. The chase had ended. After twenty-seven and one-half months on the run, Bonnie and Clyde, the elusive "phantom fugitives," had been dealt the fatal blow they had long expected, "fingered" by a trusted friend.[93]

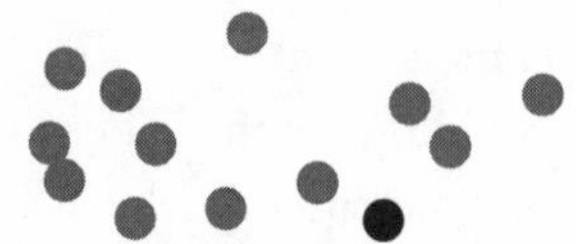

The Road to Gibsland

The specifics of the ambush are difficult to piece together. Down through the years rumors, innuendo, and hearsay have all combined to create a myriad of conflicting reports about the circumstances leading up to that morning in May 1934. Nevertheless, many accurate accounts do exist. From these, one is able to see how six lawmen, four of whom were operating beyond their jurisdiction, happened to choose the precise time and location that Bonnie and Clyde would pause long enough to be shot and killed. Ironically, it was Barrow's decision to carry out the Eastham raid that sealed his fate.

Following that raid, General Manager Lee Simmons, swimming in a sea of Texas bureaucracy, traveled from department to department in Austin trying to drum up support for an all-out effort to ambush Bonnie and Clyde.[1] Governor Miriam Ferguson was reluctant to direct such a move on her own. The adjutant general had no money to sponsor a special agent, nor did the highway patrol. Simmons was finally told to handle the job on his own. After much pencil work, the director found the state could afford one extra man on its payroll.[2] It did not take long for him to decide who to use—Frank Hamer.[3]

Just six weeks away from his fiftieth birthday, Hamer was a larger-than-life legend. Standing six feet, two inches tall and weighing more than two-hundred pounds, he had begun his career when Texas lav men still patrolled the state on horseback. Quiet, reserved, and wholly unimpressed by publicity and authority, he was widely known for having exposed the inherent corruption and incidents of murder resulting from the Texas Banking Association's long-standing offer of five thousand dollars for "dead bank robbers."[4] His opposition to the policies of a powerful group like the Texas Banking Association reinforced Frank Hamer's image as a tough, single-minded individual, prone to work against the grain.

Hamer's personal interpretation of the law can best be illustrated by an incident occurring on May 7, 1929. Judge George Calhoun, of Travis County, Texas, was forced to dismiss a case against an accused criminal because a piece of crucial evidence had been obtained illegally by Hamer. In a statement to the court Judge Calhoun severely admonished the Ranger captain for conducting an unwarranted search of the defendant's residence, pointing out that such actions were "illegal under the constitution." Afterward Hamer was asked by the press if the judge's remarks were going to make him change his methods.

"No," he replied.[5]

In November 1932, upon the election of Miriam Ferguson to the office of governor, Frank Hamer either resigned his commission or was fired.[6] Down through the years the reasons for his departure from state service have been listed variously as a personal dislike of the Fergusons,[7] an aversion to female governors,[8] and an invitation to leave his post because of prior insubordination.[9] Regardless, Hamer remained a cunning and intelligent officer—fearless, methodical, and well informed. An expert in the use and maintenance of a wide variety of weapons, he had made the delicate transition to the modern world of criminology with the ease of a master. He was a loner, noted for taking his own course in matters of law enforcement;[10] but most of all, to the underworld he remained the very embodiment of death itself, with at least fifty-three killings attributed to him in the course of his long career.[11]

Because of the lawman's prior differences with the Fergusons, Simmons feared that his plan would be blocked.

"Frank Hamer's OK with me," said Governor Ferguson.[12] Simmons was pleased. On February 1, 1934, armed with a briefcase full of signed authorizations, Lee Simmons met with Frank Hamer. "I want you to put Clyde and Bonnie 'on the spot'," he told Hamer, "and shoot everyone in sight."[13]

Hamer accepted the job immediately. The concept of tracking someone like Clyde Barrow fascinated him. By his own admission, he felt that no man, not even the infamous John Dillinger, could match Barrow's "cleverness, desperation and reckless bravado."[14] Ten days after meeting with Simmons, the lawman loaded his car and drove to Dallas. There he conferred with Sheriff Schmid and was introduced to Bob Alcorn, by then a Barrow authority and the only lawman in the state who could identify Clyde on sight. Schmid agreed that Alcorn should join forces with Hamer. Hamer was added to the Dallas County payroll as a bailiff, thus camouflaging his occasional appearances in town.[15]

On February 19 the Texans arrived in Bienville Parish, Louisiana, in search of Henry Methvin's parents. Hamer and Alcorn met with the local sheriff, Henderson Jordan. Jordan knew of the Methvins. Indeed, he had already been approached by an acquaintance of theirs, John Joyner, who informed Sheriff Jordan that Henry Methvin was ready and willing to betray Bonnie and Clyde in exchange for a full pardon from the state of Texas.[16] These events occurred prior to the Grapevine murders and before the killing of Cal Campbell in Oklahoma.

Hamer and Alcorn asked for a meeting with Joyner. At the meeting, attended by special agent Lester Kendale of the Department of Justice, Joyner reiterated the original offer, adding that any and all agreements must be made in writing and signed by the governor of Texas. Hamer and the others expressed their amenability to such a proposal, immediately drafting the text of an agreement guaranteeing Henry Methvin a full pardon should he successfully deliver Bonnie and Clyde.[17]

Shortly thereafter Governor Miriam Ferguson signed the agreement (not to be confused with the actual pardon, issued on August 14, 1934). The contract was then returned to Sheriff Jordan, who promptly signed the paper and summoned John Joyner.[18] After examining the fully executed document, Joyner informed the Methvins. A tedious waiting game then ensued. Finally, after two weeks of relative silence, it was beginning to look as though Henry Methvin had changed his mind. Then came Easter Sunday.

Aroused by the senseless murders of his men, L. G. Phares, director of the Highway Patrol, sought a place on Barrow's trail full time.[19] At that point he was informed of the activities of Hamer and Alcorn and given a chance to join forces with them. Hamer asked to make his own choice from outside the patrol force. Phares agreed, promising to give the man a technical post in the Highway Patrol as a cover.

Hamer picked an old friend and former ranger associate, B. M. "Manny" Gault. Gault, like Hamer, had resigned from the Rangers after opposing Miriam Ferguson in the election of 1932.[20] He had been working odd jobs since then, and, frankly, he needed the money. On April 6 he was put on the payroll.

Alcorn began pressing "Smoot" Schmid for a partner of his own, namely Ted Hinton, who stood next to Alcorn during the failed Sowers ambush of November 22, 1933. Having one deputy on the road was hard enough to pay for. Two was nearly unthinkable. However, the concept of being involved in the capture of an outlaw like Clyde Barrow played heavily on Schmid's political mind, especially in that election year of 1934. After much thought the sheriff finally consented to the addition of the twenty-seven-year-old Hinton to the "special force." He would leave Dallas sometime between April 1 and May 4.[21]

Shortly after the April 6 murder of Cal Campbell, Henderson Jordan received word that Henry Methvin was most anxious to carry out his end of the bargain.[22] No doubt the contract in Jordan's office was beginning to look more and more attractive to Henry.

On May 21 John Joyner arrived suddenly at Sheriff Jordan's office. Joyner told the Sheriff that Henry, along with Bonnie and Clyde, had just paid a visit to Ivy and Avie Methvin. Henry told his parents he would slip away from Barrow and Parker that night at the Majestic Cafe in Shreveport.[23]

Telephoning Dallas, the Louisiana lawman informed "Smoot" Schmid of the impending move on Bonnie and Clyde. Schmid then placed a call to the Inn Motel in Shreveport, where Alcorn, Hinton, Hamer, and Gault had been waiting—playing cards, writing letters, and generally longing for something to happen.[24] Schmid's call was just what they had been waiting for.

In Arcadia, Gault and Hinton were introduced to Sheriff Henderson Jordan and a sixth man, Bienville Parish Deputy Sheriff Prentiss M. Oakley.

The Cole farmhouse, where Bonnie and Clyde had been staying, was located in a thickly forested area, ten miles southwest of Gibsland.[25] Only one road led in or out of that part of the country. Therefore, it was recognized that Bonnie and Clyde would have to use it in their search for Henry. Jordan described an area just south of Mount Lebanon, several hundred yards beyond the Sutton's pond cutoff,[26] where the officers would have an unobstructed view of at least a half mile of the road in either direction. It was the ideal place for an ambush. At 9:00 P.M. on May 21 the lawmen drove to the prescribed location. Large, moss-covered oaks and evergreen pines choked the area. Chiggers and mosquitoes abounded. Concealing their cars in the woods directly behind their position, the officers mounted the embankment and peered out across the gravel-topped road stretching before them.[27] The air was humid, the countryside serene.

After constructing a blind of dried brush and vines, the six officers settled down for a long wait, spending their time cleaning, loading, and positioning their great arsenal of weapons. All day Tuesday the twenty-second the officers waited, but nothing happened.[28] Hardly a soul passed their position. As a decoy Ivy Methvin had parked his Model A logging truck facing northeast in the southbound lane of the Ringgold Road.[29] By the morning of the twenty-third Methvin and the lawmen were becoming discouraged. They had been stalking their prey for two nights, fighting the tedium by scraping swarms of voracious insects from their bodies.

As dawn broke they were beginning to question the value of waiting much longer.[30] For all they knew, Bonnie and Clyde were a thousand miles away. By 9:10 A.M., the officers were ready to give up, when in the distance, the high-pitched whine of a powerful engine cut through the silence.

Hinton and Alcorn straightened up—they had heard that sound before. Straining to pick up every nuance and tone, the Dallas Deputies listened intently to the steady roar of the rapidly moving vehicle. In the thirty-six hours since their arrival on that road, the officers had seen no more than two or three slow-going logging trucks and a couple of farmers. The sound of the still unseen automobile told each man present that no ordinary driver approached. Nobody but Clyde Barrow would take a gravel road at that speed. The officers gripped their weapons.

With their eyes trained on the crest of a long curve that banked on a hill less than half a mile to the northeast, the six-man team ducked behind their blind of twigs and brush. Bob Alcorn was first in line, because he was the only man in the group who could identify Barrow on sight. Hinton, crouching next to Alcorn, had known Buck and Clyde only marginally in his days as a messenger boy for Western Union. Later, however, he would develop a particular fondness for Bonnie Parker, whiling away his spare time by drinking coffee and flirting with the popular young waitress of "the courthouse cafe." He carried that fondness with him on May 23. He would carry it for the rest of his life.[31]

To the left of Hinton and Alcorn, Prentiss Oakley knelt, followed by Henderson Jordan, Manny Gault, and Frank Hamer. Each man packed a high-powered rifle (Hinton carried a Browning automatic) and some also had shotguns and sidearms.[32] There was no doubt in Hinton's mind that a gunfight was imminent. Neither he nor his fellow Texans doubted that Clyde Barrow would have to be killed to be stopped. Initially, however, Jordan and Oakley wanted to make some attempt to take Barrow alive, but the Texans were quick to veto the idea.[33] "Ain't no way that boy's going to give up," said one of the officers. "He's done shot his way out of a dozen battles. He ain't doing it again." Out on the road, less than twenty feet from the waiting guns, Ivy Methvin stood, ready to signal should the occupants of the approaching car prove to be Bonnie and Clyde. Seconds later the V-8 popped into view. Alcorn raised a pair of field glasses to his eyes.[34]

"It's him, boys," he called out quietly. "This is it—it's Clyde."[35]

On the approach, the outlaw applied his brakes and eased alongside Methvin and the supposedly disabled truck, shifting to neutral as he stopped. Both Bonnie and Clyde were looking northwest, chatting with the old man. Suddenly Methvin cupped his hands around his abdomen and backed away toward the woods.[36] It was the signal the officers had been waiting for. At that very moment, however, a pulp wood truck appeared, less than five-hundred yards to the south.[37] Barrow shifted to first and started to pull over.

Oakley stood up, followed shortly by the other five officers. Barrow was twenty feet from the barrels of six automatic rifles. The Ford eased past the truck. Bonnie suddenly screamed—"like a panther," Hamer would later say.[38] Oakley fired two shots prematurely, so tense was the situation.[39] Hinton saw Clyde's head snap back. Then all six officers opened fire. The car began rolling away.

"My God!" Hinton thought. "After all this, he's still getting away!"[40]

Discarding his rifle, Hinton grabbed a shotgun and emptied five rounds of .00 buckshot into the rear of the moving vehicle. He then drew his pistol and jumped into the road, firing at the car, Alcorn at his side, screaming for everyone to stop shooting. Hinton later realized they had both run directly into the line of fire. Amazingly, neither he nor Alcorn were hit.[41]

The wheels of the V-8 kept digging into the gravel as the car wobbled unpredictably down the road. It continued for a hundred yards, then pulled gently to the left and slid up against an embankment on the south side of the road. Hinton could not imagine anyone living through such an attack. However, considering Clyde's reputation, the impetuous deputy had no idea what to expect as he approached the stalled automobile.

Hinton could see two bloodied forms slumped forward on the front seat as he tried to crawl between the vine encrusted embankment and the driver's side of the car. There was not enough room to get the door open, so he dove across the hood and threw open the door on the passenger side just as Alcorn came running up. Bonnie, her limp body stitched full of seeping red holes, fell into the lawman's arms. Hinton tried to stand the young woman on her feet, secretly praying she was still alive.[42] Caressing her for a moment, he placed her body on the seat. Bonnie's bright red dress was blotched and splattered, her mouth ripped apart by a steel-jacketed bullet. Several fingers of her right hand had been blown away.[43]

A partially consumed sandwich lay in her lap. A blood-soaked Louisiana map fluttered in the breeze. Bonnie's stylish red hat, apparently shot away, was found in the back seat. A pair of purple-tinted sunglasses stared at Hinton from the dash. Their owner, the man who had escaped countless police traps and wreaked untold havoc throughout the Midwest for more than two years, was slumped just a few inches away. His head, a bleeding mass, dipped through the large hoop-like steering wheel of the tan Ford. Blood trickled past Barrow's cheeks and collected on his upper lip. Against the door on the driver's side a sawed-off shotgun was propped upright, a spent bullet lodged in its firing mechanism.[44] The muzzle of another shotgun rested against Barrow's right leg.

Hinton produced a sixteen-millimeter movie camera and started taking a few overall views of the car, the road, and the surrounding area. By accident, Hinton caught the camera-shy Frank Hamer and Sheriff Henderson Jordan on film as they began to inventory the considerable contents of the car. Three Browning automatic rifles, two sawed-off shotguns, one Colt .32 automatic pistol, one Colt .38 automatic pistol, one Colt .45 double action revolver (purchased for Commerce, Oklahoma, City Marshall Percy Boyd), seven Colt .45 automatic pistols, one-hundred Browning automatic rifle clips and three thousand rounds of ammunition were recovered.[45] In addition, fifteen sets of license plates and a number of magazines, road maps, and blankets were found among stacks of clothes and make-up. Barrow's saxophone was also in the car.[46]

Bienville Parish resident Cleo Sneed had been cutting timber less than a mile away when guns went off. Frightened but curious, Sneed emerged on the Ringgold Road and traipsed toward the small crowd he saw gathering in the distance.[47]

Sneed recognized Ivy Methvin. Someone was trying to help him fix his Model A. To the south, he saw a pulp wood truck turning around in the middle of the road, apparently heading back in the direction from which it had just come. Several men were carrying guns and examining a fancy Ford V-8 that had driven up against a brush-covered embankment one-hundred yards from Ivy Methvin's truck. Sneed and his friends strolled over to the car. They soon wished they had not.[48]

Jordan and Oakley left for Arcadia to summon Dr. J. L. Wade, the

The death car on Ringgold Road, Louisiana, minutes after the ambush, May 23, 1934. Bonnie and Clyde are still in the car and a crowd has begun to gather. Some of Barrow's weapons can be seen on the roof of the car, placed there by members of the ambush team. (Courtesy of L. J. Hinton.)

parish coroner.[49] Ted Hinton and Frank Hamer drove to Gibsland to secure a wrecker with which to haul the bullet-riddled V-8 into Arcadia.[50] Hinton stopped at a filling station in Gibsland to call "Smoot" Schmid in Dallas.

A local resident, Mert Davis, was standing nearby passing the time of day with a bottle of ice-cold Coca-Cola when he overheard the one-sided telephone conversation. Minutes later four carloads of Gibslanders led by Davis arrived at the scene of the ambush.[51] Methvin had not yet removed his truck. Davis vividly remembers the jack under the axle and the tire lying on its side in the middle of the road. Davis and his friends could see the V-8 sitting one-hundred yards south of the truck. The doors on the passenger side were open and a handful of people were milling around. As Davis moved in, the officers closed the doors. Someone opened the door on Bonnie's side.

"Shut that door," a lawman shouted.

The man complied, accidentally slamming the door on Bonnie's already mutilated right hand. The latch failed to hold, causing the man to slam the door again and again, each time mashing the bloody right hand. Seeing this, Davis stepped over to the car and lifted Bonnie's wrist to her lap. In doing so, he saw the nickel-plated Colt .45 automatic, the magazine, and the partially eaten sandwich. But most of all, he noted her ashen color and the terrible hole in her face.[52]

By the time the coroner arrived, the gravel thoroughfare was clogged with parked cars and pedestrians. Souvenir hunters had chipped away nearly all of the bullet-shredded safety glass on Clyde Barrow's side of the car and had trampled the shrubbery in search of bullet fragments and spent shell casings. Some were feverishly whittling a number of nearby trees in hopes of retrieving one or two bullets. Others had turned their cutlery on the bodies of the slain couple, slicing off pieces of bloody clothing. A man had to be restrained after trying to cut off one of Clyde's ears.[53] Another man wanted to do the same with Barrow's trigger finger.[54] Someone else had taken scissors to Bonnie's hair.

The wrecker driver backed his rig up to the grille of the V-8 and looped a series of chains around its bumper and frame. The police vehicles moved in behind, followed by nearly two-hundred local cars and trucks.[55]

Sheriff Jordan stopped the entourage in front of the local school in Gibsland. The sheriff wanted to show the gathering students what ultimately becomes of legendary outlaws like Clyde Barrow and Bonnie Parker.[56] Children began running from their classrooms. Thinking it was lunch time, and swept along by the crowd, twelve-year-old Polly Palmer was among the first to reach the car. She was not exactly sure what was happening. Everyone was chattering about a pair of bandits from Texas, but Polly had never even heard of Bonnie and Clyde.

Without a thought as to what she would find, Polly hopped onto the running board of the tan Ford and peered through the open window. There, just inches away, were the vacant staring eyes of Bonnie Parker, a portion of the dead woman's lip dangling across her open mouth. The terrible vision, precipitating countless bad dreams and sleepless nights for years thereafter, remained with her always. "I wish I had never gone out to that car," she said. "It still bothers me."[57]

In Arcadia sixteen thousand people waited. Soon the population of Bienville Parish tripled. The V-8 was slowly dragged to the entrance of Conger's Furniture Store, a one-story retail outlet that doubled as the parish's only funeral parlor. It was nearly 11:30 A.M., and already the sun was blazing with unseasonable furor. The smell of hot, drying blood began to mix with a multiplicity of perfumes and colognes as the mass of reporters and thrill seekers squeezed in around the car. Undertaker "Boots" Bailey and his assistants had to force their way through the crowd in an attempt to take the bodies by stretcher from the car to the back room of the furniture store.[58]

Dewey Kendrick, Sr., who had driven over from Gibsland, moved in close to see what a pair of dead fugitives might look like. Suddenly the door on the passenger side was opened, and Bonnie's leg slipped limply to the running board. Kendrick stared in disbelief at the tiny foot falling into view. His conception of the larger-than-life outlaws far surpassed the pitifully small figures before him.[59]

"Prentiss Oakley told me Clyde and Bonnie got no word of warning out on that road," Kendrick revealed. "[The lawmen] just reared up and let them have it. I know they were outlaws and killers, but I just think they should of gotten a better deal than that—they should have been given a chance to give up."[60]

Someone tried to remove Roy Thornton's gold wedding band from Bonnie's finger. Still others tugged at the remaining fingers of her right hand. "God damn!" Someone said as Clyde was being lifted out of the car. "He was nothing but a little bitty fart!"[61]

Emma Parker was spending a quiet morning in Dallas with her son Buster and daughter-in-law Edith. The family had been drawn together by the May 19, arrest of Bonnie's little sister, Billie. Incredibly, she and Floyd Hamilton had been charged with the Easter Sunday murders of Highway Patrolmen Wheeler and Murphy. The phone rang and Bonnie's mother answered.

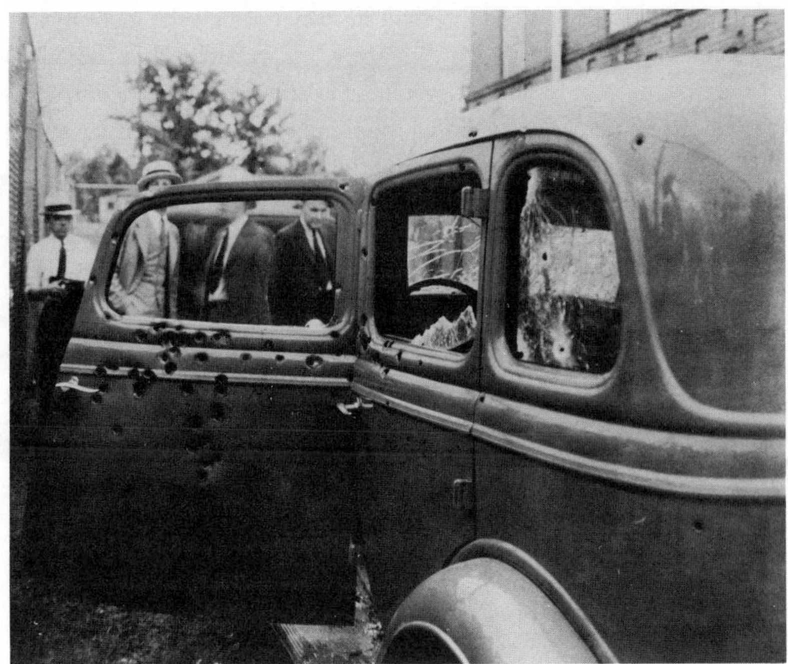

The death car after it had been towed to Arcadia, May 23, 1934. Note the condition of the rear door glass as compared to the photograph on page 208. Souvenir hunters had chipped away the shards of glass and were trying to dismantle other parts of the car, prompting Sheriff Jordan to park the vehicle behind a chain-link fence. (Courtesy of the Dallas Public Library Texas/Dallas History Archives Division, Hayes Collections.)

Emma screamed and fell to the floor. The news of her daughter's death had been related to her by a Dallas reporter.[62]

Newlywed Marie was driving home to Cement City from her parents' place when she heard the news on her car radio. She turned around and drove back to the Star Service Station. Cumie could not bring herself to make the trip to Arcadia. The memory of Buck's death was too fresh. She could not bear the thought of looking upon the naked, bullet-mangled body of her beloved Clyde.[63] Henry would go alone.

Henry Barrow, whose only car was a broken-down Model T, had to be chauffeured to Louisiana by a family friend.[64] He arrived in the midst of a raucous display and had to fight his way through the mob to view his son. He chatted quietly with anyone who approached him, but most of the time he kept to himself, watching as several people tried to scale a stack of plush new caskets lining the thin plywood wall that separated the embalming room from the rest of the store.[65]

Dr. Wade hastily assembled a six-man jury for the coroner's inquest. Recording his notes in pencil, Wade hurried through the procedure, fearful of the madness surrounding him. As the minutes ticked by the coroner's notes became less and less legible. What was left of the outlaws' clothes were removed and set aside. Clyde's diamond stick pin disappeared immediately. However, a gold wristwatch and $505.32 found in his pockets somehow remained intact.[66]

Wade's description of Clyde Barrow's body begins by detailing Barrow's many tattoos for purposes of identification. Wade goes on to describe the two head wounds, probably inflicted by Oakley, and the eight wounds from the base of Barrow's neck to his spine. Another wound that revealed Barrow's broken back is also mentioned.[67]

Wade's notes on Bonnie Parker are much longer and include such details as the Catholic crucifix worn beneath her dress. Parker's tattoos are described, followed by a lengthy list of wounds, including the three shots that struck her in the head and face. Wade also noted the rather substantial scar tissue from the burns sustained in the Wellington crash.[68]

Concluding the inquest, Wade prepared a short statement for Deputy Bob Alcorn to sign. Two days later Alcorn appeared before newsreel cameras to read a brief statement on behalf of himself and the other five members of the ambuscade.

"I regret that we couldn't have taken them alive, but that was impossible," the deputy said, stammering nervously beneath the bright lights. "I further regret that there was a woman that had to be killed, which couldn't have been helped."[69]

The lawmen were quite obviously disturbed by the shooting of Bonnie Parker. In the years that followed, a number of isolated statements attributed to each of them would confirm this. Prentiss Oakley would confide to at least two close friends that Bonnie's inclusion in the death trap preyed upon his own mind from the moment the guns fell silent on that May morning.[70]

Ted Hinton often told friends and relatives that he viewed the outlaw couple as "two love-sick kids who happened to choose the wrong path to follow." At times in his book, *Ambush*, Hinton seems caught up in the aura of romanticism that somehow exudes from the memory of Bonnie and Clyde. A strange, lilting admiration for Barrow drifts throughout Hinton's memoir, and of his apparent love for Bonnie, there can be little doubt. Even the normally tight-lipped Frank Hamer would venture to say, "As [Bonnie and Clyde] drove up that day and I pulled down on Barrow, knowing that some of my rifle bullets were going to snuff out her life along with his . . . I hated to have to shoot her."[71]

After the inquest undertaker "Boots" Bailey tried to treat the bodies, intermittently showering the crowd with embalming fluid to make the people back away. King Murphy, a local photographer, took several pictures of the undraped bodies.[72] Dallas photojournalist Denny Hayes, of the *Daily Times Herald*, pulled a blood-soaked sheet up to Bonnie's chin and snapped a number of now-famous pictures of Bill Decker and other Dallas officials viewing the two slain fugitives.

By then Arcadia was packed with people. Newsmen from all over the country were arriving hourly, seeking interviews with the ambush team. Hamer and the other five members of the "death squad" refused to talk about the ambush in depth. Not only were they fearful of revealing the truth about Henry Methvin, they seemed genuinely disinterested in glorifying their deed. To complicate matters, the officers could barely hear; their ears were still ringing with the sound of gunfire. They finally consented to pose for a group picture. Hinton was suddenly sick. Shaking uncontrollably, he rushed away.

Late on the afternoon of May 23 the poorly embalmed body of Clyde Barrow was finally released to his father. Through it all Henry Barrow remained quiet and reserved. But he was not the resigned figure of age and grief many observers thought him to be. By talking to whomever approached him, he was able to gather information about the Methvins and their relationship to the death of his son. The empty, noncommittal remarks of both Hinton and Alcorn, coupled with the conspicuous absence of Henry Methvin, confirmed the elder Barrow's suspicions. Climbing

The six officers who ambushed and killed Bonnie and Clyde, May 23, 1934. Standing left to right: Bienville Parish Deputy Sheriff Prentiss Oakley, Dallas County Deputy Sheriff Ted Hinton, Dallas County Deputy Sheriff Bob Alcorn, retired Texas Ranger Manny Gault. Kneeling, left to right: retired Texas Ranger Frank Hamer, Bienville Parish Sheriff Henderson Jordon. (Courtesy of Ken M. Holmes, Jr., and the Jenkins Publishing Company.)

into the ambulance with the body of his son, the old man departed for Dallas.

It was 10:00 P.M. before Bonnie's brother, Buster, finally arrived in Arcadia. He had confused the town of Arcadia, in northern Louisiana, with the like-sounding community of Acadia, located in the marshy bayou country of far south Louisiana.[73] When he finally arrived at Conger's Store, it looked as if a herd of cattle had stampeded through it. Footprints and torn fabric marred every piece of fine furniture in the building. A few panes of glass were broken and cigarette butts were ground into the rugs.[74] The scene in Dallas, however, would make up for what he missed in Louisiana. A man identified only as "a showman" contacted the Barrow family in hopes of purchasing Clyde's corpse for fifty thousand dollars. He wanted to mummify the body and put it on tour with a traveling tent show. The Barrows never replied.[75]

Early on Thursday morning, May 24, crowds began gathering in front of the Sparkman-Holtz-Brand Funeral Home, at 2110 Ross Avenue. As the day progressed, nearly ten thousand Dallasites trampled across the finely manicured lawn in hopes of getting a glimpse of the slain Clyde Barrow. They shouted, screamed, cajoled, and pounded on doors and windows. When that did not produce results, the mob began tearing shrubs out of the ground and heaving them through the air.[76]

Eventually Henry Barrow arrived. He reluctantly agreed to let the crowd file past his son's body. Amid hoots and cat calls the people moved past an indignant Henry Barrow and the inexpensive broadcloth-lined casket containing his infamous son. Clyde, dressed in a crisp, light grey suit and matching tie, wore a large pearl stickpin in place of the diamond

Dallas County Sheriff Richard Allen "Smoot" Schmid, Texas prison system General Manager Colonel Lee Simmons, Warden Waid, of Huntsville's Walls Unit, and Chief of Detectives Bill Decker, of the Dallas County Sheriff's Department, April, 1935. Schmid and Simmons started tracking Bonnie and Clyde independently; then they joined forces, perhaps at the suggestion of their field officers, Bob Alcorn and Frank Hamer. (Courtesy of Johnny Hayes.)

ornament stolen in Arcadia. A trio of drunk men staggered through the open doors, mashing cigarette butts into the plush new carpet.

"I'm glad he's dead," said one of the men.[77]

Henry Barrow, in a rare show of emotion, became so enraged he chased the men out of the room and ordered the doors closed. L. C. blocked the door with outstretched arms. The remaining lines grudgingly dispersed and trudged homeward, urged on by a growing number of police sentries.

It had always been assumed that Bonnie and Clyde would be buried side-by-side—as predicted in Bonnie's poem, "The End of the Line" (also known as "The Story of Bonnie and Clyde"). Therefore, it came as a bit of a shock when it was announced that Clyde would be laid to rest beside Buck in Western Heights Cemetery on the twenty-fifth, long before the final arrangements had been made for Bonnie.

Actually, many factors contributed to the decision to separate the two. Lawyers for Billie Parker were still working feverishly to have their client released from the Tarrant County jail, where she was being held for the Easter Sunday murders in Grapevine, so that she could attend her sister's funeral. The Parkers had to wait for a court decision on the matter.[78] However, the most significant reason for the decision to separate Bonnie from Clyde was Emma Parker herself. Although publicly honoring her promise to Bonnie to never slander Clyde's name, Mrs. Parker apparently refused to consider burying her daughter with the man she held most responsible for the agony she felt.

"He had her for two years," said Mrs. Parker angrily. "Look what it got her. He's not going to have her anymore. She's mine now."[79]

At five o'clock on the afternoon of May 25, after a short service, the Barrow family filed out of the funeral home to the waiting cars and followed the black hearse across the viaduct to the cemetery. Throngs of onlookers awaited the arrival of the entourage. Jerking and tugging, the spectators actually prevented many of the family members from reaching the graveside ceremony.

Groping hands lifted clods of dirt and snatched bouquets of flowers, hauling them off as keepsakes. The noise was so great that the minister was forced to shout throughout the proceedings. A light plane flew overhead. Then, swooping low over the grave, the pilot released several bunches of flowers. A cascading shower of petals and stems descended upon the people. The accompanying note read: "from a flyer friend."[80] Spectators knocked one another down to retrieve the flowers as souvenirs.

One anonymous face in the crowd, drawing little or no attention at all, belonged to a sickly looking young man with protruding ears and horrible stomach cramps—Joe Palmer. At the time he was the most wanted outlaw in the Southwest, but he braved the crowds to bid farewell to a trusted friend. It angered the escaped convict to see vandals ripping Clyde's grave apart. He turned away before the service was complete.[81]

It has long been the tendency to criticize Clyde Barrow for having been little more than a petty thief. It seems ludicrous to criticize a criminal for not having been more of a criminal, or for not having been the type of criminal people expected him to be. But such is the substance of American popular culture.

Clyde Barrow never set out to become a popular folk hero, or antihero, depending on one's view. Nor did he care that much for money. Indeed, he gave most of his ill-gotten gains to family and friends. To Clyde Barrow, money was a vague and abstract concept; it was something one needed only to make daily expenses, nothing more, nothing less. It was certainly not the root of happiness. No, the seed of what grew inside Clyde Barrow was sown and nurtured to full maturity in prison.

From the moment Barrow first set foot on the soil of a Texas prison farm, his one burning desire, the thing he wanted most in the world, was to raid that farm—not to free Raymond Hamilton, as so many believe, but to implement the plan that he and Ralph Fults had outlined long before Hamilton entered the picture. Despite numerous setbacks, Barrow worked steadily, single-mindedly toward that end. Following the Eastham raid, however, life for Clyde Barrow became anticlimactic, despite the loyal companionship of his beloved Bonnie. Only death remained, and he knew it.

Across town in the McKamy–Campbell Funeral Home, at 1921 Forest Avenue (later renamed Martin Luther King Jr. Blvd.), the body of Bonnie Parker went on display. In fewer than twenty-four hours twenty thousand people filed past her bier, and gazed at the filmy white veil that did little to mask her bullet-torn face.[82] Surprisingly, the people remained orderly, almost sedate and dignified—a far cry from those gathered earlier on Ross Avenue.

One dozen lilies, the gift of an anonymous admirer, had been placed carefully on Bonnie's ornate, silver-trimmed casket. A blue silk negligee was draped over her stark, pale body. What was left of her hair had been cut to an even length and curled.

Among the people to view Bonnie on Friday were Mr. and Mrs. Roy L. Worley, of Lancaster. Roy was the truck driver who encountered Clyde Barrow, Raymond Hamilton, and Henry Methvin on a south Dallas County road shortly after the Lancaster bank robbery of February 27. Worley was not particularly interested in seeing Clyde, but Bonnie was an entirely different matter. He had known her three years earlier at "the courthouse cafe." Like Ted Hinton, Worley liked the tiny blonde waitress. Memories of her fresh smile and friendly manner continually came to mind. When at last he and his wife were able to make their way up to the casket, Worley could not bring himself to gaze upon Bonnie's stone-cold features.[83]

On Saturday morning, May 26, after initial ballistics reports indicated that the weapons recovered from Clyde Barrow's car were the ones used to kill Wheeler and Murphy in Grapevine,[84] Billie Parker was granted a brief leave of absence from the Tarrant County jail to attend her sister's funeral. Moving fast, the family made arrangements for the service to commence at two o'clock that afternoon.

Under the watchful eyes of Tarrant County deputies, Texas Rangers, and other officers,[85] Billie arrived in front of the McKamy–Campbell Funeral Home. A solemn crowd of three-hundred or more onlookers gazed curiously at the sister of the dead fugitive. She disappeared quickly inside where 150 close friends and relatives waited. Five minutes later Emma Parker arrived, accompanied by her son and daughter-in-law.

Inside the chapel the Parkers listened tearfully as the minister spoke. Then six pallbearers, one of whom was L. C. Barrow,[86] carried the casket bearing the body of Bonnie Parker to the hearse. Billie had to lean on two close friends as she stumbled repeatedly behind the remains of her sister.

Between West Dallas and Cement City, not far from the Krause farm where Bonnie had lived with her grandparents, the funeral procession stopped in front of the historic Fishtrap Cemetery.[87] There, adjacent to the tiny graves of Billie Parker's own two youngsters, victims of food poisoning in 1933, was an open pit.

The presence of newsreel cameramen and still photographers prompted the immediate family to witness the graveside ceremony from the sanctuary of the limousine. When someone occasionally peeked through the drawn curtains of the big automobile, newsmen, poised for action, would leap into view, popping flashbulbs and shouting orders. L. C. Barrow, dressed in a flashy blue suit, invariably moved between the many camera lenses and their intended subjects.[88]

Throughout the ceremony Henry and Cumie Barrow could be seen at graveside. Nearby, several children scaled the towering superstructure of a gravel sifter to gaze past the Parker limousine to the grave beyond. Great carloads of flowers continued to arrive during the brief outdoor service. The largest floral contribution was from a group of Dallas city newsboys—a form of thanks for the multiplicity of marketable news items generated by the outlaw pair in the course of their criminal careers. Their deaths alone had sold more than half a million papers in Dallas.[89]

Finally, at 3:45 P.M. on May 26, 1934, Bonnie Parker, the once-popular, vivacious waitress of three Dallas area cafes, was lowered into the soil of Fishtrap Cemetery. She was twenty-three years old. For many it appeared as though at long last the nightmare was over—but it was not. It was far from over.

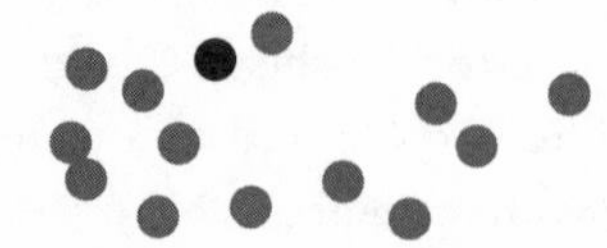

Escape from the Death House

Between the time of his arrest in Kemp, Texas, in April 1932 and the ambush of Bonnie and Clyde, in May 1934, Ralph Fults had spent most of his prison term behind the walls of the main unit at Huntsville, gradually working his way from the woodpile to the much-sought-after position of floor manager of the West Building. He had already established a thriving black-market business selling cigarettes, gambling paraphernalia, and weapons. But as floor manager he controlled the most lucrative commodity, cells.

Huntsville's inmates were forever scheming and looking for opportunities to get together, often to plan escapes. For cash, merchandise, or some future favor, Fults allowed the men on his floor to switch cells. Occasionally a convict from another floor would ask to trade places with someone under Fults's supervision. Such clandestine activities were common occurrences.

Truckload after truckload of new prisoners flooded Fults's block. Almost all of them would eventually need something Fults had to offer. His income and wealth was soon greater than many of the guards watching over him. Some of them were on his payroll.

His activities sometimes exceeded that of a humble prison merchant, however. There was a convict on his floor who had staged a series of petty armed robberies with another man. During one of the holdups the convict killed a man, the owner of a country store. Shortly thereafter he and his partner were apprehended and charged with murder.

The convict, who had actually committed the murder, offered to testify against his partner in exchange for immunity from the electric chair. The deal was arranged, and the second man was subsequently sentenced to death—solely on the testimony of the convict, the actual killer, whose life was spared. With his former associate relegated to the death house, the convict roamed Fults's cell block, bragging about his feat.

"Yeh," he said laughing aloud, "I pulled the best move you ever seen. I turned 'state's evidence' and drawed life, while my partner, he gets 'the chair.' And it's me that done the killing!"

"You can't play both sides down the middle," Fults thought. Many other prisoners in the West Building felt the same. One afternoon after lunch Fults spotted the convict walking in the upper yard, not far ahead. A number of other prisoners lingered in the yard, making use of their exercise period. When the convict rounded the corner of the South Building, the place everyone called "the jail," a man stepped up to him, presumably to ask for a light. A lone guard, patrolling north and south along the walkway, was just passing by. As soon as the guard rounded the corner, a ring of prisoners closed in.

Fults rushed forward. A swarm of hands pinned the convict's arms against his body. Someone grabbed the man by the hair and jerked his head back with a snap. A knife flashed. In an instant, the blade sank deep into the victim's throat. The assassins scattered. The convict dropped to the ground, his lungs filling with his own blood. A few minutes later the guard found the body.

On May 15 Fults was called into the Warden's office. He had long suspected Fults of carrying on more than the usual underground prison trade.

"Boy," said the Warden, leaning back in his big swivel chair, "you been moving prisoners around on your floor. You've been letting them buddy up and the like. We know that!"

Fults made no reply. "I see that arm of yours done healed up real nice," said the warden, indicating the gunshot wound that left Fults's arm in a sling for eighteen months. "Guess we'll be shipping you out to Eastham, give that arm a little exercise."

The next day Fults was hoeing cotton in the blazing Texas sun.

Not long after his transfer to Eastham Fults was told about the ambush of Bonnie and Clyde. Then just a few days later he received word of another ambush. Back in Huntsville, Ted Rogers, Lake Dallas gang member and admitted killer of Hillsboro merchant John N. Bucher, was stabbed in the back as he showered in the west cell block of the main prison. His killer, a San Antonio murderer named Pete, was placed in cell no. 1 of the death house for his own protection. Although Pete had friends among the guards, Ted had been popular with his fellow inmates, and reprisals were a certainty. Indeed, Fults, through the prison grapevine, suggested that someone heave five gallons of gasoline through the death house door and drench the killer. "Throw a match on the rat," Fults commanded. "Burn his ass to a crisp." Nevertheless, the plot was uncovered, and its would-be participants were dispersed to various farms. Pete was thus left to roam freely within the prison confines.

On May 25, while Clyde Barrow was being lowered into a West Dallas grave, Raymond Hamilton arrived in Huntsville, fresh from a Dallas mistrial and a ninety-nine-year sentence in Denton. For three long days he worked on the woodpile inside the walls unit, hoping to be forgotten by Lee Simmons and the rest of the world—but it was not to be. On the twenty-eighth, a Walker County Grand Jury handed down an indictment against Hamilton, listing him as a habitual criminal—a capital offense.[1] A trial date of June 12 was set. The state, at Simmons's request, would seek the death penalty. James Mullens, the drug addict who helped plant the weapons used in the Eastham raid, arrived in court with assurances from federal, state, and local authorities that all charges against him would be dropped if he testified about the killing of Major Crowson.[2] Afterward, witnesses to the murder of John N. Bucher were called to testify against Hamilton, and affidavits of Hamilton's conviction in the Carmen State Bank robbery were also entered into evidence. It was nearly dark before the trial was handed to the jury. Three hours later, on the fourth ballot, the panel reached its decision.

A hush fell over the crowd as the twenty-one-year-old prisoner was led into the courtroom, his chains and shackles clanking and jingling with each step taken. Among the reporters and photographers on hand for the reading of the verdict was Harry McCormick, the leathery *Houston Press* reporter whose blistering exposés of prison graft and brutality had by then made him an unwelcome sight in Huntsville.[3] Ray caught a glimpse of McCormick and grinned.

"Say, how come you never came by to see me after Eastham?" Harry asked.

"Hell, you never asked me to," answered Ray. "I'd have sure come by if I'd have known you wanted me to!"[4]

Suddenly the jury appeared, followed shortly by Judge Dean.

"Have you reached a verdict?" Dean asked the foreman.

"Yes, we have your honor," announced Reverend George Montgomery. "We find the defendant, Raymond Hamilton, guilty. We hereby affix a penalty of death in the electric chair."[5]

Hamilton, visibly shaken, tried to stammer through a statement. He apparently wanted to send a telegram to someone but spoke in a tone too soft to hear.[6] Ignoring the condemned man, Judge Dean dismissed the jury and motioned for Hamilton to be led away. Momentarily Ray perked up. He looked over his shoulder, toward McCormick.

"I'll break out of the death house," he called out. "And when I do, I'll come by to see you."[7]

McCormick smiled nervously, thinking Hamilton's prediction outrageous. Few had ever escaped from the walls at Huntsville, and no one had ever broken out of the death house. Those within earshot of Hamilton roared with laughter.[8]

On his way to the walls Ray asked if he could see his girlfriend, Mary O'Dare. The request was ignored. Hamilton was taken two blocks from the courthouse, marched through the prison gates and led to 7 level, Death Row. The smell of disinfectant was strong.[9]

Two days later the news of Joe Palmer's capture hit the streets.

At 9:30 A.M. on June 14 Palmer was making a painful attempt to walk the city streets of Davenport, Iowa. He really looked bad. His brand new grey suit, the one given to him by Bonnie Parker less than six weeks earlier, was soiled and ragged. Moreover, the ravages of an ulcerous stomach had greatly altered his physical appearance. The only other items still in his possession were the two Colt .45s tucked in his belt—the ones Clyde had passed to him just prior to the Sac City, Iowa, robbery.

Patrolman Elmer Schleuter could not help noticing the shabby-looking man trying with difficulty to make his way along the sidewalk.[10] Schleuter crossed the street to investigate. Before he could utter a word to the suspicious looking stranger, however, the officer found himself on the business end of a pair of automatics. Palmer was in the process of disarming the lawman when a local citizen named Al Schultze drove up, as if to offer assistance. He wound up assisting Palmer's flight from Iowa.

"Get in," Joe said, waving the patrolman into Schultze's car. "We're gonna ride."[11]

Fifteen miles west of town, however, Palmer started complaining about the way Schultze's car performed. Spotting another car, he sped up, overtaking Dr. W. H. Finch. The doctor's vehicle was a small coupe. Only three people could fit in the cab; Palmer, exhibiting his disdain for all lawmen, locked Officer Schleuter in the cramped rumble seat.

"Move over," Palmer ordered.[12] The doctor moved. At 3:30 on the morning of June 15 Palmer drove into St. Joseph, Missouri. Stopping the car, he turned to his captives. "I'll leave the car with y'all if you promise to turn right around and head back to Iowa," Joe said,[13] stuffing his pistols in his belt. Palmer then exited the car and started walking peacefully down the street, as if nothing had happened.

Retrieving Schleuter from his cramped confines, Finch and Schultze drove straight to the headquarters of the St. Joseph police. Minutes later a squad car full of officers located the unkempt kidnapper wandering along the same street where Finch, Schultze, and Schleuter had last seen him. The Texas outlaw offered no resistance as the cuffs were applied to his wrists.

At first, the St. Joseph authorities were unaware of their prisoner's identity. However, a check of his fingerprints soon revealed Palmer's lengthy record. He was immediately transferred to Texas, where Lee Simmons waited.[14]

On June 29 a Walker County jury quickly convicted Joe Palmer of the murder of Major Crowson.[15] He was sentenced to death and removed to the death house. Raymond Hamilton jumped to his feet when Palmer was led past his cell.

"Well?" Ray inquired. "What is it?"

"I got 'the hot squat'," Joe said, laughing.[16]

For Lee Simmons the events of May and June 1934 heralded the culmination of a desperate six months of hard work. In his memoir, *Assignment Huntsville*, he wrote: "The Barrow gang was out of the picture—'liquidated,' one would say now."[17] Simmons's personal promise to the mortally wounded Major Crowson had been fulfilled—his murder was "avenged."[18] For the first time since the Eastham break Simmons felt like relaxing. The loose ends were all tied up, the pressure removed. Then along came Charlie Frazier.

Few people knew much about Charlie Frazier, except that he was one of the most vicious and troublesome men ever to pass through the prison gates at Huntsville. In the space of sixteen years he had been convicted of a dozen crimes under four different names and escaped no less than nine times from three separate prisons across the south. On September 10, 1933, Frazier and eleven other inmates had battled their way to freedom in the notorious Angola prison break, one of the bloodiest escapes in Louisiana penal history.[19]

Recaptured in Texas, the slippery Frazier avoided extradition to Louisiana by accepting a life sentence in Texas for a series of Houston County robberies.[20] Lee Simmons would soon regret the day Charlie Frazier stepped into his professional life.

On January 13, 1934, while Clyde Barrow, Floyd Hamilton, and James Mullens were still ironing out the details of the Eastham raid, Frazier and two other men put a ladder against Huntsville's prison walls.[21] A guard spotted the convicts and opened fire, creasing Frazier's shoulder. Charlie and his cohorts were then placed in solitary confinement. Undaunted, Frazier was soon at it again. On March 7, 1934, Frazier and four other inmates, including Bonnie Parker's estranged husband, Roy Thornton, tried to place another ladder against the red brick prison walls.[22] Buckshot began spewing from two nearby guard towers, catching the prisoners in a cross fire. Frazier was struck just above the heart. He tumbled backward into the yard, gasping for breath. A second man was killed outright, while yet another was seriously wounded. Horrified, Thornton, who had been convicted of a series of burglaries the year before, raised his hands, a fifth convict doing the same. Though not expected to survive his wounds,[23] Frazier somehow pulled through, slowly regaining strength in the prison hospital. Lee Simmons would later observe that, next to Frank Hamer, Charlie Frazier had more lead in his body than anyone else in Texas.

In the weeks following the thwarted March 7 escape attempt, as he lay in the prison hospital convalescing from his near-fatal gunshot wound, Frazier became chummy with a convicted bank robber named Whitey Walker. Walker, also nursing a bullet wound, was a former member of the notorious Kimes gang of Oklahoma. He and his buddies, Irvin "Blackie" Thompson and Roy Johnson, had escaped from the Oklahoma State Penitentiary and staged a series of armed robberies in Texas.[24]

Walker, wounded at the time of his capture, and Johnson received life terms. "Blackie" Thompson was sentenced to death. In the prison hospital Walker told Frazier he wanted to save his friend Thompson from the electric chair. Charlie, of course, had just the plan.

Frazier discovered that a Huntsville guard was heavily in debt. When Charlie offered him five-hundred dollars to bring three guns into the prison, the guard jumped at the chance.[25]

The convict's outside contacts were an enigmatic pair of Texas sisters named Dot and Stella Houston. Not much is known about them, but their notoriety had spread throughout the underworld. Fults remembered hearing about them long before the summer of 1934. Authorities strongly suspected their involvement in a number of bank robberies but could never make the charges stick.[26] Dot and Stella had no trouble acquiring the cash and weapons for their good friend, Charlie Frazier, passing the items to the Huntsville guard sometime around the middle of July.

On Sunday afternoon, July 22, a baseball game between the Humble Oilers and the Prison Tigers was scheduled in the prison stadium, adjacent to the walls. It was a boiling hot day—just one in a long series of hot days that would lead to the more than 265 heat-related deaths across the Midwest in 1934. The general inmate population, eager for a break in the tedium of confinement, crowded enthusiastically into the red brick stadium for the ball game. Charlie Frazier was supposed to be among the spectators at the game, as were Roy Johnson and "Hub" Stanley, but they hid out and avoided detection. Soon the prison compound was empty. By 2:00 P.M., not a soul was in sight except for W. G. McConnell, the lone yard guard; a half-dozen picket guards were on the walls.[27]

At 3:30 a pair of black Ford V-8s moved slowly north along Avenue I. They casually parked less than two blocks from the buttressed red brick walls of the prison's southwest corner. The vehicles were driven by a pair of young women.[28] Inside the ballpark, it was the top of the ninth inning. The prison team led the oilfield crew by a score of 5 to 1. Sitting in the stands, Lee Simmons was pleased. His disposition would soon change.

At 4:10, ten minutes late, trusty Lee Brazil and two convict stewards arrived at the yard entrance of the death house. They bore dinners for the condemned men housed within. Brazil unlocked the heavy door, let the stewards pass, then stepped inside. He had just turned to close the door when a Colt .45 automatic pistol appeared in front of his face.

"Keep quiet," announced a voice from behind, "and don't hit that alarm."[29] Brazil saw Charlie Frazier glaring at him, a loaded gun in each hand and another tucked in his belt.

"Give me the keys," the desperado snapped.

Brazil relinquished the keys and backed away, the stewards frozen in place. Frazier made one of them unlock Thompson's cell door, then Palmer's. Frazier then handed Thompson a gun and forced Brazil and his assistants into the empty cells.[30] With a twist of the key, they were locked in.

Palmer asked about Hamilton. Frazier was going to leave him, but Palmer pointed out that Hamilton had helped him escape from Eastham, which was not entirely true. Frazier darted over to the twenty-one-year-old convict's cell and inserted the key.

"Anybody else?" he called out. Two remaining prisoners, a fellow named Rector and Ted's Roger's killer, Pete, who was still being kept on Death Row for his own protection, declined the offer.[31] Considering Frazier's disposition, it is amazing that he did not kill Pete right there. But he was pretty busy and in a hurry.

The four escapees dashed from the death house and joined Whitey Walker, Roy Johnson, and "Hub" Stanley in the yard. Moving to the picket station at the entrance to an area called the lower yard, they rushed the guard there, W. G. McConnell, and forced him to accompany them.[32]

"Keep your mouth shut or we'll drill you," Frazier said.[33]

They broke the lock on the gate to the lower yard and ran to the machine shop. There Walker grabbed a pair of bolt cutters, made available by some unknown accomplice, and led the men over to the fire house, applying the cutters to a light chain that secured an extension ladder. The convicts hustled their hostage down to picket station no. 7, in the southwest corner of the lower yard.[34] It was manned by Carey Burdeaux.

"Hey, you up there," Frazier called out. "Throw up your hands—we got your man down here."[35] Burdeaux, looking down, spotted the convicts and his colleague, McConnell, below. He raised his hands, and the ladder was placed against the wall.

"OK," Frazier declared, "death cell prisoners first."[36]

Hamilton scrambled up the ladder and jumped to the picket platform, taking Burdeaux's pistol as the guard stood with his hands raised. Palmer was next to arrive, followed by Thompson, who took Burdeaux's rifle.[37] The three convicts had already started descending the stairway from the picket station to the street below when suddenly three shots rang out. Guard Ed Roberts at no. 8 picket, 150 yards north of Burdeaux, had spotted Frazier scaling the wall and opened fire, knocking him to the ground.[38] Outside, Hamilton and Palmer continued down the stairs, but Thompson returned to the summit of the wall, drawing fire from Guard H. P. George at no. 6 picket, 150 yards east of Burdeaux. Thompson fired at George, momentarily stunning the guard with a glancing shot across the temple. Frazier tried to scale the ladder a second time, but Roberts shot him again. He toppled to the ground, dragging Roy Johnson with him.[39]

Thompson, who had once again started down the stairs leading to the street, returned to the summit of the wall for a second time. There he fired on Ed Roberts, who was advancing along the rim of the wall toward Burdeaux's station. Thompson fired the last round from his rifle, miss-

The remodeled southwest corner of the Walls Unit, Huntsville, Texas, 1994. On July 22, 1934, Raymond Hamilton, Joe Palmer, and Blackie Thompson scaled the wall at this point and became the only prisoners in Texas history to escape from the death house. (Photo by John Neal Phillips.)

ing Roberts. The convict drew his .45 automatic pistol and fired, soon emptying that weapon as well. Thompson threw the pistol at Roberts and ran down the stairs to the street, Palmer and Hamilton preceding him.[40]

"God, it looks like we're gone," cried Walker, halfway up the ladder.[41] A moment later, a Winchester slug ripped through his skull, killing the bank robber. "Hub" Stanley took one look at the carnage at his feet and ran behind a stack of firewood next to the pump house, Guard McConnell right behind.[42] Guard Roberts, on the wall, trained his weapon on Raymond Hamilton, who was already at street level, but he only managed to graze Hamilton slightly on the foot. Roberts then saw Frazier trying to climb the ladder to Burdeaux's station a third time. Astonished, the guard aimed and fired another bullet into the convict.[43]

Meanwhile, one block west of the prison, Huntsville resident Clyde Hall was at the front door of his lumber yard office watching the ensuing battle. Two figures had descended the stairs at the southwest corner of the prison wall, just outside Carey Burdeaux's station. A third man stood on top of the wall. He fired several shots with a pistol, then tossed the weapon aside.

The three men then darted down the fire escape as a pair of black Ford V-8s pulled up.[44] A gun went off. One man cried out and started limping. Another man was tearing off his prison clothes.[45] They dove into the first car, turning to watch their friend hop into the second car. With engines screaming and tires squealing, the Fords roared away, the first car nearly overturning as it slid around the corner of Fourteenth and Avenue J on two wheels.[46] The cars were last seen on Highway 75 north of town.

Lee Simmons and Warden Waid rushed from the ballpark to the southwest picket station. They climbed the stairs and looked into the lower yard. Whitey Walker was lying in a pool of his own blood. Charlie Frazier was being taken by stretcher to the hospital. Roy Johnson and "Hub" Stanley were being hustled away to solitary confinement. Fearing the worst, Simmons and Waid entered the compound. The first thing they saw was the open door of 7 Level.[47] Inside instead of "Blackie" Thompson, Joe Palmer, and Raymond Hamilton they found Lee Brazil and the two stewards. For the second time in seven months, the blond kid from West Dallas and the sickly Palmer had escaped from a Texas maximum security facility.

Ironically, Simmons had personally thwarted another escape attempt just thirty minutes before the death house break. He had been informed that two men were tunneling from the prison print shop, and he left the baseball game just long enough to assist in apprehending the pair. Simmons remembered seeing Frazier in the prison yard just after the incident. He had been forewarned that Frazier was not in attendance at the game. Simmons realized later that as he passed Charlie Frazier, the prisoner was no doubt carrying the three pistols used in the death house escape.[48]

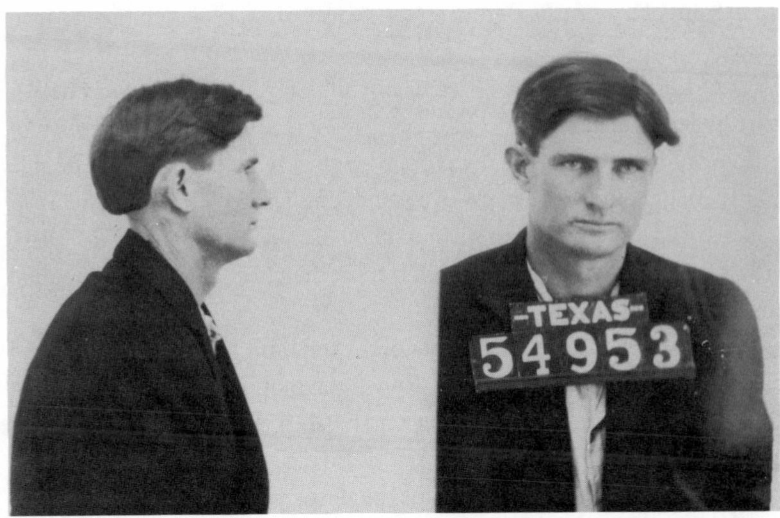

Charlie Frazier, 1934. Frazier was mastermind of the escape from the death house. (Courtesy of the Texas Prison Archives, Criminal Justice, Institutional Division [TDCJ-ID].)

On August 8, three weeks after the break, Joe Palmer was captured in Paducah, Kentucky. At first, Paducah authorities thought they had nabbed Alvin Karpis.[49] Proper identification was further complicated by the fact that Palmer had mutilated his fingerprints by rubbing them on concrete until they were virtually unrecognizable.

"You've got my picture," said Joe. "Now find out who I am on your own."

The following morning an anonymous caller suggested that Chief of Police Bryant refer to a certain detective magazine for the answer to his riddle. A full-page story about the escape from the Texas death house told Bryant everything he needed to know. Within a week Joe Palmer was back in Huntsville.

Three and a half months later Amarillo police got word that "Blackie" Thompson was using a local residence as his base of operations. For ten days city and county officials kept the house under surveillance—waiting for Thompson.[50] On the evening of December 6 a black Ford V-8 rolled up in front of the house. Before anyone could react, however, the car sped away.

The officers took to their cars. For fifteen miles Thompson held a narrow lead but then lost it all when lawmen cut loose with a volley of gunfire and punctured the tires of the bandit's vehicle. Forced to the side of the road, he decided to make a stand, emptying the contents of a .45 and a sawed-off shotgun at his pursuers. He was reaching for his 30.30 rifle when a line of gunfire struck him in the chest and face.[51] He died instantly.

With Palmer and Thompson out of the way, only one convict remained absent from his cell on Death Row—Raymond Hamilton. Lawmen throughout the country were put on the alert, but Ray had left a trail as cold as ice. Even the U.S. Bureau of Investigation failed to turn up a clue. Although alleged sightings of the desperado poured in daily from all parts of the country, it would be several months before lawmen would again come face to face with Hamilton.

Initial reports of the death house escape, filled with embellishments and twisted facts, filtered back to Ralph Fults. Some said no fewer than five guards had been killed outright as scores of prisoners scaled the walls. Eventually, however, the story was clarified, and Fults was able to understand the events of July 22.

It came as no surprise to anyone that Charlie Frazier was behind the break. His repeated attempts to escape had become legendary, plunging the Lee Simmons administration into one of the most embarrassing positions of its tenure. The damage to public relations caused by the Eastham raid had almost been repaired. Then the impossible happened. Three dangerous convicts, Hamilton and Palmer included, escaped from Death Row. "I could just hear the people say, 'Here we go again!'" Simmons would later observe.[52] But a lot more was being said.

To the delight of Fults and his fellow inmates, the nationwide publicity generated by the death house break set into motion a series of events that would lead to the eventual exposure of the rampant brutality present in the Texas Prison System.

Throughout the fall of 1934 rumor spread of Charlie Frazier's solitary confinement on 7 Level, in a death cell specially modified to eliminate any possibility of human contact. He was being fed only bread and water and was prevented from bathing, shaving, or even cutting his hair.[53] He tried several times to smuggle messages out of the prison. Most were intercepted, but some slipped through, finding their way to Harry McCormick by way of the prison chaplain, Father Hugh Finnegan.[54]

McCormick asked for an interview with Frazier, but the request was steadfastly denied. Nevertheless, his articles, charging the prison system with overt brutality and corruption, began to produce tiny ripples in the hallowed halls of state government. Governor Miriam Ferguson commissioned Mrs. J. E. King, of San Antonio, to tour the prison units. King had once chaired the Prison Advisory Board. Her testimony before a joint committee of the Texas House and Senate in 1925 had exposed the extent of the brutality and horrible living conditions in existence throughout the Texas Prison System at the time. Among other things, she had characterized the Wynne Unit as "the tuberculosis farm."[55] Not much had changed in nine years.

It is not known what King found in Huntsville regarding Charlie Frazier, but at Eastham a bizarre incident occurred. Fults remembered seeing King, whom he and the other convicts always referred to as "Colonel" King, speaking informally with the prisoners at Camp 2.

"Do any of you men have any complaints about the treatment you've received here at Eastham?" she asked. The men murmured to themselves, glancing toward the shotgun ring nearby. Then two men stepped forward. "We have some things we'd like to talk about," said one of the men. King jotted down their names, along with their prison numbers, and promised to return the following weekend with an assistant to take a deposition.

Later in the week, however, "Boss Killer" made a sudden appearance at Eastham. Fults was working in the double drainage ditch, clearing it out for the coming winter rains, when he noticed the guard and two other men moving toward the convicts who had spoken to King.

"Come here, boys," called "Boss Killer." "The warden wants to see you."

The men were marched beyond a low rise. Seconds later, several shots shattered the still morning air. Fults kept on working, a shotgun trained on his back. He was not the least bit surprised.

On the following Sunday King returned to an entirely different situation at Eastham. The men were reserved, unwilling to talk.

"Where're the two boys I saw last weekend?" she asked.

"Oh, them two?" a guard said. "Why, they done tried to escape, ma'am. We had to shoot them dead." Not another man spoke, their willingness to aid in the investigation poignantly squelched. Soon the convicts dispersed. The governor's probe was over.[56]

Later that fall Miriam Ferguson was voted out of office. It is doubtful that she would have had enough time to make use of "Colonel" King's findings had she been able to uncover anything substantial. Nevertheless, the governor and her husband seemed determined to do something for Texas's inmates before her term expired on January 15, 1935. Together they began reviewing the individual cases of a select number of convicts with the idea of issuing conditional pardons for each man, one of whom was Ralph Fults.

With the help of the state representative from McKinney, Fults's papers were pushed through the red tape. He was then transferred from Eastham to Imperial, a minimum security farm near Sugarland, Texas. At that point his imminent release loomed before him like a dream. Just a few weeks from his twenty-fourth birthday, Fults was ready to leave his past behind and start anew.

Bonnie and Clyde were dead. Joe was on death row. Methvin had been arrested by Oklahoma authorities. Ted had been stabbed to death. Jack, Fuzz, and Bybee were serving long sentences, and Johnny had completely disappeared. Of the old gang, only Raymond Hamilton remained at large, and he was the last person Fults wanted to see.

Not long after the new year 1935 the Fergusons paid a visit to Imperial. It was not an unusual sight.[57] Both Miriam and her husband Jim made frequent visits to the state's many prisons to talk with the inmates. Some have implied that a convict with enough cash could have bought his way out of prison while Miriam Ferguson was in office. The phrase: "Pardon me, 'Ma' did!" became a familiar joke in Texas. Nevertheless, Fults recalls a great many poor men who were pardoned—himself included.

"Don't you do us like Buck did," Mrs. Ferguson warned. "Don't get caught up in that outlaw life again."

"No, ma'am. You don't have to worry about that," said Fults.

On January 10, 1935, Ralph Fults walked through the front gates of the Imperial Farm,[58] a wrinkled suit on his back and ten dollars in his pocket. In Sugarland he caught the overnight bus to McKinney. He celebrated his twenty-fourth birthday at home.

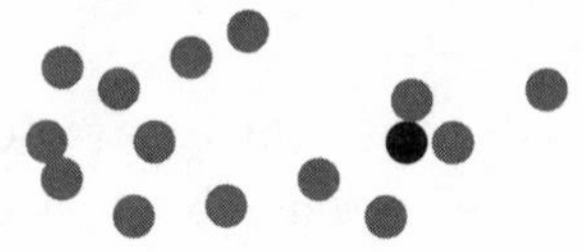

Ambush in McKinney

Following their escape on July 22, 1934, Hamilton, Palmer, and Thompson spent several days on the open road together. They traveled cross-country from Texas to Indiana to Kentucky before splitting up.

Throughout the summer and fall, while his former companions succumbed to their separate fates, Raymond Hamilton settled down in Dallas, apparently moving about at will. Later he relocated to Longview, in northeast Texas, and there resumed his criminal career.[1]

One night Floyd Hamilton introduced his younger brother to a stranger, a gorgeous young woman named Katie. Katie, a twenty-three year-old candy store clerk, had become mildly infatuated with the young bandit after discovering that a fellow employee was, in reality, one of Hamilton's younger sisters. She asked to meet Ray, and Floyd agreed to arrange it. Ray took one look at the lovely, auburn-haired lady and stood transfixed, no doubt puzzled by her interest in a man like himself. Nevertheless, as Floyd later said, "electricity flowed."[2]

"Tell my boss I won't be back to work," Katie said with a laugh, deciding to leave with Ray.[3]

On January 26, 1935, Floyd and Raymond slipped on a pair of greasy overalls, donned felt hats, and went out to make a discreet inquiry about the availability of a small frame duplex at 2614 Harrison Street, one block from Grand Avenue in south Dallas.[4] The owner, Mrs. M. B. Brown, found the two immensely polite strangers to be above reproach. Thinking them to be "factory workers with rather attractive wives," Mrs. Brown decided to let the two young couples rent the house.

At 9:15 A.M. on the morning of February 4, 1935,[5] Ray, Floyd, and a friend named John robbed the bank in Carthage, Texas.[6] Outside of town the trio switched from their Ford V-8 to John's four-cylinder Model A, hoping the police would not expect bank robbers to use such a vehicle.[7] They also traded their suits for a pair of well-worn coveralls. Raymond donned a ten-gallon hat. The three men then split the $970 haul and started back to Dallas. At some point John parted company with the brothers. Raymond and Floyd continued on in the Model A.

At 10:15 P.M. on February 4 the Model A turned down the alley behind the Harrison Street house. The duplex looked quiet as Raymond pointed the nose of the car toward the narrow driveway parallel to the house. Floyd got out, walked around to the rear of the building, and tapped out a prearranged code on the back door glass. Suddenly, heavy foot-steps thundered across the pier-and-beam flooring, echoing like drums in Floyd's ears.

"Police!" he shouted, whirling around. "Duck!"[8]

The words had barely rolled off the end of his tongue when a succesion of explosions shot a shaft of flame past his head. Feeling as if he were moving in slow motion, Hamilton dove from the unpainted wooden steps of the house and tried to take cover behind the Model A less than five feet away. A shotgun blast roared past his shoulder. He recovered just in time to prevent a second load of buckshot from ripping his body in half.[9]

Raymond tumbled from behind the wheel of the Model A just as a charge of buckshot burst through the windshield and ripped through the upholstery on the driver's side. On the way down Hamilton felt something hot slam into his neck. It felt like someone's fist, but it was not. A 30.30 slug had found its mark. With blood staining his shirt collar, Raymond pulled himself around behind the mutilated car, drew his .45, and pumped several shots into the darkened house. Floyd, joining his brother, also opened fire.

When a figure appeared at the threshold of the side door, both brothers raised their weapons. A volley of well-placed shots struck the officer's shotgun, wrenching it from the startled man's fingers.[10] Taking advantage of the momentary windfall, Floyd and Raymond bid each other farewell and took off through the alley, traveling in opposite directions. They would never meet again.

Someone spotted Floyd in Shreveport. Minutes later, as he prepared to board a bus, a half-dozen armed men closed in. Hamilton was arrested and promptly returned to Dallas, where he faced charges of felonious assault and conspiracy to harbor federal fugitives. As he awaited arraignment in the Dallas County jail, he learned the details of the Harrison Street ambush.

While the Hamiltons were in Carthage, Floyd's wife, Mildred, and Raymond's girlfriend, Katie, were spending a leisurely afternoon in downtown Dallas. At the end of the day the two young women hailed a taxi and returned to 2614 Harrison Street. The cab driver recognized Mildred. Knowing Floyd was wanted by the Justice Department, and hoping to claim a reward, the driver notified the police.[11]

Inspector E. V. Bunch and Captain Will Fritz, of the Dallas police, contacted special agent Frank Blake, of the U.S. Bureau of Investigation, for the purpose of organizing a deadly reception for Floyd Hamilton. Reasoning that Floyd and Raymond were together, the lawmen assembled eleven colleagues and drove to 2614 Harrison. Six officers took control of the house. Three men with high-powered rifles were positioned at the end of the street, and two others concealed themselves under the railroad platform at a nearby switching yard.[12] Bunch, Fritz, and Blake would cruise the neighborhood in a powerful Ford V-8. At 10:15 P.M. all was in readiness.

Suddenly headlights appeared in the alley. Was it Hamilton or just the next-door neighbor? From inside the house it was difficult to tell what was going on. The car was an old Model A, not a big V-8 as the lawmen expected. Notwithstanding, the lawmen braced themselves. A knock rattled the back door. J. F. Daniel rushed to the window and raised his weapon, his fellow officers doing the same. Before anyone could react, though, a voice cried out, "Police, duck!"

The lawmen fired. Officer Daniel stepped outside, peering at the car. Without warning a burst of gunfire erupted from behind the Ford, tore the shotgun from his hands, and nicked him on the finger.[13] A moment later footsteps echoed through the alley and faded in different directions.

While Floyd chased down a freight train two blocks away, Raymond sprinted south across roadblocked Grand Avenue to the offices of the Dallas Gas Company. Bleeding from the neck, he spotted a line of bright red service trucks, keys in place, parked in front of the company's maintenance building. Ray got behind the wheel of the first truck, drove right past the federal agents at Harrison and Grand, and escaped.[14]

The next morning Hamilton stole a newspaper from a rural mailbox and read about his brother's arrest in Shreveport.[15] He also learned of the detention of Mildred and Katie, the former being charged with conspiracy to harbor, the latter reportedly being held at some secret location without charges or legal representation.

Raymond knew the police were trying to force him into the open by eliminating his contacts.[16] What no one expected, though, was the appearance of a McKinney ex-con whose close association with both Clyde Barrow and Raymond Hamilton was not widely known—Ralph Fults.

One week after the Harrison Street ambush, Ralph Fults rode the Interurban train to Dallas, intent on doing anything to get away from the claustrophobic streets of McKinney. While in town, he took a bus to West Dallas, hoping to find Clyde's father and mother at home. As the bus rumbled over the dusty, rutted surface of Eagle Ford Road, he could see the old man seated beneath the distant canopy of the familiar old service station.

"Clyde bought that place down there in Louisiana," Henry Barrow told Fults. "He showed me the papers and everything. I know old man Methvin done set my boy up. Them 'laws' didn't even give him a chance. They just laid up in them bushes and shot him—him and little Bonnie. You should of seen that messed up deal in Arcadia. 'Bug-eyed' vultures gawking at my boy's body. Tearing up stuff and all."

While the old man spoke, Fults noticed a teenaged boy approaching from a side street. He had seen the youngster before, hanging around

Clyde, L. C., and Raymond. His name was Gilbert.

"Hi, Mr. Barrow," Gilbert said cheerily. Then turning to Fults he asked, "Wasn't you and Clyde in the joint together?"

"Maybe," Fults replied.

"Well, there's a friend of yours around the corner that wants to see you for a minute. Can you come?"

Fults shrugged his shoulders and nodded, bidding Henry Barrow farewell. He followed the boy down the street to a small house with curling leaves of ancient white paint flaking from its walls. Pulling back the sagging screen door, Gilbert ushered his guest inside. Standing beside the front window was Raymond Hamilton, a cocked .45 automatic clutched in his hand.

"Raymond," Fults said, shaking his head, "you're going to get in a spot if you hang around town like this."

"I need your help, Ralph," Hamilton said. "I got to get some guns. I had to leave everything—shotguns, automatic rifles, and ammunition—over on Harrison Street. All I got's this .45."

"Well, don't look at me," Fults replied. "I'm trying to stay clean."

"Man, I got my back against the wall," Hamilton said. "I just need a hand with one job, then I'll be clear."

"The biggest favor I can do for you is back off," Fults said. "I can help you get down to South America, where there ain't no extradition treaty. You're just buying time around here. My god, Ray, you've got 'the chair'!"

"Come on, Ralph," Hamilton said, "Me and Gilbert are going to knock over an armory in Beaumont, but I need somebody to go inside with me."

"I don't know," said Fults, remembering it was he and Clyde who first talked Ray into switching from car theft to armed robbery. Fults felt responsible for Ray's predicament.

"Well, OK," Fults said. "I'll help y'all get them guns."

Later that same night the trio left Dallas, speeding toward Beaumont, in far southeast Texas. Seven miles from their destination Gilbert was left on a side road with the backup car. Hamilton and Fults continued on to Beaumont in a stolen delivery truck.[17]

Shortly after midnight on February 16, 1935, the two bandits rolled up to the grey granite facade of the National Guard Armory on Wall Street, four blocks from the Beaumont police station. Fults and Hamilton jumped from the truck and used a crowbar to twist the padlock off the front door.[18] Inside they found a long, musty corridor. To one side was a padlocked storeroom. Forcing their way in, the intruders found a rack of Browning automatic rifles.

"Shhh!" Fults said. "Footsteps."

Fults drew his weapon; Hamilton, too. The burglars then burst into the corridor and aimed their pistols at wrinkled G. T. Owens, the night watchman. Fults sat the old man in a chair, tied his hands and feet with a length of rope, and placed a handkerchief over his eyes.[19]

After loading eight BARs and twenty-five clips into the rear of the panel truck, the two men broke the lock on a munitions chest and took three cases of steel-jacketed 30.06 shells, totaling 4,500 rounds of armor-piercing ammunition.[20] Slamming the rear doors, Fults and Hamilton jumped in the front seat of the truck and sped away, rendezvousing with Gilbert and the getaway car north of Beaumont. By morning the three of them were back in Dallas.

Fults parted company with Raymond and Gilbert and took the Interurban to McKinney.

A week later, on Saturday, February 23, Fults was enjoying eggs and grits for breakfast at his usual hangout, the City Cafe. As he scanned the pages of a newspaper, the door rattled open, and a young man stepped in. His name was Royce. A local bootlegger with strong ties to certain members of the city and county law enforcement community,[21] he was not the type of man Fults liked to associate with for very long. Royce's loyalties seemed to lie where the greatest gains were to be made. He walked over to his table and pulled up a chair.

"Somebody wants to see you," announced Royce in a low tone.

"Well, here I am," said Fults, looking up from his eggs.

"He's too 'hot' to come into town," the bootlegger explained. "I've got to take you out to him."

Fults was skeptical, but he went along nevertheless. Along a spur of the old Sherman road, just north of town, Royce maneuvered his four cylinder Model A. In the distance a black V-8 idled on the pavement.

Fults immediately recognized the youth at the wheel.

"C'mon, Ralph," Raymond Hamilton said with a smile, "ride with me to Oklahoma today. I'll bring you back tomorrow night."

"No, Ray," said Fults, stepping out of Royce's car. "I'd be doing you and me both a favor by staying out of that car of yours."

"C'mon," Hamilton pleaded. "We'll go up to Tulsa, do some messing around. I've got to be back tomorrow night. Royce, here's, holding some of my guns. I'm going to pick up a couple of them, then, because one of these I'm carrying is jammed."

Fults looked at Royce. "Oh yeh?" he snapped. "How come he can't get his guns now, Royce?"

"Because me and Lewis done stashed them in the wall of a house in town," replied the bootlegger excitedly. "It'll take us some time to get them out."

Fults was also acquainted with Lewis. He trusted him about as much as he trusted Royce. And he did not trust Royce at all.

"Well, what time are you two going to have them?" Fults demanded.

"Tomorrow night at seven sharp," Royce said.

"OK, Ray," Fults said, climbing in beside Hamilton. "I guess I'm up for a little ride." Hamilton shifted to first and took off.

"You shouldn't be messing with them bootleggers," Fults warned as he and Raymond sped north through Collin County.

"Them boys are okay," Hamilton said.

"They don't play in this kind of league," Fults said. "They're small time liquor runners, and they're friendlier with the law than they are with their own mothers."

"No," replied Ray, "you're wrong about them two."

By early afternoon the two Texans were browsing through the clothes racks at Dodge and Bonds Department Store in Tulsa, Oklahoma. Raymond picked out a dark blazer and a matching pair of trousers. Fults purchased a heavy leather jacket and an expensive white Stetson hat. The two unlikely tourists then checked into a small downtown hotel. Throughout the night all was quiet in Tulsa.[22]

Sunday, February 24, dawned cloudy and bitterly cold. Bad weather was approaching. Fults and Hamilton were up early. They ditched their

Texas car and stole a grey 1935 Ford V-8 coupe, later stopping in the Arbuckle Mountains to switch the car's license plates.[23]

At 6:45 P.M. Hamilton and Fults rode through the town of Anna, Texas, Fults's birthplace. Fults gripped a loaded .45 and scanned either side of Highway 75 in search of unusual movement. Within minutes the car was approaching the Weston cutoff, the planned rendezvous point for the meeting with Royce and Lewis.

The Weston cutoff was a seldom-used stretch of road traversing the Trinity River bottoms five miles north of McKinney. At one time it was part of Highway 5, the old road between Dallas and Sherman. When the more direct Highway 75 was constructed, it eliminated the need for the serpentine curves of the old road, much of which was totally abandoned. One of the loops, however, remained in use as a bypass linking the new highway to the nearby Weston Road.

Southbound motorists like Hamilton and Fults could simply turn right from Highway 75 onto the old road, cross the East Fork of the Trinity River, and merge onto the gravel-topped Weston Road. The strip, perhaps a mile in length, was remote and rarely traveled.

Flakes of sleet and snow began flashing in the glow of the coupe's headlamps as Hamilton made the slow turn from Highway 75 onto the cutoff and eased toward the distant concrete culvert where Royce and Lewis were supposed to be parked. The darkness made it difficult for Fults to see through the flurry of wind-driven ice. The temperature had dropped considerably in the previous hour, and it looked as if the roads would soon glaze over. Briefly, though, the weather gave way just long enough for the coupe's high beams to scan the road ahead. Tall, slender pines and broad-leafed oaks, their branches beginning to sag under the weight of the freezing rain, were all Fults could see.

"I don't like this," he said. "Those boys should have been here by now."

"They're here," said Raymond reassuringly.

"I don't see another car anywhere," said Fults. "I think something's going down. Better speed up."[24]

The coupe rolled gently toward the concrete culvert. Beyond that, perhaps two hundred yards away, an old wood-frame bridge across the

East Fork of the Trinity River loomed like a skeletal creature in the distance. As the wheels of the V-8 reached the culvert, Fults spoke again.

"There's something phoney here. We'd better step on it."

Hamilton shifted to second gear. Suddenly, without warning, the ditch on either side of the culvert lit up with a spurt of fire and flame, and the ear-splitting sound of high-powered weapons filled the air. For a terrifying moment the car seemed to stand still as if suspended on a thread. Shards of flying glass and twisted metal instantly filled the interior of the outlaw car, covering its occupants with debris.

Hamilton mashed the gas pedal to the floorboard. Gradually the V-8 pulled away, but not fast enough. A thunderous volley of steel-jacketed slugs drilled through the rear of the stolen Ford, passing between Fults and Hamilton and exiting through the dash. The radio exploded, and the clock above the rear-view mirror disintegrated. Waves of bullets poured into the heavy steel body of the car as it rocked with the resounding thuds of buckling doors, fenders, and wheel wells.

Raymond slumped over the wheel, a stream of blood dribbling from his forehead. Fults lurched toward his wounded friend and reached for the steering wheel. By then the car had nearly stopped. Unexpectedly, Hamilton straightened up.

"I'm okay," he said, shaking his head.

The outlaw gunned the engine and accelerated toward the narrow wooden river bridge. Fults pulled himself over the seat, grabbed a BAR, and poked the barrel through the shattered rear window. Gunfire was still erupting from the distant culvert. He pulled the trigger, but only three or four shots rang out. He had picked up the jammed rifle. Taking the second weapon, he then raked the dark river bottom with a sweeping, circular motion. He felt something hot brush past his head. Fults jammed clip after clip into the magazine and unleashed more than eighty rounds toward his unseen assailants. Only then did the shooting from the culvert stop.

As Hamilton made a wide loop onto the Weston Road, Fults sank low in the rear seat. Freezing rain and blasts of cold air poured in through the shattered windows. The interior of the once-comfortable Ford looked as if it had been hit by a tornado. Everything in sight was either broken or shredded.

Fully expecting more officers to pop into view at any moment, Fults and Hamilton peered anxiously into the deep shadows along the road. Car lights suddenly appeared just ahead of them. The driver of the innocent-looking vehicle seemed in no hurry. Perhaps it was only a farmer. Fults raised his weapon and glared cautiously at the approaching vehicle.

"It's that SOB, Royce!" Fults said. "The bastard set us up, and now he's on his way down for a look at the kill." Fults heaved the still-warm rifle through a jagged hole in the side window.

"No, Ralph," shouted Raymond, whirling around, "his wife's with him!

The McKinney, Texas, constable who organized the attempted ambush of Raymond Hamilton and Ralph Fults, February, 1935. He holds the Remington Model 8 he used in the ambush and stands before the bullet-riddled Ford V-8 in which Hamilton and Fults were riding when the officers opened fire. Note the bullet holes in the windshield where Fults was seated. (Courtesy of Cecil Mayes.)

You'll kill her too!"

Fults peered through the sleet as the bootlegger's car passed. A young woman was indeed seated on the passenger side. Fults sank down in the cold, wet rear seat. Within minutes the car reached the village of Weston. In the icy distance a Model T rattled north, just beyond the square.

"Let's take that guy," said Raymond, speeding up.[25]

Twenty-year-old L. B. Harlow, behind the wheel of the target Model T, had just pulled out onto the road when the grey V-8 rolled up beside him. Harlow knew instantly that something was wrong. Two men were staring at him with great intensity as they drew alongside. A multiplicity of large holes festooned the coupe's contoured body. Not a single piece of glass remained intact in the car. Suddenly the Ford swerved in front of Harlow's little car, forcing it to stop. As the two desperate men emerged, young Harlow slid over on the seat of his own machine. By chance, he had been stopped in front of a friend's house.

"Perhaps," he thought, "I can make a run for it."

Although the house stood less than twenty feet away, Harlow's plan failed when Ray, nearly dwarfed by the rifle he carried, hurried up to the driver's side of the Model T, a pronounced limp in his stride. By then Fults had crowded in on the passenger side.

"C'mon with us," Ray said. Harlow stepped to the frozen pavement between the two gunmen and climbed aboard the V-8. The appearance of the car's wrecked interior startled him. The seat cushion under him was stitched with giant holes, the radio was crushed, and the rear view mirror was a twisted piece of jagged metal.[26]

"They must of hit the gas tank," Hamilton said. "We're running on fumes."

Just then a Model A passed them on the slick road and traveled slowly in the opposite direction. Hamilton whipped around and started after the unsuspecting motorist. A block and a half away Ray overtook the little four-cylinder Ford and forced a bewildered sixteen-year-old J. C. Loftice into the ditch.

Hamilton jumped from the car and ran up to Loftice. Fults grabbed Harlow by the arm and outflanked the Model A, preventing Loftice's escape on foot.

"Get in back," Ray ordered Harlow as he opened the Ford's rumble seat. "Get down on the floor."[27] Ray and Fults then approached the driver.

"Get over," they told the frightened Loftice. The boy slid to one side and relinquished the wheel to Hamilton, Fults squeezed in on the opposite side. Harlow was about to leap to freedom when Ray backed out of the ditch, shifted to first gear, and took off. Within seconds the car was traveling much too fast to jump from.[28] He would have to wait until the car stopped again. A mixture of rain, sleet, and snow pelted the young hostage in the face as the coupe literally skidded over the narrow gravel road between Weston and Celina.

"This weather's getting pretty rough," said Fults. "We ought to hole up some place for the night." Less than two miles away the lights of a farmhouse popped into view.

"D'you know these folks?" Ray asked the wide-eyed J. C. Loftice.

"Yes sir," he answered, "that's the Mayes place."

Ray turned in and drove around behind the house.[29]

"Go to the back door and ask this Mr. Mayes to come on out here," Hamilton ordered Loftice.

A strong wind whipped around the large rambling house as Loftice stepped to the kitchen door and knocked. The door opened, and an elderly man with a heavily wrinkled brow appeared. It was Bill Mayes, owner of the farm. Raymond rushed out from the shadows. "OK," he said, "get inside." Ray then followed Loftice and the old man into the kitchen. Momentarily Fults and Harlow appeared, carrying the rifles and a sack full of clips.

"Just call me 'Gabe,'" Fults announced, removing his hat politely. At that point he saw the brim, tattered and dangling by a few threads. A pair of large bullet holes were visible in the crown. He suddenly realized what he had felt whistling past his hair during the ambush. Two slugs had come within inches of tearing the top of his head off.

"Here," Fults said with a shaky smile, handing the hat to old man Mayes, "I won't be needing this anymore."[30]

In the kitchen Fults and Hamilton found Sally Mayes hovering over a gurgling cauldron of beans. Her twenty-two-year-old son, Roy, retreated to the bedroom to shield his toddler daughter from the unknown gunmen invading his parents' home.[31]

"Anybody else in the house?" Ray asked excitedly, his eyes darting nervously about the room.

"Yeh," answered Mrs. Mayes, "my daughter-in-law, Cecil. She's sick in bed with the flu."

"Show me," Hamilton demanded, waving everyone into an adjoining bedroom. The hostages crowded around the thickly blanketed bed containing the pale form of a sick woman, the wife of young Roy Mayes.

"Ma'am," Ray began, removing his leather gloves. Streaks of blood trickled down the side of his face. "I'm Raymond Hamilton. We're not going to hurt none of you folks. We'd just like to hole up here for the night and let this weather pass."[32]

The announcement startled L. B. Harlow. Neither he nor any of the other hostages had the slightest idea that the small, soft-spoken youth standing before them was the notorious badman they had all heard so much about, by then called "Public Enemy No.1" in the Southwest.[33]

"We don't want your valuables," Ray added. "We rob banks, insurance companies, and oil refineries. We ain't never robbed a poor man."[34] Hamilton then raised his right hand to his head and shook broken glass from his thinning blond hair. Sally Mayes appeared with a pan of hot water and soap and gently sponged the outlaw's wounds as he spoke. She then offered Hamilton and Fults a plate of beans, biscuits, berry cobbler, and coffee.[35]

Hamilton spoke about his mother and brother. He said he felt bad about the trouble he had caused them. Several newspapers would later imply that Raymond reacted callously to queries about his family, but such statements contradicted what the hostages reported.[36]

"The 'feds' have them on trial, you know," Ray said, "for harboring me, and Clyde, and Bonnie. They've even got my father-in-law in court. He ain't never seen me on the lam."[37]

After supper Ray took one of the BARs and moved into the living room.

"I'm gonna try and fix this thing," he said, turning to young Roy Mayes. "Would you sit by that window, there, and watch the road? Let

Key players in the saga of Bonnie and Clyde, on trial for harboring their slain companions, 1935. Left to right: Hilton Bybee (obscured), Floyd Hamilton, S. J. W., L. C. Barrow, Henry Methvin, W. D. Jones, Joe Bill, James Mullens (Jimmy LaMont), and J. C. Floyd Hamilton later commented that at the time of this photo no one suspected Henry Methvin's involvement in the ambush of Bonnie and Clyde, hence the friendly rapport between Methvin and L. C. Barrow. (Courtesy of the Public Library, Texas/Dallas History Archives Division, Hayes Collection.)

us know if a car turns in."[38]

Fults decided to visit the desperately ill Cecil Mayes. The young woman watched weakly as the tall, lean intruder pulled up a chair and sat down. He had a Colt .45 automatic pistol tucked in his belt and a Browning automatic rifle resting on his knees.

"Don't worry none, ma'am," he said, reassuringly. "We ain't going to hurt nobody. If a car pulls in here, we won't be having any shooting in this house. We'll go out to the barn and make a stand there."[39]

Mrs. Mayes's eyes brightened.

"I was born over in Anna," Fults said. "Do you know a woman by the name of Agnes Comer?"

Mrs. Mayes nodded. "Well, that's my aunt," he said with a smile. Fults then walked to the front room. Raymond was working on the damaged rifle. Fults and Hamilton were both on edge. They understood the vulnerability of their position. The house was of the classic Prairie pier-and-beam style, constructed above ground. Numerous windows and storm shutters made a variety of strange sounds as they creaked, groaned, and slammed with the windy blasts of the ferocious winter storm. More than once a crashing shutter sent the two outlaws leaping to their feet, weapons drawn.[40]

"What was that?" they would shout, eyes bulging.[41]

Nevertheless, shortly after midnight both Hamilton and Fults dozed off. No one in the house made a move to disturb them.[42]

At 6 A.M. the fugitives decided to get on the road.

"We'll take you two," said Hamilton, pointing to Harlow and Loftice, "and Mr. Mayes can drive us in his new Chevy."

"Oh no," interrupted Roy, the old man's son, "don't take my Dad. He'll get you killed on them icy roads. You'd best let me drive that car."[43]

"OK," said Raymond, "we'll take you instead."

Harlow, Loftice, and Mayes helped their heavily armed captors load the late-model Chevrolet with weapons and ammunition. The teenaged Loftice pilfered one of the machine gun clips as a souvenir. While the engine was warming up, Raymond approached Sally Mayes.

"Ma'am," he said, "I'm afraid I ain't got enough money to pay for your hospitality, but I promise to return one day and pay y'all back. I promise."[44]

Roy Mayes, at the wheel of his father's car, eased out to the main road and turned west toward Celina. Harlow occupied the passenger side of the sedan's front side while Loftice sat in back between Fults and Hamilton.

"In Celina," Fults said, "turn toward Frisco, then take Highway 24 to Lake Dallas."

Mayes followed the instructions implicitly, stopping at a lakeside filling station just south of Denton.[45]

"How about that Ray Hamilton giving them McKinney police the slip last night?" asked the attendant. Everyone smiled and nodded as if amazed.[46] At 7:30 A.M. the car slipped onto the main square of Denton and pulled up to a newspaper stand not far from the two banks Fults and Clyde Barrow had planned to rob in 1932.

Raymond handed Harlow a half-dollar and asked him to pick up a newspaper and a pack of cigarettes.[47] On the way out of town Fults scanned the headlines.

"That constable from McKinney and five of his buddies was all that was hiding under that culvert," he said. "Listen to this—"Smoot" Schmid and the Department of Justice was supposed to have five carloads of cops on that road, but they got the call too late."[48]

"Anything in there about them bootleggers?" Ray asked.

"Well," Fults said, "they say they've got somebody in custody and that they've recovered the Beaumont guns from this guy's house."[49]

"Royce." Ray said.

Just when and how Raymond Hamilton became acquainted with Royce and Lewis is unclear. Nevertheless, at some point following the National Guard Armory raid in Beaumont, Hamilton paid them to hide six of the eight Browning automatic rifles taken from the armory. Somehow, a McKinney, Texas Constable discovered the Beaumont guns stashed in Royce's house and recognized the golden opportunity of his life. Royce and Lewis were offered the chance to put Hamilton on the spot in exchange for the freedom to continue bootlegging in the county without legal interference.[50]

"It'll be a cinch," the Constable told the whiskey sellers. "You set up Hamilton, and we'll kill him outright. After that you can sell your liquor in this county forever because I'll run for sheriff and win. Hamilton'll be dead, so will Fults. Nobody'll be the wiser. We'll make it a Clyde-and-Bonnie-type ambush."[51]

Royce and Lewis had no choice. They could either finger Hamilton or face federal charges of conspiracy for harboring and accepting stolen goods. They readily agreed to the deal. The constable then contacted five trusted colleagues and got down to work. There was little doubt that he and his men fully intended to kill both Hamilton and Fults.[52]

To avoid criticism, the McKinney constable arranged for Dallas County Sheriff "Smoot" Schmid and agents of the U.S. Bureau of Investigation to be on standby with five car loads of officers to back them up.

The move was purely superficial. To shut out the other officers and thus claim all the credit for himself,[53] the constable planned to give Schmid and the Justice Department men the wrong time for the meeting and then claim Hamilton showed up earlier than expected. However, by the time Sheriff Schmid and the others arrived on the evening of February 24, the outcome of the attempted ambush had already been determined, and the constable's plans lay in ruin.[54]

At 9:30 the following morning the 1929 Chevrolet bearing Hamilton, Fults, and their trio of hostages rolled up to Marguerite's Cafe at 1523 East Lancaster in Ft. Worth. It was very cold inside the car, and the travelers had decided to pick up some hot coffee and eggs to warm up. Ray waited outside with Harlow and Loftice while Fults led Roy Mayes up to the door of the little restaurant. Cafe owner Marguerite Raney watched curiously as young Mayes stepped inside and made his way to the counter. Another man, tall and lean, stood outside and peered occasionally through the ice-caked glass.

"Let me have five bacon-and-egg sandwiches, coffees, and a bottle of milk," Mayes requested.

The two took the food and drink back to the car, and all of the five youths settled down for a quick feast. The troupe then began prowling the city streets in search of a fast car for Fults and Hamilton to steal. Not far away Earl Penix had just started his new Ford V-8. He intended to let the engine warm up for five or ten minutes while he dashed back inside his home for another cup of coffee.[55] The car only had four hundred miles on it, and Penix was still breaking it in. Mayes rounded the corner just as the unsuspecting motorist jumped from his car and ran back to the warmth of his house.

"Hold up," Ray said, "here's my chance."[56] Without another word the bandit exited the Chevy and raced over to Penix's Ford. He was already pulling away before anyone saw what was happening.

"Follow him," Fults ordered Mayes.

The Weston boy quickly drove up behind the brown V-8, sticking close to the tracks it made in the fresh ice and snow. Thirteen miles southeast of Ft. Worth, near the town of Mansfield, Raymond pulled over.

"OK," the gunman announced, hiking back to the Chevrolet as it rolled to a stop behind him, "we'll leave y'all here. Now promise us that y'all won't tell anybody about this 'till you get back home. We need some lead time."

Mayes and the others agreed, watching with relief as Fults slid from the back seat and started transferring weapons to the new car.

"Can we have some money for gas back home?" Roy asked. "We're busted." Hamilton laughed as he pulled a small amount of silver from his pocket.

"I ain't got much either," he sighed. "Here's two bucks. That'll get y'all back to Weston."[57] Hamilton then removed his gloves and necktie. "Y'all can have these too, as souvenirs. Something for y'all's grandkids." Within minutes, he and Fults were gone. It was two in the afternoon.

Meanwhile, back in McKinney, the embarrassed constable there tried hurriedly to cover his tracks.[58] On the twenty-sixth, Texas Governor James Allred added to the rising swell of criticism by personally admonishing the McKinney officers, saying, "The Hamilton trap was badly bungled."[59] J. Edgar Hoover, angered by the apparent attempt to exclude his own agents, severely chastised McKinney's constable. He later revealed to U.S. Congressman Halton W. Summers that his men intended to "kill Ray."[60] In the interim, while all of Texas was looking for Hamilton and Fults, the outlaws were actually cruising the northern reaches of the Midwest.

In Minnesota they robbed a small town bank of several thousand dollars. Their escape was greatly inhibited by the onset of one of the worst ice storms in Minnesota history. A deluge of sleet and snow swept across the state, snapping power lines, freezing water pipes, and halting all traffic.

On a country road Hamilton and Fults were forced to pull over as twenty-foot snowdrifts surrounded their car. As the fuel tank was nearly full, the two desperadoes left the motor running so that they could take advantage of the heater. Before long the blower burned out, and the temperature within the car plummeted. Faced with the prospect of freezing to death, the outlaws searched the cab for something to fuel a fire. The few old newspapers they carried did not last long; neither did their road maps and other assorted papers. Wrapping themselves in blankets, Fults and Hamilton acquiesced to using a most unusual fuel for their fire—money. Throughout the night the bandit duo nursed the tiny, glowing fire, that burned before them on the floorboard of their car. They fed the flame with wads of ones and fives stolen from the Minnesota bank.

The following day a snow plow pushed its way past the stranded V-8 and forged a path to the main road. Raymond cranked the engine and pulled in behind the giant road machine. Before long he and Fults were speeding south toward Texas and a warmer climate. It was time, they decided, to implement Hamilton's long-ago-promised visit to Harry McCormick.

On Monday, March 18, Hamilton and Fults pulled up to a sandwich stand in the Houston, Texas Heights. One of the waitresses was the younger sister of Dot and Stella Houston, the women who had aided in the death house break eight months earlier. Through them, it was hoped that a meeting could be arranged with McCormick. Later that same evening the telephone rang at the reporter's home.

"Mack?" a woman said, "there's a man here that wants to talk to you. He's got some news from Huntsville. Meet me at the intersection of Shepard Drive and Eleventh."[61] Twenty minutes later, as McCormick approached the prescribed corner, someone stepped into view. The newsman slowed.

"Tail my sister," said Dot, as she hopped in beside McCormick. The reporter then recognized Stella at the wheel of a 1935 V-8 that waited across the road. She turned west on Eleventh, McCormick close behind. Within minutes the two cars were speeding northwest on Hempstead Road. At Satsuma they turned left onto a seldom-used dirt road. The travelers rattled over the graded lane for more than a mile before stopping. Stella flashed her headlights. Not far away another car flashed its lights. Stella proceeded toward the phantom vehicle, McCormick imitating every move.[62]

"There's your story, Mack," said Dot,[63] nodding toward the darkened vehicle. The newspaperman climbed from his vehicle and walked over to the other V-8. In the front seat a tall, lean man was gripping the steering wheel and scanning the moonlit countryside. In the back was Raymond

Hamilton, a Browning automatic rifle lying across his knees.

"Hello, Harry," he said, removing his hat. "I'm sorry it took me so long to get here to talk to you, but when your life is on the line you have to be mighty careful. Everything is jam up," Hamilton went on to say. "Get in here with me. Did you bring plenty of pencils and paper?"

"I don't need either, Raymond," McCormick answered,[64] maneuvering past a great arsenal of weapons as he slid over next to Raymond.

"I want to tell you how thankful I am to you and Mefo [*Houston Press* editor] for the things you've tried to do to get humane treatment for the boys in 'the joint.' I know you'll be fair and tell the truth. A good many folks out there are on my side. They know I never killed nobody. But before we get into that, we better move on. It's not safe to hang around in one place for too long."[65]

Fults cranked the engine and started driving, Stella following in the second V-8. Dot drove McCormick's car.

"I can't tell you who this man is," Ray announced, pointing to Fults. "He'll speak for himself."

Harry McCormick, 1948. As ace reporter for the *Houston Press*, McCormick risked his career to expose the brutality of the Texas prison system. He also risked his life to meet Raymond Hamilton and Ralph Fults for the purpose of transferring a large quantity of stolen cash to a Houston lawyer for Joe Palmer's defense. (Courtesy of the Fults family.)

"Hell," Fults said, "I may as well tell you everything. Them cops know who I am, anyway. I'm Ralph Fults, from McKinney, and I've run with Clyde, Bonnie, and Raymond off and on since '32. Ma Ferguson gave me a conditional pardon last January, and I was riding with Raymond when them double-crossing bootleggers put us on the spot. The papers all say 'unidentified companion,' but them lawmen know it was me in that car with Ray. I was the bait, and them bootleggers fingered us. I mean to ride with Raymond to the finish now. Hell, they mean to kill me anyhow."[66]

"How in the hell did you guys get out of that McKinney deal alive?" McCormick asked.

"Man," said Hamilton, "they shot a couple o' holes in Ralph's hat and grazed me across the temple. Nearly knocked me for a loop. Ralph jumped in the back and let them have it with a Browning."[67]

As Hamilton spoke, the three cars zipped through a succession of villages—Cypress, Hockley, and Waller. At Hempstead the cars turned north on State Highway 6, moving over that road for several miles before taking a virtually unknown cutoff near an unincorporated gathering of farmhouses known locally as Retreat.[68] Four miles from the main highway Fults, Stella, and Dot extinguished the lights of their respective vehicles and coasted into an open pasture.

"Now," said Raymond, turning to McCormick, "how're we going to do this? Ralph says it's OK to use his name, but what about the women? I don't want no heat coming down on them."[69]

"I always protect my sources," said McCormick. "I won't even mention them. It'll be as if they're not even here."

"Fine," said Ray. "Ask me whatever you want. I may not answer, but ask all the questions you want."

"How did you manage that death cell break?" McCormick asked.

"Well, of course, I got all the credit for that, but to tell you the truth, I had very little to do with that escape," admitted Raymond.[70] "It was Charlie's baby all the way, and now I'm out, and he's rotting in that hole. Joe put in a good word for me, and they let me in on it, which brings me around to something." Hamilton reached for a large grocery sack and handed it to the reporter.

"This here's the real reason for this little get together. Me and Ralph want you to give this to Joe's lawyer. There's a couple of grand in there. We nearly froze to death getting it, too! We hope it'll buy a stay of execution. It's the least we can do. And there will be more money coming soon. We're planning a job in Mississippi. Maybe we can buy Palmer a life sentence. Who knows? Anyhow, I'm telling you this because I know you'll keep your yap shut."[71]

"I couldn't believe we was free," Hamilton went on to say, returning to the escape from the death house, "after talking about it so often. Blackie just laughed and said he'd live to be eighty. You know, Clyde used to talk that way too, and now they're both dead. Me, I don't like to talk about it much—living, dying—superstitious I guess."[72]

"Ray," Fults broke in, surveying the dark terrain, "there's a car out there."

"It's 3:30," Ray said. "We'd best wrap this up." Fults started the car and pulled out to the little dirt road. A lone white church stood nearby. "To keep the feds off of you, we best make out like we kidnapped you and held you against your will," Hamilton said. As Dot brought McCormick's car up, he and Fults bound and gagged the reporter.

"We better make this look real," Ray said, severing the wires of the horn and hurling the butt of his BAR through both headlights.

"Give me a hand with him," Fults said, turning to Stella. "Grab his feet so we can lift him into his car."

"Well, you asked for this, Mack," she said, laughing. "You sure do look funny."[73]

Hamilton carefully planted a full set of fingerprints all over the hood, dash and, windshield of McCormick's car. Then he and Fults and the Houston sisters drove off, leaving the reporter tied up in his own vehicle.

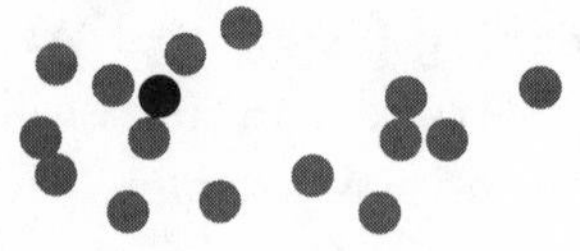

Mississippi

A few hours after leaving Harry McCormick securely trussed inside the cab of his own car, Hamilton, Fults, and the Houston sisters robbed a large San Antonio grocery store of several hundred dollars, enough to finance the Mississippi heist.[1] The wire services had already picked up the story of Raymond's arrant kidnapping of the Houston reporter, but no one in San Antonio suspected the outlaw's presence in their city. Two days would pass before Raymond Hamilton and Ralph Fults were positively identified as the San Antonio hijackers. On March 21, 1935, Texas Governor Allred revoked Fults's conditional pardon.

On their way to Mississippi the quartet of thieves picked up one of the twelve hundred U.S. dailies carrying Harry McCormick's interview with Hamilton and Fults, a nationwide scoop for the veteran crime reporter. True to his word, McCormick published only that which Hamilton and Fults had preapproved. He could have exposed the Houston sisters, blown the Mississippi plan, and revealed the story behind the stolen money for Joe Palmer. Instead, Harry revealed the involvement of Royce and Lewis in the McKinney ambush, adding that both Hamilton and Fults were angered by the double-cross and fully intended to return the favor.[2] For the time being there remained but one task for Hamilton, Fults and the two sisters—getting their hands on as much cash as possible for Joe Palmer's legal defense.

The thought of pulling a job in Mississippi never really appealed to Fults. "Mississippi and Louisiana's got the worst roads in the country," he advised. "Ain't nothing but logging roads and swamp trails leading nowhere." Nevertheless, the others convinced Fults to go along with the plan. Thus began one of the wildest escapades in U.S. criminal history.

The Bank of Blountville was located in an unimposing, one-story building on the main square of Prentiss, Mississippi, sixty miles south of Jackson. Among its former employees was a forty-two-year-old former socialite named Bergie.[3] She had once been charged with counterfeiting and held in a Monroe, Louisiana, jail.[4] There she had met Dot and Stella.

To them Bergie confided that she held a grudge against the directors of a bank in her home state of Mississippi. She often thought about getting even with everyone concerned by robbing the bank, but she had no contacts in that particular area of the underworld. Dot and Stella, of course, knew just what to do. However, when the death cell break failed to produce their friend Charlie Frazier, the sisters put the bank job on the back burner, and later they prevailed upon Hamilton and Fults to help them pull it off.

Shortly after crossing the Louisiana line, en route to Mississippi, the four outlaws found themselves gliding through the sleepy streets of Gibsland. They decided to take a look at the spot where Bonnie and Clyde had died. Pulling up to a filling station, the outlaw band obtained directions to the site from a man who seemed tired of reciting the same speech over and over again. To him the strangers were nothing more than another bunch of sightseers on holiday. After handing the attendant enough cash to cover the gas, Raymond proceeded through town and turned south on Main. The car then swept past the very school where a swarm of Bienville Parish children had come face to face with the sickening, lifeless forms of Parker and Barrow less than ten months earlier. At Mount Lebanon Hamilton turned right onto "Ringgold Road", just as Clyde had done on that fateful morning. No one spoke as the Ford sped over the winding, gravel-topped lane.

"This must be it," Raymond said, as the car rounded a long curve with two low hills standing in the distance. Hamilton coasted to a stop on the exact spot where the officers opened fire. The scene was quiet and peaceful. There was little to indicate the terrible violence of that May morning—only the rutted tire marks where countless tourists had stopped their cars, gazed at the surroundings, and turned around.

For several minutes the quartet absorbed what they could from the sight. Despite his many disagreements with Barrow, Raymond still seemed close to the slain outlaw. Fults, too, often thought of Bonnie and Clyde. Although he had always known they would eventually be killed, the reality of their deaths was somehow made more complete by paying a visit to that hilltop in Bienville Parish.

On or about March 23 the four fugitives arrived in Prentiss, Mississippi. After stashing their gear at Bergie's house, Hamilton and Fults made several visits to town. They memorized the layout and got the feel of the local routine. The bank looked harmless enough. There was a time lock on the safe, but Bergie assured the desperadoes it would not be in use during regular business hours. The outlaws' spent the rest of their time cruising the roads in search of an appropriate escape route, which proved chilling. Fults had been right. Very few roads actually led anywhere. Most were nothing more than wagon trails winding through marshy woodlands and disappearing altogether beneath the waters of some bog. It became frighteningly clear that the getaway would have to be accomplished in the opening moments of the flight, affording little opportunity for evasive, back-country driving.

On Wednesday night, March 27, the outlaws went to Hattiesburg, Mississippi, and stole a bright red car to use during the robbery.[5] They hoped to confuse any pursuers by switching to a black Ford V-8 two miles from town. The heist would be staged the following morning.

As dawn's filtered grey light inched its way across the tree-lined horizon on Thursday morning, March 28, Hamilton and Fults were busy tuning the engines of the two automobiles and cleaning the assemblage of heavy weapons. At 9:00 A.M. Dot and Bergie climbed aboard the black V-8. Stella slid behind the wheel of the bright red Hattiesburg car and prepared to chauffeur the two men to town.

Two miles southeast of Prentiss,[6] Dot and Bergie split off from the two-car procession and turned down a side road adjacent to an open field. Minutes later, at 9:30 A.M., nineteen-year-old Stella brought the getaway car to a stop beside the Bank of Blountville.[7] Leaving the cumbersome Browning automatic rifles, Fults and Hamilton took the less visible Colt .45s, got out of the car, and walked quickly around to the front of the building and through the open doors of the bank. Moving rapidly through the cramped little lobby, they passed Fred Dale, the bank's sole customer, and forged a path to the rear of the teller's cage.

"OK," said Raymond, calmly opening his blazer to reveal the blue-steel weapon tucked in his belt, "this here's a stickup." Cashier R. C. Williams looked first to the Colt .45, then to the two strangers staring intently in his direction. Neither outlaw had drawn a weapon, preferring to keep everything as quiet as possible.

"Now," Ray commanded, popping open a pair of pillow cases, "let's fill these with cash." Dale and Williams, along with assistant cashier John Burrow and the bank's accountant, Lona Winburn,[8] watched the small bandit toss currency and silver into the bags, his tall, lean companion standing nearby, glaring at the quartet.

Suddenly a woman appeared in the lobby, moving toward the teller's station with a wad of money clenched tightly in her right hand. Fults moved around to intercept her. "Ma'am," he said, raising his fingers to his forehead in a courteous gesture, "may I help you?"

"Yes," the woman answered. "I'd like to make a deposit."

Carefully the outlaw unbuttoned his suede coat and moved his pistol into view. "Ma'am, this is a holdup."

Surprisingly placid, Alma Rogers extended her hand. "Do you want my money?" she inquired.

"No ma'am," replied Fults. "You haven't deposited it yet. It's not insured yet. We just want what's covered by federal insurance. Now, you just sit down over here 'till we're ready to go."[9] Gratefully, Alma Rogers backed away from the bandit and settled into a nearby chair.

"OK, let's go to the vault," Raymond said, shoving the last of the change into the already bulging sack.

"We can't do that," replied Williams. "The time lock is in effect. It's not due to open 'til two this afternoon."

Hamilton and Fults looked at each other. They knew they had missed their chance to rake in forty or fifty thousand dollars, despite Bergie's assurances that the time lock was never in use during business hours.

"OK," Ray said. "Don't try and follow us 'til you hear the car pull away."

Raising the sacks of loot to his shoulder, Hamilton followed Fults through the lobby to the front doors and motioned for Stella to bring the car around. In a flash she was breezing up to the curb with the back door open. Fults and Hamilton dove in and, amidst the sound of squealing tires, were soon speeding southeast through the town square to the open country beyond.

Two miles from town Stella turned onto the Hattiesburg road and drew alongside Dot and Bergie. Quickly transferring the weapons and cash to the black V-8, the group then concealed the red car in a grove of trees and took off in the Ford. Dot was driving.[10]

The plan was to double back through the Whitesand community to Bergie's place west of Prentiss. Before long, however, they began running across small bands of armed men assembled at various points along the way. Several carloads of possemen passed the V-8, but they paid no attention to a woman driving a black Ford. The hunters were on the lookout for two men in a red car. Nevertheless, Fults and Hamilton knew that a fight was imminent.[11]

"Pull over," Ray suddenly commanded. "We'll get out here and get in them woods. Y'all go on to the house. We'll get another car and get to a safe place. When we do we'll phone or come get you."

Hamilton and Fults pulled everything out of the Ford and slogged into the thick underbrush of the heavy forest. In addition to his .45 Fults carried a Browning and a pillow case full of silver. Raymond was hauling fifteen hundred rounds of ammunition in a zipper pouch, the other Browning, and the currency. It was slow going through the woods. Briars continually slapped them about the face, and armadillo holes lay everywhere like booby traps. Both fugitives stumbled repeatedly.[12] Eventually they emerged at a farm-to-market road. A large, Queen Anne–style farmhouse stood nearby. In the yard three farm hands were busying themselves with a few light duties. In the garage the rear bumper of a car was visible.

"We'll have better luck walking up on that house if we ditch these big guns," said Ray. Fults did not like the idea of abandoning the heavy weapons, but he was inclined to agree with Hamilton's assessment. Stepping back ten or twenty yards from the road, the bank robbers dug a shallow pit in the moist earth, wrapped the Brownings in a blanket, and placed them carefully in the hole. Ray then dropped the ammunition on top of the blanket. Fults then heaved the bulky pillow case in the hole and started raking dirt and leaves over it and the weapons. Brushing the mud from their hands, they trekked out to the road and turned toward the house.

The outlaws smiled pleasantly as they approached the trio of workmen laboring in the barnyard.

"Howdy," Raymond said, pulling his pistol. "Let's take a hike around to the front of this house."

Tal Polk was sitting on his front porch when he spotted the strangers and his employees mounting the steps. The guns told him everything he needed to know.

"Hand over the keys to that car there," Hamilton demanded.

"Th'ain't no keys," answered Polk. "My boy, he's got them, and he's done gone to town."[13] Meanwhile, an auto approached.

"Hold these guys while I get us that car," Hamilton told Fults. Hamilton then dashed out to the shoulder of the country lane and raised his weapon. J. M. Hand, a surveyor for the Mississippi State Highway Department, was traveling to a job site. Thinking the gunman meant to shoot him, he pulled over and jumped out of the car, diving into a ditch full of tall reeds.[14] Ray, thinking the surveyor had a gun, called to Fults.

"Give me a hand with this guy," he pleaded.

Fults turned away from his captives and hurried down to the graded road. Just as he reached the automobile, he spotted the surveyor crouching in the ditch ten feet away.

"Get your hands up and get back in this car," Fults called out, taking aim on the state employee. Raymond ran around to the other side of the car and helped the prisoner from the ditch. Suddenly a shotgun blast ripped through the air, and something slammed into Fults's back, throwing him face down across the gravel.[15]

Rolling over, Fults caught a glimpse of Tal Polk, double-barrelled, open-bore shotgun in hand, aiming at Hamilton.[16] The farmer realized that he had not completely disabled Fults. Dropping the muzzle, he pulled the trigger again. The shot raked across Fults's right arm and face. Ricocheting chips of rock and clay filled his eyes, blinding him temporarily.

Wrestling the surveyor to the floorboard of the halted car, Hamilton whirled and fired at Polk. The old man threw his empty weapon aside and rushed to his house, and the three hired hands scattered toward the woods. Raymond poured two clips into the structure, striking Polk's daughter-in-law in the shoulder as she reached for the telephone.[17]

Thinking Fults had been killed, Hamilton jumped into the surveyor's car, jammed the stick into first gear, and started to pull away. When he heard the back door swing open with a jolt, he looked over his shoulder. There, hanging by one hand to the chrome door latch was Fults, bloodied and half-blind.

"Man, I thought they got you for sure!" exclaimed Raymond, applying the brakes. Without a word, Fults pulled himself onto the back seat and closed the door. With the captive surveyor huddled at his feet, Fults stretched out, a bloody, aching mess, in the back. Hamilton then pulled away from the Polk house and steered south toward Columbia. He had driven less than a mile, though, when he called quietly to Fults.

"Man, looky there," he said.

Fults reared up and peeked over the top of the seat. Two cars were blocking the road not more than seventy-five yards away. Behind that a line of armed men stood.

"Just turn around real slow," he told Raymond. "They haven't seen me or this other fellow yet. They'll think you're a local."

Hamilton took the advice, easing the surveyor's machine over to the side of the road and slowly cutting the wheels. The plan worked beautifully. Not a single posseman raised his weapon as the car made a rather nondescript about-face and disappeared unobtrusively in the opposite direction. At that point, however, they were headed straight back to Prentiss. In fact, within minutes they approached the outskirts of the little town.

"OK, mister," Hamilton said, pulling over. "You better drive. We'll just be passengers."

Hand rose from the floorboard, stepped around to the driver's side of the car, and took the wheel. Raymond slid over on the seat and placed his left foot above the surveyor's right foot, ready to punch the accelerator should the need arise.[18] Minutes later the two outlaws rode comfortably through the heart of the city, and cruised past the very bank they had robbed that morning, four hours earlier.

"It can't be more than thirty minutes 'til that time lock opens," Fults said, waving innocently to an unknown man strolling through the square. "What would you say to hanging around here for a spell and taking that bank again?"[19]

Raymond shook his head. "Hell," said Fults, gazing at the empty shops and distinct lack of vehicles around the courthouse, "ain't nobody left here in town. They're all out looking for us. It'd be a cinch to knock that bank over."

"Naw," Raymond replied, "I guess I'm superstitious."

Before long the outlaws were back on the road, speeding north toward Newhebron. Several carloads of men passed the fugitives, but no one seemed the least bit interested in the surveyor's car or its occupants. Eight miles from Prentiss, however, Hand's automobile started handling poorly. Hamilton decided to pull off the road and stash the malfunctioning machine in the trees.

"Come on," Fults ordered, dragging the state worker from the front seat. The three men tramped through the thickets for several minutes before arriving behind a cotton farmer's house.[20] Two men stood in the yard as Hamilton and Fults approached, flanking a dazed J. M. Hand.

"Howdy," Fults said.

"How do?" the younger man replied.

"We got a load of corn liquor broke down, over on the highway," Raymond announced. "We'll pay y'all five bucks to carry us there."[21]

"Well, I don't know," the young man said. "Somebody done robbed the bank in Prentiss, and I'm afraid that we'll run across the posse or the robbers."

"Naw," said Fults. "Them robbers are long gone by now."

"OK," the tall fellow said. "We'll take y'all folks to the highway. Come on, Grandpa, let's ride."[22]

The farmers mounted the front seat of their ancient Model A sedan while Hamilton, Fults, and J. M. Hand settled down in the back seat. A pair of hens cackled as the car clattered through the barnyard and swung onto the muddy farm road.[23]

Four miles down the road, beyond a sharp curve, a posse was assembled.[24] The first thing Fults saw was seven or eight cars parked along the dirt lane and several groups of men milling about. Some were sitting casually in their vehicles; others moved from house to house, questioning the occupants. No one seemed to notice the two cotton farmers pulling up in a Model A. Everyone apparently recognized the driver.

"It might be possible," Fults said, "to back right out of this situation before anyone knows what's happening." But suddenly, the driver and his grandfather bailed out of the stalled automobile, each man running, wild-eyed, in opposite directions.

"Oh boy," said Raymond, peeking over the top of the front seat. The gathering of men suddenly seemed curious about the Model A but still showed no visible signs of alarm.

"What do you think?" Hamilton asked.

"Maybe they don't know what's going on here," Fults said. "Nobody knows what we look like, do they?"

Hamilton nodded in agreement.

"Get down," Fults told J. M. Hand. "We're going to start shooting now."[25]

Deliberately aiming high, the desperate pair launched the assault, filling the air with smoke and lead. Caught by surprise, the lawmen dove for cover; they seemed unsure of what was taking place.[26] Following a brief moment of indecision, a few members of the posse began returning the fire. Bullets started slamming into the old Ford with a terrible force. The car rocked with each impact. A shower of glass engulfed the cab as slugs battered hardware and upholstery on either side of Fults and Hamilton.[27]

"Looks like we're gone, this trip," Fults said as he jammed his last clip of ammunition into his pistol.

Raymond agreed, likewise reloading with the last of his shells. Then Fults happened to spot a large man behind a nearby tree. He wore a black hat, and he was a skilled marksman. His shots continually produced shards of glass that carved bloody designs on Fults's face. The outlaw raised his weapon, drew a bead, and squeezed off a round. The gunman lurched backward, dropping his rifle and clutching the top of his head.[28]

At the same instant Raymond stood up and fired several rounds into one of the parked cars. One of the bullets sailed through the windshield and creased the forehead of Sheriff Ennis Crawford, of neighboring Covington County.[29] Tumbling from the automobile, Crawford cast his weapon aside and raised his hands. His companion, Simpson County Sheriff Joe Duckworth, did the same. Apparently confused, the rest of the posse ceased firing.

"Let's get out and take them all," Ray said, gripping the door latch. Taking advantage of the brief lull in the fighting, the bandits darted headlong into the midst of the gunmen. By then, Fults had forgotten all about the bird shot still buried in his face and back, saying later: "I done got healed right quick." He darted between two cars and disarmed six open-mouthed possemen without firing a shot. Meanwhile, Raymond walked up with eight or nine more prisoners, their hands held high.

"Hold them while I check the cars," Fults said. Rushing from door to door, the outlaw jerked several more men to their feet and confiscated their weapons.

"Better drop them," he called out to yet another man, crouching inside his car. "We got all your buddies." The unknown man let his rifle tumble to the mud and then stepped into the open. As a precaution, Fults leaned over and peeked inside the vehicle. Sure enough, hiding on the front floorboard was a second man.

"Better watch him," he called to Ray. "There's another one in there." Hamilton whirled around and faced the automobile.

"Get out of there, buster," he shouted.

The man lifted himself onto the seat.

"Oh no," Fults commanded. "You crawl out of there."

Without protest the prisoner dropped to his hands and knees and backed out of the car. Raymond moved the captives into the open and held them at bay with a couple of discarded weapons. Fults gathered the two wounded men, including Sheriff Crawford, who was still dizzy from the crease above his ear, and helped them rejoin their fellow citizens.

Hamilton and Fults then began stacking commandeered weapons in a haphazard pile just beyond the cars. The stack of guns soon looked like cordwood freshly cut and ready for the stove. The outlaws were trying to decide what to do with all those rifles and shotguns when another carload of possemen drove up. Unaware of what had transpired, the new arrivals smiled reassuringly as Fults walked over to greet them.

"Howdy," Fults greeted, returning the smile. "What're y'all doing?"

"We're out looking for the bank robbers!" the man behind the wheel announced cheerily.

"Well," said Fults, raising his .45, "you just found them!"

The men were forced to join the other captives, which by then included two sheriffs, one deputy sheriff, a state senator, and a judge— thirteen prisoners in all.[30]

Then yet another car pulled up, a Ford V-8 coupe. County Extension Agent M. E. Smith and his good friend Ralph Baylis were using the excitement in town as an excuse to blow the afternoon and roam the countryside in search of the bandits. They were not even armed.[31]

"OK," said Hamilton, dashing over to the car. "Stay right there."

Fults hurriedly gathered up the commandeered guns and stashed them in the trunk of Smith's V-8. Then he stepped over to the passenger side of the car and motioned for Baylis to get out.

"Let me in there."

Baylis got out and watched as Fults and Hamilton slid in next to Smith.

"C'mon," Ray called to Baylis. "Get up here on my lap. You're coming with us."

Baylis sat on Hamilton's knees.

"OK," Raymond commanded, waving his pistol. "Let's scram." The Ford coupe roared away with the outlaws' fourteenth and fifteenth captives of the day, leaving behind a very embarrassed posse. They could not even follow their former captors. Fults had the keys to their vehicles in his pocket.

The bandits and their captives had not ridden very far, however, when they encountered another roadblock. Five men, armed with pistols, shotguns, and rifles, were standing in the middle of the road, ready for action.

"D'you know these guys?" Fults asked.

Smith nodded.

"You better tell them something."

Slowing down, Smith poked his head through the window. "Put the guns down, boys," he shouted. "They've got us." Reluctantly the officers tossed their weapons aside. Raymond had Baylis slide into the rear of the cab while he and Fults got out to pick up the guns. Neither bandit knew that a sixth man had ducked behind a tree beside the road and was aligning the sights of a Springfield rifle with Fults's skull.[32] Suddenly a hot slug whistled past the bank robber's ear and blasted a jagged hole in the roof of Smith's car, just above Baylis, seated in back.[33] The shot came so close to Fults's head that his ears were ringing.

Raymond spun around and fired several well-placed shots at the sniper, stinging his face with chunks of wood and bark from the very tree he sought to hide behind. Soon the assailant was pinned down, afraid to move. Momentarily Fults ordered the five lawmen to mount the running boards of the V-8 to act as shields. Baylis was also made to act as a human rampart, stepping up beside the others as Fults and Hamilton settled in beside Smith.

"Let's hook'm," Hamilton ordered.

Smith shifted to first and took off. Just north of Newhebron two of the hostages were freed. Later, near the community of Shivers, the three remaining possemen were left by the side of the road. Baylis was then forced to rejoin Hamilton in the cab of the V-8 where he sat in the outlaw's lap for the next several hours.[34] M. E. Smith, still at the helm of the car, was also retained as a hostage.

Crossing the Pearl River at Georgetown,[35] the foursome turned north on Highway 51, the main road between New Orleans and Jackson. They had driven less than a mile when a column of National Guard troop carriers passed them in the southbound lane. The troops had been mobilized earlier in the day by Mississippi Governor Sennett Conner in an attempt to apprehend Fults and Hamilton. With smiles stretched across their faces, the outlaws waved heartily at the Prentiss-bound soldiers, who returned the friendly gestures with equal gusto.[36]

Just outside Terry, twenty miles south of Jackson, Fults and Hamilton had Smith turn off the highway and park in a secluded forest. There the outlaws counted and divided the money while the hostages relaxed. The $1,117 was divided equally between Hamilton and Fults, $558 each.[37] The odd dollar posed a problem.

"What about this?" Raymond asked, holding the bill.

Fults shrugged. The bill was partially torn, so Hamilton ripped it in half and gave Smith and Baylis each a portion as a souvenir.[38] The men laughed and tucked the mementos into their pockets. Afterward the outlaws and their hostages returned to the road.

Just north of Jackson, Smith was ordered to stop at a roadside snack shop. There a copy of the *Jackson Daily News* was purchased, as well as a sack of sandwiches and cold drinks. Raymond scanned the paper. Governor Conner, relating the details of the robbery, described the scene in Prentiss as "a reign of terror."[39] He also tried to explain how two men could rob a bank, switch to five different cars, disarm two heavily armed posses, take a total of fifteen prisoners and slip through a cordon of one-hundred-and-fifty local vigilantes and two-hundred troops of the Mississippi National Guard without being caught. Ray was pleased. He loved creating headlines.

Raymond gave Smith nine dollars to cover any expenses incurred through the use of his car. "We're sorry for the inconvenience," he said. "We're kind of in a jam, and we've got to make it the best way we can. I'll guarantee one thing, though, we ain't coming back to Mississippi. Not if we can help it."[40] The desperadoes then took turns catnapping. Later, just before daybreak, they changed the plates on Smith's car and prepared to leave.

"I'll drive the rest o' the way," Hamilton announced, turning to Smith. "You're too slow."[41] Taking the wheel, Raymond zipped at top speed through Batesville, Grenada, and Sardis as if they were not there. Before long the red needle of the speedometer was bobbing back and forth across the one-hundred-mile-an-hour mark.

"Do you mind if I take a drink?" Smith suddenly asked, watching as the road thundered beneath the wheels of his coupe.

"I'm sorry," Ray replied, "we don't carry no liquor. Don't like it much at all."[42]

"No," the county agent replied. "I mean I always keep a half pint in the glove box."

"Oh!" said Ray. "OK, go ahead."

With a lurch, the man raided the tiny compartment and fished through a mass of jumbled maps until he located the flask of whiskey. After taking a good, long drink, he offered the bottle to the other occupants of the car. Hamilton and Fults declined, but Baylis, normally a teetotaler, grabbed the bottle and downed a hefty swallow.[43] Tears billowing in his eyes confirmed his assertion that he was not much of a drinking man.

Twenty miles south of Memphis, near the town of Hernando, Hamilton and Fults removed the large cache of captured weapons from the rear of the car and carried them to the banks of a nearby brook. Choosing four or five pistols each, the outlaws discarded the rest of the guns and returned to the car.[44] Smith and Baylis had not moved.

"I'm sorry, fellas," he said, "but y'all had better ride back here in the trunk 'till we get into Memphis. We can't afford to have anybody spotting us all together."

The men reluctantly crawled into the trunk.

Just after daybreak the coupe roared across the Tennessee state line and proceeded unnoticed into the very heart of downtown Memphis.[45] Turning down Linden Street, not far from the Chisca Hotel, Hamilton pulled over.[46] Stepping cautiously from the car, the fugitives moved around to the trunk.

"I'm going up the street to fetch us a car," Ray called to the men. "My partner will be sitting on the running board 'til I get back, so don't try to escape. We'll let y'all go when we get outside the city limits."[47] Following the brief speech, the bank robbers nodded to one another and quietly moved away from the car. Stepping casually to the sidewalk, they were quickly swallowed by the anonymity of the Friday morning rush. It was 9:30—exactly twenty-four hours after the Prentiss robbery.

It did not take long for Smith and Baylis to start getting hot in the cramped confines of their automotive prison. Using a piece of metal, the hostages removed the screws from the lock on the trunk and stepped into the cool air. Fearing that Fults and Hamilton were still lurking nearby, both men lunged into the street and hailed a cab.[48]

Upon hearing of the release of the Prentiss hostages in the midst of his own city, Chief Inspector Will Griffin issued orders to shoot Hamilton and Fults on sight.[49] Notwithstanding, the Texas outlaws moved undetected through Memphis for more than twenty-four hours.

After leaving the coupe on Linden Street, the outlaw duo purchased a change of clothes and checked into the State Hotel, registering as Joe E. French and George Harper.[50] An employee of the hotel was suspicious of the pair and hurried to notify the police. Fults and Hamilton, equally suspicious, stayed just long enough to shower and change their clothes. By 11:00 A.M. they had slipped down the fire escape and disappeared into a downtown theater.[51] After sitting through three screenings of *The Last Mile*, starring Clark Gable, the hunted men emerged from the theater. At a distance of twenty-five feet apart, they moved along the busy city sidewalk—Raymond on the inside, hugging the buildings, while Fults flanked the outside, near the curb.

Every corner newsstand was filled with newspapers bearing the headline, "Inspector Griffin Issues Shoot to Kill Orders on Mississippi Bank Robbers."[52] Pictures of Hamilton were posted everywhere, accompanied by descriptions of Fults and his wounded face.

Fults and Hamilton located another hotel and checked in without arousing suspicion. While relaxing in their room, they heard a radio bulletin about the capture of Dot, Stella, and Bergie. Apparently their car had become mired in a muddy ditch, forcing the three women to strike out on foot through an open field.[53] A pair of deputies picked them up.

The following morning, March 30, Fults donned a pair of thick, horn-rimmed glasses, poked a cigar in his mouth, and accompanied Raymond to Union Station. After shipping a pair of suitcases to Tulsa, Fults stepped up to the ticket counter and purchased a pair of first class seats on the next train to Louisville. En route to the loading platform, however, both outlaws spotted four plainclothes officers posted at the gate.

"Let's go to the freight yard," Raymond suddenly said.

"Oh no," Fults answered. "I'm too damned stiff and sore to hop some boxcar. I'm taking my chances on that Pullman car, right there."

"Well," Ray said, looking around, "maybe we'd best split up for a while. Everybody's looking for two guys. Maybe we can get out of this by busting up."

"Okay," Fults replied.

"All right," Hamilton said, "we'll meet in Tulsa on April 30. One month from today."

"Raymond," Fults said, "you ain't going to try and go back to Texas, are you?"

"Hell, no," he said, turning away.

"You've got 'the chair'," Fults said. "They'll burn you if you go back."

"No," Hamilton said, "they'll never burn me. I ain't never killed nobody, and they know it!"

"You're fooling yourself," Fults said. "Don't go to Texas. Don't go home."[54]

As soon as Raymond was out of sight, Fults pulled the brim of his brand new grey felt Stetson low across his face and started toward the loading gate. The officers were scrutinizing every face that passed. Nearby, Fults could see a line of taxis parked on Union Avenue. If a lawmen tried to lay a hand on him, he would draw two pistols and make a break for the cabs.

Fifteen feet from the gate Fults pulled a handkerchief to the right side of his face, as if to clean his glasses. His left hand gripped one of the five guns he carried. Without incident, however, the bandit breezed past the sentries and climbed aboard the train, shielding himself behind a large man as he walked. He did not stir from his car until the Louisville station popped into view a few hours later.

In Kentucky Fults spent a great deal of his time listening to the radio and wondering if the footsteps outside his door belonged to a policeman. He slept fitfully and did not eat well. Some of the wounds in his face, throat, and shoulders were becoming infected. With a penknife he carved out as many of the pellets as he could, tossing them down the lavatory drain in his room. Some of the shot tumbled to the floor, however. Fults was able to retrieve a few of the lead balls, but just as many remained somewhere on the floor. Fearing that the cleaning woman might discover the shot, the weakened outlaw decided to vacate his room after only three or four days.[55]

Limping stiffly to the train station, Fults caught the first Pullman back to Memphis. From there he rode a bus to Little Rock, Arkansas, stole a car, and steered north to Springfield, Illinois. By switching to so many different modes of transportation, Fults hoped to shake the federal men who were on his trail. The plan worked like a charm. In Illinois he settled into relative obscurity. No one suspected that the quiet southerner was, in reality, one of the most wanted men in the nation.

A few hours after his arrival in Springfield, Fults sat down at the lunch counter of a small cafe not far from his hotel. A radio was on. A news bulletin interrupted the regularly scheduled program.

"Ladies and gentlemen," the announcer began, "we have received a report that Texas death house fugitive Raymond Hamilton was surprised and taken prisoner in a Ft. Worth, Texas, train yard today. Not a shot was fired."[56]

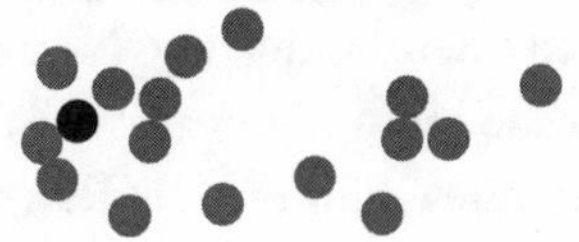

The Last Ride

After leaving Fults at the Pullman gate in Memphis, Ray hurried to the freight yard in hopes of losing the law. Almost immediately he encountered a small group of hoboes, including a teenaged runaway from Tupelo named Noland.[1] Hamilton, still wearing a three-piece suit and fine Stetson hat, approached the boy.

"Say, buddy," Ray smiled, eyeing the kid's nap sack, "you got another pair of them overalls?"

"Sure do," Noland answered.

"I'll give you ten bucks for them," Ray said.

"OK," said the youngster.

"You want to ride with me?" the outlaw asked, watching a line of boxcars rolling past.

"Sure," said Noland, "I ain't got nothing else going."[2]

Hamilton and his new-found companion picked out a car and hopped aboard, sliding onto the rods so the freight detectives would not spot them. At some point along the way Raymond noticed a newspaper article stating that his mother had been released from prison after serving a thirty-day sentence for harboring Clyde Barrow and Bonnie Parker. Against all odds and the advice of Ralph Fults, Hamilton decided to go home for a visit.[3]

On Thursday morning, April 4, Hamilton and Noland arrived in Ft. Worth's East Belknap switching yard. By then they had befriended an Illinois transient named Glen.[4] Glen, like Noland, had no idea that the small blond man with the big wad of cash was one of the most wanted men in America. They knew him only as Ray, never suspecting that a bank robber would be riding the rods like a penniless bum.[5] The trio disembarked from the southbound freighter, stretched their aching muscles for several minutes, and walked over to a gathering of fellow travelers huddled behind a nearby tin shed.[6]

On Friday morning Raymond sent young Noland into West Dallas to arrange a meeting with his mother. Knowing that his road companion could neither read nor write, Hamilton scrawled a simple message on the back of a discarded envelope and handed it to the boy. Noland was supposed to deliver Raymond's message to a West Dallasite known only as Lester,[7] but for some reason the teenager had difficulty locating the address furnished by Hamilton. Unsure of his destination, he instructed a cab driver to cruise aimlessly through the dusty little neighborhood.

Among the many curious people who saw Noland that day were a trio of county detectives named Bill Decker, Bryan Peck, and Ed Castor.[8] The sight of a taxi in that part of town was strange enough, but the disheveled passenger in the back seat was too much for the lawmen to overlook. After watching the car for several minutes as it turned in and out of side streets and narrow alleys, the deputies moved in.

"What are you doing, son?" asked Decker.

"A friend of mine over in Ft. Worth asked me to deliver this note," said Noland,[9] offering the folded piece of paper to his inquisitors. Upon viewing the contents of the message, the lawmen hustled Noland downtown. There, they grilled him about his pal in Ft. Worth. They quickly produced a mug shot of Raymond Hamilton and pushed it beneath his nose.

"Yeh," said the boy, "that's the guy that's waiting for me. What did he do?"

"Do you mean to say you don't know who this is?" asked one of the officers skeptically.

"No," said Noland. "I ain't got no idea."

"Will you show us where this man is waiting?" another deputy asked.

"Yes sir," Noland agreed, reluctantly, "I guess so."[10]

It was nearly dark when the lawmen assembled in front of the Rock Island terminal. Noland led "Smoot" Schmid, Bill Decker, and a five-man squad of officers to the edge of the railroad yard. They could see a tin shed where Hamilton and a half dozen transients stood not more than fifty yards away. By chance, the outlaw's back was turned toward the officers. Dressed in a pair of greasy overalls, a brown vest, and a brown hat, he did not exactly look the part of the Southwest's Public Enemy No.1.

"Go on over to him." Decker told Noland, as darkness closed in. "We'll be right behind you."

Cautiously the young Mississippi youth slid down the embankment and approached his traveling companion of the previous six days. Before Raymond could turn around to greet his hobo friend, however, seven automatic pistols were thrust into his back.

"Hoist 'm, Ray," said Bill Decker, jabbing the cold barrel of his .45 into the fugitive's ribs. Hamilton complied without a show of resistance. A strange smile flickered across his lips.

"Well, Bill," Ray started, "why don't you go ahead and kill me?"

"Oh no," Decker replied. "You'll stand hitched."[11]

By the time the cars containing Hamilton, Schmid, and the others arrived from Ft. Worth, the corridors of the Dallas County Jail were jammed with hundreds of people spilling out to Houston Street and blocking traffic. Men and women in evening attire moved among farmers, merchants, and reporters—all surging forward to get a look at the notorious bandit.[12] He looked tired, ragged, and somehow relieved. Nevertheless, nearly concealed by the much larger officers, he managed to force a dimpled grin as he was led through the doors and down the hall.

"Ray," a reporter shouted, "how'd you get out of Mississippi?"

"Just as fast as I could," the youth replied.[13]

Laughter erupted, and suddenly he was gone, ushered upstairs. In the cell block curious prisoners were pressing their faces up to the bars, trying to catch a glimpse of the infamous outlaw personality.

"Hell," a voice suddenly cried out, "he ain't nothing but a damned little kid."[14]

"Smoot" Schmid broke away long enough to call Lee Simmons in Huntsville.

"I've got your little bad boy," the sheriff shouted over the long distance wire.[15] Simmons immediately took off for Dallas, Warden Waid at his side. Schmid then brought Raymond out into one of the jail's corridors to mingle with the newspapermen and photographers.

"How about Ralph Fults?" a voice in the crowd called out.

"He croaked," Raymond answered. "I planted him in Mississippi."[16]

"Do you want to see Katie?" someone else asked.

"Sure, I want to see her," he answered quickly. "She's the sweetest girl in the world. True blue. I'd do anything under the sun for her. You know they kept her in jail for three weeks, but she wouldn't squeal on me, not that girl."[17]

"What about Mary O'Dare?" came another question.

"That girl 'ratted' on me to save her own neck," Raymond said bitterly.

"How about Bergie and the two sisters?" another newsman inquired.

"I'm not squealing on any women," Hamilton mused. "Women have enough trouble without men heaping more on them."[18]

"What about the chair?" another reported asked.

Hamilton flashed a painful look. "Take me back to my cell. I don't feel like talking anymore."

A few hours later Simmons and Waid arrived from Huntsville.

"It'll be a great pleasure to take him back," Simmons said.[19]

At 10:30 the following morning Hamilton was escorted to a car parked in the alley beside the county jail. Throughout the night the crowds had grown to mammoth proportions.

"Goodbye, Ray," someone shouted.

Hamilton raised his shackled hands and smiled. Three hours later, he was back in Huntsville, on Death Row, facing the dingy little cell from which he had fled so joyously nine months before.[20] The first person he saw was Joe Palmer.

"How are you, Joe?" Raymond smiled. "You're looking well."

"Sure," said Palmer without stirring. "I'm fine. Nothing to do all day but lie around with a bunch of Negroes to wait on you. Nothing to worry about."[21] Before the end of the day he would be sentenced to death in Judge S. W. Dean's court. Before Judge Dean could verbalize his decree, however, Palmer tried to clear Hamilton of the Crowson affair. Turning to young Max Rogers, the Walker County district attorney, Joe mounted into a surprisingly thoughtful soliloquy.

"You will remember, Mr. Rogers, that you used one set of witnesses to prove that I killed Crowson and another set to prove that Hamilton killed him. You know the testimony against Hamilton was perjured. I believe that the guards who were instrumental in this case committed perjury, and I believe you solicited it. . . . When calamity walks shoulder to shoulder with you, the law of averages will take its toll from you for convicting an innocent man. I killed Major Crowson . . . because of mistreatment to convicts . . . and I am making this statement for the sake of my own conscience."[22]

Despite repeated attempts by the judge to interrupt Palmer, the statement was read into the record in its entirety. Only then did Joe relinquish the floor to Dean.

"Your honor," he said casually, "I am ready to be sentenced."

"Do you have any preference as to date?" the Judge asked.

"Yes," Palmer answered. "Make it 1999."[23]

Dean affixed May 10 as the date of execution. At 3:00 P.M. on Monday, April 8, Raymond Hamilton appeared in the packed Walker County Courtroom.[24] More than two-hundred people jammed the gallery as Hamilton was seated in a chair directly across from the bench. Max Rogers strolled up to the outlaw and seated himself in an adjacent chair. Within minutes the greying, sixty-six-year-old Judge Dean arrived. Hamilton rose from his chair.

"Judge," he said. "let me call my lawyer in Dallas. . . . He's got something new that'll help me."

"I know what he's going to say," said Dean, "but you can call him."[25]

"Get A. S. Baskett, in Dallas," Hamilton told a deputy. "I wonder why he's not here. He told me the other day he'd be here." Suddenly it was announced that Baskett was on the line. Ray rushed for the receiver.

"Can't you get down here?" he asked. "Oh," Hamilton then said, his

April 8, 1935. Judge Dean, standing far left, sentences Raymond Hamilton, far right, to death in the electric chair. (Courtesy of Cecil Mayes.)

voice trailing to a whisper. "Well, what should I do?" he inquired. "You mean, take it? Okay."[26] He hung up the earpiece and trudged back to the bench.

"Raymond Hamilton," the Judge decreed, "you are here now to be sentenced, friendless and without money. Have you anything to say as to why sentence should not be passed?"[27]

"Yes, I have," answered Raymond. He then turned to face the crowd. "People," he began, "I hope I have a few friends among you. . . . I want you to know I never killed anyone. . . . Crowson was going to be killed no matter what I did . . . and I want to tell you that whenever Simmons and the others get after you together, you don't get fairness. . . . They're afraid they can't hold me, that I'll break out and call more attention to them, so they get me 'the chair'. . . . I don't know if there's anything like 'haunts' but if there are, I sure do want to come back and kick this whole bunch out of bed every night."[28] Hamilton then turned toward the bench. "All right, your honor," he said. "I'm ready."

Dean read the death pronouncement and affixed the date as May 10.

"Is that the same night as Joe's going over?" the condemned man asked.

"Yes," Dean replied, "it is the same."

"Thank you, your honor," Hamilton said. "That's the way I wanted it."

Then, turning away, Hamilton saw Lee Simmons sitting nearby. Probably recalling reporter Harry McCormick's lament over having been barred from the prison by Simmons because of his scathing editorials, Hamilton said,"Excuse me, your honor. Don't I get to pick five witnesses to my execution?"

"Yes," Judge Dean answered, "that's the law."

"Tell McCormick I want him to be there," Raymond said, grinning at the poker-faced Simmons.[29] A bailiff then grabbed Hamilton by the arm.

As the once-dapper bandit was being led past the crowd, several young women pressed against the railing, some trying to touch the gunman. Looking over his shoulder, Hamilton raised his manacled hands to wave farewell, a smile on his face.[30]

As soon as he heard the news of Raymond's capture, Ralph Fults was on the move. Grabbing the first bus south from Springfield, he rode all the way to Ft. Worth and arrived sometime on the morning of the eighth. Making his way to a nearby factory, he picked out a beautiful, new, tan Ford V-8 and drove north to Denton.[31] There he made contact with an ex-con he had known at Eastham.

"I need someone to help me raid the National Guard Armory over in Mineral Wells," Fults confided in his friend.

"Well," the ex-con said, "I'm trying to stay clean, but I think 'One-eyed' Max is still knocking around town."

Fults had known Max for nearly ten years—first in Gatesville, then inside the walls at Huntsville. He seemed the perfect choice.

"I know it's a long shot," Fults told Max, "but I'm going to try and bust Raymond loose. I need some heavy artillery, though. Will you help me knock over the guard armory in Mineral Wells?"

"Sure," Max answered, without hesitation, "I'll help you hit that armory. I got some guns myself, but they're only rifles and shotguns. I could use a couple of them Brownings. Meet me in an hour, out on the highway. You can follow me down to Dallas. We'll pick up my weapons and head on over to Mineral Wells."

It was well past dark when the two cars containing "One-eyed" Max and Ralph Fults roared down Denton Drive past Dallas's Love Field. In the second car Fults watched intently as Max approached the intersection of Denton and Mockingbird Lane. Suddenly a pair of county squad cars appeared from behind a large billboard. Their tires dug into the dirt as they tried to force Fults's V-8 into the ditch. Fults mashed the accelerator to the floorboard and looked around. Max had vanished. Fults knew he had been betrayed.[32]

Turning left onto Mockingbird, the outlaw sped east, barely outdistancing his pursuers. One of the lawmen, an exceptional driver, stuck close to Fults's bumper, although the cars attained speeds in excess of ninety miles-per-hour.

Fults's gloved hands were perspiring heavily as he blasted across Lemmon Avenue. The luminous glow of a distant guard railing signaled the curve to Highland Park. The fugitive nearly lost control of the car as he took the turn on two wheels, scraping whitewash from the wooden railing. Still the lawmen followed.

With the darkened Neoclassical buildings of Southern Methodist University looming on his left, Fults cut his lights, veered off of Mockingbird, and whipped down a series of residential streets, eventually emerging behind both county vehicles. The move apparently baffled the officers completely, for they had reduced their speed considerably and seemed lost.[33]

The following evening, April 9, Fults was back in Denton. There he was able to enlist the aid of a young man named John "Red" Otis. Otis had long been associated with a variety of Denton and Dallas County underworld figures. Unlike the other Red, who had abandoned Fults and Barrow in Electra, the trustworthy Otis was virtually unknown to anyone other than the local authorities.

Red agreed to drive Fults to McKinney, in neighboring Collin County, for the purpose of visiting the outlaw's mother and father. A few blocks west of the McKinney town square Otis turned from Lee Street onto

Bass, stopping beside a small white frame house on the southwest corner of the intersection.[34] Fults emerged from the passenger side of the car and closed his coat over the sawed-off shotgun dangling by a strap from his shoulder. The neighborhood looked clean, but the house could be filled with lawmen ready to open up on the six-foot outlaw at any moment. Tensely gripping the modified stock of his weapon, Fults cautiously approached the innocent-looking house. Red waited in the car, engine running, .45 automatic pistol in hand.

Mounting the creaking wooden steps of the back porch, Fults opened the screened-in rear entrance and tapped lightly on the kitchen door. Footsteps rapped lightly across the floor, and the face of a middle-aged woman appeared at the door. It was Fults's mother.

"Oh, son," Sophie cried, rushing to open the door. "Please give up before it's too late."[35]

"I'm not sure what to do, Momma," Fults replied. "I think that bunch down in Huntsville mean to kill me if I go back there. And besides, Mississippi can hang me for the Prentiss job. I just come by to let y'all know I'm still alive. Raymond was only saying that he buried me to keep the hounds off my trail. Did you get my letter from Kentucky?"

"Yes, son," Sophie answered, "please be careful and try not to think about running much longer. You know you can't go on forever. You'll either be killed or captured."[36]

"You shouldn't worry about the likes of me," Fults said.

Seconds later he was gone.

Fults had Red drive him to the domino parlor on Tennessee Street. Across the street customers sat quietly at the City Cafe. Through the alley, to the east, a small number of prisoners dozed in the McKinney jail.

Fults slipped casually from the passenger side of Red's car, turned the brim of his Stetson down, and surveyed the dark, empty sidewalk before him. The ground floor of the building was occupied by a jewelry store, next to which stood Larson's gun shop. Darkened and ominous, both establishments were closed for the evening. Between the two businesses, opening onto the street, there appeared a lone door, behind which a flight of steps ascended to the domino parlor above the jewelry shop.

A lot more went on in that little second-story room than games of dominoes, however. Bookies and bootleggers used the parlor as a base of operations. Fults knew the place would be packed, probably with a number of people he had known since childhood. For the time being, though, there were only two men he wanted to see when he topped that landing—Royce and Lewis.

Poking his right hand through the hole cut in the pocket of his overcoat, Fults grabbed the little 16-gauge shotgun and heaved himself through the door leading to the domino parlor. Sprinting to the top of the stairs, the determined desperado rounded the corner and squared off before a room full of startled gamesmen. Ralph Fults was the last person any of them expected to see.

"Any of y'all seen them bootleggers?" Fults said loudly, sliding a menacing barrel through the opening in his coat. "Well?" he asked, peering through a blanket of cigar smoke at the milk-white faces. Silence.

"We ain't seen hide nor hair of either one of them boys since that night you and Raymond was jumped," someone said. Fults glowered at the speaker.

"Honest, Ralph," another man conceded, "them boys done lit out of here, and they ain't been back since. And that's the gospel."

"Well," said Fults, backing toward the stairwell, "if you happen to see them slithering out from under some rock, tell them I'm looking for them." With that, he vanished.

Two days later, on April 11, Fults sent Red back to McKinney in search of Royce and Lewis. Red was to pose as a go-between to arrange a meeting between the two bootleggers and the alleged owner of a number of Oklahoma speakeasies. The club owner, of course, would turn out to be Fults, who meant to gun down both men.

At 11:30 Fults was cruising Foote Road eight miles west of McKinney.[37] He was looking for Red, hoping to verify the time and place of his meeting with the bootleggers. For some reason, however, a farmer named Henry Bales pulled in behind Fults's V-8 and started tailing him. Bales was haunting the back roads between McKinney and Frisco in hopes of catching his daughter with a young man he had tried to keep her from seeing. Apparently he thought Fults was his man.[38] Thinking

Bales was a lawman, Fults hit the accelerator. To the fugitive's surprise, however, the farmer had no trouble keeping up. Fults slid a .45 from his belt, cocked the hammer, and placed the weapon in his lap.

Suddenly the road disappeared—a bridge was out. Fults hit the brakes too late. The V-8 slid headlong over the embankment at nearly eighty miles per hour and plummeted into the dry creek bed.[39] The force of the crash threw him forward, shattering glass and ripping the doors wide open. Amazingly, he was bruised but otherwise unhurt by the jolt.

Quickly regaining his wits, Fults located his .45, tumbled from the thoroughly wrecked vehicle, and moved painfully toward a nearby grove of mesquite. He knew the other car would be along at any moment; rather than risk a shootout with what he perceived to be a carload of officers, he opted to strike out on foot.

A terrible dust storm had passed through the area earlier in the day, and a lingering cloud of topsoil tinged the night sky.[40] Slowly picking his way across open fields and through patchy clusters of oak and gum, Fults worked his way toward the Frisco highway.[41] At 4:00 A.M. he eased through yet another thicket of gnarled mesquite trees and suddenly heard a voice not more than ten feet ahead of him.

"Got a match?" the unseen speaker whispered. Dust swirled past the desperado's eyes as he strained to locate the source of the question. Out of nowhere a match flicked, revealing four men crouched directly in front of him. Fults knew then that a posse was combing the area. He quietly retraced his steps and out-flanked the heavily armed men.

Day was just beginning to break when an exhausted Ralph Fults emerged from the woods behind a farmhouse not far from the Frisco highway, near Allen, twenty-five miles north of Dallas. Through the mist the bandit spotted the form of Vick Howell,[42] bucket and three-legged stool in hand, trudging toward the corral for the morning milking. Fults stood up and approached the farmer.

"G'morning," Fults said as he stepped into the barnyard.

"G'morning," Howell replied warily.

"I wonder if you can give me a lift into McKinney?" the tattered youth inquired. "Some hijacker done kidnapped me last night, took my car, and let me out in them woods back yonder. It was prob'ly that damned Fults boy that's been running around with Ray Hamilton."[43]

"My boy's heading that way in just a few minutes," Howell stated. "You can ride in with him." Soon Fults and twenty-five-year-old Cecil Howell were rambling toward McKinney.[44] At the Dallas cutoff, however, the fugitive pulled his .45.

"Let's go south," he demanded, shoving a cold barrel into Howell's ribs. The young man did as he was told, turning right at the fork.

"How much do you make per day at your job," he asked Howell.

"Two bucks," the young man replied.

"Well, I ain't got much on me," Fults then said, "but here's a five. Now you're working for me."[45]

Five miles down the road, near the town of Renner, Fults spotted a good-looking V-8 parked in front of a farmhouse.

"Pull up here," the kidnapper demanded. "Leave the motor running and walk up on that Ford—see if the keys are in it."

Howell walked up the dirt drive and examined the car. He saw the keys in the ignition and signaled to Fults. The fugitive jumped from the farm boy's car and ran up to the vehicle.

"I'm going to take this car," Fults told Howell. "You go on back home and tell the 'coppers' anything you want."

Fults drove south to Houston in hopes of locating the younger sister of Dot and Stella. Though not directly associated with the darker world of her siblings, she had nonetheless been driven underground by the events in Mississippi. The McKinney bandit was unsuccessful in locating her.

Doubling back to the Red River Valley the harried outlaw slipped into Oklahoma to cool off. He arrived in Ardmore on the evening of the thirteenth. By chance, Fults met a twenty-four-year-old ex-con whom he had known in prison.[46] The man offered to help Fults burglarize the Mineral Wells armory, but only if he was paid a large sum of money. Fults, more desperate than skeptical, agreed to the arrangement.

The following day, April 14, the two men drove to Graham, Texas, and robbed the Lesage Oil Refinery of nine-hundred dollars.[47] After taking his share of the money, Fults's new partner stepped into a corner market for a pack of cigarettes. He never returned.

Alone again, Fults ventured first to Denton, then to Dallas in search of a contact, to no avail. In Dallas the outlaw found that a reporter with the *Dallas Morning News* was referring to him as "Chump No.1" for being used as a decoy to lure Raymond Hamilton into the McKinney ambush. "He doesn't know the half of it," Fults mused to himself.

Actually, the less-than-complimentary moniker originated with the McKinney, Texas constable who organized the failed ambush. He was still mad about the way Hamilton and Fults had spoiled his one and only chance at stardom.[48]

Fults toyed with the idea of kidnapping the reporter and taking him on a mad dash through the Midwest—perhaps depositing him on some Minnesota back road not far from the Canadian border. In fact, he was about to pull over to a pay phone and scan the city directory for the newsman's address when a pair of squad cars rolled past. Thinking he had been spotted, Fults left town immediately.

He spent the night on Lake Dallas, rising early the following morning, Wednesday, April 17. The bandit then got in his V-8 and drove north toward the town of Prosper, eighteen miles west of Denton. He planned to rob the bank there. Suddenly an unmarked car passed him in the southbound lane. The three occupants looked closely at Fults as they passed.[49] In the rear-view mirror Fults saw the car make a high-speed U-turn. Fults knew he had been spotted. He punched the accelerator. Within seconds he left his pursuers in a cloud of dust, a thousand yards or more beyond his taillights. The speedometer danced madly between seventy-five and eighty miles per hour as Fults bobbed along the graded road in search of a cutoff to the main highway.

Not far down the road, beyond a wide curve, the road suddenly split. To the right there appeared a seldom-used trail leading down to the end of a peninsula known locally as "Millionaire's Island." It was a dead end. To the left was the connection to the main highway, but a pair of squad cars blocked the road. A number of officers were spread out, their rifles and shotguns jutting into the air like lances. Unable to negotiate such a blockade, the outlaw turned right.

Fults knew he was speeding headlong toward the water's edge but hoped to somehow continue driving along the shore. If he could make it to the woods, not far away, then perhaps he could escape on foot.

Shots rang out just as Fults spotted the sun-dappled water stretching out before him. A line of .44 slugs ground into the body of the Ford as he slowly executed a hairpin turn onto the clay embankment, picked up speed, and pulled away. He drew his pistol and placed it on his lap, anticipating the upcoming flight through the woods. Glancing in the mirror, he could barely see the Denton officers through the clouds of dust kicking up in the wake of his speeding auto. They were gaining on him. Then a yawning wash appeared in the embankment directly in the path of Fults's Ford. At high speed the V-8 careened over the edge of the ten-foot ravine; when it hit bottom the car was a twisted hulk of raw, jagged steel and glass.[50] For the second time in five days Fults was hurled about the cab of a crashing automobile, breaking the wheel in half and smashing his head against the rear-view mirror. Dust and steam rose around the dazed bandit as he fumbled around in the wreckage. Above a high-pitched ringing in his ears, Fults could barely make out the sounds of garbled words echoing in his head.

"Get out here and get them hands up!" Denton city policeman Roy Moore was shouting.[51]

Fults looked up. His bleary eyes slowly focused on the open bore of a "thumb-bustin' .44 hogleg" leveled just inches from his face. Ignoring the weapon, he reached further beneath the seat.

"Hey there," snapped Moore, dragging the dazed fugitive from the smoldering wreck. "What are you looking for?"

"My pistol," Fults answered faintly, dusting off his cap. "It was on my lap."

Just then officers Sam Gentry and Luther Allen rushed in.[52] While Moore handcuffed his captive, Allen and Gentry located the .45, lodged deep behind the seat. Fults was taken first to the Denton County jail, then to Dallas.

Among others who wanted Fults, federal authorities insisted that only Alcatraz could restrain the slippery McKinney gangster. Nevertheless, Dallas County Chief of Detectives Bill Decker, who six years earlier had transferred a severely beaten Ralph Fults from the Dallas City Police Station to the Dallas County Jail, released the outlaw to the Texas Rangers.

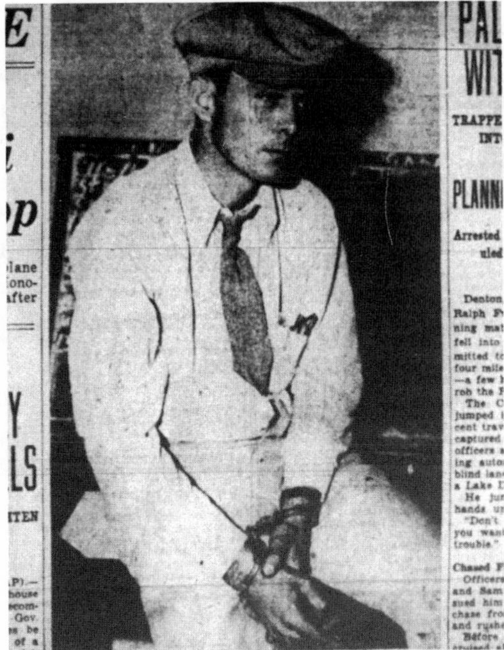

Ralph Fults, April 1935. A handcuffed Fults sits in the Denton County jail shortly after his capture. (Courtesy of the Fults family.)

Ranger Captain Fred McDaniel drove Fults to Austin.[53] There the outlaw was interviewed about his experiences with Clyde Barrow and Raymond Hamilton. Fults, in turn, probed the Rangers for information about the ambush of Bonnie and Clyde.

"Yeh," McDaniel said, "they approached me and Hickman and Gonzuales on that Clyde and Bonnie deal. We told them 'no thanks, we don't ambush people and we don't shoot women.' "[54]

On April 20 Ralph Fults was taken to Huntsville in chains, shackled and surrounded by a half-dozen prison guards. They put him in solitary confinement in the South Building. Lee Simmons was not taking any chances.

From the main prison yard the most direct route to solitary was actually through Death Row on 7 Level. On the way Fults got one last glimpse of Raymond Hamilton.

Sandwiched between two guards, Fults was led through the door of the death house. As soon as he drew up alongside cell No.7, he dropped to one knee, as if to tie a shoe lace. Hamilton, seated on his bunk with his hands clasped, seemed in reasonably good spirits.

"Thanks, Ralph," he said.[55]

Before Fults could reply, one of his escorts poked him in the back with a bat.

"Git along there," he said. Fults started walking. He did not even get to see Joe Palmer.

Fults spent the next several days wondering what would happen to him. He lost all track of time, isolated as he was. His cell, measuring a scant four feet by four feet, was void of light and oppressively hot. It was impossible to stretch out. The toilet consisted of a hole in the floor, the stench of which thickened the already stagnant air. A bucket in the corner provided water. After ten days a quartet of guards dropped in on the prisoner.

"C'mon with us," one of them said. Fults had to shield his eyes as he was led into the light and marched toward the prison administration building. He knew where he was being taken—to the office of a high-ranking prison official, an official he had dealt with before.

"Mr. Fults," the official said quietly, as Fults was led into his office. " I know you're from McKinney. That's just a whistle-stop from my home town. Why, I even know your family physician, and he tells me what wonderful people your mother and father are and how supportive they are of you. I feel like you would go straight if given half a chance, and I'm in a position to help you a great deal. I can make life much easier for you while you're serving your term. I could prevent the state of Mississippi from extraditing you, which they are trying to do right now. They want to hang you. All you have to do is come clean about the kidnapping of Harry McCormick so the feds can file harboring charges against him."[56]

The official stared at Fults earnestly. Despite the capture and imminent execution of Raymond Hamilton, April had not been a good month for the Texas Prison System. On the third of the month Chairman W. A. Paddock, of the Texas Prison Board, conducted a four-man tour of the

Retrieve Farm, near Angleton, after reported incidents of the severe brutality there grew too numerous to ignore.[57] What he found would shake the very foundation of prison management; the revelations would finally expose the subhuman conditions that certainly contributed to the vicious and destructive natures of men like Clyde Barrow and would accomplish the very thing Harry McCormick had been working for since 1930.

Three convicts who worked in one of Retrieve's sweltering hot fields were found to have deep, festering lacerations lining their bare backs. Four others, their hands and feet mutilated by self-inflicted axe wounds, testified that they had cut themselves in hope of being admitted to the prison hospital in Huntsville, in order to avoid being killed by the sadistic Retrieve guards. Yet another man had attempted to achieve the same ends by injecting himself with kerosene.[58] Disgusted by what he saw, Paddock ordered general manager Simmons and Warden Waid to meet him at Retrieve and explain themselves as soon as possible. A telegram was sent to Governor Allred, who responded by dispatching Texas Ranger Captain Fred McDaniel to the farm.[59]

On April 4 Lee Simmons met with reporters.

"We found two men who had cut their legs with axes," Simmons admitted, "but that's nothing new in the prison system. I say give them more axes if they need them."[60] The general manager would soon regret his remarks.

"Simmons Offers Convicts 'More Axes' To Chop Selves," blared the headlines. The prison director's position grew more tenuous with each passing day. On April 9 State Representative Kenneth McCalla introduced a House resolution calling for an investigation into the growing charges of brutality within the prison system.[61]

"It challenges the human imagination to conceive that men would maim and cripple themselves for life without adequate cause," said McCalla.[62]

On April 10 excerpts from the Osborne Association's annual report on U.S. prisons began appearing in the *Houston Press*, most of which lambasted the Texas Prison System as an institution whose "methods of punishment are unworthy of a prison system which claims to be taking advantage of modern methods of handling prisoners."[63] References were made to the night sixteen men were found "riding the barrel" at Retrieve, the leg wound of one of the inmates festering during the course of the punishment.

"They work these men like dogs all day and stand them on the barrel all night," W. R. Dulaney of the prison board stated in dismay. "No wonder they chop off their legs to get out of it."[64]

Finally, touching on the irrevocable incorrigibility of men like Charlie Frazier, Blackie Thompson,and Clyde Barrow, the Osborne Association best summed up its findings by adding that "atrocious legal punishments are bound to develop more atrocious and far more barbarous illegal acts."[65]

By the time Ralph Fults was summoned to the prison administration building on May l, Texas prison officials were no doubt searching desperately for a way to discredit their critics, in particular Harry McCormick. Indeed, investigations were mounting daily, mostly as a result of McCormick's editorials. The chance to charge him with harboring Raymond Hamilton would have been perfect. Facing the obstinate Fults, on May 1, waiting for his answer, the prison official must have had but one thought on his mind—get Harry McCormick.

"Well," Fults said, returning the official's gaze, "I surely don't want to lie about that McCormick deal."

The official's eyes brightened in anticipation.

"But he was kidnapped all right," the convict announced brazenly, "Sure as I'm standing here, we kidnapped Harry McCormick."

The official's lips tightened. "No," he shouted, "I know better. He's guilty of harboring you and Raymond. With your testimony we could convict him."

Fults said nothing.

"Now look, you bastard," the official snapped. "I'm going to ship you out to Central Farm if you don't play along. Things are already at a boil on Central. Somebody could get hurt there. I can make it easy on you, or I can make it tough. What's it gonna be?"

No reply.

"Get him out of here," the official shouted.[66]

Fults was hurried down to the yard and loaded in the rear of "Uncle Bud's" truck. Minutes later he and a dozen other men were on their way to Central Farm, twenty-two miles southeast of Houston. It was a bad place to be in the spring of 1935.

Inmates and guards alike were edgy, feeling the effects of an incident that had occurred just prior to Ralph Fults's arrival. A convict named Beaumont King had attacked and brutally stabbed a hated guard, who, in his dying breath, had managed to shoot the convict assailant between the eyes. By the time Fults stepped from Uncle Bud's truck, the situation on the farm had blossomed into a powder keg of emotions.

Fults, a noted troublemaker, was the only man in stripes. When the camp manager viewed the new arrivals, he zeroed in on the McKinney outlaw. "There ain't but two bad men in the whole world," the manager shouted, "and I'm both of them."

Fults nearly laughed, but it was no joke. Later he found himself hoeing next to the man who had smuggled the three guns to Charley Frazier and Whitey Walker, thus precipitating the only escape in history from the Texas death house.

"Are you sorry you helped those guys?" Fults asked.

"Hell, no," the former guard replied. "I knew they'd never rat on me. It's my own damned fault I got caught. If I had it to do again, I'd still help them."

On the morning of May 10 a mounted guard rode up to Fults.

"Raymond and Joe went over, just past midnight," he said.

Fults made not reply.

Everyone knew Joe's fate was sealed. He seemed to welcome death. But Raymond fought it. Indeed, public sentiment was leaning strongly in his favor, with thousands working to have his sentence commuted to life imprisonment. By April 17 the Houston area alone had gathered more than ten-thousand signatures on a petition calling for Governor Allred to make just such a move.[67] The petition, however, was summarily ignored, as were the many personal pleas of Raymond's mother. Hamilton was doomed. Eight days before his execution, Katie arrived in Huntsville.

"Your girl's here for a visit," the Warden said to Raymond. "But before we can let her see you, we got some papers for you to sign."

Hamilton examined the documents. They rescinded his request that Harry McCormick attend his execution.[68] Having failed with Fults, prison officials were now trying a new way to discredit the Houston reporter. Thinking only of his beloved Katie, Raymond affixed his signature. Smiling broadly, the Warden then led his prisoner into the tiny visitor's cubicle where a tearful Katie waited.

"So you're Katie?" the Warden said. "Well, I'm going to give you both thirty minutes together. I want you to take a good look at your boy, now, because this'll be the last time you'll ever see him as he is. We're gonna shave a little round spot on top of his head and shoot plenty of juice through that hard little body of his."[69]

The young woman sobbed uncontrollably.

On May 9 Governor Allred and the Court of Criminal Appeals rejected all motions for a stay of execution. Hamilton would die in less than six hours.

Harry McCormick was told that Raymond had been forced to sign a retraction to his earlier request, allowing Harry to witness the execution—this, in exchange for a brief visit with Katie.

"Don't go to Huntsville," prison Chaplain Father Hugh Finnegan warned. "They're going to embarrass you by waving that sworn statement in front of everyone and announcing to the world that Raymond doesn't want you there."[70] McCormick refused to back down. Through his many friends in the state legislature, he was able to contact Governor Allred. Lee Simmons received a phone call from the governor and the doors to the prison opened to Harry McCormick.[71]

As midnight approached, special admittance cards were issued to the half-dozen newsmen to be allowed within the death chamber, including Harry McCormick and his editor Royal Roussel, also a staunch advocate of prison reform. In addition to these men, nearly fifty officers and prosecutors from across the nation had been given cards. The death of Raymond Hamilton would be the judicial event of the year.

At 11:55 P.M. the main gates swung open. The entourage poured through, at first proceeding in a somber, orderly fashion, then becoming a swirling mass of lumbering figures, each bent on beating the next man to the death house for a better seat.[72] Reaching their destination, however, they found the spectator section already packed with state legislators and other special guests who had been admitted in advance.

People rushed for the open door, crashing through at a rate of two and three bodies at a time, grumbling and shoving as they fought each other for a place to stand, stoop, or kneel. Some slipped beneath the railing to press up against Father Finnegan, Dr. W. B. Veazey, and the men of the death squad.[73] "Smoot" Schmid was there, as was Ted Hinton. Standing to one side was a man whose interest in both Raymond Hamilton and Clyde Barrow had begun on one particularly bloody August night in 1932, Sheriff C. G. Maxwell, of Atoka County, Oklahoma.

At midnight Father Finnegan and a delegation of prison officials approached Joe Palmer. Palmer, who had spent the previous hour with Raymond Hamilton, picking through a final meal of fried fish, ice cream, and chocolate cake, grasped his fellow prisoner's right hand firmly and threw his thin, pale arm over the boy's left shoulder.

"Goodbye, old pal," Joe said. "We're going to be happy in a few minutes. "We'll meet on the other side."[74]

He walked through the green door.

A few minutes later the handful of prison officials and designated guards arrived before cell no.7. Raymond Hamilton, the top of his head shaved smooth, looked up.

"Is Joe . . . gone?" he asked.

Father Finnegan nodded. At 12:19 A.M. on May 10 Raymond appeared in the death chamber. He had declined the use of the usual prison "death suit" of dark broadcloth in favor of his own monogrammed blue silk shirt and autumn brown jacket. One leg of his matching trousers had been opened at the seam to afford greater accessibility to the condemned man's shaved left ankle.

"Hello, Harry," Raymond said, strolling calmly into the room.

"Got something to say?" the Warden asked quickly.

"Yes sir," the blond youth replied. "The governor's office has asked me for information about the Hillsboro murder. I didn't do that job. The man who killed Bucher is dead now, but even if he wasn't, I wouldn't tell you people anything about it."[75]

He then turned to the priest.

"I hope you have a pleasant trip to Ireland, Father Finnegan," he said jovially, referring to a forthcoming vacation. Then, looking over his shoulder, he eyed the chair. Grinning, he hoisted himself onto the contraption with a jaunty little skip, dropping into the seat like an impetuous child. The guards moved in, securing a complex system of medieval-looking straps to Hamilton's body—three leather harnesses for each arm and one per leg. His head was then drawn tight against the high, straight back of the apparatus and tied in place by yet another strap. Father Finnegan leaned forward and spoke softly as the star-shaped copper electrodes were strapped to Hamilton's skull and left ankle, a piece of brine-soaked organic sponge separating the metal from his bare skin.[76] A final pull on the chin strap wiped the grin from Hamilton's face.

Silence fell over the room as the guards and Father Finnegan backed away.

"Well," Hamilton barely uttered, the leather mask dropping before his face, "goodbye all."[77]

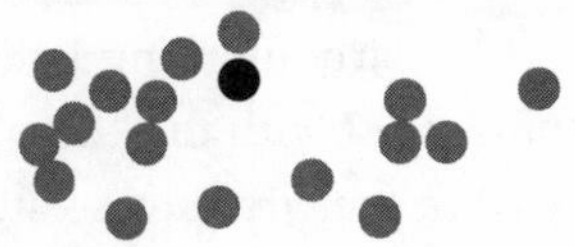

"Boss Killer" and the Shadow of the Gallows

In the summer of 1935, five convicts died of heatstroke in a single week on Central farm.[1] The conditions were atrocious, but the weather was not the only thing heating up.

One evening in late June, 1935, a trusty slipped up to Ralph Fults's bunk at Central Farm. "The word's out," he said. "Ain't nobody supposed to fraternize with you."

Fults gazed into the trusty's eyes.

"And there's something else," the convict said, showing a dirk knife. "I'm supposed to pick a fight with you. I ain't going to do it, though. I ain't nobody's hit man. Watch yourself; keep your eyes peeled."

The next morning two men were severely beaten for openly talking to Fults. Later Fults was taken to the farm manager.

"Well, boy," the manager said, "you want a beating too?"

"You're the doctor," Fults replied.

The manager leaned forward in his chair, returning the prisoner's stare. "Get on back to work," he shouted, waving a big right hand at the door. Fults departed.

For the next several days the situation continued to deteriorate. Fults was a marked man, and he knew it. Prison management was closing in. Then on June 29, a particularly stiflingly hot morning, it happened. On his way to the fields Fults chanced to look up. There, sitting astride a big bay horse not more than a hundred yards away, was "Boss Killer",—sunglasses glistening in the early morning light. Fults did not have to guess what was happening—not with the "Boss" prowling like the grim reaper just down range from the virtually isolated convict.

"Why doesn't he get it over with?" Fults thought to himself.

At that very moment a pair of strange cars drew up in front of the prison compound. Several men got out and disappeared into the main office. Minutes later the men emerged, the farm manager leading them into the fields. The manager was pointing toward Fults and talking over his shoulder.

"Fults," the farm manager called out, "these men are from Mississippi. Governor Allred's released you into their custody. You're to leave immediately for Jackson."[2]

Fults turned toward the group of officers hiking through the furrows, then passed a glance over his shoulder. "Boss Killer" had disappeared.

Later that day the two-car escort transporting Fults from Texas to Mississippi was approaching Houston when suddenly a tall, lean man leaped from a vehicle parked along the highway and began flailing his arms in the breeze. Fults knew the man. Prentiss Sheriff William "Uncle Billy" Mathewson knew him as well.

"This guy's a reporter named McCormick," said "Uncle Billy." "I told him he could have a few minutes with you."

The Mississippi cars pulled over. Harry was accompanied by a photographer, and Fults was helped out of the car for an interview and a quick picture. Mathewson told McCormick that Mississippi had a good capital case against Fults and that the authorities there had guaranteed Texas they would hang the outlaw.[3] Among other things, Fults and McCormick briefly discussed Texas prison management, then focused on the deaths of Raymond Hamilton and Joe Palmer. Harry then gave Fults a carton of cigarettes and had his cameraman make a few shots of the notorious gunman.

"Let my mother know where I'm being taken," said the prisoner as he was escorted back to the car. McCormick agreed to do so.

Arriving in Jackson, Fults was placed on the top floor of the newly constructed five-story jail—Death Row. Settling into cell no.5, the bandit began surveying his new surroundings. He was immediately struck by the pristine condition of the jail. The paint was fresh, void of the usual graffiti. Jackson authorities were proud of their new prison, promoting it as "moth proof and escape proof."

Not far from Fults's cell was a federal prisoner named Bobby. Bobby had a girl friend who sent him gifts on a regular basis. Fults contracted with Bobby to smuggle some hacksaw blades to Death Row, via his girl friend. Fults had the woman buy a pound cake that was prepackaged in cellophane. He told her how to steam the wrapping off, slip the blades inside the cake, and reseal the package. So perfect was her work, the Jackson guards suspected nothing. Fults had the blades within hours of his request.

Breaking the blades into short pieces, sometimes no more than one or two teeth, Fults went to work. He fashioned a makeshift handle from a discarded wooden stick and mounted the broken blades on it. Two weeks passed before any noticeable progress was made on the bar.

Fults was often interrupted by visitors, some official, some merely sightseers.[4] A number of agents from the U.S. Bureau of Investigation came and went. They always wanted the same thing—information about the activities of Bonnie, Clyde, and Raymond.

Fults refused to cooperate. "Now, we know you were in on that armory job in Beaumont, Texas," said one of the investigators. "How about this one in Minneapolis?"

"Hey," Fults said, "I'm not going to do your job for you. Get out and dig that answer up for yourself."

"C'mon, Fults," the agent said. "At the very least, you're going to get life imprisonment for that Prentiss bank heist. Why not confess to a couple of the unsolved cases in our files?"

"Man, I don't know what y'all do for a living," Fults answered. "You couldn't catch Clyde, you couldn't catch Raymond, you couldn't catch me. Man, you guys couldn't catch a cold!"

The agents left and never returned.[5]

Throughout the remainder of the long, hot summer of 1935 Fults continued working on the bar. As September neared, he was convinced that another thirty minutes work would finish the job. He had accumulated a large quantity of sheets with which to make the five-story descent once he severed the bar. Before he could make another move, however, three Bible-toting strangers arrived on his floor. They were part of a group holding Sunday services in the jail. Until that moment Fults had no idea what day it was, so strong was the taste of freedom in his mouth. Reluctantly he turned to face the men.

"We are three laymen messengers from God," the men said in unison.

"I'm Chalmers Alexander," said one. "I have surrendered all to Jesus. I am afraid of nothing on this earth, but I fear hellfire and eternal damnation." Alexander then arranged his wire glasses and stared at Fults pleasantly. Slight of build with a fair complexion, he was a banker with an interest in law.[6]

"I'm Ike Garber," the second man announced. "I used to be a drunkard before I gave myself to God. Today I'm one of the most successful contractors in Jackson."[7]

The third man was a short, stocky insurance broker named Billy Gilbert. He said,"Since accepting Christ as my savior, I've been blessed in many ways. I was broke and cursed with illness, but now that I have mended my ways, things are so much better. You need help more than anyone we know. The state is out to hang you, but in life or in death there is no better haven for man than God."[8]

Though far more interested in the window behind him, Fults found himself strangely drawn to the words of these men. Their gentle candor intrigued him.

"I need help, all right," Fults said. "And nobody knows it better than I do. But it don't seem right to wait until I get in the worst jam of my life before calling on the Lord."[9] The three men smiled and chose not to argue. They merely signed a copy of the New Testament and handed it to the prisoner.

"We'll be back," they said as they turned to leave.

A few moments later, much to Fults's dismay, a group of officers arrived from Prentiss. They had come to transport Fults south for the trial.

"The fates are playing tricks on me," Fults muttered to himself.

Slipping a couple of hacksaw blades in the soles of his shoes, Fults quietly joined the Prentiss-bound entourage. By late afternoon he found himself shut in on the upper level of the musty, ancient, two-story red brick Jefferson Davis County jailhouse—a mere stone's throw from the Bank of Blountville. The sight of a decrepit old gallows trap situated just outside of his cell did little to lift Fults's spirits. The mechanism, rusting and dented, looked as if it had not been used in years. Overhead, dangling through a steel ring mounted in one of the ceiling joists, hovered a rotting piece of rope.

Fults could not help but wonder how many men had fallen to their deaths through that hole—their ankles, thighs, and wrists firmly secured. He suddenly visualized muslin hoods concealing anonymous faces, with heavy knots of hemp crushing throats and snapping vertebrae. He thought of his childhood and the day he skipped school to watch that hanging in Collin County. The sight of the condemned man's head nearly pulled from his body by the fall was etched deeply in his mind.

"You're a lucky feller," a deputy said, seeing Fults staring at the old trap. "They're going to build you a brand new scaffold, right out there in the square. This old thing probably won't even work."

Fults made no response. He was hoping to get a chance to pull out a hacksaw blade and get down to work, but the deputy never went away. Later that night the deputy was relieved by yet another lawman. A twenty-four-hour guard had been posted just outside of his cell and would remain there for the duration of his stay—quite possibly his last stay anywhere.

Late one afternoon Fults heard children's voices outside his window. Looking out, he noticed a handful of little girls gazing open-mouthed in his direction. They seemed too bashful to say anything. Fults smiled and waved, but the youngsters darted off. The following day, however, they were back. Fults called to one of them.

"What's your name, little one?" he asked quietly.

The girl, perhaps ten or eleven, looked down shyly and started shuffling her feet.

"Vivian," she replied. "These are my school pals," she then added, gaining confidence. "This here's Mary and Gertrude and Linda. . . . "[10]

"Well, I sure am glad to see y'all," Fults said. "I hope that y'all will be good kids and mind your folks and teachers so you won't get into trouble like me. If I'd have minded my Mom and Pop when I was your size, I wouldn't be here today."

"Yes, Sir," said Vivian. "Now, we want to sing you a song." The group then broke into a high-pitched rendition of "Now the Day is Over." Fults knew the song well. He had sung it often as a boy in McKinney, long before leaving home to strike out on a crime-ridden, ten-year trek to Death Row.

In time, others visited Fults's cell. They usually turned out to be lawmen or members of the posse Fults and Hamilton had routed, but one day Alma Rogers dropped by.

"Do you remember me?" she asked as Fults sat up to greet her.

"Yes, Ma'am," he answered. "You're the lady that walked into the bank."

"That's right," said Mrs. Rogers. "And do you know that half this town is mad at me?"

"Yeh?" asked Fults. "How's that?"

"Well, I told everybody that you wouldn't take my money and that you boys were the nicest bank robbers I've ever met. Now everybody's mad at me! Well, I told them you shouldn't be sentenced to death, and I'm going to keep on telling them that!"

On September 1, the day before the trial, Fults's parents arrived from Texas. They were accompanied by an attorney named Luther Truett, one of the three attorneys who had defended Fults in Wichita Falls. As soon as he saw the faces of his parents, Fults realized just how much the whole ordeal had affected them, especially his father. He looked tired, grey, and considerably older than when last they had met. After a brief introductory conversation, Truett left for a conference with Harvey McGehee, the judge who was to hear the case. Fults and his parents looked at each other for several minutes before speaking.

"How much is this costing you?" Fults asked.

"We don't care," Audie replied evasively. "We only want to save your life."

"Pop, how much?" Fults insisted.

"Around a thousand dollars," Audie finally admitted.[11]

Fults sank into his bunk in dismay.

"What's this thing?" Audie asked, scraping his feet over the trap in front of the cell.

"That?" Fults asked. "That's a gallows trap. That's where they hang men."

Audie winced and backed away, nervously glancing up at the frayed rope stretched above his head. Several minutes later Luther Truett returned from Judge McGehee's chambers.

"Ralph," he said excitedly, "I want you to change your plea from not guilty to guilty and throw yourself on the mercy of the court. Judge McGehee will accept such a plea."

"Well, Mr. Truett," Fults answered, "I figure they're going to hang me no matter what I do."

"Now, Ralph," Truett interjected, "I've been doing a lot of research, and I can't find a single instance in this state where a man was sentenced to death after entering a guilty plea. Besides, I reminded McGehee that a jury trial could last a long time. The cost would be astronomical. He would like to avoid that."

Fults looked over to his father. "It sounds good to me, son," Audie said.

"OK," the prisoner said. "We'll do it your way."

The following morning, September 2, Fults was up early. Truett had told him to be sure to look his best for the trial, so he shaved carefully and dressed in the new suit his parents had brought with them from Texas. Just as the armed escort arrived from the courthouse, Fults caught sight of his copy of the New Testament, the one given to him in Jackson by the three reformed sinners. Touching it fleetingly, he stepped through the opened door of his cell and joined the lawmen for the short walk across the street to the weathered red brick courthouse. He tried not to look at the battered old gallows trap as he made his way to the stairs.

The square outside was choked with automobiles and horse-drawn buckboards. All eyes were on the prisoner as he was led to the courtroom and seated next to his lawyer. Throughout the reading of the indictment, Fults could feel the cold blue eyes of Judge McGehee trained on him like a pair of lasers etching into his very soul. Suddenly the Judge spoke, startling the prisoner.

"Ralph Fults," McGehee called in a surprisingly soft, gentle voice. "You will please rise."

Fults pushed his chair back and stood up straight.

"You have heard the charges in the indictment," the judge said. "What is your plea?"

"I plead guilty to the charges, Judge McGehee," Fults announced. "And I wish to throw myself on the mercy of the court."

Silence fell over the courtroom as McGehee gazed upon Fults's face, his deep blue eyes searching for some unknown clue.

"The court sentences you to fifty years for bank robbery," McGehee suddenly stated.

Fults caught his breath.

"For kidnapping," McGehee added, "the court sentences you to another fifty years."[12]

"Thank you, judge," Fults stammered, his legs turning to rubber. Sheriff Mathewson stepped forward and took him by the arm. As he was being led from the courtroom, Fults looked over to his mother. Tears were streaming down her face. He had never seen his mother cry before.

At the jail, as he gathered his few belongings for the trip to the penitentiary, Fults once again caught sight of the book from the three lay ministers. He opened it, randomly turning to John 3:15: "That whosoever believeth in him should not perish, but shall have eternal life."[13] Fults closed the book and tossed it in his duffel bag.

On his way through the foyer of the jail, en route to the waiting prison transport, Fults overheard a radio broadcast coming from the sheriff's office. A news bulletin was being read over the air. Col. Lee Simmons had just resigned as general manager of the Texas Prison System.[14]

Epilogue

Robert F. "Bob" Alcorn remained as Dallas County Deputy Sheriff for several years before retiring. Afterward he worked briefly in sales, then became a court bailiff.

In the 1950s Ralph Fults, by then living in Dallas, chanced to meet Alcorn. The two men established a friendly rapport. Alcorn spoke briefly but guardedly about the ambush in Louisiana. He stated without hesitation that neither he nor any of the other officers involved in the shooting said a thing when Bonnie and Clyde pulled alongside their position on the morning of May 23, 1934. Alcorn died in 1964.

Aubrey was finally paroled in the 1950s. He borrowed one of Ralph Fults's automobiles to take his driving test and went to work for one of Fults's friends. Not long after his parole, however, he contracted a terminal disease and died without ever revealing the reason behind his absence from that field on the morning of January 16, 1934.[1]

Bergie was acquitted of all charges in the Prentiss bank robbery.[2]

Blanche refused to cooperate with the authorities following her arrest in Dexfield Park, leading Department of Justice investigators on a merry chase with false names and misinformation. A frustrated J. Edgar Hoover flew to Iowa to take charge of her interrogation. Gazing at the young woman's bandaged face, Hoover threatened to gouge out her other eye if she did not cooperate.[3] Blanche sat in silence. Hoover finally gave up.

Blanche was sentenced to the Missouri State Penitentiary for a period of not less than one year and not more than ten for her part in the Platte City gunfight.[4] In 1935 she was sentenced to a year and a day for harboring Bonnie and Clyde.[5] After serving six years, during which time she became close friends with Platte City's Sheriff Holt Coffey, Blanche was granted a full pardon.

"I don't think Clyde felt bad about leaving Buck and me in Dexfield Park," she said once. "At least I hope he didn't. You see, we were all just little kids then, but we were still in full control of our own lives. Clyde never held a gun to my head. I was there because I wanted to be, plain and simple."[6]

Blanche spent the last years of her life in Texas, fishing and hoping to be forgotten. In 1988 she died of cancer.

At the 1935 trial for harboring her son, Cumie T. Barrow was asked by Judge Atwell what punishment she should receive. "Maybe sixty days," the judge said. "Well, I'm needed at home," Cumie said. "Can't you make it thirty, like Mrs. Parker?"

"Then we'll make it thirty," the Judge decreed.[7]

In 1938 Cumie Barrow was accidently struck by a shotgun blast intended for her son, L. C. She recovered and continued to live behind the Star Service Station until her death on August 14, 1942. She is buried just a few feet from Clyde and Buck.

Henry Barrow continued to operate the Star Service Station until advancing age forced him to retire. He died on June 19, 1957, at the age of eighty-three.

"Boss Killer" committed suicide in Houston, Texas in the 1940s.[8]

Hilton Bybee, in addition to his other lengthy sentences, was given ninety days for harboring Bonnie and Clyde.[9] Although standing as close to Major Crowson as Joe Palmer and Raymond Hamilton when the guard was shot, Bybee was never tried for that killing, nor was Henry Methvin.

In 1937 Bybee once again escaped from Eastham. On July 22, 1937, however, he was gunned down by a posse in Arkansas.[10]

Bill Decker was sworn in as sheriff of Dallas County on January 2, 1949.[11]

One day in the early 1950s Ralph Fults got an unexpected phone call. "If you don't come down to my office and drink some coffee," said the familiar voice, "I'm going to send one of my deputies out there to fetch you." It was Bill Decker. Fults accepted the sheriff's invitation and the resulting visit blossomed into a fond friendship.

Fults and Decker traded many tales, but most of all the lawman asked about the ordeal of an ex-con trying to go straight. He and Fults also spoke of prison conditions and the need to separate first offenders from hardened criminals—one of Fults's pet causes. In 1955 Decker spoke out in favor of such action at the tenth Regional Conference of the National Jailer's Association in San Antonio. Decker remained as sheriff until declining health forced him to retire in 1970. He died shortly thereafter.

Charley Frazier, weak, unkempt, and grossly underweight, was interviewed by Harry McCormick shortly after the resignation of Lee Simmons. Neither his hair nor his beard had been shorn in months, and he appeared unwashed as well. McCormick wrote that Frazier "looked and walked like a fugitive from the grave."[12] Shortly thereafter Frazier was transferred to Louisiana, where he received a life sentence for his part in the bloody prison break at Angola in 1933. On October 18, 1936, the indomitable renegade was shot six times at close range during yet another escape attempt.[13] Amazingly, he survived. Years later, Frazier was pardoned. By then he had converted to Christianity. He spent the rest of his life preaching.

Fuzz was sentenced to a lengthy term for the Celina burglary and abductions, even though he had not participated in those crimes. While in prison, he became involved with organized crime. A bogus criminal charge was filed against Fuzz in a western state under mob control. He was extradited there, tried, convicted and quietly pardoned.

Over a period of years, Fuzz rose to great heights in the criminal structure, eventually becoming the manager of a vast labor force. To a friend he admitted his involvement in at least one gangland slaying, and he is suspected of many others. In the 1970s Fuzz became entangled in a gangland rivalry and was shotgunned to death.[14]

Manny Gault avoided all publicity.

Frank Hamer granted few interviews and refused to cooperate in the production of any book or motion picture that dealt with his life. As a result, Hamer remains an enigmatic figure and a supreme giant in Texas folklore. He maintained a home in Austin and accepted occasional commissions in the field of law enforcement.

During the infamous 1948 U.S. senatorial campaign between former Texas Governor Coke Stevenson and Lyndon Johnson, Hamer became embroiled in the fight to gain access to the pivotal ballot box no. 13 in Jim Wells County, the one supposedly containing the few votes needed by Johnson to win the election. Stevenson demanded to see the actual votes, but election officials in Jim Wells County refused to let him. Stevenson went to Alice, the county seat, with his lawyers. He also brought his close friend Frank Hamer. The ballot box was being kept under armed guard, but when Stevenson approached with the sixty-four-year-old Hamer, who made it known he was heavily armed and quite ready to use force, the box was made available for inspection. Supposedly, many discrepancies were noted by Stevenson's attorneys, but nothing was resolved. The ballot box disappeared shortly after the incident, and Johnson was deemed the winner of the election.[15]

Hamer died in 1955.

Floyd Hamilton received two years in Leavenworth for harboring Bonnie and Clyde.[16] Following his release, in 1938 he embarked on an extensive Midwestern bank-robbing spree, netting him, like his younger brother, the ominous title of Public Enemy No. 1. In August 1938 he was recaptured in Dallas. Texas subsequently sentenced him to twenty-five years, and the federal government sentenced him to thirty.[17]

Hamilton was transferred to Alcatraz in 1940. In 1943 he tried unsuccessfully to escape—a fiasco that got him thrown into solitary for nine years.[18] During that time of virtual isolation, Hamilton's next-door neighbor was Robert Stroud, "the Birdman of Alcatraz." In 1958, after twenty-two years in prison, Floyd Hamilton was freed.

With the help of Bill Decker and Ted Hinton, Hamilton was offered a job with a Dallas car dealership. He remained with the same company until his retirement. Well read in eastern philosophy, Hamilton believed strongly in the concept of reincarnation. He often said he had been a wicked priest in a prior life and was being forced to pay for that wickedness. On July 24, 1984, Floyd Hamilton died.[19]

Ted Hinton, an experienced pilot, trained flyers during World War II. After the war, he continued to fly, formed a trucking company, and operated a motel in Irving, Texas, not far from the sight of his first brush with Bonnie and Clyde in 1933. At the time Ralph Fults was managing a tire store nearby and was often visited by the former deputy, who loved to socialize. One day Fults asked Hinton if he and the others had truly called to Bonnie and Clyde on that May morning in Louisiana. A broad, toothy grin broke across Hinton's face, but he said nothing. He did not have to.[20]

Dot Houston was acquitted of all charges in the Prentiss bank robbery.[21]

Stella Houston received a light sentence in the Prentiss bank robbery because she was seen driving the getaway car.[22]

Jack, for a time Lee Simmons's personal driver until an altercation with the general manager landed him in a hoe squad at Eastham, was a witness to Fults's confrontation with a high-ranking prison official in 1935.[23]

Using money earned through piecework in the prison craft shop, Jack was able to get his sentence greatly reduced, or as he said, "buy the sentence down." After his release he relocated to a North Texas town, married, and, like Ralph Fults, settled down to raise a family. He never broke the law again.

Johnny disappeared.[24]

W. D. Jones, convicted as an accessory in the January 6, 1933, death of Fort Worth Deputy Malcolm Davis received a fifteen-year sentence. In 1935, another two years were added for harboring Bonnie and Clyde.[25] Following his release from prison, Jones married and settled in Houston. In the late 1960s, after the sudden death of his wife, Jones became addicted to paregoric (an opium-based drug), which he consumed in a liquid form called "Black Jack." The paregoric was mixed with Jack Daniels whiskey and drunk straight from the bottle to conceal the presence of the drug. In 1971 Jones's drug supplier turned him in. He was sentenced to several months in a federal institution near Fort Worth, basically to dry out. On August 20, 1974, Jones was gunned down in Houston.[26]

Henderson Jordan refused to return the so-called "death car" of Bonnie and Clyde to its rightful owners. Jordan said he and the other five officers involved in the ambush deserved to keep the car because they had risked their lives to make it famous. It took a court order to make Jordan return the car.

Jordan often intimated to friends that the ambush of Bonnie and Clyde bothered him. He and Oakley both had wanted to try taking the outlaws alive.[27]

John Joyner was paid one thousand dollars by the state of Texas for his part in the ambush of Bonnie and Clyde. In 1942, Joyner murdered his wife and then committed suicide.[28]

Katie moved to the western United States and became the road manager for a successful professional boxer.

Lewis disappeared.

Marie was sentenced to one hour in the custody of a U.S. Marshall for harboring Bonnie and Clyde. The sentence did not take into account the weeks spent in jail awaiting trial.[29]

Harry McCormick moved to Dallas, where he worked for a time on the city desk of the *Dallas Dispatch*. Later he joined the staff of the *Dallas Morning News*. Remembered by colleagues as loud, foul-mouthed, and by far one of the best reporters in the business, McCormick often risked his life to get a story.[30] On one occasion a volatile gunman had barricaded himself in a Dallas house. He was holding a number of hostages and had already killed a policeman who tried to approach the premises. After several hours of stalemate, McCormick stepped from the crowd, proceeded through the police lines, and eased up to the front door. There he engaged the gunman in conversation while the hostages escaped through a rear window. McCormick finally persuaded the killer to surrender.[31]

In 1947 McCormick appeared with Ralph Fults on the nationally broadcast CBS radio program, *We the People*. The two men spoke of the Barrow gang and reenacted the famous "kidnapping" of March 19, 1935—carefully sticking to the original version for Harry's protection. The program laid the groundwork for a proposed biography of Fults, to be penned by McCormick. The chain-smoking newspaperman was still working on the manuscript when cancer took his life in 1967.[32]

Henry Methvin was sentenced to death for the slaying of Oklahoma officer Cal Campbell. In 1936, following the disclosure in court of Methvin's part in the ambush of Bonnie and Clyde, an Oklahoma court of appeals commuted the condemned man's sentence to life imprisonment.[33] Methvin served ten years, during which time he suffered a near-fatal stabbing inflicted in an apparent reprisal against the man who "fingered" Bonnie and Clyde.

One day Ralph Fults passed through Bossier City, Louisiana, where Methvin resided after his parole. He had not seen Henry since the early days on Eastham, and he longed to find out about the final weeks in the lives of Bonnie and Clyde. Fults stepped into a bar to ask about the former outlaw.

"Well, he's around town, all right," said the bar tender, "but I don't know for how long. He's taken to carrying a scattergun and trying to throw his weight around."

Two weeks later, on April 19, 1949, Methvin's body was found on the railroad tracks outside of town, cut in half by a passing train.[34]

Iverson "Ivy" Methvin was killed in an automobile accident in 1946.[35]

James Mullens received immunity from prosecution in return for his testimony against Joe Palmer and Raymond Hamilton. For harboring Bonnie and Clyde he received a four-month sentence. In 1938 Mullens was sentenced to seventy-five years in prison for a thirty-six dollar holdup.[36]

Prentiss Oakley, like Henderson Jordan, was very disturbed by the events on May 23, 1934, and remained so all his life.[37]

Mary O'Dare was sentenced to one year and one day in the federal prison at Alderson, West Virginia, for harboring Bonnie and Clyde.[38] In 1938 she was sentenced to five years for trafficking narcotics.

"One-eyed" Max was killed in Los Angeles by Fuzz after Max tried to ambush him in a gangland dispute.[39]

Billie Parker, acquitted of all charges stemming from the Grapevine killings, received one year and one day in the federal prison at Alderson, West Virginia, for harboring her sister and Clyde Barrow.[40]

Bonnie Parker's grave was moved from Fishtrap Cemetery in 1945.

Emma Parker received thirty days for harboring Bonnie and Clyde.[41]

Royce, ironically, wound up living across the street from Fults and his young wife during their stay in McKinney. Fults assured Royce that his anger had long since subsided, and the two men established a cordial, but distant, relationship. Out of curiosity, Fults asked Royce about the setup with the McKinney constable, but the bootlegger would only say that it was Lewis, not he, that arranged the ambush. In the mid-1970s Royce was gunned down by McKinney officers following an unknown altercation.[42]

Bud Russell retired from the Texas Prison System in May 1944 at age sixty-nine. For the rest of his days he worked on his stock farm near Blum, Texas. He sometimes reminisced about his life as the most legendary transfer officer ever to handle prisoners in Texas. In slightly more than thirty-nine years Russell traversed 3,900,000 miles and moved 115,000 convicts.[43] His larger-than-life appearance, dark glasses, and economy of words won him the respect of not only his fellow peace officers but of the prisoners as well. Even today, ex-convicts who knew him speak almost reverently, if not mythically, of the man.

Richard Allen "Smoot" Schmid served as sheriff of Dallas County until the last day of 1946. Between 1947 and 1953 he served on the State Board of Pardons and Paroles. He died on July 1, 1963.[44]

West Dallas remains starkly depressed, shamelessly neglected, and branded with the same social prejudices that plagued it half a century earlier. Recently it was discovered that several lead smelters situated there were releasing enough toxic emissions into the atmosphere to severely poison the neighborhood residents. Despite this, it took nearly two years before the City of Dallas and the Environmental Protection Agency terminated lead production in West Dallas. By then, schools and other public and private facilities had been forced to close because of the staggeringly high levels of lead found in West Dallas soil samples, including those taken from playgrounds.[45]

In 1984, when a comprehensive proposal designed to upgrade the level of public housing in West Dallas was introduced to the Dallas City Council, one councilman discounted the idea, adding that conditions had always been bad in that part of the city and they were going to remain that way no matter what was done.

Roy Thornton, Bonnie Parker's estranged husband, was convicted of burglary in 1933. Upon his arrival in prison, he quizzed Ralph Fults about the nature of his wife's relationship with Clyde Barrow. It became a matter of unceasing interest to him. When Bonnie and Clyde were ambushed, however, Thornton said he was glad they died together.

Thornton was involved in a series of escape attempts, at least one of which was masterminded by Charlie Frazier.[46] On October 4, 1937, Thornton was killed trying to escape from Eastham.[47]

Ralph Fults began serving his two fifty-year terms on September 2, 1935. Although his chances for a parole were virtually nonexistent, he was nonetheless relieved, having escaped both the gallows, in Mississippi, and the reprisals of Texas prison officials. His glee, however, would be short-lived.

On May 5, 1936, Fults, in utter desperation, led a prison strike at Camp 5 of the Mississippi State Penitentiary, near Parchman.[48] Commandeering the barracks and dining hall, he and the other inmates hoped to win an audience with the governor and expose the many murders and incidents of sadistic brutality[49] perpetrated by the camp manager, whose hatred of Texans was both bizarre and all-consuming. "The whole state's populated with nothing but criminals," he often said. "An electrified fence should be put up along its borders to keep the bastards away from the rest of us." Two of Fults's friends, both Texans, had already been killed. Fults was told that he was next on the list. A strike was quickly organized.

Instead of the governor, however, Fults and his band of insurgents found themselves face-to-face with the National Guard—indeed, the same troops that let Fults and Raymond Hamilton slip through their fingers following the Prentiss bank robbery. Thus, thirty-six hours after it started, the strike was ended. Fults was beaten and placed in solitary confinement. He felt like a failure, doomed to death. The National Guard remained at the prison camp for several weeks, ostensibly to maintain the peace, but its presence prevented the camp manager from making any moves against Fults. Then, suddenly, the manager was fired. An investigation had revealed his hand in a scheme to sell penitentiary goods for personal profit. The strike and the immense publicity it generated had achieved its purpose after all.[50]

The new manager at Camp 5 was N. G. Briggs, a retired sheriff from eastern Mississippi. His arrival at the state penitentiary would signal a major turning point in the life of Ralph Fults. Although a staunch disciplinarian, Briggs was exceedingly fair. His efforts to implement humane treatment for the convicts in his charge soon won him the respect and admiration of everyone at Camp 5. The inmates eventually began referring to the seventy-year-old Briggs as "the old gentleman."[51]

Each morning Briggs would accompany the work crews to the fields. "Men," he would say, pacing off a section of land, "we've got to do this much work today. If you finish early, you can do what you like with the spare time. We're not going to have any sixteen- and twenty-hour work days while I'm in charge." Fults, who had never known a farm boss like Briggs, responded favorably. Within a year he was made a trusty. Within two years he was moved inside to the kitchen.

"You're a pretty tough customer," Briggs said after reviewing Fults's file.

"I used to think so," Fults answered.

"Well, I'm getting along in years," Briggs said. "I don't have much time left. But if I can help just one fellow get himself straightened out in this world, then my life will have been worth it. I'd like to make you that fellow." Fults was speechless.

Briggs then began petitioning for Fults's release. His petition was met with much opposition, but eventually Harvey McGehee, the judge who sentenced Fults for his part in the Prentiss bank robbery, heard about the plea. By then McGehee was a member of the State Supreme Court, and through his considerable influence, a conditional pardon was granted to Ralph Fults in January 1944—nine years after Fults had entered the Mississippi State Penitentiary.

Upon his release Fults tried to enlist in the armed forces. "You've already been to war someplace else," said the army doctor as he examined the scars of five gunshot wounds and a knifing. Fults failed the physical exam and was exempted from service. Disappointed and unsure of what to do, Fults turned to Briggs for help. Through him he was able to secure a position at a shipyard in Pascagoula, Mississippi. There he worked long hours, saved his money, and avoided all contact with the underworld.

By chance Fults met a young waitress named Ruth. Initially unaware of his terrible past, Ruth began seeing Fults on a regular basis. Eventually, however, Fults felt compelled to reveal the story of his ten fast years on the run. With tears streaming down her face, Ruth listened as Fults recounted his days with Clyde Barrow and Raymond Hamilton. He withheld nothing, speaking at length about the persons, places, and events that contributed to the many physical and psychological scars he still carried. "Are you through with that life?" Ruth asked. "As God is my witness, I swear to you that I am," Fults replied. "Then I'm with you," Ruth said.[52] Shortly thereafter, Ruth and Ralph Fults were married.

Ironically, Ruth had been born and raised less than twenty miles from Prentiss, the scene of Fults's infamous bank robbery and escape of March 28, 1935. When she mailed pictures of the groom to friends and relatives back home, she was soon flooded with congratulatory letters and telegrams, each remarking how familiar Fults looked.

After the war Fults invested his savings in two separate business ventures in Mississippi. It would have been very easy for him to get involved in the underworld, but with his wife's support he was able to avoid such a move. In 1947, upon the death of his father, Fults sold his interests and moved back to Texas to help his mother resettle.

Because of his past, Fults found it difficult to socialize in McKinney. He conducted his business and tended to his mother as quietly as possible, continually worried about what the townspeople thought of him and how it affected his family's well-being. He even traveled all the way to Dallas each day to work as a carpenter on the construction of the new Dr. Pepper headquarters on Mockingbird, not far from the spot where he outmaneuvered those two county squad cars in 1935.

Ruth Fults, a devout Southern Baptist, tried repeatedly to get her husband to accompany her and their children to church, but Ralph refused. "Those people won't accept me," he said. "Besides, I ain't been right with the Lord in so long, it'd be hypocritical."

One day the minister of the little church paid a visit to Ralph. "You don't understand," said Fults. "You ain't been here too long. You don't know what I mean to these people. You've got a former cop in your choir. He and five others tried to kill me in 1935. Nobody'll accept me in your church."

"It's not my church, Ralph." the minister said. "It belongs to anyone who believes in Jesus Christ. Please come to the next service. I'll introduce you. If that congregation doesn't accept you, I'll resign."

Fults attended the next scheduled service, pacing nervously in the foyer of the little church as he awaited the moment of his introduction. When his name was called by the minister, Fults walked slowly toward the pulpit. He was as scared as he had ever been with Bonnie and Clyde. He could barely bring himself to look up from the floor. He saw his wife smile broadly. Then he looked at the other faces. To his amazement, they too were smiling. From both sides of the aisle, hands reached out to him, shook his hand, patted him on the back. He barely made it to the pulpit when the whole congregation crowded around him. Then up stepped the officer who had been part of the ambush team that tried to kill Fults and Raymond Hamilton in 1935. Fults tensed up. The former officer approached. He extended his hand and with a big grin said, "I'm proud of you, Ralph. Proud to have you back in town and proud to have you join this church."

Seven years later, in 1954, the State of Mississippi granted Ralph Fults an unconditional pardon. Ironically, the pardon was signed by Governor Hugh White, who had ordered the Mississippi National Guard to stop Fults and the others involved in the prison uprising of May 5–6, 1936.

By then Fults lived in Dallas and was the proud father of three children. He began lecturing regularly to church and civic groups in hopes of fostering a greater understanding of the circumstances that would lead a youngster down the road to imprisonment. He neither sought nor accepted monetary compensation for these engagements. Soon men like State Representative Davis Clifton would seek his advice on prison matters. Fults's recommendations, and those of others like him, would help bring about the separation of first offenders from hardened criminals—it being Fults's contention that he and Clyde had learned every aspect of armed robbery from the more experienced convicts they associated with on the inside.

In 1960 Ralph Fults helped create a locally broadcast television program called *Confession*. Through panel discussions, Fults, along with representatives from the Texas prison system and State Board of Pardons and Paroles, established a dialogue between businessmen, legal professionals, and former inmates. The result was a greater public awareness of the unique needs of former prisoners and of the importance of offering jobs to these men and women. For a time, through his considerable influence, Norman Vincent Peale succeeded in having the program nationally syndicated.

Later, after delving into real estate and outside sales, Fults settled into a permanent position at the Buckner Home for Boys, a hundred-year-old orphanage in Mesquite, Texas. From the start the once hardened gunman easily identified with the wild and rebellious nature that he saw in many of the children. Ralph spoke of his life in Gatesville and of his days with Bonnie, Clyde, and Raymond, emphasizing always the futility and waste of that kind of life. To redirect the nervous energy of the boys he dealt with, Fults managed a number of sports activities, including boxing. On several occasions, he led his band of orphans to the state Golden Gloves finals, winning two titles.

After he retired in 1984, Fults lived the quiet life of a congenial grandfather. Few of his neighbors knew of his past. When he was diagnosed with inoperable cancer in 1992, he looked upon it philosophically. "I can't be concerned about that," he said. "The way I see it, I lived sixty-some-odd years longer than I should have. I was given a second chance, and I've had a really great life."

Fults died in 1993. Hundreds of people attended his funeral in Dallas. Most were former Buckner students or ex-cons whom he had helped at some point in their lives.[53]

Lee Simmons, citing personal and financial hardships,[54] but facing an ever-increasing number of investigations into allegations of brutality and corruption within the walls of the prisons under his control, announced his resignation from the post of general manager of the Texas Prison System on September 2, 1935. Within days, however, State Representative

Ralph Fults, 1984, a changed man. (Photo by John Neal Phillips.)

Jeff D. Stinson initiated a drive to have the prison board not only refuse the resignation, but reinstate Simmons at a 67 percent annual wage increase, saying, "For every $1,000.00 paid to Lee Simmons, he saves the state $10,000."[55] Apparently overlooking the findings of the Osborne Association, the *Dallas Morning News* said, "The Texas (prison) system has been given the highest rating in the country. One of the best jobs of public service done in Texas in twenty-five years has been done by Lee Simmons. If Simmons cannot be persuaded to withdraw his resignation, his retirement will be regretted by all citizens who are conversant with penitentiary affairs."[56]

In response to this Colonel W. R. Dulaney, of the Texas Prison Board said, "Lee Simmons is attempting to leave the prison system in a blaze of glory when in fact, the losses of the prison system under his management are a disgrace to Texas . . . and credit for the new buildings constructed during Simmons's managership is due to the state legislature, not Simmons."[57]

On September 6, 1935, State Senator T. J. Holbrook, chairman of the Senate Prison Committee, urged the prison board to accept Simmons's resignation, stating vehemently that the whole episode "was a phoney." Of Simmons's contention that he had been forced, in his own words, "to make a financial sacrifice . . . by attending to the state's business instead of my own," Holbrook scoffed that Simmons was "a hopeless failure and making more money now than ever before."[58]

Despite the many assurances of Representative Stinson that Simmons's resignation would cost the state hundreds of thousands of dollars, the fact remained that $3.5 million dollars had already disappeared, and a number of strong voices in the state legislature were making their displeasure known. Indeed, the revelations of the Osborne Association's report and the findings of the prison board's probe into charges of rampant brutality on the Retrieve Farm, coupled with the regrettable "give them more axes" statement (amid strong allegations that Lee Simmons and the manager of the Retrieve Farm had conspired to remove sixteen inmate witnesses from that facility prior to the prison board's April investigation),[59] seemed destined to reverse the countenance of many of the director's strongest supporters.

By September 7, when the prison board convened to consider the Simmons question, some of its members were already predicting that his resignation would be accepted without debate. So it came as no surprise when two days later, on September 9, a South Texas businessman named Dave Nelson was voted the new prison manager.[60] At his first press conference Nelson said he intended to make sweeping reforms in the methods and procedures of handling convicts. As his first official act he promised to disarm trusties, abolish the use of "the bat", and discontinue the punishment called "riding the barrel". Then, looking directly at reporter Harry McCormick, Nelson went on to say that as long as he remained general manager, no reporter would ever be denied access to the prison system.[61] Nelson then extended a personal invitation to McCormick, offering him a tour at his earliest convenience. McCormick readily accepted.

"Fine," Nelson replied. "And who would you like to interview first?"

"Charley Frazier,"[62] the reporter said.

If Simmons's resignation was, indeed, nothing more than a bluff, it certainly backfired. But perhaps his actions were sincere. We may never know, despite the 1957 publication of Simmons's autobiography, *Assignment Huntsville*, dealing largely with his years as general manager of the Texas Prison System. Unfortunately, many items, including the events surrounding his resignation, are treated only superficially.

After retiring, Lee Simmons returned to the management of his considerable business interests in Sherman, Texas. In 1938 he headed the unsuccessful gubernatorial campaign of Clarence Miller. Simmons died in 1957 at the age of 84.[63]

The State Juvenile Training School at Gatesville, termed "a training school for outlaws" by District Judge R. T. Brown in 1951, was closed.

The Texas Prison System, now the Texas Department of Criminal Justice, Institutional Division, or TDCJ-ID, made some progress toward reform in the decades after the departure of Col. Lee Simmons, but it has been a difficult accomplishment.

The grand hope of sweeping prison reform promised in 1935 by General Manager Dave Nelson, Lee Simmons's successor, was dashed when Nelson suffered a massive heart attack and died just sixteen days into his administration.

Barely three years later, on August 17, 1938, Houston County Attorney Leon Lusk filed murder charges against an Eastham dog sergeant after six of eight unarmed convicts died during an attempted escape.[64] Three were gunned down while trying to surrender. Two others drowned. A sixth convict bled to death after being held down and stabbed.[65]

In the early 1940s the Texas Prison System was once again named as one of the nation's worst penal institutions.[66] Under the leadership of O. B. Ellis, however, from 1947 to 1961, the prison system made significant improvements.

Ellis was reform-minded and once spoke at a program with Ralph Fults. Ellis even brought Fults a copy of his prison mug shot as a gift. "Here," said Ellis as he handed the picture to Fults. "I wanted your wife to see how you look without grey hair." The two men exchanged ideas about prison reform, and Ellis went on to implement many broad plans, including salary increases for guards, better education for inmates, and segregation of first offenders from hardened criminals.[67] Fults often cited low pay as incentive for guards to accept bribes from convicts or to be overzealous with respect to bringing in escapees, dead or alive, for the reward money. In the 1920s and early 1930s the reward was nearly a month's salary. A lot of convicts died. If an alleged escapee was dead, he could not testify that he was lured into the escape attempt or that he was not even trying to escape at all.

A system of inmate education was actually started by Lee Simmons, but, as Fults pointed out, when an inmate is worked from before sunrise until after dark, six days a week, not much time or energy is left for education. Fults also maintained that he and Clyde Barrow learned everything they knew about armed robbery, particularly bank robbery, from their fellow inmates at Eastham. Under Ellis, these and many other inequities were addressed.[68]

No doubt Ellis would have carried his ideas further, but in 1961 he suddenly died. His successors were not as interested in reform.

Officials of the prison system, by then renamed the Texas Department of Corrections, tried to undermine inmate-attorney relations by censoring their correspondence,[69] an old practice. In 1972 a court order banned such censorship. Also in the same year, inmate David Ruiz filed a handwritten petition that would eventually result in a class action suit, *Ruiz v. Estelle* (1981), leading to vast, court-ordered reforms in the Texas Department of Corrections, particularly regarding questions of overcrowding, health care, and inhumane treatment of prisoners,[70] All had been issues in the time of Clyde Barrow and Ralph Fults.

In 1973 the sixty-third Texas State Legislature finally outlawed the use of inmate trusties, or building tenders—armed convict guards of the type that beat and sodomized Clyde Barrow at Eastham. The use of building tenders continued in secret, nevertheless.[71]

In 1981 U. S. District Court Judge William Wayne Justice issued his final decree in *Ruiz v. Estelle*, giving broad relief[72] to Texas prisoners in all areas covered by the initial 1972 suit. The following year Texas Department of Corrections attorneys admitted that building tenders were still being used in Texas prisons.[73]

By 1983 much of the so-called "old guard" of the Texas Department of Corrections had either resigned or been removed. Nevertheless, investigations revealed continued abuse of prisoners, apparently sanctioned by Texas Department of Corrections officials.[74]

On September 27, 1983, an escapee from the Coffield Unit was recaptured and deliberately trampled under a horse on the orders of the camp manager,[75] the very thing an Eastham highrider tried to do to Clyde Barrow in 1930.

In 1983 an Ellis Unit inmate named Eroy Brown was cleared of murder charges after proving he had killed that facility's warden and assistant warden in self-defense. The prisoner had been transported to a well-known secluded area of the farm where he was beaten and threatened with a gun. Brown got possession of the weapon and killed both men.[76]

On December 27, 1983, a pair of Texas convicts won a fourteen-thousand-dollar settlement after charging prison guards with using them as decoys in the training of attack dogs.[77] On August 16, 1984, in a statement reminiscent of the late Lee Simmons, Texas Governor Mark White, in response to the growing incidents of prison violence, stated: "I'd rather have the inmates cutting themselves in prison than out on the streets cutting you and me."[78]

A former Texas Department of Corrections general manager and a farm manager were both investigated on charges of graft after it was found they owned stock in the construction company that built a dairy facility at Eastham.[79]

Inmates who testified in *Ruiz v. Estelle* or in other court cases against the Texas Department of Corrections were harassed and threatened, particularly at the Wynne Farm.[80] Eastham guards were still beating prisoners who refused to work, just as guards had beaten two inmates with railroad trace chains near Fults and Barrow at the same facility a half century earlier. The practice was still being referred to as a "tune up".[81] In 1984 alone two-hundred disciplinary actions were taken against Texas Department of Corrections officials for use-of-force violations.[82]

By 1990, however, the principal parties in *Ruiz v. Estelle* began working toward ending court supervision of the Texas Department of Corrections, saying it was at last in compliance,[83] sixty years after Clyde Barrow and Ralph Fults bitterly planned to free as many inmates as possible from "that hell-hole," Eastham.

Notes

Preface

1. Jack [pseud.], interview by John Neal Phillips, 20 February 1982. Others called it "Burnin' Eastham" or "Hell-Hole of Texas." Harry McCormick, "The Impossible Interview," 68.

2. Texas Prison System, File no. 70383, Ralph Fults.

3. *McKinney (Tex.) Courier-Gazette*, 25 April 1932.

4. Lee Simmons, *Assignment Huntsville*, 132, 170; Bud Russell, "Clyde Barrow-Bonnie Parker Harboring Case," 7.

5. Buried behind lead stories about Hamilton and Fults was a small column stating that Joe Palmer had been granted a stay of execution. *Houston Press*, 20 March 1935.

6. Harry McCormick, unfinished manuscript about Fults, 179.

7. Osborne Association, "Annual Report on U.S. Prisons," quoted in *Houston Press*, 10 April 1935.

8. Simmons, *Assignment Huntsville*, 168.

9. *Houston Press*, 3 April 1935, 4 April 1935, 9 April 1935, 10 April 1935; *Daily Times Herald*, 9 April 1935.

10. *Houston Press*, 2 September 1935; *Dallas Morning News*, 2 September 1935; *Dallas Daily Times Herald*, 2 September 1935.

Chapter 1

1. Others remembered the use of this tactic, particularly at Eastham. Floyd Hamilton, interview by John Neal Phillips, 18 July 1981; Jack interview, 20 February 1982; "Doc" [pseud.], interview by John Neal Phillips, 24

August 1984.

2. Stated by Joe Palmer in court prior to the reading of his death sentence. *Dallas Dispatch*, 9 April 1935.

3. Simmons, *Assignment Huntsville*, 63, 132; Russell, "Barrow-Parker Harboring Case," 7.

4. Simmons, *Assignment Huntsville*, 132.

5. *Methvin v. Oklahoma*, A=9060 (1936); Simmons, *Assignment Huntsville*, 132; Russell, "Barrow-Parker Harboring Case," 7; *Dallas Morning News*, 14 August 1934; *Dallas Daily Times Herald*, 14 August 1934.

6. There is a difference of opinion as to the total number of people killed by Barrow and his accomplices. Depending on the source, the number may range from ten to thirteen or more. Probably thirteen deaths can be attributed to the Barrow Gang, with Clyde Barrow himself committing five murders, including that of "Big Ed," the Eastham building tender.

7. Marie Barrow, interview by John Neal Phillips, 24 August 1984; Floyd Hamilton interview, 18 July 1981; *Dallas Morning News*, 17 January 1934; *Dallas Dispatch*, 16 January 1934.

8. Raymond Hamilton stated in court prior to the reading of his death sentence, "[W]henever Simmons and the others get after you, you don't get fairness." *Houston Press*, 9 April 1935. In a chapter titled "Resettling Accounts"' Simmons himself uses terms such as "liquidated" to describe his dealings with the Barrow Gang. Simmons, *Assignment Huntsville*, 168.

9. The Barrow family also noticed a marked difference in Clyde's post-prison demeanor. "Something awful sure must have happened to him in prison, because he wasn't the same person when he got out." Marie Barrow interview, 15 September 1993.

Chapter 2

1. Texas Prison System, File no. 70383, Ralph Fults; Blanche Barrow, interview by John Neal Phillips, 18 November 1984.

2. Russell usually travelled out of state by train. For some unknown reason, however, on this trip he used his "one-way wagon."

3. Edmund Stillman, *The American Heritage History of the 20's and 30's*, ed., Ralph K. Andrist, 156. The economy was already exhausted by the time Hoover took office in 1929, especially in the farming industry. He happened to be in office at the time of the disastrous October 1929 crash and therefore took the blame.

4. Indeed, others described Clyde Barrow as looking like a "schoolboy." Kermit "Curley" Crawford, interview by John Neal Phillips, 19 April 1983; Roy L. Worley, interview by John Neal Phillips, 18 August 1983.

5. The case of "Two-Gun" Stillman is an example. Other such incidents have been described. Mrs. J. E. King, quoted in *Dallas Morning News*, 11 February 1925; Floyd Hamilton interview, 18 July 1981; Jack interview, 20 February 1982; "Doc" interview, 24 August 1984.

6. The sentence included five counts of burglary and two counts of auto theft, two years on each count, to run concurrently; it was changed to a full fourteen years after Barrow's escape from the Waco jail. Barrow's mother got the decision overturned by the Texas Supreme Court. Cumie T. Barrow, unfinished manuscript.

7. Blanche Barrow interview, 18 November 1984.

8. Marie Barrow interviews, 24 August 1984, 15 September 1993; Cumie T. Barrow, unfinished manuscript, n.p.

9. William Thompson, of the Texas Prison System, to Doug Walsh, of the Dallas police, 17 May 1932, Dallas, Dallas Public Library, Texas/Dallas History Archives Division "Smoot" Schmid scrapbook. In the letter Thompson apologizes for not having informed the Dallas police of Buck Barrow's escape and subsequent return to prison.

Chapter 3

1. United States, Census, 1920.

2. Ruth Fults Rutledge, interview by John Neal Phillips, 22 July 1983.

3. A book of Audie Fults's quips and one-liners was published and sold in Collin County in the 1920s.

4. Robert C. Trojanowicz and Merry Morash, *Juvenile Delinquency*, 52, 53, 54; Peter C. Kratcoski and Lucille Dunn Kratcoski, *Juvenile Delinquency*, 54; Eugene D. Wheeler and S. Anthony Baron, *Violence in Our Schools, Hospitals, and Public Places*, 154, 155; Jack Katz, *Seductions of Crime*, 9. These sources also cite television violence as a major contributor to aggressive behavior. Although he and his contemporaries were certainly not watching television, Fults lists the quantity and type of motion pictures he watched (westerns mostly) as a major influence on his outlook that crime and violence was something romantic and exciting. Other studies indicate, however, that there are genetic causes for violent, antisocial behavior. See Lawrence Taylor, *Born to Crime*.

5. Jimmy Beldon, interview by John Neal Phillips, 15 February 1981.

6. Richard Lingeman, *Small Town America*, 103; Roderick Nash, *The Nervous Generation*, 2, 3; Robert S. McElvaine, *The Great Depression*, 13, 21; Donald Worster, *The Dust Bowl*, 10.

7. See Eliot Asinof, *Eight Men Out*.

8. Andrist, *American Heritage History*, 64–72; See Russell, *The Shadow of Blooming Grove*.

9. Nash, *The Nervous Generation*, 143, 144; McElvaine, *The Great Depression*, 12. One of the worst race riots of the time occurred in Chicago during the summer of 1919.

10. Nash, *The Nervous Generation*, 126; McElvaine, *The Great Depression*, 23.

11. Lingeman, *Small Town America*, 412, 413; Robinson, *World Cinema*, 103.

12. Bryan Sterling, *The Best Of Will Rogers*; H. T. Webster, *The Best of H. T. Webster*; See also the writings of H. L. Mencken, Ring Lardner, and Sherwood Anderson.

13. Ralph Fults, interviews by John Neal Phillips, 10 December 1980, 1 February 1981.

14. Mrs. Eugene McDowell, interview by John Neal Phillips, 5 May 1981; *Dallas Morning News*, 18 April 1935.

15. McDowell interview, 5 May 1981.

16. Fern Robertson, interview by John Neal Phillips, 5 May 1981.

17. Harry McCormick, unfinished manuscript, 11.

18. Sentenced as Raymond Johnson, *Dallas Morning News*, 18 April 1935.

Chapter 4

1. Upon Fults's arrival at the main prison in Huntsville in 1929, Assistant Warden N. A. Baughn made it a point to show in the prison records just how many of Fults's friends had "graduated" from the Texas State Juvenile Training School, at Gatesville, to the penitentiary. In 1951, based on the testimony of Fults and others, District Judge R. T. Brown termed the reformatory "a training school for outlaws" and recommended that it be closed. Ralph Fults interview, 10 December 1980.

2. McCormick, unfinished manuscript, 30.

3. *Dallas Dispatch*, 22 July 1934; *Dallas Morning News*, 22 July 1934; *Daily Times Herald*, 22 July 1934; *Houston Press*, 22 July 1934.

4. L. L. Edge, *Run the Cat Roads*, 63–70, 74–79, 176–83.

5. Ibid., 20, 118.

6. McCormick, Unfinished manuscript, 54–56.

7. *General and Special Laws for the State of Texas*, Bill 21, Chapter 84, Section 3, 64. The statute states that "they (the trustees) shall make rules as may be deemed proper for same, having in view reformation, education and discipline." Among the rules implemented was corporal punishment in the form of whippings with a leather strap called "the bat." The same practice was also in use at Texas prison units.

8. McCormick, unfinished manuscript, 23.

9. Ibid., 24.

10. Ibid., 24, 25.

11. Ibid., 43, 44.

12. Ibid., 44.

13. Ibid., 45.

14. Ibid., 46, 47.

15. Beldon interview, 15 February 1981. Collin County authorities would later make a deal with two area bootleggers to help ambush Ralph Fults and Raymond Hamilton in exchange for the freedom to continue bootlegging without interference.

16. *Dallas Daily Times Herald*, 16 April 1929.

17. Jack interview, 20 February 1982; David A. Shannon, ed., *The Great Depression*, 16; Worster, *The Dust Bowl*, 10.

18. United States, Census, 1920, 1930. The population went from 158,976 in 1920 to 294,734 in 1930.

19. William L. McDonald, *Dallas Rediscovered*, v, 7.

20. Philip Lindsley, *A History of Greater Dallas and Vicinity*, 72–74.

21. Executions by electrocution in the state of Texas involved the administration of three successive currents of electricity by means of a dial, not by means of a switch, as was popularly believed. The voltages were 1200, 800, 500. Dr. Robert Pierce, interview by John Neal Phillips, 6 November 1993; Lt. Lonny Johnson, interview by John Neal Phillips, 5 November 1993; Lt. Gene Stewart, interview by John Neal Phillips, 5 November 1993.

Chapter 5

1. Simmons, *Assignment Huntsville*, 184; Robert H. Russell, interview by John Neal Phillips, 10 February 1985.

2. Simmons, *Assignment Huntsville*, 183.

3. Ibid., 184.

4. Jack interview, 20 February 1982; Russell interview, 10 February 1985; Harry McCormick, statement to Ralph Fults, 1948 (Ralph Fults interview, 5 November 1980).

5. Jack interview, 20 February 1982; Floyd Hamilton interview, 18 July 1981. Ralph Fults also described this (Ralph Fults interview, 10 November 1980).

6. Simmons, *Assignment Huntsville*, 180–84.

7. Jack interview, 20 February 1982; Floyd Hamilton interview, 18 July 1981; Russell interview, 10 February 1985.

8. McCormick, "The Impossible Interview," 55, 63, 64, 66, 67.

9. Simmons, *Assignment Huntsville*, 66.

10. Pierce interview, 6 November 1993; Johnson interview, 5 November 1993; Lt. Gene Stewart, interview by John Neal Phillips, 5 November 1993; Walker, *Penology For Profit*, 14–17.

11. Simmons, *Assignment Huntsville*, 66.

12. McCormick, "The Impossible Interview," 68.

13. Ibid., 67.

14. Pierce interview, 6 November 1993; Jack interview, 20 February 1982; Ralph Fults interview, 10 December 1980.

15. Texas Prison Board, Minutes, 1 August 1929. The board recommended that he be replaced.

16. *Ruffin v. Commonwealth*, 62Va (1871), 790–96.

17. Simmons, *Assignment Huntsville*, 117.

18. "Doc" interview, 24 August 1984.

19. McCormick, unfinished manuscript, 54–56. Not all of the other

prisoners in solitary confinement (there were five) wanted Fults involved, thinking him too young. The most vocal was Earl Thompson, whose younger brother Blackie had staged a few burglaries with Fults in 1927. When Fults mentioned this, the older Thompson's attitude changed. Blackie Thompson would later play a major role in the 22 July 1934 death house escape in Huntsville, Texas. McCormick, unfinished manuscript, 54–56.

20. Texas Prison System, File no. 70383, Ralph Fults.

21. The Texas Prison System used a hybrid foxhound-Walker-bulldog.

22. McCormick later exposed the horrible conditions at Retrieve. McCormick, unfinished manuscript, 60–62; *Houston Press*, 4 April 1935; *Dallas Daily Times Herald*, 4 April 1935.

23. Jay Robert Nash, *Bloodletters and Badmen*, 177.

24. During this trip, made by rail in a boxcar, Fults witnessed people boiling rats in Kansas City's own version of "Hoover Town."

Chapter 6

1. Bud Russell was widely respected by those on both sides of the law. Joe Palmer, at the time of his execution, asked that Bud and his son, Roy, escort him to the electric chair, saying he wanted "the only two honest lawmen he knew" to do it. Russell interview, 10 February 1985.

2. Simmons, *Assignment Huntsville*, 54, 55.

3. Ibid., 55; Harry McCormick, statement to Ralph Fults (Ralph Fults interview, 14 March 1981).

4. Texas Prison Board, Minutes, 1 August 1929.

5. Simmons, *Assignment Huntsville*, 52.

6. Steve J. Martin and Sheldon Ekland-Olson, *Texas Prisons*, 10; *Dallas Morning News*, 11 February 1925; *Daily Times Herald*, 27 September 1929.

7. Texas Prison System, File no. 70383, Ralph Fults.

8. *Dallas Morning News*, 7 May 1929.

9. *Dallas Daily Times Herald*, 5 November 1929.

10. Simmons, *Assignment Huntsville*, 61.

11. Ibid., 63.

12. *Dallas Morning News*, 11 February 1990. The farm manager reinstated by Simmons was placed in charge of Eastham. Upon his arrival at Eastham with Ralph Fults in 1930, Clyde Barrow was greeted by this manager in a way he would never forget; Martin and Ekland-Olson, *Texas Prisons*, 14.

13. This was not a new concept in Texas. See Walker, *Penology For Profit*, 13, 14.

14. Paul Lucko, quoted in *Dallas Morning News*, 11 February 1990; Texas Prison Board, Minutes, 19 May 1930.

15. Fifty years later guards at Eastham were still practicing the "tune-up." Martin and Ekland-Olson, *Texas Prisons*, 226.

16. Ralph Fults interviews, 5 November 1980, 1 February 1981, 10 May

1981.

17. Ralph Fults interview, 10 May 1981. Several years later the guard who beat Fults was dragged by a prisoner from his horse in the cotton fields of Eastham and stabbed to death. In retaliation the prisoner was held down and murdered by a camp official who rammed the prisoner's own knife—blade, handle, and all—into the prisoner's rectum with the heel of his boot. "Doc" (pseud.) interview, 24 August 1984.

18. Ralph Fults interview, 10 May 1981.

19. Katz, *Seductions of Crime*, 21.

20. Some say Clyde was actually born in 1910. Indeed in his mother's unfinished manuscript 1910 is listed as his date of birth. In subsequent pages, however, 1909 is the date recorded. Cumie T. Barrow, unfinished manuscript; Marie Barrow interview, 24 August 1984, 15 September 1993, 25 September 1993.

21. Rumors that Buck had a twin brother who died at birth have been confused with the fact that Buck himself once fathered twins that died. Only seven children were born to Cumie and Henry Barrow. Marie Barrow interview, 24 August 1984.

22. Cumie T. Barrow, unfinished manuscript.

23. Marie Barrow interview, 15 September 1993.

24. W. D. Jones, "Riding with Bonnie and Clyde," 160. The Barrows also camped in such places. Jones first met Clyde Barrow under the Houston Street Viaduct in Dallas. Clyde's younger sister, Marie, also remembers meeting Jones, commenting on his good looks and adding that he had "a bunch of good-looking brothers, too!" Blanche said she remembered the two best-looking boys were Ralph Fults and W. D. Jones, but she said that Jones was "the best-looking of them all!" Marie Barrow interview, 25 September 1993; Blanche Barrow interview, 3 November 1984.

25. Floyd Hamilton, *Public Enemy No. 1*, 13, 14; Ted Hinton, *Ambush*, 161; Marie Barrow interview, 24 August 1984, 15 September 1993.

26. It was later paved and renamed Singleton.

27. The levee gave way the following year. *Dallas Daily Times Herald*, 21 March 1957.

28. Marie Barrow interview, 25 September 1993; Jones, "Riding," 160.

29. Floyd Hamilton interview, 18 July 1981.

30. Hinton, *Ambush*, 7; Marie Barrow interview, 15 September 1993, 25 September 1993.

31. Marie Barrow interview, 24 August 1984, 15 September 1993.

32. Cumie T. Barrow, unfinished manuscript.

33. Buck's full name was Marvin Ivan Barrow.

34. Cumie T. Barrow, unfinished manuscript; Marie Barrow interview, 15 September 1993.

35. Floyd Hamilton interview, 18 July 1981; Marie Barrow interview, 24 August 1984.

36. Ken M. Holmes, Jr., interview by John Neal Phillips, 18 January 1994.

37. Holmes interview, 18 January 1994. Fifty years later, the note was found during remodeling of the old farmhouse. The case against Barrow was dropped 28 February 1928. United States, Department of Justice, report, 8 June 1934.

38. Mrs. John W. Hays, interview by John Neal Phillips, 20 April 1980.

39. Cumie T. Barrow, unfinished manuscript. In later years Clyde Barrow, who had relatives all over East Texas, frequented Broddus with Bonnie. They were seen in town at dances and in the company of a local bootlegger whom Barrow had befriended in 1926. Most residents seemed to know who they were. No one said a thing to the authorities.

40. Frank is credited by Nell Barrow Cowan as the person most responsible for Clyde's plunge into crime. Cumie Barrow thought it was "fast women," including Bonnie. Marie Barrow is convinced that no individual person or event shaped her brother's criminal life, with the possible exception of prison. Jan I. Fortune, *Fugitives*, 27; Cumie T. Barrow, unfinished manuscript; Marie Barrow interview, 15 September 1993.

41. Cumie T. Barrow, unfinished manuscript.

42. Ibid.

43. Marie Barrow interview, 24 August 1984, 15 September 1993.

44. Cumie T. Barrow, unfinished manuscript. Floyd Hamilton said, "I always thought that bunch in Waco wanted Clyde along because he was so little he could fit in all those tight windows." Hamilton interview, 18 July 1981.

45. Cumie T. Barrow, unfinished manuscript; Hamilton interview, 18 July 1981.

46. Fortune, *Fugitives*, 75.

47. Texas Prison Board, Minutes, 3 March 1930; Simmons, *Assignment Huntsville*, 58; *Dallas Morning News*, 4 March 1930.

48. *Dallas Morning News*, 30 January 1930.

49. Blanche Barrow interview, 3 November 1984; Marie Barrow interview, 15 September 1993.

50. On 27 September 1983, the manager of the Collier Unit was forced to resign when he ordered a prisoner similarly trampled. Martin and Ekland-Olson, *Texas Prisons*, 227.

51. Texas Prison Board, Minutes, 1 August 1929.

52. Three decades later Fults would learn that McCormick had exposed the planned killing, too late to save Stillman's life. Harry McCormick, statement to Ralph Fults, 1961 (Ralph Fults interview, 5 November 1980).

53. Ralph Fults interview, 10 December 1980; Marie Barrow interview, 24 August 1984, 15 September 1993.

54. Fortune, *Fugitives*, 87. Barrow told his family the stabbing was done by "a lifer." They never knew the full story.

55. Cumie T. Barrow, unfinished manuscript; Marie Barrow interview, 24 August 1984; Floyd Hamilton interview, 18 July 1981; Hinton, *Ambush*, 35; Fortune, *Fugitives*, 89.

56. Cumie T. Barrow, unfinished manuscript.

57. Almost every other source says Barrow did this to get out of working in the fields, but Clyde told Fults he did it to get transferred to the prison hospital in Huntsville to see Buck. Ralph Fults interview, 5 November 1980.

58. Beldon interview, 15 February 1981.

Chapter 7

1. Hinton, *Ambush*, 15–17; Hamilton, *Public Enemy No. 1*, 18.

2. Raymond Hamilton's older brother, Floyd, supplied the satchel of tools used by Fults. Floyd Hamilton interview, 18 July 1981.

3. Jones, "Riding with Bonnie and Clyde," 160; Marie Barrow interviews, 24 August 1984, 15 September 1993.

4. In November 1982 Dallas City Councilman Robert Medrano alerted his fellow members of the council to the dangerous levels being emitted into the atmosphere by a West Dallas smelter. Medrano was ignored, some members literally laughing as he spoke. A subsequent federal investigation into the EPA's handling of the matter prompted a cleanup.

5. Cumie T. Barrow, unfinished manuscript; Marie Barrow interview, 15 September 1993.

6. Clyde was employed at United Glass and Mirror, on Swiss Avenue in Dallas.

7. Many years later Fults would be astonished to find that Clyde had first tried working as a mechanic at his father's service station, then ventured all the way to Framington, Massachusetts (sometimes mistakenly listed as Farmington; Hinton says Worcester), under an alias to find work and leave his past behind. Barrow returned after only two weeks, homesick. Fults interview, 5 November 1980; Cumie T. Barrow, unfinished manuscript; Marie Barrow interview, 15 September 1993. One source has Barrow returning to Texas on 17 March 1932 or 18 March 1932. Fortune, *Fugitives*, 93.

8. Blanche Barrow interview, 3 November 1984.

9. Fort Worth Police File no. 4316, Clyde Barrow. He was arrested and charged with something called "general principals [sic]."

10. Several people witnessed this statement. It came as no surprise to Clyde's mother. Fults said she despised the way the Dallas police and Dallas County Sheriff's Department treated ex-cons—especially those holding jobs. She did make her son promise to never take his own life, a promise Marie and others thought he would never keep. Marie Barrow interview, 25 September 1993; Blanche Barrow interview, 18 November 1984; Cumie T. Barrow, unfinished manuscript.

11. Clyde lost the gun. Blanche Barrow interview, 18 November 1984.

12. Hamilton, *Public Enemy No. 1*, 11.

13. Floyd Hamilton interview, 18 July 1981.
14. Hamilton, *Public Enemy No. 1*, 12.
15. Floyd Hamilton interview, 18 July 1981.
16. Ibid.
17. Hamilton, *Public Enemy No. 1*, 18.
18. *McKinney* (*Tex.*) *Daily Courier-Gazette*, 28 January 1932. The criminal docket for the 59th District Court listed 4 February 1932 as the proposed date of Hamilton's trial. The case was never heard.
19. The policeman's involvement was later discovered by Fults during a series of conversations with fellow inmates, both at Huntsville and at Eastham. Jack interview, 20 February 1982.
20. Lawrence Erdang, *The Timetables of History*, 319. Other sources say five-thousand banks closed between the years 1930 and 1932. Shannon, *The Great Depression*, 72.
21. On 19 May 1933 Clyde would return to Okabena and rob the bank that he and Hamilton and Fults had given up on. *Fairmont* (*Minn.*) *Daily Sentinel*, 19 May 1933.
22. Fults's statements concerning this bank robbery were corroborated by three other sources. A Lake Dallas gang member, Jack, mentioned the "big bank haul" that Barrow, Fults, and Hamilton made "up in the plains, somewhere." He also berated Hamilton for backing out of the planned raid on Eastham. Floyd Hamilton recalled that his brother had left Dallas with Barrow and Fults and had returned alone with "several thousand dollars." Blanche recalled that shortly before and immediately after Fults's capture, with Bonnie Parker in Kaufman County, Clyde had discreetly given away a lot of cash to friends and relatives in West Dallas. He gave his parents enough to purchase the property adjacent to the Star Service Station. There remains, however, some question as to the location of the bank involved and the amount stolen. This is the only point in Fults's testimony that cannot be verified by hard evidence. Nevertheless, it is included in the text exactly as Fults has stated, not only because of his detailed description of the incident, but because every aspect of the rest of Fults's testimony, the whole ten years, checks out perfectly. Jack interview, 20 February 1982; Floyd Hamilton interview, 18 July 1981; Blanche Barrow interview, 18 November 1984; Ralph Fults interviews, 5 November 1980; 4 December 1982, 22 February 1985.
23. Hinton, *Ambush*, 105, 111; Jack interview, 20 February 1982.
24. Hamilton had to abandon a brand new car, a rack of new clothes, and the rest of his share of the Lawrence bank robbery loot when he was trapped in a road block near Wichita Falls, Texas.
25. Hinton refers to it as the "American Cafe," but no such cafe is listed in the city directory for the years in question. There is a well-known photograph in circulation showing a cafe called the "All American Cafe," which was in business in the early 1920s on Houston Street, but it is on the east side. The cafe where Bonnie worked, according to five witnesses, was on the

west side of Houston Street, where the Post Office Annex now stands. This photograph usually is cropped so the marquee reads "American Cafe." Hinton, *Ambush*, 7; Marie Barrow interview, 24 August 1984; Blanche Barrow interview, 18 November 1984; Worley interview, 18 August 1983; *Worley's Dallas City Directory*, 1914–1935.

26. Fortune, *Fugitives*, 92, 93.

27. The episode took place at Kemp, Texas, 19 April 1932 and at Prentiss, Mississippi, on 28 March 1935.

28. Malsch, *Lone Wolf.*

29. Ken Adams, interview by John Neal Phillips, 10 May 1981. As a boy, Adams saw Gonzuales demonstrate his ability with a pistol at the Henderson County Fair, shooting from the hip and lighting matches from a distance of twenty-five feet.

30. Now Lake Lewisville.

31. Blanche Barrow interview, 18 November 1984.

32. *Wichita (Wichita Falls, Tex.) Daily Times*, 14 April 1932.

33. Ibid.; *Electra (Tex.) Gazette*, 21 April 1932; *Denton (Tex.) Record Chronicle*, 15 April 1932.

34. *Wichita (Wichita Falls, Tex.) Daily Times*, 9 April 1932. Floyd had killed a former Oklahoma Deputy Sheriff on 7 April 1932. He was believed to be headed for Texas when Barrow and Fults arrived in Electra on the fourteenth.

35. *Wichita (Wichita Falls, Tex.) Daily Times*, 14 April 1932.

36. Ibid.

37. Captain Tom Hickman, statement to Ralph Fults, 1948 (Ralph Fults interview, 4 December 1982).

38. *Wichita (Wichita Falls, Tex.) Daily Times*, 14 April 1932.

39. Ibid.

40. *Electra (Tex.) Gazette*, 27 April 1932; *Wichita (Wichita Falls, Tex.) Daily Times*, 11 May 1932.

41. *Electra (Tex.) Gazette*, 21 April 1932.

42. Ibid.

43. Ibid.

44. *Denton (Tex.) Record Chronicle*, 15 April 1932.

45. *Electra (Tex.) Gazette*, 21 April 1932.

46. Among other exercises, Barrow practiced driving full speed in reverse until he perfected his ability to spin around, shift to second, and continue forward in one flowing motion.

47. Oris K. Helms, interview by John Neal Phillips, 17 January 1983; Mrs. John W. Hays interview, 20 April 1980. Both knew Barrow before he had a criminal record. They concur with Bonnie's feelings.

48. Fortune, *Fugitives*, 42; U.S., Department of Justice, Memo to Doug Walsh, of the Dallas Police Department about the activities of Clyde and Buck Barrow in Nacogdoches County, Texas, 4 May 1933; Leo Muckleroy,

quoted in Sitton, *The Loblolly Book*, 58. Muckleroy was Clyde's cousin. Bonnie and Clyde frequently hid in Martinsville, Texas, at Muckleroy's farm house. Bonnie once nicked two of her toes when a pistol she was handling accidentally discharged. When that happened, Bonnie and Clyde left and never returned.

49. Jones, "Riding with Bonnie and Clyde," 162. Nonetheless, Her involvement in the Joplin shooting cannot be disputed.

50. Hargraves Cafe, at 3308 Swiss Avenue; Marco's Cafe, at 702 main Street; "courthouse cafe" (American Cafe?), on Houston Street.

51. Rose Myers, interview by John Neal Phillips, 19 January 1983; Hinton, *Ambush*, 8; Fortune, *Fugitives*, 47.

52. Fults always maintained that Bonnie's parents were divorced, saying that Bonnie herself said this. Emma Parker said under oath that her husband (Bonnie's father) was dead and that she was not divorced. Russell, "Barrow-Parker Harboring Case," 25.

53. Santerre, *The White Cliffs of Dallas*.

54. Charlie Conn, interview by John Neal Phillips, 11 January 1983.

55. "Death seemed to cling to Roy like smoke to a flannel suit." Floyd Hamilton, *Public Enemy No. 1*, 16.

56. Fortune, *Fugitives*, 49, 55, 56.

57. Johnny Hayes, interview by John Neal Phillips, 28 April 1983; *Dallas Daily Times Herald* reporter Bill Duncan told Hayes, then a darkroom assistant, that he viewed the undraped body of Bonnie Parker in Louisiana. Neither he nor anyone else present could verify the rumors of her pregnancy. Moreover, the coroner, Dr. Wade, made no indication in his autopsy notes of a pregnancy. Bienville Parish, Louisiana, Coroner's Inquest, 23 May 1934.

58. Myers interview, 19 January 1983.

59. Ibid.

60. Ibid.

61. Fortune, *Fugitives*, 47.

62. Gus Marco later took a job as a waiter at the Jefferson Cafe.

63. It is interesting that Barrow and Parker never met before January 1930. Both knew many of the same people, including Roy Thornton and the Mace brothers.

64. Fortune, *Fugitives*, 61–72; Marie Barrow interviews, 24 August 1984. 15 September 1993.

65. Fortune, *Fugitives*, 76; Cumie T. Barrow, unfinished manuscript; Marie Barrow interview, 24 August 1984.

66. Fortune, *Fugitives*, 77.

67. Ibid., 92, 93; Marie Barrow interview, 15 September 1993; Cumie T. Barrow, unfinished manuscript.

68. This reinforced Fults's assertion that Barrow had taken that job to impress Bonnie's mother. Fortune, *Fugitives*, 93.

69. Walter M. Legg, Jr., interview by John Neal Phillips, 13 March 1981.

70. Ibid.

71. Ralph Fults interview, 10 November 1980. According to Walter M. Legg, Jr., they were "show mules," trained to buck (interview by John Neal Phillips, 13 March 1981).

72. Legg interview, 13 March 1981.

73. Ibid.

74. Ibid.; Walter M. Legg, Jr., interview by John Neal Phillips, 15 September 1993.

75. Legg interviews, 13 March 1981, 15 September 1993. Legg stated during one of the interviews that, from their vantage point Barrow and Fults could have easily shot several members of the posse but fired over their heads, apparently to try and scare them away.

76. Ibid.; *Dallas Evening Journal*, 18 March 1935.

77. Walter M. Legg, Jr., letter to the author, 1 September 1982. Legg states that few realized until later that another man was in the ravine with Fults and Parker. The two men reloading their weapons were so involved in the task at hand that they failed to notice Barrow running between them.

Chapter 8

1. Blanche Barrow interview, 18 November 1984; Ted Rogers, statement to Ralph Fults and Jack (Jack interview, 20 November 1982; Ralph Fults interview, 12 November 1980).

2. Legg, to author, 1 September 1982.

3. Legg, interview, 13 March 1981.

4. Legg, to author, 1 September 1982.

5. *McKinney (Tex.) Daily Courier-Gazette*, 21 April 1932.

6. Ibid.

7. Ibid., 23 April 1932.

8. Ibid., 21 April 1932.

9. Ibid.

10. *Denton (Tex.) Record Chronicle*, 21 April 1932.

11. *McKinney (Tex.) Daily Courier-Gazette*, 21 April 1932; Blanche Barrow interview, 3 November 1984.

12. Ibid.

13. *Denton (Tex.) Record Chronicle*, 22 April 1932.

14. Jack interview, 20 February 1981.

15. *Denton (Tex.) Record Chronicle*, 22 April 1932.

16. Ted Rogers, statement to Ralph Fults and Jack (Jack interview, 20 February 1981; Ralph Fults interview, 12 November 1980).

17. There is a discrepancy as to the number of vehicles approaching the officers. The newspaper reported two vehicles driving up to the camp site. Jack said only he and "Fuzz" approached. The second car had been abandoned at the camp by Clyde, Ted and Johnny. Ted Rogers, statement to Ralph

Fults and Jack (Jack interview, 20 February 1982; Ralph Fults interview, 12 November 1980).

18. *Denton (Tex.) Record Chronicle*, 22 April 1932; Jack interview, 20 February 1982.

19. *Denton (Tex.) Record Chronicle*, 23 April 1932.

20. Ibid.; *McKinney (Tex.) Daily Courier-Gazette*, 25 April 1932.

21. McKinney is the Collin County seat serving Celina.

22. Although Police Chief Taylor identified the weapon as his own, Fults said that he had paid a McKinney man to dispose of it. The man later told Fults that he had thrown it down a water well.

23. *McKinney Daily Courier-Gazette*, 25 April 1932.

24. Wichita Falls is the Wichita County seat serving Electra.

25. Blanche Barrow interview, 3 November 1984.

26. *Wichita (Wichita Falls, Tex.) Daily Times*, 12 May 1932.

27. Ibid.

28. Ibid.

29. During the trial no mention was made of Owens's request that Barrow and Fults burn his car.

30. *Electra (Tex.) Gazette*, 5 May 1932. Following the shooting in Hillsboro, Barrow's picture was circulated throughout the state. Chief Taylor identified him as Fults's accomplice.

31. Fults knew that Barrow had given away most of the cash from their Lawrence bank robbery. This is borne out by a newspaper report that likened Barrow to a modern "Robin Hood," because of the money he frequently gave to friends and relatives in West Dallas. *Dallas Dispatch*, 15 January 1933; Marie Barrow interview, 24 August 1984; Blanche Barrow interview, 18 November 1984.

32. Cumie T. Barrow, Unfinished manuscript.

33. Ibid.

34. *Dallas Morning News*, 1 May 1932.

35. Ibid.

36. Hill County, Texas, wanted poster, J. W. Freeland, Sheriff, 1 May 1932.

37. Hamilton, *Public Enemy No. 1*, 19. According to Hamilton, the robbery was prearranged by Bucher's son. However, Ted Rogers told Ralph Fults, Buck Barrow, and Jack that no such arrangement existed and that he pulled the trigger. Jack interview, 20 February 1982; Blanche Barrow interview, 18 November 1984.

38. *Dallas Morning News*, 1 May 1932.

39. Ibid.; Hill County, Texas, wanted poster, J. W. Freeland, Sheriff, 1 May 1932.

40. Ted Rogers, statement to Jack (Jack interview, 20 February 1982).

41. Texas Prison System File no. 70383, Ralph Fults.

42. Fortune, *Fugitives*, 97–102. During her stay in the Kaufman County

Jail, Bonnie Parker wrote the poem "Suicide Sal."

43. Marie Barrow said that of all her siblings, Buck had the hottest temper and was quickest to get into fights, despite his size. She rarely, if ever, saw the gregarious Buck that Ralph Fults describes. On the other hand, Marie apparently only saw her brother Clyde when he was at his very best, never as the sullen killer Fults describes. Marie Barrow interview, 19 April 1995.

44. Hinton, *Ambush*, 35; Floyd Hamilton interview, 18 July 1981; Marie Barrow interview, 24 August 1984. However, Blanche said Buck harbored no such guilt feelings. Blanche Barrow interview, 3 November 1984.

45. Floyd Hamilton interview, 18 July 1981.

46. Ibid.

47. Hamilton, *Public Enemy No. 1*, 18.

48. Ibid.

49. Noted by Ralph Fults and Floyd Hamilton on 18 July 1981. Blanche, who knew Rogers well, also noted the resemblance. Blanche Barrow interview, 18 November 1984.

50. *Dallas Dispatch*, 30 July 1932.

51. Floyd Hamilton interview, 18 July 1981. It is interesting that Barrow would have anything to do with Raymond Hamilton after Hamilton's refusal to join him and Ralph Fults on the raid against Eastham. For some reason Barrow let Hamilton take more liberties with his friendship than he did others. Eventually, though, Hamilton would cross Barrow one time too many.

52. Henry Nuehoff, Jr., interview by John Neal Phillips, 10 January 1983. The Nuehoff brothers had moved to Dallas from Nashville that year.

53. Elsie Wullschleger Karlen, interview by John Neal Phillips, 10 January 1983.

54. *Dallas Daily Times Herald*, 26 January 1933.

55. Ibid.

56. Nuehoff interview, 19 January 1983.

57. Ibid.

58. Ibid.

59. Ibid.

60. Fortune, *Fugitives*, 112.

61. Ibid., 110.

62. Ibid., 112.

63. Ibid., 113; *Daily Oklahoman*, 7 August 1932.

64. Floyd Hamilton interview, 18 July 1981.

65. Hamilton, *Public Enemy No. 1*, 20; Hinton, *Ambush*, 76, 115. Fults said that Barrow disliked any mood altering substance, adding that he rarely even drank coffee. However, it is known that when Barrow felt safe and comfortable enough he would occasionally take a drink. As a general rule, though, Barrow liked to stay very alert.

66. *Daily Oklahoman*, 6 August 1932.

67. Ibid., 8 August 1932.

68. Ibid., 7 August 1932.

69. Ross took a bus to McKinney, Texas. The fourth man, later found wounded in Denison, Texas, escaped by unknown means.

70. *Roswell (N. Mex.) Daily Record*, 4 August 1932.

71. Fortune, *Fugitives*, 124.

72. Ibid.; Hinton, *Ambush*, 22; Hamilton, *Public Enemy No. 1*, 21; *Roswell (N. Mex.) Daily Record*, 15 August 1932.

73. Fortune, *Fugitives*, 124; Hinton, *Ambush*, 22.

74. *Roswell (N. Mex) Daily Record*, 15 August 1932.

75. Ibid.

76. *Dallas Morning News*, 15 August 1932.

77. They made 1,000 miles in 13 hours at an average speed of 77 miles per hour. *Roswell (N. Mex.) Daily Record*, 15 August 1932.

78. *San Antonio Express*, 16 August 1932.

79. *Dallas Morning News*, 16 August 1932.

80. Ibid.

81. *Amarillo (Tex.) Sunday News Globe*, 12 June 1933. Sergeant Bert Whisnand, of the Texas Rangers, and Dallas County Chief of Detectives Bill Decker both shared this view, the latter saying that "it is a common occurrence for criminals to lead their victims to believe they are some well-known outlaw, in order to aid them in avoiding apprehension."

82. Fortune, *Fugitives*, 107, 128; Marie Barrow interview, 24 August 1984.

83. *Dallas Morning News*, 12 October 1932.

84. Ibid.

85. Some sources mention the presence of a woman. Another source said Hall attacked the robber with a knife. There is no evidence to indicate either. Moreover, the shooting took place in front of the store, not the rear, and no woman is mentioned.

86. *McKinney (Tex.) Courier-Gazette*, 25 April 1932.

87. Barrow was parked in the alley.

88. Simmons, *Assignment Huntsville*, 182, 183.

89. Jones, "Riding with Bonnie and Clyde," 151; W. D. Jones, Voluntary Statement B–71.

90. Jones, "Riding with Bonnie and Clyde," 151; W. D. Jones, Voluntary Statement B–71.

91. Jones, "Riding with Bonnie and Clyde," 160; W. D. Jones, Voluntary Statement B–71. Fults remembers Jones hanging around the Star Service Station in 1932. He would sometimes steal license plates for Barrow.

92. Jones, "Riding with Bonnie and Clyde," 160; W. D. Jones, Voluntary Statement B–71.

93. Jones, "Riding with Bonnie and Clyde," 160; W. D. Jones, Voluntary Statement B–71.

94. Jones, "Riding with Bonnie and Clyde," 160; W. D. Jones, Voluntary Statement B–71.

95. *Dallas Daily Times Herald*, 26 November 1933.

96. Ibid.

97. Jones, "Riding with Bonnie and Clyde," 160.

98. *Dallas Evening Journal*, 26 December 1932.

99. Jones, "Riding with Bonnie and Clyde," 160.

100. Ibid.

101. *Dallas Morning News*, 26 December 1932.

102. *Dallas Evening Journal*, 26 December 1932; Fortune, *Fugitives*, 134.

103. Jones, "Riding with Bonnie and Clyde," 160; Jones, Voluntary Statement B–71.

104. *Dallas Evening Journal*, 26 December 1932.

Chapter 9

1. Richard B. Morris, *Encyclopedia of American History*, 402.

2. *Dallas Dispatch*, 30 December 1932.

3. Ibid., 7 January 1933; *Dallas Evening Journal*, 7 January 1933; *Dallas Daily Times Herald*, 9 January 1933.

4. *Dallas Morning News*, 8 January 1933; *Dallas Daily Times Herald*, 19 January 1933.

5. The street was later renamed Winnetka.

6. Because Dallas County Deputy Sheriff Ed Castor had paid a visit to McBride earlier in the day, she and her sister were wary.

7. Hinton, *Ambush*, 31; *Dallas Morning News*, 7 January 1933; *Dallas Daily Times Herald*, 7 January 1933; *Dallas Evening Journal*, 7 January 1933; *Dallas Dispatch*, 7 January 1933.

8. Hinton, *Ambush*, 31; *Dallas Morning News*, 7 January 1933; *Dallas Daily Times Herald*, 7 January 1933; *Dallas Evening Journal*, 7 January 1933; *Dallas Dispatch*, 7 January 1933.

9. It is unlikely that Barrow was driving a Chevrolet, despite Bradberry's description. By then Barrow used Fords exclusively unless nothing else was available. Other witnesses said it was a Ford and that Barrow had bolted a police siren to the dash. Marie Barrow interview, 15 September 1993.

10. Hinton, *Ambush*, 32; *Dallas Dispatch*, 7 January 1933.

11. Cumie T. Barrow, unfinished manuscript.

12. *Dallas Dispatch*, 8 January 1933; *Dallas Evening Journal*, 7 January 1933.

13. *Dallas Dispatch*, 8 January 1933.

14. *Dallas Evening Journal*, 7 January 1933.

15. *Dallas Dispatch*, 7 January 1933.

16. Hamilton, *Public Enemy No. 1*, 22; Fortune, *Fugitives*, 127.

17. *Dallas Daily Times Herald*, 26 January 1933.

18. The bank teller actually managed to conceal a great deal of cash from Hamilton's view. *Dallas Daily Times Herald*, 26 January 1933.

19. He was also known as Gene O'Day.

20. *Dallas Daily Times Herald*, 25 November 1932. It was a common trick to use a brightly colored car in town and switch to the more common black Ford outside of town.

21. *Dallas Evening Journal*, 7 January 1933.

22. Hamilton, *Public Enemy No. 1*, 21; *Dallas Dispatch*, 25 November 1932. Hamilton supposedly told the teller that he had returned for the money hidden from him during the first robbery.

23. Hamilton, *Public Enemy No. 1*, 22.

24. *Dallas Daily Times Herald*, 15 December 1932.

25. Ibid.

26. Hill County, Texas, wanted poster, J. W. Freeland, Sheriff, 1 May 1932. Initially, another man was charged. Upon Hamilton's capture the focus shifted to him. Mrs. Bucher first said Hamilton was not the right man, but the Hill County authorities were persistent, and she eventually changed her mind. Floyd Hamilton interview, 18 July 1981.

27. *Dallas Daily Times Herald*, 9 January 1933.

28. Jones, Voluntary Statement B–71.

29. Marie Barrow interview, 24 August 1984, 15 September 1993; Cumie T. Barrow, unfinished manuscript.

30. Fortune, *Fugitives*, 138; Hinton, *Ambush*, 31, 32; Jones, Voluntary Statement B–71.

31. Ibid.

32. Cumie T. Barrow, unfinished manuscript. Nell Barrow Cowan reported that Bonnie said Jones was "likely to kill people in the houses up and down the street." Fortune, *Fugitives*, 139, 140.

33. Fortune, *Fugitives*, 140; Jones, Voluntary Statement B–71.

34. Marie Barrow interview, 25 September 1993.

35. Cumie T. Barrow, unfinished manuscript.

36. Jones has stated that Barrow could be quite charming and polite, traits he used to his advantage when necessary. Jones, "Riding with Bonnie and Clyde," 164; Fortune, *Fugitives*, 59; *Joplin Globe*, 13 April 1975; Wilma Blohm interview, 5 May 1983.

37. Jones, "Riding with Bonnie and Clyde," 164; Fortune, *Fugitives*, 144, 145.

38. Ibid.

39. Cumie T. Barrow, unfinished manuscript.

40. *Dallas Dispatch*, 7 January 1933.

41. Hinton, *Ambush*, 100.

42. *Dallas Dispatch*, 16 January 1933.

43. *Dallas Morning News*, 11 January 1933.

44. *Dallas Daily Times Herald*, 26 January 1933.

45. Neuhoff interview, 19 January 1983.

46. *Dallas Evening Journal*, 30 March 1933.

47. Ibid.

48. *Dallas Daily Times Herald*, 18 March 1933.

49. Fortune, *Fugitives*, 145; Floyd Hamilton, *Public Enemy No. 1*, 23; Hinton, *Ambush*, 36.

50. Blanche Barrow interview, 3 November 1984.

51. Floyd Hamilton interview, 18 July 1981. Despite Hamilton's statement, Fults remembers no such expressions of guilt on the part of Buck Barrow. In Fults's ten-month association with Buck, any references made to Clyde were usually in praise of his criminal deeds. Marie said that one of the stipulations of Buck Barrow's pardon was that he try to get Clyde to turn himself in. Marie Barrow interview, 25 September 1993.

52. Raymond Hamilton often asked to go with Buck and Blanche when they staged robberies, but neither of them trusted him. Blanche Barrow interview, 3 November 1984.

53. Marie Barrow interview, 15 September 1993, 25 September 1993; Cumie T. Barrow, unfinished manuscript.

54. *Dallas Evening Journal*, 16 April 1933.

55. Blanche Barrow interview, 3 November 1984.

56. *Joplin Globe*, 13 April 1975.

57. Ibid.

58. Blanche Barrow interview, 3 November 1984.

59. *Joplin Globe*, 15 April 1933.

60. Several cases of liquor had been taken, so the authorities used that reason for obtaining the warrant.

61. Blanche Barrow interview, 3 November 1984; Marie Barrow interview, 24 August 1984.

62. W. D. Jones, Voluntary Statement B–71.

63. Marie Barrow interview, 15 September 1993, 25 September 1993; Cumie T. Barrow, unfinished manuscript.

64. Jones, Voluntary Statement B–71.

65. Cumie T. Barrow, unfinished manuscript.

66. Reported to be Clyde, but Jones said it was Buck. Jones, Voluntary Statement B–71.

67. *Joplin Globe*, 15 April 1933.

68. Cumie T. Barrow, unfinished manuscript.

69. Hinton, *Ambush*, 38; *Joplin Globe*, 13 Apr. 1933; Hounsell, *Lawmen and Outlaws*, 48.

70. Blanche Barrow interview, 3 November 1984; Cumie T. Barrow, unfinished manuscript.

71. Ibid.

72. DeGraff, statement to Trey Ford (Ford, interview by John Neal Phillips, 6 June 1984); Newton County Missouri, Coroners Inquest, 14 April 1933.

73. Cumie T. Barrow, unfinished manuscript; Blanche Barrow interview, 3 November 1984.

74. Ibid; Jones, "Riding with Bonnie and Clyde," 162; Newton County, Missouri, Coroner's Inquest, 14 April 1933; Neosho County, Missouri, Coroner's Inquest, 13 April 1933.

75. Blanche Barrow interview, 18 November 1984.

76. *Joplin Globe*, 15 April 1933.

77. Ibid.

78. Blanche Barrow interview, 3 November 1984.

79. Ibid.

80. Ibid.; Marie Barrow interview, 24 August 1984; Cumie T. Barrow, unfinished manuscript. The story of a hysterically screaming Blanche first appeared in *Fugitives* at a time when Blanche still could have been charged with the killings in Joplin. It may have been included in an attempt to make her look like an unwilling accomplice, although it is certain she fired no shots.

81. *Joplin Globe*, 15 April 1933; Fortune, *Fugitives*, 152; Cumie T. Barrow, unfinished manuscript.

82. Cumie T. Barrow, unfinished manuscript.

83. *Joplin Globe*, 15 April 1933.

84. Jones, "Riding with Bonnie and Clyde," 165; *Dallas Dispatch*, 26 November 1933.

85. Blanche Barrow interview, 3 November 1984.

86. Ibid; Jones, "Riding with Bonnie and Clyde," 165.

87. Blanche Barrow interview, 3 November 1984; Jones, "Riding with Bonnie and Clyde," 165.

88. Cumie T. Barrow, unfinished manuscript.

89. *Joplin Globe*, 15 April 1933; Hinton, *Ambush*, 39; Fortune, *Fugitives*, 153.

90. Blanche Barrow interview, 3 November 1984.

91. Marie Barrow interview, 24 August 1984; Cumie T. Barrow, unfinished manuscript.

92. Jones, "Riding with Bonnie and Clyde," 164.

93. Quoted in a number of newspapers and magazines.

94. Robert F. Roseborough, interview by John Neal Phillips, 11 July 1984.

95. *Ruston (La.) Daily Leader*, 27 April 1933.

96. Ibid.; Frank X. Tolbert, "Tolbert's Texas," *Dallas Morning News*, 18 March 1968.

97. "Tolbert's Texas," *Dallas Morning News*, 18 March 1968.

98. Ibid.

99. *Ruston (La.) Daily Leader*, 28 April 1933; "Tolbert's Texas," Dallas Morning News, 18 March 1968. Blanche said they desperately needed another car because the one they were traveling in was literally falling apart,

which is not surprising, considering the way Clyde drove. The suspension, among other things, was faulty. After the outlaws picked up Stone and Darby, Clyde hit at least one parked car. "We damn near got killed in that car," Blanche said. Blanche Barrow interview, 3 November 1984.

100. Blanche Barrow interview, 3 November 1984.

101. Ibid.

102. *Ruston (La.) Daily Leader*, 28 April 1933; "Tolbert's Texas," *Dallas Morning News*, 18 March 1968.

103. *Ruston (La.) Daily Leader*, 28 April 1933.

104. Blanche Barrow interview, 3 November 1984; Cumie T. Barrow, unfinished manuscript.

105. *Ruston (La.) Daily Leader*, 28 April 1933. *Fugitives* has quite a different twist to this story. Fortune, *Fugitives*, 161, 162.

Chapter 10

1. *Dallas Daily Times Herald*, 2 February 1933.
2. *Dallas Dispatch*, 5 May 1933.
3. *Dallas Morning News*, 3 June 1933.
4. Ted Rogers, statement to Jack, Fuzz and Ralph Fults (Jack interview, 20 February 1982).
5. Jones, Voluntary Statement B–71.
6. Ibid.
7. Jones, "Riding with Bonnie and Clyde," 164.
8. Fortune, *Fugitives*, 168.
9. Jones, "Riding with Bonnie and Clyde," 164, 165.
10. *Amarillo (Tex.) Sunday News-Globe*, 12 June 1933.
11. Ibid.
12. Ibid.
13. Ibid.; *Dallas Morning News*, 12 June 1933.
14. *Amarillo (Tex.) Sunday News-Globe*, 12 June 1933.
15. *Dallas Morning News*, 12 June 1933.
16. *Amarillo (Tex.) Sunday News-Globe*, 12 June 1933.
17. Fortune, *Fugitives*, 172; Jones, "Riding with Bonnie and Clyde," 165.
18. Mrs. Pritchard statement to Ken M. Holmes, Jr. (Ken M. Holmes, Jr., interview by John Neal Phillips, 25 September 1993).
19. Ibid.; Fortune, *Fugitives*, 172; Russell, "Barrow-Parker Harboring Case," 15, 41.
20. Jones, "Riding with Bonnie and Clyde," 165. The fact that Buck was possessed of such a vicious nature is borne out by Marie, who remembered him as "the meanest, most hot-tempered," of all her siblings. Marie Barrow interview, 19 April 1995.
21. *Ft. Smith Southwest American*, 24 June 1933.
22. *Dallas Dispatch*, 24 February 1935.
23. Jones, "Riding with Bonnie and Clyde," 165.

24. Marie Barrow interview, 24 August 1984; Cumie T. Barrow, unfinished manuscript. In another book about the Barrow brothers, it was stated that witnesses often saw Clyde carrying Bonnie because she was drunk. In reality, her burns required that she be carried.

25. Russell, "Barrow-Parker Harboring Case," 25. Clyde didn't trust Billie. Marie Barrow interview, 15 September 1993.

26. *Dallas Dispatch*, 24 February 1935.

27. *Ft. Smith Southwest American*, 24 June 1933.

28. Jones, Voluntary Statement B–71; *Ft. Smith Southwest American*, 26 June 1933. Initially thought to have been struck by machine gun fire, Humphrey was actually wounded by shotgun pellets, according to his attending physicians. Buck later admitted killing Humphrey, but he may have said so to discount Jones's involvement. *Dallas Dispatch*, 24 February 1935.

29. *Dallas Dispatch*, 24 February 1935.

30. Jones, "Riding with Bonnie and Clyde," 165; in a statement presented at the Federal harboring trial, Jones said both he and Buck killed Humphrey. Russell, "Barrow-Parker Harboring Case," 15, 27.

31. Jones, "Riding with Bonnie and Clyde," 165; Russell, "Barrow-Parker Harboring Case."

32. Jones, "Riding with Bonnie and Clyde," 165; Russell, "Barrow-Parker Harboring Case"; *Ft. Smith Southwest American*, 24 June 1933.

33. There is a report that Buck Barrow and W. D. Jones assaulted a woman near Mt. Vista for not giving them the keys to her car. She claimed to have been beaten with a chain and almost raped. *Ft. Smith Southwest American*, 26 June 1933. Neither man ever exhibited such tendencies before or after this incident. Moreover, Barrow and Jones were expert car thieves. They did not need the keys to start a car. Fortune says the woman willingly offered the keys, but Buck, still dazed from the wreck, backed the car over a stump. Hinton ignores the incident entirely. Fortune, *Fugitves*, 179; Hinton, *Ambush*, 57; Crawford County, Arkansas, wanted poster, Sheriff Albert Maxey, 30 June 1933.

34. Jones, Voluntary Statement B–71.

35. Cumie T. Barrow, unfinished manuscript; Marie Barrow interview, 15 September 1993, 25 September 1993.

36. Jones, Voluntary Statement B–71.

37. Jones, "Riding with Bonnie and Clyde," 162.

38. Blanche Barrow interview, 3 November 1984.

39. William R. Searles, interview by John Neal Phillips, 20 April 1983; Russell, "Barrow-Parker Harboring Case," 15.

40. Jones, Voluntary Statement B–71.

41. Searles interview, 20 April 1983.

42. Crawford interview, 19 April 1983.

43. Ibid.

44. Ibid.

45. Blanche Barrow interview, 3 November 1984.

46. *The (Platte City, Mo.) Landmark*, 20 July 1933, 21 May 1982, 11 June 1982.

47. Crawford interview, 19 April 1983. Crawford was a personal friend of Captain Baxter.

48. Ibid.; Searles interview, 20 April 1983.

49. Crawford interview, 19 April 1983.

50. Searles interview, 20 April 1983.

51. Ibid.; *The (Platte City, Mo.) Landmark*, 28 May 1982.

52. Crawford interview, 19 April 1983.

53. Ibid.; Searles interview, 20 April 1983; Hinton, *Ambush*, 63.

54. Blanche Barrow interview, 3 November 1984.

55. Ibid.

56. Jones, Voluntary Statement B–71.

57. Crawford interview, 19 April 1983.

58. Ibid.; Jones, Voluntary Statement B–71.

59. Crawford interview, 19 April 1983.

60. Ibid.

61. Searles interview, 20 April 1983.

62. Crawford interview, 19 April 1983; *The (Platte City, Mo.) Landmark*, 28 May 1982.

63. Crawford interview, 19 April 1983.

64. Jones, Voluntary Statement B–71.

65. Crawford interview, 19 April 1983.

66. Ibid.; Blanche Barrow interview, 3 November 1984; Cumie T. Barrow, unfinished manuscript.

67. Blanche Barrow interview, 3 November 1984.

68. Ibid.

69. Crawford interview, 19 April 1983. Blanche said she did not think the shooting stopped until Clyde had driven her and the others well away from the motor courts. Blanche Barrow interview, 3 November 1984.

70. Ibid.; *The (Platte City, Mo.) Landmark*, 28 May 1982.

71. Ibid.

72. Jones, Voluntary Statement B–71; Debra Sanborn, "The Barrow Gang's Visit to Dexter," n.p.; Russell, "Barrow-Parker Harboring Case," 15; *Dexter (Ia.) Sentinel*, 5 October 1967.

73. Jones, Voluntary Statement B–71; John Love, interview by Diane Hutzell and Cheri Rupp, Dexter, Iowa n.d.

74. Jones, Voluntary Statement B–71; Love interview, n.d.; Wilma Blohm, interview by John Neal Phillips, 5 May 1983.

75. Belonging to Edward Stoner.

76. Sanborn, "The Barrow Gang's Visit to Dexter," n.p.; Love interview n.d.

77. Jones, Voluntary Statement B–71; Love interview, n.d.; Wilma

Blohm, interview by John Neal Phillips, 5 May 1983.

78. Blohm interview, 5 May 1983.
79. Ibid.
80. Ibid.
81. Sanborn, "The Barrow Gang's Visit to Dexter," n.p.
82. Jones, Voluntary Statement B–71.
83. Sanborn, "The Barrow Gang's Visit to Dexter," n.p.; Love interview, n.d.
84. Ibid.
85. Blohm interview, 5 May 1983.
86. Ibid.
87. Ibid.
88. Love, interview, n.d.
89. Sanborn, "The Barrow Gang's Visit to Dexter," n.p.
90. Ibid.
91. Jones, Voluntary Statement B–71.
92. Blanche Barrow interview, 3 November 1984.
93. Jones, Voluntary Statement B–71.
94. Just as he and Fults had done in Kemp, Texas, on April 19, 1932.
95. Marvelle Feller, interview by John Neal Phillips, 5 May 1983.
96. Love interview, n.d.
97. Jones, Voluntary Statement B–71.
98. Ibid.; Blanche Barrow interview, 3 November 1984; *Dexter* (*Ia.*) *Sentinel*, 5 October 1967.
99. Jones, Voluntary Statement B–71.
100. *Dexter* (*Ia.*) *Sentinel*, 5 October 1967.
101. Feller interview, 5 May 1983.
102. Blanche Barrow interview, 3 November 1984; Fortune, *Fugitives*, 193.
103. Feller interview, 5 May 1983.
104. Robert Creager, quoted in *Dexter* (*Ia.*) *Sentinel*, 5 October 1967.
105. Fortune, *Fugitives*, 196.
106. Feller interview, 5 May 1983.
107. Ibid.
108. Ibid.
109. Ibid.
110. Ibid.
111. Ibid.
112. Ibid.
113. Ibid.
114. *Dexter* (*Ia.*) *Sentinel*, 5 October 1967.
115. Blanche Barrow interview, 3 November 1984.
116. Ibid.
117. *Dexter* (*Ia.*) *Sentinel*, 5 October 1967.

118. Ibid.
119. Sanborn, "The Barrows' Visit to Dexfield," n.p.
120. Ibid.
121. Fortune, *Fugitives*, 203.
122. *Dallas Dispatch*, 24 February 1935.
123. Jones, Voluntary Statement B–71.
124. Russell, "Barrow-Parker Harboring Case," 28.
125. Jones, Voluntary Statement B–71.
126. Ibid.

Chapter 11

1. *Dallas Daily Times Herald*, 24 July 1933; Hamilton, *Public Enemy No. 1*, 28.

2. *Dallas Evening Journal*, 9 August 1933; *Dallas Daily Times Herald*, 9 August 1933; *Dallas Morning News*, 9 August 1933; *Dallas Dispatch*, 9 August 1933.

3. McCormick, "The Impossible Interview," 68. Actually the total was 266, including the revocation of Hamilton's three-year suspended sentence from 1931.

4. Ibid.

5. Ibid. "Lam" means escape.

6. Floyd Hamilton interview, 18 July 1981.

7. Marie Barrow interview, 24 August 1984, 15 September 1993.

8. Ibid. Marie and her mother once rode with Clyde at top speed across an open field, and "he scared us both half to death." Sophie Stone also noted that when she was abducted by Barrow in 1933, the many weapons in the car did not scare her nearly as much as Clyde Barrow's driving. See "Tolbert's Texas," 18 March 1968. Joe Palmer told Lee Simmons of Barrow's reliance on his ability with a car, rather than weapons. See Simmons, *Assignment Huntsville*, 165.

9. Marie Barrow interview, 15 September 1993; Russell, "Barrow-Parker Harboring Case," 28.

10. Ibid.

11. Marie Barrow interview, 24 August 1984.

12. Russell, "Barrow-Parker Harboring Case," 24. Marie said her mother marked a calender every time Clyde came to Dallas. Marie Barrow interview, 15 September 1993.

13. Marie Barrow interview, 15 September 1993.

14. Ibid.; Cumie T. Barrow, unfinished manuscript, Today, as one stands atop the Esters Road overpass, watching an endless stream of traffic roaring below, it becomes difficult to imagine the remote rural scene of 1933. Motels and car dealerships line the busy highway, extensions of the large shopping mall standing less than a mile away. To the east the finger-like peaks of Dallas's downtown office complexes rise like monoliths against the horizon.

To the west the viewer is struck by the sight of a great thread of massive, wide-bodied jumbo jets drifting in from the stratosphere, each plane making its final approach to one of the busiest airports in the world. Beyond that, the flickering peaks of Ft. Worth's impressive skyline press forward like mirages in the hazy, smoke-filled atmosphere. Though choked by a half century of urbanization, it takes no scholar to understand why the intersection of Esters Road and the North Ft. Worth Pike would have been the perfect place to find Clyde Barrow in 1933.

15. Floyd Hamilton interview, 18 July 1981; Marie Barrow interview, 15 September 1993.

16. *Dallas Morning News*, 23 November 1933; *Dallas Dispatch*, 23 November 1933; *Dallas Daily Times Herald*, 23 November 1933.

17. Hinton, *Ambush*, 104. Alcorn had used a Browning automatic rifle at least once before, in Denton, Texas, during a siege in the 1920s.

18. Marie Barrow interview, 25 September 1993.

19. *Dallas Dispatch*, 24 February 1935.

20. Hinton, *Ambush*, 104.

21. Marie Barrow interview, 15 September 1993. Clyde told her this several days later.

22. Ibid. Floyd Hamilton said Barrow had seen a tin can that had been nailed to a fence post by the informant as a point of reference for the sheriff and his men. Floyd Hamilton interview, 18 July 1981.

23. Marie Barrow interview, 24 August 1984.

24. Ibid.

25. *Dallas Dispatch*, 23 November 1933; *Dallas Morning News*, 23 November 1933; *Dallas Daily Times Herald*, 23 November 1933.

26. *Dallas Dispatch*, 23 November 1933.

27. Ibid.

28. Hamilton, *Public Enemy No. 1*, 25.

29. *Dallas Dispatch*, 23 November 1933.

30. *Temple (Tex.) Morning News*, 24 November 1933. The charges were dropped 30 December 1933.

31. Barrow drafted a letter confessing to the Doyle Johnson killing. Using axle grease as ink, he affixed his palm and fingerprints to the letter. Jones's statement made the letter unnecessary. It is still in the possession of the Barrow family. Clyde Barrow, letter, 21 November 1933; Marie Barrow interview, 24 August 1984. See also Fortune, *Fugitives*, 137.

32. Jones, Voluntary Statement B–71; *Dallas Morning News*, 26 November 1933; *Dallas Dispatch*, 26 November 1933; *Dallas Daily Times Herald*, 26 November 1933.

33. Hamilton, *Public Enemy No. 1*, 25.

34. Ibid.

35. Floyd Hamilton interview, 18 July 1981.

36. Marie Barrow interview, 24 August 1984.

37. Hamilton, *Public Enemy No. 1*, 30.
38. Ibid., 29.
39. Floyd Hamilton interview, 18 July 1981.
40. Ibid.
41. Hamilton, *Public Enemy No. 1*, 31.
42. Ibid. Floyd Hamilton said he thought Barrow was "too yellow to plant those guns on Eastham." Floyd Hamilton interview, 18 July 1981. Ralph Fults said he and Barrow knew of Mullens in prison and did not trust him (Ralph Fults interview, 21 May 1983). Joe Palmer said Barrow thought Mullens was trying to set a trap. Simmons, *Assignment Huntsville*, 167.
43. Floyd Hamilton interview, 18 July 1981.
44. Marie thinks her brother planted the guns, not Floyd Hamilton and James Mullens. Marie Barrow interview, 25 September 1993.
45. *Dallas Morning News*, 17 January 1934; *Dallas Daily Times Herald*, 17 January 1934; Texas Prison System, Special Escape Report, Raymond Hamilton, 16 January 1934.
46. Simmons, *Assignment Huntsville*, 116.
47. Hamilton, *Public Enemy No. 1*, 32.
48. *Dallas Morning News*, 17 January 1934; *Dallas Daily Times Herald*, 17 January 1934; *Dallas Dispatch*, 17 January 1934; Texas Prison System, Special Escape Report, Raymond Hamilton, 16 January 1934.
49. *Dallas Morning News*, 17 January 1934; *Dallas Daily Times Herald*, 17 January 1934; *Dallas Dispatch*, 17 January 1934; Texas Prison System, Special Escape Report, Raymond Hamilton, 16 January 1934.
50. Hamilton, *Public Enemy No. 1*, 32.
51. *Dallas Morning News*, 17 January 1934.
52. Ibid., 22 January 1934; *Dallas Daily Times Herald*, 22 January 1934.
53. Joe Palmer, quoted in *Assignment Huntsville*, 167.
54. Hamilton, *Public Enemy No. 1*, 32, 33; Russell, "Barrow-Parker Harboring Case," 10.
55. Joe Palmer, quoted in *Assignment Huntsville*, 166.
56. Ibid.
57. Hamilton, *Public Enemy No. 1*, 33.
58. Joe Palmer, quoted by Simmons, *Assignment Huntsville*, 167.
59. Cumie T. Barrow, unfinished manuscript; Marie Barrow interview, 24 August 1984.
60. Joe Palmer, quoted in *Assignment Huntsville*, 167.
61. Ibid.
62. Hamilton, *Public Enemy No. 1*, 33.
63. Joe Palmer, quoted in *Assignment Huntsville*, 167.
64. Marie Barrow interview, 15 September 1993.
65. Joe Palmer, quoted in *Assignment Huntsville*, 167.
66. Worley interview, 17 August 1983.

67. *Dallas Evening Journal*, 28 February 1934; *Dallas Dispatch*, 28 February 1934; *Dallas Daily Times Herald*, 28 February 1934.

68. *Dallas Evening Journal*, 28 February 1934; *Dallas Dispatch*, 28 February 1934; *Dallas Daily Times Herald*, 28 February 1934.

69. Worley interview, 17 August 1983.

70. Ibid.

71. Ibid.

72. Ibid.

73. Ibid.

74. Ibid.; *Dallas Evening Journal*, 16 January 1934; *Dallas Daily Times Herald*, 16 January 1934. Floyd Hamilton said the Lancaster robbery netted more than five thousand dollars.

75. Cumie T. Barrow, unfinished manuscript; Marie Barrow interview, 15 September 1993.

76. *Dallas Morning News*, 26 April 1934; *Dallas Daily Times Herald*, 26 April 1934; *Dallas Dispatch*, 26 April 1934; Floyd Hamilton interview, 18 July 1981; Bud Russell, "Barrow-Parker Harboring Case," 19.

Chapter 12

1. *Dallas Dispatch*, 17 January 1934.

2. *Dallas Daily Times Herald*, 22 January 1934.

3. Simmons's own chapter heading. *Assignment Huntsville*, 164, 165.

4. Walter Prescott Webb, *The Texas Rangers*, 539.

5. *Methvin v. Oklahoma*, A-9060 (1936).

6. Fortune, *Fugitives*, 247; Simmons, *Assignment Huntsville*, 166.

7. Hamilton, *Public Enemy No. 1*, 36. This robbery is often attributed to Clyde Barrow.

8. *Dallas Dispatch*, 1 April 1934; *Dallas Morning News*, 1 April 1934; *Dallas Daily Times Herald*, 1 April 1934. This robbery is often attributed to Clyde Barrow. See Sitton, *The Loblolly Book*, 49–57.

9. Ibid.

10. Ibid.

11. *Dallas Morning News*, 1 April 1934, 2 April 1934.

12. *Dallas Daily Times Herald*, 1 April 1934.

13. *Dallas Daily Times Herald*, 2 April 1934; *Dallas Morning News*, 2 April 1934; *Dallas Dispatch*, 2 April 1934; Fortune, *Fugitives*, 230–233.

14. Russell, "Barrow-Parker Harboring Case," 12; Marie Barrow interview, 15 September 1993. The trip to Houston was a ploy by Hamilton to draw attention away from Grapevine, Texas, his actual destination.

15. Marie Barrow interview, 24 August 1984; Simmons, *Assignment Huntsville*, 167.

16. Fortune, *Fugitives*, 231.

17. *Dallas Evening Journal*, 2 April 1934. The car stolen by Hamilton in Houston also had yellow wheels. Later Floyd Hamilton met his brother

near Dallas with a set of black wheels and helped his brother install them. See Russell, "Barrow-Parker Harboring Case," 20.

18. Marie Barrow interview, 15 September 1993; Fortune, *Fugitives*, 232; Hinton, *Ambush*, 137; Floyd Hamilton interview, 18 July 1981.

19. *Dallas Morning News*, 2 April 1934.

20. Ibid.

21. *Dallas Evening Journal*, 2 April 1934; *Dallas Morning News*, 2 April 1934. There are two separate articles in the *Dallas Morning News*. One, filled with references to men dressed as women and cigar butts bearing "tiny teeth marks," has the smaller of the two assailants shooting Murphy. The other outlines the eyewitness account of the Giggals. The *Dallas Evening Journal* also ran the Giggal story, which states that the larger of two men shot Murphy. Emma Parker said that Methvin later told her that he killed both officers. See Fortune, *Fugitives*, 236.

22. *Dallas Evening Journal*, 26 May 1934. Barney Finn, Tarrant County Sheriff's Department Bertillon expert, later revealed that the print belonged to Methvin, not Barrow. *Dallas Daily Times Herald*, 6 September 1934.

23. *Dallas Evening Journal*, 2 April 1934.

24. Ibid.; *Dallas Morning News*, 2 April 1934; *Dallas Daily Times Herald*, 2 April 1934; *Dallas Dispatch*, 2 April 1934.

25. *Dallas Dispatch*, 2 April 1934.

26. *Dallas Evening Journal*, 3 April 1934.

27. *Methvin v. Oklahoma*, No. A-9060 (1936).

28. Ibid.

29. Ibid.

30. Ibid.; Boyd positively identified Methvin as the killer of Cal Campbell. *Dallas Daily Times Herald*, 17 September 1934.

31. *Methvin v. Oklahoma*, No. A-9060 (1936).

32. Ibid.

33. Ibid.

34. *Dallas Morning News*, 8 April 1934.

35. Simmons, *Assignment Huntsville*, 166.

36. *Dallas Morning News*, 8 April 1934.

37. Ibid., 7 April 1934.

38. *Dallas Dispatch*, 8 April 1934; *Dallas Morning News*, 8 April 1934; *Dallas Daily Times Herald*, 8 April 1934.

39. Leon Charping, interview by John Neal Phillips, 16 May 1984; Cleo Sneed, interview by John Neal Phillips, 16 May 1984; Dewey Kendrick, Sr., interview by John Neal Phillips, 16 May 1984; Louise Polly Palmer, interview by John Neal Phillips, 16 May 1984; Carrol Y. Rich, "The Day They Shot Bonnie and Clyde," 37.

40. *Dallas Daily Times Herald*, 3 June 1934; Marie Barrow interview, 24 August 1984; Billie Jean Parker, *The Truth about Bonnie and Clyde*, sound recording.

41. Charping interview, 16 May 1984; Sneed interview, 16 May 1984; Kendrick interview, 16 May 1984; Palmer interview, 16 May 1984.

42. Simmons, *Assignment Huntsville*, 166.

43. Ibid.

44. *Dallas Morning News*, 9 April 1934. The actual letter, a photocopy of which appeared in the newspaper, differs from the facsimile on page 38 of *Public Enemy No. 1*.

45. Cumie T. Barrow, unfinished manuscript; Marie Barrow interview, 24 August 1984.

46. *Dallas Morning News*, 26 April 1934; Hamilton, *Public Enemy No. 1*, 39.

47. *Dallas Daily Times Herald*, 25 April 1934; *Dallas Evening Journal*, 25 April 1934.

48. *Dallas Morning News*, 26 April 1934.

49. *Dallas Morning News*, 26 April 1934; *Dallas Daily Times Herald*, 26 April 1934.

50. *Dallas Morning News*, 26 April 1934; *Dallas Daily Times Herald*, 26 April 1934.

51. *Dallas Morning News*, 26 April 1934; *Dallas Daily Times Herald*, 26 April 1934.

52. *Dallas Morning News*, 26 April 1934; *Dallas Daily Times Herald*, 26 April 1934.

53. *Dallas Morning News*, 26 April 1934; *Dallas Daily Times Herald*, 26 April 1934.

54. *Dallas Morning News*, 26 April 1934; *Dallas Daily Times Herald*, 26 April 1934.

55. Floyd Hamilton interview, 18 July 1981.

56. Joe Palmer, quoted in *Assignment Huntsville*, 165.

57. Jim Muckleroy, United States, Department of Justice, report on Clyde Barrow in East Texas, 30 March 1933.

58. Marie Barrow interview, 15 September 1984; Joe Palmer, quoted in *Assignment Huntsville*, 165, 166; Cumie T. Barrow, unfinished manuscript; Schott, "Death's Used Car," 25 May 1980.

59. Schott, "Death's Used Car," 25 May 1980; Joseph L. Schott, interview by John Neal Phillips, 10 June 1980.

60. He referred to a gunfight near Reed Springs, Missouri on 12 February 1934.

61. Dallas, Texas, Police Department File no. 6048, Clyde Barrow.

62. Marie Barrow interview, 24 August 1984.

63. Fortune, *Fugitives*, 226; Hinton, *Ambush*, 155, 156.

64. They also robbed banks in Iowa and Oklahoma. Joe Palmer, quoted in *Assignment Hunstville*, 165; *Dallas Dispatch*, 15 June 1934. Palmer admitted aiding Barrow in both robberies.

65. Joe Palmer, quoted in *Assignment Huntsville*, 165.

66. Ibid.

67. Fortune, *Fugitives*, 239.

68. The Ford, stolen from a Marshall, Texas insurance agent, was later used in the bloody Joplin escape. The car appeared in many of the snapshots printed from the film left by the fleeing outlaws. The owner of the car was nearly arrested. Luckily, he had reported it stolen and knew the local sheriff well. When the car was recovered in Oklahoma, thirty days after the Joplin gunfight, the bipod of a Browning automatic rifle was still bolted to the dash. Roseborough interview, 24 June 1984.

69. Fortune, *Fugitives*, 240.

70. *Dallas Daily Times Herald*, 10 May 1934; *Dallas Dispatch*, 10 May 1934; *Dallas Evening Journal*, 10 May 1934; *Dallas Morning News*, 10 May 1934.

71. *Dallas Dispatch*, 20 May 1934.

72. Cumie T. Barrow, unfinished manuscript; Marie Barrow interview, 25 September 1993.

73. *Dallas Morning News*, 8 August 1934.

74. *Dallas Daily Times Herald*, 14 May 1934.

75. Pat Askins, interview by John Neal Phillips, 4 June 1980; Alton Askins, interview by John Neal Phillips, 4 June 1980.

76. *Methvin v. Oklahoma*, A-9060 (1936).

77. Hinton, *Ambush*, 158.

78. Ibid. Hinton qualifies the cafe story by introducing it as "the story Bryant (Shreveport chief of police) related to us." Lorraine Joyner, an in-law of John Joyner and the Methvins, maintains it was a laundry, not a cafe. Lorraine Joyner, interview by Dr. Robert Pierce, 13 May 1992.

79. Hinton, *Ambush*, 158–67.

80. Kendrick interview, 16 May 1984; Charping interview, 16 May 1984. Another eyewitness said the cafe was called "Rosie's." Mert Davis, *Ringgold (La.) Record*, 26 April 1968.

81. Charping interview, 16 May 1984; Sneed interview, 16 May 1984; Davis, *Ringgold* (*La.*) *Record*, 26 April 1968.

82. Hinton, *Ambush*, 165–68. Ivy and Avie Methvin, Henry's parents, sometimes appear as Iverson and Mildred. Lorraine Joyner interview, 13 May 1992.

83. Kendrick interview, 16 May 1984; Charping interview, 16 May 1984.

84. Charping interview, 16 May 1984; Sneed interview, 16 May 1984; Davis, *Ringgold* (*La.*) *Record*, 26 April 1968.

85. Charping interview, 16 May 1984; Sneed interview, 16 May 1984; Davis, *Ringgold* (*La.*) *Record*, 26 April 1968; Parker, *The Truth about Bonnie and Clyde*, sound recording.

86. Davis, *Ringgold* (*La.*) *Record*, 26 April 1968.

87. Hinton, *Ambush*, 169.

88. Bienville Parish, Louisiana, Coroner's Inquest, 23 May 1934.

89. Ibid.
90. Hinton, *Ambush*, 169.
91. Cumie T. Barrow, unfinished manuscript.
92. Hinton, *Ambush*, 169, 170.
93. *Methvin v. Oklahoma*, A-9060 (1936); Davis, *Ringgold (La.) Record*, 26 April 1968. Three months later the governor of Texas issued a full pardon to Henry Methvin, saying that it was in return for Methvin's part in the ambush of Bonnie and Clyde. *Austin American Statesman*, 14 August 1934.

Chapter 13

1. *Dallas Dispatch*, 24 May 1934.
2. Simmons, *Assignment Huntsville*, 132.
3. In 1948 Fults met Ranger Captain Tom Hickman at a function where both men were featured speakers. After the function they talked. Hickman spoke of a number of things, including the stake-out in Denton, Texas, the ambush in McKinney, Texas, and the ambush of Bonnie and Clyde. Hickman said both he and Lone Wolf Gonzuales had been approached by Simmons—before Hamer. Both said no to the plan, adding, "We don't ambush people and we don't shoot women." Captain Fred McDaniel related a similar story when he transferred Fults to Austin in 1935. Ralph Fults interviews, 14 March 1981, 22 February 1985.
4. *Dallas Morning News*, 13 March 1928.
5. *Dallas Daily Times Herald*, 7 May 1929.
6. *Dallas Dispatch*, 29 May 1934.
7. Webb, *Texas Rangers*, 539.
8. *New York Daily News*, 4 June 1934.
9. Ranger Captain Fred McDaniel, statement to Ralph Fults, 20 April 1935.
10. Simmons, *Assignment Huntsville*, 133; Webb, *Texas Rangers*, 531. Webb refers to "Hamer's inflexible adherence to right, or what he thinks is right."
11. "Not counting Mexican bandits," Hamer added. Zarko Franks, "Bonnie and Clyde—Fresh Insights into Their Deaths," 31 July 1977; *Texarkana (Tex.) Press*, 24 May 1934.
12. *Dallas Dispatch*, 24 May 1934.
13. Simmons, *Assignment Huntsville*, 132.
14. *Dallas Evening Journal*, 6 June 1934.
15. *Dallas Daily Times Herald*, 10 April 1935.
16. *Methvin v. Oklahoma*, A-9060 (1936). According to John Joyner (misspelled as "Joiner" in transcript) and Avie Methvin, the date of their contact with Sheriff Jordan was 1 March 1934. Hamer said he and Alcorn arrived in Bienville Parish on 19 February 1934 and immediately began planning the ambush. See Newell, *Texarkana (Tex.) Press*, 24 May 1934. Bud Russell, who knew Simmons well, maintains that Henry Methvin was not in on the

ambush. Russell, "Barrow-Parker Harboring Case," 7.

17. *Methvin v. Oklahoma*, A-9060 (1936); Russell, "Barrow-Parker Harboring Case," 1, 2.

18. *Methvin v. Oklahoma*, A-9060 (1936).

19. *Dallas Daily Times Herald*, 2 April 1934; *Dallas Morning News*, 2 April 1934; *Dallas Dispatch*, 2 April 1934; *Dallas Evening Journal*, 2 April 1934.

20. *New York Daily News*, 3 June 1934. Texas Ranger Clint Peoples said Governor Ferguson offered him a commission in the Ranger force in exchange for five hundred dollars. He declined. Clint Peoples, interview by John Neal Phillips, 30 September 1983.

21. Hinton said both he and Alcorn were commissioned to track Bonnie and Clyde full time in November 1933. Hamer said that after meeting with Simmons, he drove first to Dallas. Sheriff Schmid later admitted "lending" Alcorn to Hamer. According to Joyner, Hamer and Alcorn were the only Texans present in Sheriff Jordan's office on 1 March 1934. On 6 April 1934, Hinton was reportedly in Wichita Falls recovering stolen saddles. See Hinton, *Ambush*, 111; *New York Daily News*, 3 June 1934: *Dallas Evening Journal*, 6 June 1934; *Dallas Daily Times Herald*, 6 April 1934, 23 May 1934; *Methvin v. Oklahoma*, A-9060 (1936).

22. *Methvin v. Oklahoma*, A-9060 (1936).

23. Ibid.

24. Hinton, *Ambush*, 158.

25. Charping interview, 16 May 1984; Sneed interview, 16 May 1984; Kendrick interview, 16 May 1984; Davis, *Ringgold (La.) Record*, 26 April 1968.

26. Charping interview, 16 May 1984.

27. Hinton, *Ambush*, 163. Almost every other report has the officers taking their positions at the intended ambush site on the evening of 22 May 1934, including Simmons, although he inadvertently listed the date as 22 April 1934. Hinton and historian Carrol Y. Rich maintain that the stake-out lasted two nights, beginning 21 May 1934. See Rich, "The Day They Shot Bonnie and Clyde," 38.

28. Hinton, *Ambush*, 165.

29. Charping interview, 16 May 1984; Sneed interview, 16 May 1984; Davis, *Ringgold (La.) Record*, 26 April 1968.

30. Hinton, *Ambush*, 167.

31. Mrs. Ted Hinton, interview by John Neal Phillips, 15 April 1980; Larry Grove, interview by John Neal Phillips, 2 April 1980; John W. "Preacher" Hays, interview by John Neal Phillips, 20 April 1980; Johnny Hayes interview, 14 October 1981, 28 April 1983.

32. Hinton, *Ambush*, 167–169.

33. Dr. T. C. Kirby, married to Prentis Oakley's cousin, said Oakley once told him this. See Thomas E. Aswell, *The Story of Bonnie and Clyde*, 23.

34. Despite assertions that Hinton identified the occupants of the approaching car, most contemporary accounts have Alcorn performing that

duty. Moreover, in a 1934 film documentary featuring a recreation of the ambush in which both Hinton and Alcorn appear, it is Alcorn who identifies the occupants of the approaching car. See *Bienville (La.) Democrat*, 24 May 1934; Jamieson, *The Retribution of Bonnie and Clyde*, motion-picture documentary.

35. Jamieson, *The Retribution of Bonnie and Clyde*, motion-picture documentary.

36. Davis, *Ringgold (La.) Record*, 26 April 1968.

37. Ibid.; Hinton, *Ambush*, 172.

38. *Daily Oklahoma Times*, 21 May 1984.

39. Kendrick interview, 16 May 1984.

40. Hinton, *Ambush*, 169.

41. Ibid.

42. In relating this story to writer Larry Grove, Hinton was on the verge of tears. "He was so fond of Bonnie," Grove said. "He spoke of feeling her breathe her last breath, but you know she had to have been dead already—shot like she was." Grove interview, 2 April 1980.

43. Bienville Parish, Louisiana, Coroner's Inquest, 23 May 1934.

44. Some say that Barrow had a Browning automatic rifle in his lap and that a bullet had struck it, rendering it inoperable. Three eyewitnesses saw two sawed-off shotguns, muzzles down, the stocks resting on Barrow's legs, as was his custom. A pistol was in Bonnie's lap. Later, the officers discovered the BARs beneath a blanket in the back seat. Charping interview, 16 May 1984; Sneed interview, 16 May 1984; Davis, *Ringgold (La.) Record*, 26 April 1968.

45. Webb, *Texas Rangers*, 543.

46. *Bienville (La.) Democrat*, 24 May 1934; Hinton, *Ambush*, 173; *The Retribution of Bonnie and Clyde*, motion-picture documentary.

47. Sneed interview, 16 May 1984.

48. Ibid.

49. *Bienville (La.) Democrat*, 24 May 1934.

50. Hinton, *Ambush*, 178; Rich, "The Day They Shot Bonnie and Clyde," 39.

51. Davis, *Ringgold (La.) Record*, 26 April 1968.

52. Ibid.

53. Rich, "The Day They Shot Bonnie and Clyde," 39.

54. Kendrick interview, 16 May 1984.

55. *Bienville (La.) Democrat*, 24 May 1934; Hinton, *Ambush*, 182.

56. Kendrick interview, 16 May 1984.

57. Palmer interview, 16 May 1984.

58. Rich, "The Day They Shot Bonnie and Clyde," 40, 41.

59. Kendrick interview, 16 May 1984.

60. Ibid.

61. Rich, "The Day They Shot Bonnie and Clyde," 41.

62. Fortune, *Fugitives*, 246.
63. Marie Barrow interview, 24 August 1984.
64. Ibid.
65. *Bienville (La.) Democrat*, 24 May 1934; Rich, "The Day They Shot Bonnie and Clyde," 41.
66. Marie Barrow interview, 24 August 1984.
67. Bienville Parish, Louisiana, Coroner's Inquest, 23 May 1934.
68. Ibid.
69. Jamieson, *The Retribution of Bonnie and Clyde*, motion-picture documentary.
70. Kendrick interview, 16 May 1984; Aswell, *The Story of Bonnie and Clyde*, 23.
71. *Dallas Evening Journal*, 6 June 1934.
72. Rich, "The Day They Shot Bonnie and Clyde," 42.
73. Fortune, *Fugitives*, 247.
74. Rich, "The Day They Shot Bonnie and Clyde," 41.
75. *Dallas Daily Times Herald*, 23 May 1934.
76. *Dallas Evening Journal*, 23 May 1934; *Dallas Morning News*, 23 May 1934; *Dallas Daily Times Herald*, 23 May 1934.
77. *Dallas Evening Journal*, 23 May 1934.
78. Fortune, *Fugitives*, 246.
79. Hinton, *Ambush*, 190.
80. *Dallas Morning News*, 26 May 1934; *Dallas Daily Times Herald*, 26 May 1934; *Dallas Evening Journal*, 26 May 1934. The airplane and flowers were arranged for by a notorious Dallas racketeer who actually never met Clyde Barrow. Marie Barrow interview, 15 September 1993.
81. Simmons, *Assignment Huntsville*, 166.
82. Fortune, *Fugitives*, 254.
83. Worley interview, 17 August 1983.
84. *Dallas Daily Times Herald*, 27 May 1934.
85. Parker, *The Truth About Bonnie and Clyde*, sound recording.
86. *Dallas Morning News*, 27 May 1934; *Dallas Daily Times Herald*, 23 May 1934; *Dallas Evening Journal*, 27 May 1934; *Dallas Dispatch*, 27 May 1934.
87. *Dallas Morning News*, 27 May 1934; Fortune, *Fugitives*, 255; Hinton, *Ambush*, 192.
88. *Dallas Daily Times Herald*, 27 May 1934.
89. Ibid.

Chapter 14

1. *Dallas Evening Journal*, 28 May 1934.
2. *Dallas Daily Times Herald*, 1 June 1934.
3. McCormick "The Impossible Interview," 68.
4. Johnny Hayes interview, 10 October 1981, 28 April 1983.

5. *Dallas Dispatch*, 12 June 1934; *Dallas Daily Times Herald*, 12 June 1934; *Dallas Morning News*, 12 June 1934; *Dallas Evening Journal*, 12 June 1934.

6. Ibid.

7. Johnny Hayes interview, 10 October 1981, 28 April 1983; McCormick "The Impossible Interview," 68.

8. Johnny Hayes interview, 10 October 1981.

9. *Dallas Dispatch*, 12 June 1934.

10. *Dallas Dispatch*, 15 June 1934; *Dallas Daily Times Herald*, 15 June 1934.

11. *Dallas Dispatch*, 15 June 1934; *Dallas Daily Times Herald*, 15 June 1934.

12. *Dallas Dispatch*, 15 June 1934; *Dallas Daily Times Herald*, 15 June 1934.

13. *Dallas Dispatch*, 15 June 1934; *Dallas Daily Times Herald*, 15 June 1934.

14. *Dallas Daily Times Herald*, 15 June 1934.

15. Ibid., 29 June 1934; *Dallas Dispatch*, 29 June 1934.

16. *Dallas Daily Times Herald*, 29 June 1934; *Dallas Dispatch*, 29 June 1934.

17. Simmons, *Assignment Huntsville*, 168.

18. Ibid.

19. *Dallas Dispatch*, 11 September 1933; Tattersall, *Conviction*, 176–200.

20. Simmons, *Assignment Huntsville*, 170–73.

21. *Dallas Morning News*, 13 January 1934; *Dallas Daily Times Herald*, 13 January 1934; *Dallas Dispatch*, 13 January 1934; *Dallas Evening Journal*, 13 January 1934.

22. *Dallas Morning News*, 7 March 1934; *Dallas Daily Times Herald*, 7 March 1934; *Dallas Dispatch*, 7 March 1934; *Dallas Evening Journal*, 7 March 1934.

23. *Dallas Dispatch*, 7 March 1934.

24. *Dallas Morning News*, 23 July 1934. According to Dr. E. R. Milner of the University of North Texas, Clyde Barrow is mistakenly listed as the perpetrator of one of their crimes, the McMurray Oil Refinery robbery of 8 January 1933. See Hinton, *Ambush*, 97. Dr. E.R. Milner, interview by John Neal Phillips, 4 August 1984.

25. *Dallas Daily Times Herald*, 14 August 1934; Simmons, *Assignment Huntsville*, 155.

26. McCormick, "The Impossible Interview," 68.

27. *Dallas Daily Times Herald*, 23 July 1934; *Dallas Dispatch*, 23 July 1934; *Dallas Morning News*, 23 July 1934; *Dallas Evening Journal*, 23 July 1934; Texas Prison System, Special Escape Report, Joe Palmer, 22 July 1934.

28. McCormick, "The Impossible Interview," 68.

29. Lee Brazil, quoted in Texas Prison Board, Minutes, 24 July 1934,

303.

30. Ibid.

31. Ibid.

32. W. G. McConnell, quoted in Texas Prison Board, Minutes, 24 July 1934, 304.

33. *Dallas Morning News*, 23 July 1934; *Dallas Daily Times Herald*, 23 July 1934; *Dallas Evening Journal*, 23 July 1934; *Dallas Dispatch*, 23 July 1934. There is a debate as to which corner of the prison the prisoners escaped from. Because the numbering of the pickets has changed over the years, it is hard to determine the location of picket no. 7. However, references to the southwest corner appear in the Texas Prison Board Minutes, and eyewitness Clyde Hall said the prisoners scaled the wall at the southwest corner. W. G. McConnell, quoted in Texas Prison Board, Minutes, 24 July 1934, 304; Hall interview, 10 December 1983.

34. *Dallas Morning News*, 23 July 1934; *Dallas Daily Times Herald*, 23 July 1934; *Dallas Evening Journal*, 23 July 1934; *Dallas Dispatch*, 23 July 1934.

35. *Dallas Morning News*, 23 July 1934; *Dallas Daily Times Herald*, 23 July 1934; *Dallas Evening Journal*, 23 July 1934; *Dallas Dispatch*, 23 July 1934.

36. Carey Burdeaux and W. G. McConnell, quoted in Texas Prison Board, Minutes, 24 July 1934, 304, 305.

37. Ibid.

38. *Dallas Morning News*, 23 July 1934; *Dallas Daily Times Herald*, 23 July 1934; *Dallas Evening Journal*, 23 July 1934; *Dallas Dispatch*, 23 July 1934; D. W. Roberts, quoted in Texas Prison Board, Minutes, 24 July 1934, 305.

39. H. P. George and D. W. Roberts, quoted in Texas Prison Board, Minutes, 24 July 1934, 304, 305.

40. Hall interview, 10 December 1983.

41. Simmons, *Assignment Huntsville*, 154; Lee Simmons, quoted in Texas Prison Board, Minutes, 24 July 1934, 296–300.

42. W. G. McConnell, quoted in Texas Prison Board, Minutes, 24 July 1934, 304.

43. D. W. Roberts, quoted in Texas Prison Board, Minutes, 24 July 1934, 305.

44. Hall interview, 10 December1983.

45. *Dallas Dispatch*, 23 July 1934.

46. Hall interview, 10 December 1983.

47. Simmons, *Assignment Huntsville*, 153.

48. Simmons, quoted in Texas Prison Board Minutes, 24 July, 296–300.

49. *Dallas Morning News*, 13 August 1934.

50. Ibid., 7 December 1934; *Dallas Evening Journal*, 7 December 1934; *Dallas Daily Times Herald*, 7 December 1934; *Dallas Dispatch*, 7 December 1934.

51. Ibid, 7 December 1934; *Dallas Evening Journal*, 7 December 1934; *Dallas Daily Times Herald*, 7 December 1934; *Dallas Dispatch*, 7 December

1934.

52. Simmons, *Assignment Huntsville*, 154.

53. McCormick "The Impossible Interview," 68; Russell interview, 2 February 1985; Pierce interview, 5 November 1993.

54. Simmons, *Assignment Huntsville*, 168; Harry McCormick, *Bank Robbers Wrote My Diary*, 109, 110; McCormick later revealed to Ralph Fults that Father Finnegan was the one supplying the smuggled information. Fults interviews, 4 December 1982, 22 February 1985, 29 April 1985.

55. Martin and Ekland-Olson, *Texas Prisons*, 10; *Dallas Morning News*, 11 February 1925.

56. This was not the only time this happened to King. Her testimony before a joint Texas State House and Senate committee revealed a similar incident in 1925. Martin and Eckland-Olson, *Texas Prisons*, 10; *Dallas Morning News*, 11 February 1925.

57. Maisie Paulissen, "Pardon Me, Governor Ferguson," 152, 153.

58. *Houston Press*, 31 March 1935.

Chapter 15

1. Hamilton, *Public Enemy No. 1*, 54.

2. Ibid., 62.

3. Ibid.

4. *Dallas Morning News*, 18 January 1935; *Dallas Evening Journal*, 18 January 1935; *Dallas Daily Times Herald*, 18 January 1935; *Dallas Dispatch*, 18 January 1935.

5. *Dallas Morning News*, 4, 5 February 1935; *Dallas Evening Journal*, 4, 5 February 1935; *Dallas Daily Times Herald*, 4, 5 February 1935; *Dallas Dispatch*, 4, 5, February 1935.

6. *Dallas Morning News*, 4, 5 February 1935; *Dallas Evening Journal*, 4, 5 February 1935; *Dallas Daily Times Herald*, 4, 5 February 1935; *Dallas Dispatch*, 4, 5, February 1935.

7. Floyd Hamilton interview, 18 July 1981.

8. Ibid.

9. Ibid.

10. *Dallas Evening Journal*, 5 February 1935; *Dallas Daily Times Herald*, 5 February 1935.

11. Mildred Hamilton, interview by John Neal Phillips, 18 July 1981.

12. *Dallas Evening Journal*, 5 February 1935; *Dallas Morning News*, 5 February 1935.

13. *Dallas Evening Journal*, 5 February 1935; *Dallas Morning News*, 5 February 1935.

14. Floyd Hamilton interview, 18 July 1981.

15. Ibid.

16. Ibid.

17. *Dallas Morning News*, 17 February 1935; *Houston Press*, 16 February

1935, 17 February 1935.

18. Ibid.

19. Ibid.

20. Ibid.

21. Although the U.S. Congress had repealed prohibition in December 1933, Texas did not vote to ratify the new amendment until August 1935.

22. Fults interviews, 5 November 1980, 12 November 1980, 12 June 1984.

23. *Dallas Evening Journal*, 24 February 1935.

24. Ted Hinton, quoted in the *Denton (Tex.) Record-Chronicle*, 17 April 1935, following an interview with Ralph Fults.

25. Ibid.

26. L. B. Harlow interview by John Neal Phillips, 17 December 1983.

27. Ibid.

28. Ibid.

29. *Dallas Morning News*, 2 February 1935.

30. Ibid. The hat was put on display in the window of a McKinney drug store, where it remained for years.

31. *Dallas Dispatch*, 25 February 1935.

32. Cecil Mayes, interview by John Neal Phillips, 12 June 1982.

33. The Federal Bureau of Investigation's "Ten Most Wanted" list was not initiated until the 1950s. Before that, pressured by reporters asking for the Bureau's thoughts on who the worst outlaws were (and partially for the publicity it generated), regional lists of "most wanted" criminals were released on a periodic basis.

34. Mayes interview, 12 June 1982.

35. Ibid.

36. Ibid.; *Dallas Morning News*, 26 February 1935.

37. Mayes interview, 12 June 1982; Russell, "Barrows-Parker Harboring Case," 22.

38. Jesse Roy Mayes, quoted by Blake, U.S. Department of Justice Report, 26 February 1935.

39. Mayes interview, 12 June 1935.

40. Ibid.

41. Ibid.

42. Ibid.

43. Ibid. Newspaper reports list the car as a 1928 model, but Mrs. Mayes recalled that it was a brand new 1935 model.

44. Ibid.

45. Mayes, quoted by Blake, U. S. Department of Justice Report, 26 February 1935.

46. Harlow interview, 17 December 1983.

47. Ibid. Some reports incorrectly list Loftice as the man making the purchases. According to Harlow, he was the one who walked up to the news

stand.

48. Ibid.

49. *Dallas Morning News*, 25 February 1935.

50. Beldon interview, 15 February 1981.

51. Royce, statement, to Ralph Fults, 22 November 1955; Beldon interview, 15 February 1981; Mayes interview, 12 June 1982.

52. Royce, statement, to Ralph Fults, 22 November 1955; Beldon interview, 15 February 1981; Mayes interview, 12 June 1982.

53. Royce, statement, to Ralph Fults, 22 November 1955; Beldon interview, 15 February 1981; Mayes interview, 12 June 1982.

54. *Dallas Evening Journal*, 25 February 1935; *Dallas Morning News*, 25 February 1935; *Dallas Daily Times Herald*, 25 February 1935; *Dallas Dispatch*, 25 February 1935.

55. Mayes, quoted by Blake, U.S. Department of Justice Report, 26 February 1935.

56. Harlow interview, 17 December 1983.

57. Mayes interview, 12 June 1982; *Dallas Morning News*, 26 February 1935.

58. Beldon interview, 15 February 1981.

59. *Dallas Evening Journal*, 27 February 1935.

60. *Dallas Dispatch*, 4 March 1935.

61. McCormick, "The Impossible Interview," 69–71.

62. Ibid., 72.

63. Ibid.

64. Ibid. The truth about this incident has never been revealed. To protect McCormick, who could have been charged with harboring, the *Argosy* article is partially incorrect. Fults said McCormick told Hamilton where to meet him. There were no shadowy, clandestine arrangements. Fults also remembers McCormick had his typewriter.

65. *Houston Press*, 19 March 1935; McCormick, "The Impossible Interview," 72.

66. McCormick, unfinished manuscript, 29. McCormick mentions Fults's feelings of guilt about the trouble Raymond Hamilton was in—blaming himself and Clyde Barrow for dragging Hamilton along on those early burglaries.

67. McCormick, "The Impossible Interview," 72.

68. *Houston Press*, 19 March 1935.

69. McCormick, "The Impossible Interview," 72.

70. *Houston Press*, 19 March 1935.

71. Fults interviews, 13 February 1982, 4 December 1982, 22 February 1985. Palmer's lawyer filed the appeal the day after the Hamilton-Fults-McCormick meeting. *Houston Press*, 20 March 1935.

72. *Houston Press*, 19 March 1935; McCormick, "The Impossible Interview," 72.

73. McCormick, "The Impossible Interview," 74.

Chapter 16

1. *Dallas Dispatch*, 22 March 1935.
2. *Houston Press*, 20 March 1935.
3. *Jackson (Miss.) Daily News*, 17 April 1935.
4. *Memphis Commercial Appeal*, 1 April 1935.
5. Ibid., 29 March 1935.
6. *Prentiss Headlight*, 4 April 1935.
7. Simmons, *Assignment Huntsville*, 160.
8. *Memphis Commercial Appeal*, 29 March 1935, 30 March 1935; *Memphis Press Scimitar*, 29 March 1935, 30 March 1935; *Jackson (Miss.) Daily News*, 29 March 1935, 30 March 1935; *Prentiss (Miss.) Headlight*, 4 April 1935.
9. *Jackson (Miss.) Daily News*, 29 March 1935.
10. Contemporary news accounts imply that the transfer never occurred, due to the fabricated story the three women worked out ahead of time in anticipation of their own capture.
11. McCormick, unfinished manuscript, 149.
12. Ibid., 150.
13. *Prentiss (Miss.) Headlight*, 4 April 1935.
14. Ibid.; *Jackson (Miss.) Daily News*, 29 March 1935, 30 March 1935.
15. *Prentiss (Miss.) Headlight*, 4 April 1935; *Jackson (Miss.) Daily News*, 29 March 1935, 30 March 1935.
16. McCormick, unfinished manuscript, 151.
17. *Memphis Commercial Appeal*, 29 March 1935.
18. *Prentiss (Miss.) Headlight*, 4 April 1935.
19. McCormick, unfinished manuscript, 152.
20. *Prentiss (Miss.) Headlight*, 4 April 1935.
21. Ibid.
22. Ibid.
23. McCormick, unfinished manuscript, 152.
24. Ibid., 153.
25. Ibid.
26. *Memphis Commercial Appeal*, 29 March 1935; *Jackson (Miss.) Daily News*, 29 March 1935; *Memphis Press Scimitar*, 29 March 1935.
27. McCormick, unfinished manuscript, 153.
28. Ibid., 154.
29. *Prentiss (Miss.) Headlight*, 4 April 1935; *Memphis Commercial Appeal*, 29 March 1935; *Jackson (Miss.) Daily News*, 29 March 1935.
30. *Prentiss (Miss.) Headlight*, 4 April 1935; *Memphis Commercial Appeal*, 29 March 1935; *Jackson (Miss.) Daily News*, 29 March 1935.
31. Mrs. Ralph Baylis, interview by John Neal Phillips, 14 January 1984.
32. McCormick, unfinished manuscript, 156.
33. Baylis interview, 14 January 1984.

34. Ibid.
35. *Memphis Commercial Appeal*, 29 March 1935.
36. McCormick, unfinished manuscript, 157.
37. *Memphis Commercial Appeal*, 29 March 1935.
38. Baylis interview, 14 January 1984.
39. *Jackson (Miss.) Daily News*, 29 March 1935.
40. *Memphis Commercial Appeal*, 1 April 1935.
41. Ibid.
42. McCormick, unfinished manuscript, 157.
43. Baylis interview, 14 January 1935.
44. *Memphis Press Scimitar*, 2 April 1935.
45. Ibid.
46. *Memphis Commercial Appeal*, 29 March 1935; *Memphis Press Scimitar*, 29 March 1935.
47. *Memphis Press Scimitar*, 2 April 1935.
48. Ibid., 29 March 1935.
49. *Memphis Commercial Appeal*, 2 April 1935.
50. Ibid.; *Memphis Press Scimitar*, 2 April 1935.
51. *Memphis Commercial Appeal*, 2 April 1935, 3 April 1935, 4 April 1935; McCormick, unfinished manuscript, 160.
52. *Memphis Commercial Appeal*, 29 March 1935; *Memphis Press Scimitar*, 29 March 1935, 2 April 1935.
53. *Jackson (Miss.) Daily News*, 29 March 1935, 30 March 1935; *Memphis Commercial Appeal*, 29 March 1935, 30 March 1935; *Memphis Press Scimitar*, 29 March 1935, 30 March 1935.
54. McCormick, unfinished manuscript, 161; Fults interviews, 5 November 1980, 12 November 1982, 10 May 1981, 4 December 1982, 12 June 1984.
55. Ibid.
56. *Dallas Daily Times Herald*, 6 April 1935; *Fort Worth Star Telegram*, 6 April 1935; *Houston Press*, 6 April 1935; *New York Times*, 6 April 1935.

Chapter 17

1. Floyd Hamilton interview, 18 July 1981; *Houston Press*, 6 April 1935; *Dallas Daily Times Herald*, 6 April 1935.
2. Floyd Hamilton, interview, 18 July 1981.
3. *Houston Press*, 6 April 1935; *Memphis Commercial Appeal*, 7 April 1935.
4. *Houston Press*, 6 April 1935; *Dallas Daily Times Herald*, 6 April 1935.
5. *Houston Press*, 6 April 1935; *Dallas Daily Times Herald*, 6 April 1935.
6. *Houston Press*, 6 April 1935; *Dallas Daily Times Herald*, 6 April 1935; Floyd Hamilton interview, 18 July 1981.
7. Floyd Hamilton interview, 18 July 1981.
8. *Dallas Daily Times Herald*, 6 April 1935, 7 April 1935; *Dallas Morning News*, 6 April 1935, 7 April 1935; *Dallas Dispatch*, 6 April 1935, 7 April 1935.

9. Hamilton, *Public Enemy No. 1*, 66.
10. *Fort Worth Star Telegram*, 6 April 1935; *Fort Worth Press*, 6 April 1935; *Dallas Daily Times Herald*, 6 April 1935; *Dallas Dispatch*, 6 April 1935.
11. *Dallas Daily Times Herald*, 7 April 1935.
12. *Houston Press*, 6 April 1935; *Dallas Daily Times Herald*, 6 April 1935, 7 April 1935.
13. *Memphis Commercial Appeal*, 6 April 1935.
14. *Houston Press*, 6 April 1935.
15. *Dallas Daily Times Herald*, 7 April 1935.
16. *Memphis Commercial Appeal*, 7 April 1935.
17. *Dallas Daily Times Herald*, 7 April 1935.
18. Ibid.
19. Ibid.
20. Ibid., 8 April 1935.
21. Ibid.; Hamilton, *Public Enemy No. 1*, 71.
22. *Dallas Dispatch*, 9 April 1935.
23. Ibid.
24. *Houston Press*, 9 April 1935.
25. Ibid.
26. Ibid.
27. Ibid.
28. Ibid.
29. Ibid; Hayes interview, 10 October 1981.
30. *Houston Press*, 9 April 1935.
31. Ibid., 10 April 1935.
32. McCormick, unfinished manuscript, 170.
33. Ibid.
34. *McKinney (Tex.) Courier-Gazette*, 13 April 1935. Unknown to Fults at the time, several agents of the U.S. Department of Justice were posted in a house on the northwest corner of the intersection. The agents saw nothing.
35. Ibid.
36. McCormick, unfinished manuscript, 28.
37. *McKinney (Tex.) Courier-Gazette*, 13 April 1935.
38. Ibid.
39. *Dallas Daily Times Herald*, 17 April 1935; *McKinney (Tex.) Courier-Gazette*, 17 April 1935.
40. *Dallas Morning News*, 11 April 1935; *Dallas Daily Times Herald*, 11 April 1935.
41. *McKinney (Tex.) Courier-Gazette*, 12 April 1935, 13 April 1935.
42. Ibid.
43. McCormick, unfinished manuscript, 172.
44. Ibid.
45. *McKinney (Tex.) Courier-Gazette*, 12 April 1935, 13 April 1935.
46. *Dallas Evening Journal*, 25 April 1935.

47. Ibid.

48. Beldon interview, 15 February 1981; *Dallas Morning News*, 18 April 1935.

49. *Denton (Tex.) Record Chronicle*, 17 April 1935.

50. Ibid.; *Dallas Morning News*, 17 April 1935; *Dallas Daily Times Herald*, 17 April 1935.

51. *Denton (Tex.) Record Chronicles*, 17 April 1935; *Dallas Morning News*, 17 April 1935; *Dallas Daily Times Herald*, 17 April 1935.

52. *Denton (Tex.) Record Chronicles*, 17 April 1935; *Dallas Morning News*, 17 April 1935; *Dallas Daily Times Herald*, 17 April 1935.

53. *Dallas Morning News*, 18 April 1935.

54. This was confirmed later by both Hickman and Gonzuales to Ralph Fults. Fults interviews, 14 March 1981, 22 February 1985.

55. McCormick, unfinished manuscript, 177.

56. Ibid., 29, 178.

57. *Dallas Daily Times Herald*, 3 April 1935; *Houston Press*, 3 April 1935.

58. *Houston Press*, 3 April 1935. "Just as we drove up to the farm," a board member said, "a short convict and a big tall one mutilated each other with an axe. It was a chopping pact and the men were not angry at each other, but each helped the other with the mutilation."

59. *Houston Press*, 4 April 1935.

60. Ibid.

61. *Houston Press*, 9 April 1935; *Dallas Daily Times Herald*, 9 April 1935.

62. *Houston Press*, 9 April 1935.

63. Ibid.

64. Ibid.

65. Ibid., 10 April 1935.

66. McCormick, unfinished manuscript, 178. By chance, Jack witnessed this exchange. He had been assigned the job of personal chauffeur to Lee Simmons and was waiting in an adjoining room with the prison Chaplain Father Hugh Finnegan, who related the story to McCormick. Jack interview, 20 February 1982.

67. *Houston Press*, 17 April 1935.

68. Ibid., 10 May 1935.

69. Katie, statement, to Floyd Hamilton (Floyd Hamilton interview, 18 July 1981).

70. *Houston Press*, 10 May 1935.

71. Ibid.; McCormick, "The Impossible Interview," 68.

72. *Houston Press*, 10 May 1935.

73. Ibid.

74. Ibid.

75. Ibid.

76. Pierce interview, 16 January 1993.

77. Floyd Hamilton interview, 18 July 1935.

Chapter 18

1. *Dallas Evening Journal*, 11 July 1935.
2. *Houston Press*, 30 June 1935.
3. Ibid. Although Fults actually faced the gallows, the *Dallas Dispatch* carried a similar headline: "Fults, Ray's Pal, to Face Chair in Robbery Hearing."
4. *Dallas Morning News*, 25 July 1935; *Dallas Daily Times Herald*, 25 July 1935; *Jackson (Miss.) Daily News*, 25 July 1935.
5. Fults made a statement about the Prentiss robbery, saying Bergie and the Houston sisters had nothing to do with it. *Dallas Daily Times Herald*, 10 July 1935; *Jackson (Miss.) Daily News*, 10 July 1935.
6. McCormick, unfinished manuscript, 186.
7. Ibid.
8. Ibid.
9. Ibid.
10. Ibid., 189.
11. Ibid., 191.
12. Ibid., 194; *Jackson (Miss.) Daily News*, 2 September 1935.
13. McCormick, unfinished manuscript, 197.
14. *Dallas Daily Times Herald*, 2 September 1935; *Dallas Dispatch*, 3 September 1935.

Epilogue

1. Fults interview, 10 May 1981.
2. *Houston Press*, 29 August 1935.
3. Blanche Barrow interview, 3 November 1984.
4. Russell, "Barrows-Parker Harboring Case," 4, 5.
5. Ibid., 50.
6. Blanche Barrow interview, 3 November 1984.
7. Marie Barrow interview, 15 September 1993; Russell, "Barrow-Parker Harboring Case," 49, 50.
8. Fults interview, 21 May 1983.
9. Russell, "Barrow-Parker Harboring Case," 50.
10. *Dallas Daily Times Herald*, 22 July 1937.
11. *Dallas Morning News*, 2 January 1949; *Dallas Daily Times Herald*, 2 January 1949.
12. McCormick, "The Impossible Interview," 74. McCormick, *Bankrobbers Wrote My Diary*, 109–10, Mary Carey interview, 8 December 1985.
13. *Dallas Daily Times Herald*, 18 October 1936.
14. Jack interview, 20 February 1982.
15. Caro, *Means of Ascent*, 325–28. In case it strikes the reader as curious that I have not cited here the biography *I'm Frank Hamer* by John H. Jenkins and H. Gordon Frost (published in 1968 by Pemberton Press), I would like

briefly to explain my reasons for excluding it as a source.

The most important reason for the exclusion is that the chapters in *I'm Frank Hamer* involving Bonnie and Clyde contain flawed research. The treatment of the April 1, 1934, murders of highway patrolmen Wheeler and Murphy near Grapevine, Texas, is a good case in point.

The entire account in *I'm Frank Hamer* is based solely on the testimony of just one of the three eyewitnesses, William Schieffer, who only saw the shootings "from a distance." Moreover, he was never able to pick out pictures of Bonnie and Clyde from police mug shots while the investigation was underway. Indeed, Schieffer would eventually identify Floyd Hamilton and Billie Mace, Raymond Hamilton's brother and Bonnie Parker's sister, as the killers.

Regardless, Schieffer's story as it appears in *I'm Frank Hamer* has Schieffer not only identifying the killers as Bonnie and Clyde but crawling up close enough to the murder scene to overhear Bonnie joking about the way the head of one of the officers bounced when she fired two more shotgun blasts into his body at point-blank range.

The fact that Henry Methvin, by his own admission, was involved in the killings is completely omitted from the account. Methvin's involvement is supported not only by his own testimony but also by the identification of his thumb print on a whiskey bottle found at the scene and the statements of two other eyewitnesses who reported seeing "the larger of two men" firing into the body of the felled officer. Methvin, taller than Barrow, would have been that man.

These discrepancies, coupled with many others, including the book's inaccurate identification of photographs, cast serious doubt on the reliability of the research involved in *I'm Frank Hamer*.

16. Floyd Hamilton interview, 18 July 1981; Russell, "Barrow-Parker Harboring Case," 50.

17. Floyd Hamilton interview, 18 July 1981.

18. Hamilton, *Public Enemy No. 1*, 155.

19. *Dallas Morning News*, 24 July 1984.

20. L. J. "Boots" Hinton, interview by John Neal Phillips, 5 May 1980.

21. *Houston Press*, 29 August 1935.

22. Ibid.

23. Jack interview, 20 February 1982.

24. Blanche thought Johnny was killed in a gun battle somewhere in the Midwest. Blanche Barrow interview, 3 November 1984.

25. Russell, "Barrow-Parker Harboring Case," 50; *Dallas Morning News*, 22 February 1935; *Dallas Daily Times Herald*, 22 February 1935.

26. *Houston Post*, 20 August 1974; Christine, interview by John Neal Phillips, 25 May 1984.

27. Schott, "Death's Used Car," 22; Kendrick interview, 16 May 1984.

28. Lorraine Joyner, interview by Dr. Robert Pierce, Huntsville, Texas,

13 May 1992.

29. Marie Barrow interview, 24 August 1984, 15 September 1993.

30. Hayes interviews, 10 October 1981, 24 April 1982.

31. McCormick, *Bankrobbers Wrote My Diary*, vii, 137; *Dallas Morning News*, 8 August 1966.

32. *Dallas Morning News*, 8 August 1966.

33. Methvin v. Oklahoma, A-9060 (1936).

34. Joyner interview, 13 May 1992; *Dallas Morning News*, 5 July 1991.

35. Joyner interview, 13 May 1992.

36. *Dallas Dispatch*, 11 January 1938; *Dallas Morning News*, 11 January 1938.

37. Kendrick interview, 16 May 1984.

38. Russell, "Barrow-Parker Harboring Case," 50.

39. Jack interview, 20 February 1982.

40. Russell, "Barrow-Parker Harboring Case," 50.

41. Ibid.

42. Beldon interview, 15 February 1981; Mayes interview, 12 June 1982.

43. Simmons, *Assignment Huntsville*, 183; *Dallas Daily Times Herald*, 23 May 1944.

44. *Dallas Morning News*, 1 July 1963.

45. *Dallas Morning News*, 3 July 1983.

46. *Dallas Daily Times Herald*, 7 March 1934; *Dallas Evening Journal*, 7 March 1934; *Dallas Dispatch*, 7 March 1934; *Dallas Morning News*, 7 March 1934.

47. *Houston Press*, 4 October 1937.

48. Ibid., 8 May 1936.

49. An article in the *New York Post*, dated 9 January 1957, stated that "the state penitentiary system at Parchman is simply a cotton plantation using convicts as labor. The warden is not a penologist but an experienced plantation manager. His annual report to the legislature is not in salvaged lives; it is a profit and loss statement, with the accent on profit."

50. McCormick, unfinished manuscript, 205.

51. Ibid., 216.

52. Ruth Fults, interview by John Neal Phillips, 23 April 1984.

53. *Dallas Morning News*, 17 March 1993.

54. *Dallas Daily Times Herald*, 2 September 1935; *Dallas Dispatch*, 3 September 1935.

55. *Dallas Evening Journal*, 6 September 1935.

56. *Dallas Morning News*, 4 September 1935.

57. *Dallas Dispatch*, 5 September 1935.

58. *Dallas Evening Journal*, 6 September 1935.

59. *Dallas Dispatch*, 16 April 1935.

60. Ibid., 9 September 1935.

61. *Houston Press*, 31 October 1935; *Dallas Evening Journal*, 31 October

1935; *Dallas Dispatch*, 31 October 1935.

62. McCormick, "The Impossible Interview," 74; McCormick, *Bankrobbers Wrote My Diary*, 109.

63. *Dallas Morning News*, 17 June 1938;*Dallas Morning News*, 15 October 1957.

64. *Dallas Morning News*, 17 August 1938; *Dallas Daily Times Herald*, 17 August 1938.

65. "Doc" interview, 24 August 1984.

66. Martin and Ekland-Olson, *Texas Prisons*, xiii.

67. Ibid., xxiii.

68. Ibid.

69. Ibid., xxiii, xxiv.

70. Ibid., xxv, xxvi.

71. Ibid., xxvi, 203.

72. Ibid., xxv, xxvi.

73. Ibid., xxv, 203.

74. Ibid., 218–27.

75. Ibid., 227.

76. Ibid., 151, 269.

77. *Dallas Morning News*, 27 December 1983.

78. *Dallas Morning News*, 16 August 1984.

79. Martin and Ekland-Olson, *Texas Prisons*, 236.

80. Ibid., 221.

81. Ibid., 226.

82. Ibid., 218–27.

83. Ibid., xxx.

References

Public Documents

Dallas, Texas. Dallas Police Department. Mug book.

Dallas, Texas. Dallas Police Department. File #6048, Clyde Champion Barrow.

Dallas, Texas. Dallas Police Department. Transcript of a telephone wire tap on the Barrow and Parker households, 18–30 April 1934.

Fort Worth, Texas. Fort Worth Police Department, File #4316, Clyde Barrow.

Jones, W. D., Voluntary Statement, B-71, Dallas County Sheriff's Department, 18 November 1933.

Louisiana. Bienville Parish. Coroner's Inquest, 23 May 1934, Dr. J. L. Wade, Coroner.

Missouri. Neosho County. Coroner's Inquest. 14 April 1933.

Missouri. Newton County. Coroner's Inquest. 14 April 1933.

Oklahoma. Criminal Court of Appeals. *Methvin v. Oklahoma*, A-9060, 18 September 1936.

Texas. Texas Prison System, *Annual Report for the Year Ending December 31, 1929*. Huntsville, Tex.: Texas Prison Board, 1930.

Texas. *General and Special Laws for the State of Texas*. Austin: 20th Legislature of Texas, 1887, Bill 21, Chapter 84, Section 3, Texas State School for Boys.

Texas. Texas Prison Archives, Texas Department of Criminal Justice Institutional Division (TDCJ-ID), Prisoner Files, Huntsville, Tex.

Texas. Texas Prison System, dying statement of Major Joseph Crowson, 23 January 1934.

Texas. Texas Prison System, letter from W. M. Thompson to Doug Walsh of the Dallas Police Department, 17 May 1932. Dallas Public Library, Texas/Dallas History Archives Division, "Smoot" Schmid Scrapbook.

Texas. Texas Prison System, Minutes of the Texas Prison Board, 1 August 1929, 3 March 1930, 19 May 1930, and 24 July 1934.

Texas. Texas Prison System, Special Escape Report, Raymond Hamilton,16 January 1934 and 22 July 1934.

Texas. Texas Prison System, Special Escape Report, Joe Palmer, 16 January 1934 and 27 July 1934.

United States. Department of Commerce. Bureau of the Census. Census, 1900. Washington, D.C., 1903.

United States. Department of Commerce. Bureau of the Census. Census, 1910. Washington, D.C., 1913.

United States. Department of Commerce. Bureau of the Census. Census, 1920. Washington, D.C., 1923.

United States. Department of Commerce. Bureau of the Census. Census, 1930. Washington, D.C., 1933.

United States. Department of Justice. Bureau of Investigation. Statement of Jim Muckleroy in a memo to Doug Walsh of the Dallas Police Department concerning the activities of Clyde Barrow and Bonnie Parker in Nacogdoches County, Texas, 4 May 1933.

United States. Department of Justice. Bureau of Investigation. Report on the criminal history of Clyde Barrow, including the 1928 automobile theft charge, 8 June 1934.

United States. Department of Justice. Bureau of Investigation. Statements of L. B. Harlow, J. C. Loftice, and Jesse Roy Mayes to Agent Frank Blake, 26 February 1935.

Books and Articles

Andrist, Ralph K. *The American Heritage History of the 20's and 30's*. New York: American Heritage Publishing Co., 1970.

Asinof, Eliot, *Eight Men Out, The Black Sox and the 1919 World Series*. New York: Holt, Rinchart and Winston, 1963.

Aswell, Thomas E. *The Story of Bonnie and Clyde*. Ruston, Ca.: H. M. G., 1968.

Caro, Robert A. *Means of Ascent*. Vol. 2 of *The Years of Lyndon Johnson*. New York: Alfred. A. Knopf, 1990.

Davis, Mert. "Eyewitness Account of the Ambush of Bonnie and Clyde." *Ringgold Record*, 26 April 1968.

Edge, L. L. *Run the Cat Roads*. New York: Dembner Books, 1981.

Erdang, Lawrence. *The Timetables of History*. New York: Simon and Schuster, 1981.

Fortune, Jan I. *Fugitives: The Story of Clyde Barrow and Bonnie Parker, as Told by Bonnie's Mother (Emma Krause Parker) and Clyde's Sister (Nell Barrow Cowan)*. Dallas, Tex.: The Ranger Press, 1934.

Franks, Zarko. "Bonnie and Clyde—Fresh Insights into Their Deaths from the Last Living Member of the Ambush Party that Killed Them." *Houston Chronicle*, 31 July 1977.

Hamilton, Floyd. *Public Enemy Number 1*. Dallas, Tex.: Acclaimed Books, 1978.

Harding, David. *Weapons*. New York: St. Martin's Press, 1980.

Hinton, Ted, as told to Larry Grove. *Ambush: The Real Story of Bonnie and Clyde*. Austin, Tex.: Shoal Creek, 1979.

Hounsell, Jim. *Lawmen and Outlaws: 116 Years in Joplin History*. Joplin: Joplin Historical Society, 1993.

Jones, W. D. "Riding with Bonnie and Clyde." New York: *Playboy*, 15 no.11 (November 1968).

Katz, Jack. *Seductions of Crime: Moral and Sensual Attractions in Doing Evil*, New York: Basic Books, 1988.

Knight, James R. "Incident at Alma." *Arkansas Historical Review* 61 no. 4 (winter 1997).

Kratcoski, Peter C., and Lucille Dunn. *Juvenile Delinquency*. Englewood Cliffs, N.J.: Prentice-Hall, 1988.

Lindsley, Philip. *A History of Greater Dallas and Vicinity*. Chicago, Ill.: Lewis Publishing Co., 1909.

Lingeman, Richard. *Small Town America*. Boston, Mass.: Houghton Mifflin Co., 1980.

Malsch, Brownson. *Lone Wolf*. Austin, Tex.: Shoal Creek, 1980.

Martin, Steve J. and Sheldon Ekland-Olson. *Texas Prisons: The Walls Came Tumbling Down*. Austin, Tex.: Texas Monthly Press, 1987.

McConal, Patrick M. *Over the Wall*. Austin: Eakin Press, 2000.

McCormick, Harry, as told to Mary Carey. *Bankrobbers Wrote My Diary*, Austin, Tex.: Eakin Press, 1985.

McCormick, Harry, as told to Mary Carey. "The Impossible Interview." *Argosy*, 253 no. 2 (February 1958).

McDonald, William L. *Dallas Rediscovered*. Dallas, Tex.: The Dallas Historical Society, 1978.

McElvaine, Robert S. *The Great Depression: America 1929–1941*. New York: Time Books, 1984.

Morris, Richard B. *Encyclopedia of American History*. New York: Harper and Row, 1982.

Nash, Jay Robert. *Bloodletters and Badmen, Book 2*. New York: Warner Books, 1975.

Nash, Roderick. *The Nervous Generation: American Thought 1917–1930*. Chicago: Rand McNally Co., 1970.

Osborne Association's Annual Report on U.S. Prisons. New York: The Osborne Association, 1935.

Paulissen, Maisie. "Pardon Me, Governor Ferguson." *Legendary Ladies of Texas*. Edited by Francis E. Abernathy. Dallas, Tex.: E-Heart Press, 1981.

Rich, Carroll Y. "The Day They Shot Bonnie and Clyde." *Hunters and Healers*. Edited by Wilson M. Hudson. Austin, Tex.: Encino Press, 1969.

Robinson, David. *World Cinema, A Short History*. London: Eyre Methuen, 1981.

Russell, Francis. *The Shadow of Blooming Grove: Warren G. Harding in His Times*. New York: McGraw-Hill, 1968.

Schott, Joseph L. "Death's Used Car." *Dallas Morning News*, 25 May 1980.

Shannon, David A., ed. *The Great Depression*. Englewood Cliffs: NJ. Prentice Hall, 1960.

Simmons, Lee. *Assignment Huntsville: Memoirs of a Texas Prison Officer*. Austin, Tex.: University of Texas Press, 1957.

Sitton, Thad. *The Loblolly Book*. Austin, Tex.: Texas Monthly Press, 1983.

Sterling, Bryan. *The Best of Will Rogers*. New York: Crown Publishers, 1979.

Tattersall, Peter D. *Conviction: A True Story*. Montclair: The Pegasus Rex Press, 1980.

Taylor, Lawrence. *Born to Crime: The Genetic Causes of Criminal Behavior*. Westport, Conn.: Greenwood Press, 1984.

Tolbert, Frank X. "Taken for a Ride by Bonnie and Clyde." *Dallas Morning News*, 18 March 1968.

Trojanowicz, Robert C., and Merry Morash. *Juvenile Delinquency: Concepts and Control*. 4th ed. Englewood Cliffs, NJ.: Prentice-Hall, 1987.

Ungar, Sanford J. *FBI: An Uncensored Look Behind the Walls*. Boston, Mass.: Atlantic Monthly Press, 1975.

Walker, Donald R. *Penology for Profit: A History of the Texas Prison System 1867–1912*. College Station, Tex.: Texas A & M University Press, 1988.

Webb, Walter Prescott. *The Texas Rangers*. Austin: University of Texas Press, 1980.

Webster, H. T. *The Best of H. T. Webster, A Memorial Collection*. New York: Simon and Schuster, 1953.

Wheeler, Eugene, and S. Anthony Baron. *Violence in Our Schools, Hospitals, and Public Places*. Ventura, Calif.: Pathfinder, 1994.

Who Was Who in America: 1943–50. Vol. 2 of *Who Was Who in America*. Chicago: A. N. Marquis, 1951.

Worley's Dallas City Directory. Dallas: Worley Directory Publishing, 1914–1935.

Worster, Donald. *The Dust Bowl: The Southern Plains in the 1930s*. New York: Oxford University Press, 1979.

Newspapers

Amarillo Sunday News-Globe (Texas).

Austin American Statesman (Texas).

Bienville Democrat (Arcadia, Louisiana).
Celina Record (Texas).
Daily Oklahoman (Oklahoma City).
Daily Oklahoma-Times (Oklahoma City).
Dallas Daily Times Herald (Texas).
Dallas Dispatch (Texas).
Dallas Evening Journal (Texas).
Dallas Morning News (Texas).
Dallas Sentinel (Texas).
Denton Record Chronicle (Texas).
Des Moines Register (Iowa).
Dexter Sentinel (Iowa).
Electra Gazette (Texas).
Fairmont Daily Sentinel (Minnesota).
Fort Worth Press (Texas).
Fort Worth Star Telegram (Texas).
Greenville Evening Banner (Texas).
Greenville Messenger (Texas).
Greenville Morning Herald (Texas).
Hillsboro Mirror (Texas).
Houston Chronicle (Texas).
Houston Press (Texas).
Jackson Daily News (Mississippi).
Joplin Globe (Missouri).
Landmark (Platte City, Missouri).
McKinney Daily Courier-Gazette (Texas).
Memphis Commercial Appeal (Tennessee).
Memphis Press Scimitar (Tennessee).
New York Daily News (New York City).
New York Post (New York City).
New York Times (New York City).
Prentiss Headlight (Mississippi).
Ringgold Record (Louisiana).
Roswell Daily Record (New Mexico).
Ruston Leader (Louisiana).
San Antonio Express (Texas).
Sherman Daily Democrat (Texas).
Southwest American (Fort Smith, Arkansas).
Temple Daily Telegram (Texas).
Temple Morning News (Texas).
Texarkana Press (Texas).
Wellington Leader (Texas).
Wichita Daily News (Wichita Falls, Texas).
Wichita Times (Wichita Falls, Texas).

Unpublished Papers

Barrow, Blanche. "My Life with the Barrow Gang." Unpublished memoir. 1933–35.

Barrow, Clyde. Letter to Dallas Police admitting involvement in the Christmas Day killing of Doyle Johnson. 21 November 1933. In the possession of the Barrow family.

Barrow, Cumie T. Unfinished memoirs. 1933. In the possession of the Barrow family.

Crawford, Kermit ("Curley"). Letter to author. 21 December 1982.

Henson, S. C., a.k.a. Joe Wood. Letter to reporter Kent Biffle. 4 September 1980.

Hollandsworth, Nettie. Letters to author. 15 August 1982, 16 September 1982.

Hutzell, Diane and Cheri Rupp. Essays based on interviews with John Love and Dr. K. M. Chapler, eyewitnesses to Dexfield Park battle and its aftermath. 1983. The Dexter Historical Society.

Legg, Walter M., Jr. Letter to author. 1 September 1982.

Mayes, Cecil. Letter to author. 23 July 1984.

McCormick, Harry. Unfinished manuscript about Ralph Fults and the Barrow gang. 1956–1966. In the possession of the Fults family.

Methvin, Clemie, quoted by James R. Knight. E-mail to author. 30 July 2001.

Poteat, Beryl, quoted by James R. Knight. E-mail to author. 2 August 2001.

Russell, Bud. "The Clyde Barrow-Bonnie Parker Harboring Case." 1935. In the possession of Robert H. Russell.

Sanborn, Debra. "The Barrow Gang's Visit to Dexter." 14 May 1976. The Dexter Historical Society.

Searles, William R. Letter to author. 21 April 1983.

Author Interviews

Adams, Ken. Dallas, Tex., 10 May 1980.

Askin, Alton. Dallas, Tex., 4 June 1980.

Askin, Pat. Dallas, Tex., 4 June 1980.

Barrow, Blanche. Dallas, Tex., 3 November 1984, 18 November 1984.

Barrow, Marie. Dallas, Tex., 24 August 1984, 15 September 1993, 25 September 1993, 30 September 1993, 19 April 1995.

Baylis, Mrs. Ralph. Prentis, Miss., 14 January 1984.

Beldon, Jimmy. McKinney, Tex., 15 February 1981.

Blohm, Wilma. Dexter, Iowa, 5 May 1983.

Carey, Mary. Dallas, Tex., 8 December 1985.

Charping, Leon. Gibsland, La., 16 May 1984.

Christine. Dallas, Tex., 25 May 1984.

Conn, Charlie. Dallas, Tex., 11 January 1988.

Crawford, Kermit ("Curley"). Kansas City, Mo., 19 April 1983.

"Doc" [pseud.]. Dallas, Tex., 24 August 1984.

Feller, Marvelle. Dexter, Iowa, 5 May 1983.

Ford, Trey. Dallas, Tex., 6 June 1984.
Fults, Ralph. Dallas, Tex., 5 November 1980, 12 November 1980, 10 December 1980, 1 February 1981, 8 March 1981, 14 March 1981, 10 May 1981, 18 July 1981, 13 February 1982, 4 December 1982, 21 May 1983, 12 June 1984, 22 February 1985, 29 April 1985.
Fults, Ruth. Dallas, Tex., 23 April 1984.
Grove, Larry. Dallas, Tex., 2 April 1980.
Hall, Clyde. Huntsville, Tex., 10 December 1983.
Hamilton, Floyd. Dallas, Tex., 18 July 1981.
Hamilton, Mildred. Dallas, Tex., 18 July 1981.
Harlow, L. B. Dallas, Tex., 17 December 1983.
Hayes, Johnny. Dallas, Tex., 10 October 1981, 28 February 1983.
Hays, John W. ("Preacher"). Dallas, Tex., 20 April 1980.
Hays, Mrs. J. W. Dallas, Tex., 20 April 1980.
Helms, Oris K. Dallas, Tex., 17 January 1983.
Hinton, L. J. ("Boots"). Dallas, Tex., 5 May 1980.
Hinton, Mrs. Ted. Dallas, Tex., 15 April 1980.
Holmes, Ken M., Jr. Dallas, Tex., 9 September 1993, 18 January 1994.
Jack, [pseud.]. Denton, Tex., 20 February 1982.
Jackson, Olin. Gibsland, Louisiana, 22 May 1998.
Johnson, Lonny. Huntsville, Tex., 5 November 1993.
Karlen, Elsie Wullschleger. Dallas, Tex., 10 January 1983.
Kendrick, Dewey, Sr. Gibsland, La., 16 May 1984.
Legg, Walter, Jr. Kemp, Tex., 13 March 1981, 15 September 1993.
Mayes, Cecil. McKinney, Tex., 12 June 1982.
McDowell, Mrs. Eugene. Aspermont, Tex., 5 May 1981.
Milner, Dr. E. R. Dallas, Tex., 4 August 1984.
Myers, Rose. Dallas, Tex., 19 January 1983.
Neal, LaVohn Cole. Gibsland, Louisiana, 30 September 1993.
Nuehoff, Henry, Jr. Dallas, Tex., 20 February 1982.
Otis, John ("Red"). Denton, Tex., 20 February 1982.
Palmer, Martha. Dallas, Tex., 15 June 1984.
Palmer, Polly. Gibsland, La., 16 May 1984.
Peoples, Clint. Dallas, Tex., 30 September 1983.
Pierce, Dr. Robert. Huntsville, Tex., 5 November 1993, 6 November 1993.
Robertson, Fern. Aspermont, Tex., 5 May 1981.
Roseborough, Robert F. Marshall, Tex., 11 July 1984.
Russell, Robert H. Dallas, Tex., 11 July 1984.
Rutledge, Ruth Fults. McKinney, Tex., 22 July 1983.
Schott, Joseph L. Fort Worth, Tex., 10 June 1980.
Searles, William R. Cassville, Mo., 20 April 1983.
Sneed, Cleo. Gibsland, La., 16 May 1984.
Stewart, Gene. Huntsville, Tex., 5 November 1993.
Worley, Roy. Lancaster, Tex., 18 August 1983.

Index